ODETE LOPES MAZZA

THE COMPLETE BOOK OF THE PETIT LENORMAND

GERMAN METHOD

The Complete Book of The Petit Lenormand
Odete Lopes Mazza

1st Edition: November, 2023

Original title:
A Bíblia do Baralho Petit Lenormand
© 2022, PRH Grupo Editorial Portugal, Lda.

Translation: Tânia Regina Carvalho Leite
Proofreading: Alexsander Lepletier
Layout: Diogo Saavedra

ISBN: 978-989-33-5388-2

© 2023, Odete Lopes Mazza

All rights for this book are reserved. This means that no part of this publication, including text, design, images, or other content, can be reproduced, stored in a retrieval system, or transmitted in any form or by any means, electronic, mechanical, photocopying, recording, or otherwise, without the author's prior written permission. Any unauthorized reproduction of this book in any form is strictly prohibited and will be considered a violation of the author's copyright.

CONTENTS

Preface 9

Introduction 13
The art of learning how to read the cards 13
How to choose a deck 18
Consecrating the deck 25

Chapter 1: Origins, Cards and Suits 31
A brief history of the origins of the Petit Lenormand 31
The Anatomy of the 36 cards 61
The German Cartomancy Suits 64

Chapter 2: The meaning of the 36 cards 73
The schools or The Petit Lenormand Traditions 75
The Gypsy Cards and the Orishas 76
Reversed cards 86
Comparing Similar Tarot Cards to the Petit Lenormand 89
The Meaning of the 36 cards 91

Chapter 3: Polarity and Significator card 173
The Polarities of the 36 cards 173
The Significator Card 175
   Group 1: Significator Cards to identify People 177
     The Two Querent's Cards: The Man and The Woman 177
     The 34 Cards: The other people's cards 181
     The Theme Card according to Personality,
     Character, and Behavior 190
     The Court Card Figures 201

Group 2: Significator Cards or Theme Cards 205
Significator Cards for Love, Feelings,
Emotions, and Relationships 205
Theme Cards for Communication and News 216
Theme Cards for Work 221
Theme Cards for Finances and Money 237
Theme Cards for Travel and Vacation 249
Theme Cards for Health 251
Theme Cards for Physical Death 266
Theme Cards for Magic 269
Other topics 278

Predicting Time 299

Chapter 4: The Lopes Mazza Codes 313
Philippe Lenormand's Law 314
The Directional Facing Law 318
The Law of Position 324
The Law of Predominance 378
The Law of Movement 381

Chapter 5: Combination Technique 385
How to perform a Card Combination 386
Steps for Combining Cards 387
Two-Card Combination 398
Combining More than Two Cards 401
The Hidden Card 403

Chapter 6: Reading Methods (Drawings) 407
The Energy of the Day Method 414
The Three-Card Method 418
The Three-Card Method (Extended) 427
Should I Trust Method 434
Method to Identify Magic 438
The Grandmother's Method 442

Chapter 7: The Grand Tableau 449

   The Grand Tableau Layout 453
   The Foundations of The Grand Tableau 455
      The Philippe Lenormand Method 455
      The Timeline Method 465
      The Method of Houses 480
   The Auxiliary Techniques 525
      The Position of the Querent's Card in The Grand Tableau . 525
      The Bridge Technique 534
      Identifying a Person in The Grand Tableau 536
      The Chaining Technique 540
      The Knighting Technique 554
      The Queen's Movement Technique 561
      The Mirroring Technique 567
      The Counting of 7 573
   Introduction Step-by-step to read the Grand Tableau 582
      Step-by-step guide for a General Reading 584
      Step-by-step guide for a Specific Reading 596

References *611*
The Author *613*
Acknowledgment *615*

PREFACE

Odete Lopes Mazza is an influential Portuguese fortune teller whose knowledge and expertise have been passed down through generations. Her fascination with card reading began in childhood when she learned to unveil the mysteries of the cards with her beloved grandmother. Over the years, her practice has led her to collaborate on significant projects with renowned specialists. Her innovative books have become bestsellers and are a reference for anyone interested in the Petit Lenormand deck. Her books have been translated into multiple languages, spreading her knowledge across borders, and inspiring readers along the way.

Cartomancy, which is part of history and culture, has found its voice through the works of this remarkable author. With her strong commitment to understanding the symbolic significance of each card and honoring family heritage, she offers a distinct perspective in her practice. Her approach infuses every card with nuanced meanings and captivating stories, enriching the art of card reading and also allowing today's readers to connect deeply to the mysteries of the past.

This book takes readers on a fascinating journey through the history of cartomancy. It explores the intricacies of German suits and reveals the meanings of each card in crucial life areas. The book stands out due to its detailed and comprehensive study of the Grand Tableau, presenting a wealth of wisdom that hasn't been found in any other publication. Mrs. Mazza generously shares not only established techniques, but also her precious methods, which she has developed over years of dedicated practice. In this exceptional book, readers are warmly invited to explore the Petit Lenormand in a whole new way.

Exploring Odete Lopes Mazza's works awakened my passion for the Petit Lenormand deck while also introduced me to the German method, which is her working approach. Her teachings completely redefined my understanding of card reading and became a crucial milestone in my Petit Lenormand studies. She offers the contents in a simple and didactic way, ensuring that even beginners can grasp the nuances of the Petit Lenormand language with great precision.

It was a great pleasure and honor to have been chosen to translate her book into English. I humbly embraced this task, fully aware of the enormous responsibility of translating such a rich and captivating language as Portuguese into English. Therefore, I state with absolute conviction that Odete Lopes Mazza's work not only illuminated my path in card reading but also left an indelible impression on my heart, enriching my journey in ways I could never have imagined.

Odete Lopes Mazza's extraordinary work goes beyond the realm of mere literature, serving as a guiding beacon for aspiring fortune tellers seeking to decipher the Petit Lenormand language. Her book is a masterful combination of ancient wisdom and innovative methods, providing a valuable resource for professional fortune tellers and for those beginning into the depths of card reading. It's a work that not only teaches, but also inspires, leaving a lasting legacy of knowledge and enlightenment. Mrs. Mazza's charisma and passion permeate every page, making it a wellspring of motivation for everyone interested in Petit Lenormand.

Tânia Regina Carvalho Leite

Shaila Naisha Kumar Lopes

Dear Grandma,
I want to express my deepest gratitude for being a valuable example in my life, teaching me everything I know and imparting essential values such as humility, respect, integrity, and professionalism, especially in the esoteric realm. Today, I offer this gift in loving tribute to you, and I hope that, with your blessing, it will find its way into the hands of other professionals.

With love, your granddaughter
Detinha

"CARTOMANCY WILL BE IN THE FUTURE WHAT WE MAKE OF IT TODAY!"

ODETE LOPES MAZZA

INTRODUCTION

This book was conceived with the purpose of helping all those who want to take the first steps in the Petit Lenormand studies. The goal is to be accessible to everyone, and its content is properly organized and explained in simple language.

It's a step-by-step introduction to the topic with graphics and illustrated examples. It also addresses other fundamental areas, such as the meaning of cards and techniques to help beginners overcome challenges.

I hope with all my heart that you will know how to reap the fruits of my teachings and that you will enjoy what I offer you with lots of love. I wish you good luck and, above all, good work.

THE ART OF LEARNING HOW TO READ THE CARDS

It's necessary to have a vocation to be a fortune teller. Vocation brings us the disposition and motivation to learn, practice, and be patient on the long journey of learning. There is no point in insisting on cartomancy if there is no vocation and passion for card reading; otherwise, you'll always remain on the same level and never become a professional.

To be a fortune teller, you don't have to come from a fortune-telling or psychic family (like me). It isn't also required to have the gift. Card reading is based on interpreting a symbolic language composed of numbers and symbols (religious, cultural, astrological, etc.). The fortune teller translates this symbolic language into a language that the querent understands (English in your case and Italian in mine). Remember that no one is born a fortune teller, and every professional has gone through the same difficulties.

What you need to know to start your studies well:

1. When you choose to study The Petit Lenormand, it's important not to mix up the "schools." The Petit Lenormand isn't a Gypsy deck (although there may be similarities in the image of the cards). In Europe, the Petit Lenormand "speaks" German, Swiss-German, French, Dutch, Belgian, and Russian. Because there are subtle differences between them, they shouldn't be mixed. It's up to you to decide which "school" or "language" suits you best.

    Whether it's the traditional German school, one of the most recognized schools in Europe, or the French or Brazilian schools, they all have value. They shouldn't be undervalued or despised since each brings significant knowledge.

    In my professional travels worldwide, I've met fortune tellers from different "schools," and I've learned a great deal from each of them. For example, in 1990, a friend introduced me to different practical possibilities of working with the Petit Lenormand, and I chose to follow the German "school." At that time, the traditional "school" (Philippe's Method as it's known in Switzerland) – which has been my first "school" since 1971 – was relatively limited compared to today's traditional modern "school," which is rich in content.

2. It's important to understand that learning to read the Petit Lenormand isn't simply memorizing keywords for each card or card combination. This way of learning isn't effective, regardless of the subject. Keep in mind that haste is the enemy of perfection. It makes learning much more challenging.

    Believe me, you can't learn proper card reading in seven days or during a weekend workshop. In such a brief period, you might memorize names, numbers, and a few keywords. As previously stated, I don't think this approach will promote an accurate understanding of the cards.

INTRODUCTION

The cards aren't poetry to be memorized; they represent life and can only be fully comprehended by experiencing them daily. My master, my grandmother, used to tell me, *"My daughter, you can only understand something by living with it. Live with your problems, friends, and work every day to get to know them better and to overcome any disagreements that arise"*.

Learning the art of card reading is a gradual process that requires an extended period, so it's useless to expect immediate results after just a few days of study and practice or by reading books and online resources. In fact, no one can provide an accurate consultation with limited experience.

3. Only through consistently practicing can you truly interact directly with the cards, touching, feeling, and hearing them day after day. If you want to know your cards perfectly, you shouldn't rush the process. Instead, patience, calmness, and passion will help you to empathize with them.

   Start by learning each card's keywords, and then learn to form your own. Nothing is worse than watching a fortune teller interpret the cards using a "plastered" language resulting from memorized words and texts. Finally, you need to bring out your personality and inner beauty. How you laugh, gesture, and communicate will make you feel completely free and at peace.

4. When we hold a deck of cards and decide to make it our "friend" for divination purposes, we must take care of it and commit to learning everything about its origins, symbolism, and meanings. Each divination deck has its own methodology, which sets it apart from others. Proper preparation is one of the most important goals and prerequisites for a successful start.

   Based on my experience, I highly recommend that everyone strive to absorb as much information as possible about the subject during the study phase. It's essential to be aware of the "danger" that threatens your professional future if you take the easiest path without the necessary foundations: solid theoretical and practical preparation. Therefore, it's essential to follow a systematic study under the guidance of a Master who knows how to guide you through each step so that you can accurately assimilate all the "key concepts" that can help you improve your technique. Acquiring this knowledge plays a significant role in the psychological introduction to the cards.

A skillful interpretation lies not only on the deck's aesthetics and intuition (which is vital in a reading) but also on your deep understanding of it.

5. Professional confidence is gained through consistent practice, daily acquaintance with the cards, deepening techniques, and clarification of any doubts arising during the study.

It's important not to get discouraged or disheartened by the first unsatisfactory results. Instead, deepen your studies on the subject you want to learn, identify the problem, and strive to improve yourself. Don't be afraid to reach out to a more experienced fortune teller, describe your problem and ask for advice from those who have already dealt with a similar situation. These "mistakes" will eventually disappear with commitment and persistence, and the hard work will pay off.

Nevertheless, every professional has experienced difficult times marked by errors, uncertainties, and a lack of confidence. That's why I recommend you take an introductory course in Petit Lenormand, following the "style" or "school" (whatever you want to call it, in Europe, we call it methods) with which you most identify (Traditional, German, Swiss-German, French, Dutch, Belgian, Russian, or Brazilian). An introductory course will give you a safe start to your studies. Of course, it won't prepare you for an actual professional consultation, but it'll provide the necessary tools to continue your journey if that is your calling.

It would be best to study with someone who offers serious and professional courses and with excellent practical experience. Starting off well is crucial. Remember that no one is born a fortune teller and that every professional has gone through similar challenges and difficulties.

INTRODUCTION

6. This book is specially designed to guide step by step those who are beginning their studies or professionals who want to expand their knowledge of The Petit Lenormand.

   For beginners, I recommend not to skipping any of the learning stages provided in this book. The seven learning chapters follow a precise teaching chronology based on my professional courses of levels 1 (introduction) and 2 (advanced), which will allow you to correctly and easily learn everything related to The Petit Lenormand of the German Method.

Chapter 1
- Origins of the Petit Lenormand
- The anatomy of cards
- The suits

Chapter 2
- The Meanings of the 36 cards

Chapter 3
- The polarities of the cards
- The significator cards

Chapter 4
- Lopes Mazza's methods

Chapter 5
- Combination techniques

Chapter 6
- Reading Methods (drawings)

Chapter 7
- The Grand Tableau

HOW TO CHOOSE A DECK

Before studying the Petit Lenormand, you'll need to acquire a deck of cards. For many beginners, this can be a challenging experience due to preconceived notions, such as the belief that the deck must be stolen or gifted to be effective.

However, these myths created in the past no longer make sense nowadays, and they can now be demystified by fortune tellers and professional card readers, who daily, with their work, debunk any stories created to turn card reading into something magical and powerful. As you'll learn throughout this book, your cards' true magic and power come from the knowledge, intuition, and theoretical and practical experience you'll bring to the reading.

At the beginning of your study journey, you need to have a deck. You probably heard that the deck should be stolen or gifted to you; otherwise, it wouldn't be effective. There's no basis for such an assertion. Although my first deck was given to me by my grandmother as part of a passage ceremony – which is common in fortune-telling families - all the other decks that I've worked with or collected were designed or bought by me.

I've been working with the Blue Owl deck since 1989, which I bought at an esoteric shop in Switzerland called "The Prophet." This deck has proved to be as effective as my first gifted deck.

When purchasing a Petit Lenormand deck, here are some things to consider.

INTRODUCTION

TYPES OF DECKS AVAILABLE

1. DECKS WITH SUITS
2. DECKS WITH POEMS
3. DECKS WITH IMAGES
4. DECKS WITH SUITS, POEMS, AND IMAGES

There are four types of decks. From left to right:

1. Decks with a central symbol and a suit;
2. Decks with a central symbol and a poem;
3. Decks with a image;
4. Decks with a symbol, a suit, a poem, and a image

Nowadays, commercially available decks come in a variety of styles, including classic, modern, and thematic.

Classic decks, also called traditional decks, are replicas of historical decks or decks that keep the Petit Lenormand's traditional symbolism. Due to their simplicity and symbolic clarity, they're perfect allies for those taking their first steps in Lenormand studies as they help them become more familiar with the Petit Lenormand language.

A good example is the Lilac Dondorf Lenormand deck from 1878, which was restored by Fanu and is available on the Game of Hope blog. It's a beautiful deck with clear symbols that are easy to identify. I hold this deck in high regard, as my grandmother used it and because I received my teachings from it.

Lilac Dondorf Lenormand

Another classic deck is the Lenormand Silhouettes Deck, published in 2013 by authors Kendra Hurteau, who is a fortune teller, and Katrina Hill. In the center of each card, surrounded by a vintage-style cornice, is the silhouette of the symbol of each card (an anchor, a heart, a woman, etc.). At the bottom left, there is the number that identifies the card, and on the right, there's a card from the traditional deck. This deck is designed to be an easy-to-understand tool suitable for both beginners and experienced fortune tellers.

Lenormand Silhouettes Deck

The Blue Owl deck from 1920, <u>used in this book</u>, is a popular Lenormand deck primarily used by fortune tellers in Switzerland, Germany, and France. I bought mine in an esoteric store called The Prophet in Switzerland in 1989, and I still use it - 32 years later!

Modern decks contain the 36 symbols of the Petit Lenormand, but some authors have incorporated additional symbols related to Lenormand card meanings, such as Astrology and chakras.

Modern decks usually portray humorous or non-traditional imagery, which diverges from the classic deck. An example is the Gilded Reverie Lenormand deck, created by artist Ciro Marchetti in 2014, which is very popular worldwide as it conveys unique energy and allure.

In 2017, Ciro released a revised version of the Gilded Reverie Lenormand – Expanded Edition Deck, which included extra cards representing the querents of the same sex. In this version, Marchetti also considered the directional facing law for both cards: no. 28 The Man and card no. 29 The Woman, now facing different directions, whereas they both faced the same direction in the original version.

Gilded Reverie Lenormand

Thematic decks are inspired by movies, fables, animals, different cultures (such as Gypsy, Celtic, Viking, Arab, etc.), upcoming festive seasons (Christmas, Halloween, etc.), sexuality, and much more.

The first example is Rana George's deck. She's a fortune teller and author of a Lenormand book titled "The Essential Lenormand" (2014), published in 2017 and features scenes from everyday life in Lebanon, representing the author's cultural background.

Rana George's Lenormand

Another example is "The Celtic Lenormand" deck, inspired by Celtic culture, which was created in 2015 by Chloe McCracken, a professional fortune teller from England, and illustrated by Will Worthington. I've noticed that many of my students who are fans of Celtic culture have adopted this deck to work. Each card depicts a daily scene from Celtic life without betraying the traditional Lenormand symbolism.

The Celtic Lenormand

The third deck is "The Egyptian Lenormand", published in 2015 by American author Nefer Khepri a professional fortune teller and Reiki master from Texas. Kepri is fascinated by the Egyptian world and its mysterious and captivating culture. All thematic Lenormand decks are rich in cultural teachings, and I feel privileged to have them in my Lenormand deck collection.

The Egyptian Lenormand

Non-traditional decks differ from the traditional Petit Lenormand deck but maintain the same number and name of each card. These decks incorporate the author's style and, in some cases, deviate from the true symbolic identity of the Petit Lenormand. For example, "Melissa Lenormand" deck by the fortune teller and author Melissa Hill and Les Vieux Jours Lenormand by artist and author Pam Batista, published in 2012, are rich in symbolism, especially the second deck, in which the author incorporates symbolic imagery from the Tarot, alchemy, and others.

Melissa Lenormand

For beginners, I recommend choosing a deck that doesn't deviate too far from the classical decks, as it makes it easier to become familiar with the traditional Lenormand's symbolism before exploring non-traditional decks to avoid being influenced by an author's personal beliefs.

Many people mistakenly believe a deck will work for them just as well as for a famous fortune teller who uses it and rush out to get it. However, it's not how it works. The true "magic" behind

Les Vieux Jours Lenormand

INTRODUCTION

the effectiveness of a deck in a fortune teller's hands is their deep knowledge of the deck itself. So don't put aside the deck you love so much. Instead, dedicate your heart and soul to it by learning its language, and you'll find that you'll master it and will feel more satisfied with your readings. So don't hesitate, and start today!!

Going on...

What should be considered when buying a deck?

1. When choosing a deck, make sure that it conveys positive energy and that you enjoy its overall look (including color, images, size, and quality of the cards). It should be something that you find visually pleasing and enjoyable to touch and handle. You must feel comfortable and confident when working with it. So, choose a deck that suits your style and "speaks to you". Once you've chosen, I recommend you to work with it for at least a year to become familiar with the symbols;

2. When buying decks, pay attention to the type of cardboard used, including resistance and thickness, is essential. Some materials may make the cards hard to shuffle or handle, and you want to avoid that. I have already bought several beautiful decks, but the material was low quality and damaged after only a few days of use. I recommend investing in high-quality decks that will withstand regular use and last you a long time.

3. Another thing to consider is the deck size you plan to work with. Whether big or small, it should be practical for shuffling and holding it in our hands comfortably. I recommend using a small deck for a Grand Tableau reading due to space limitations.

4. Observe the back of the deck and make sure you like it. Everything must be in accordance with your style and preferences.

5. These days, the internet provides easy access to blogs written by professional fortune tellers and deck collectors. These blogs often provide images of each card along with detailed

information about the decks. So, before buying a deck from your favorite esoteric store or online, do some research.

6. If you follow the German tradition, it's important to respect directional facing law, especially regarding the two querents' cards: the card: The Man, card number 28, and The Woman, card number 29. The figures on these cards must face each other. This technique is important as it helps you create a timeline (past, present, and future) which will be discussed in Chapter 4 of Lopes Mazza's codes. In a relationship reading, it allows you to check the current state of the relationship and each person's true intention. Decks with extra cards representing same-sex people in a reading are now widely available, especially in the Grand Tableau Lenormand.

The figures on these cards must face each other

INTRODUCTION

CONSECRATING THE DECK

I've received several questions regarding card consecration through e-mail and my Facebook page: *"What is the card consecration? Is it really necessary to consecrate the cards?"* Consecration involves "liberating" the cards from any external influences left by others, such as by the previous owner (if it's a second-hand deck) or the workers who handled the cards during the manufacturing, among others. In addition, the ritual of Consecration purifies the deck and charges it with your energy.

"Is it really necessary to consecrate the deck?". Some people may not think so, but it's a necessary practice for religious people. Both options are respectable since everyone can choose what is best for them. However, it's important to clarify that consecration alone doesn't enable a fortune teller to "read" the cards. I believe and will continue to do so that only well-prepared people with solid knowledge gained from extensive theoretical and practical studies can become professional card readers. It takes a lot of hard work, daily and consistently, to reach the level of a professional fortune teller.

The method of card consecration varies among fortune tellers, and there are numerous ways to do it. I propose a very simple ritual that I practice myself.

To consecrate your deck, you'll need the following materials:

- A white cotton tablecloth measuring 1 meter by 1 meter. This will serve as your work tablecloth during your card readings. I use my grandmother's scarf.
- An incense stick of your choice
- Enough coarse salt to form a circle).
- A glass of water.
- Crystal stones or coins.
- A candle

Ritual step by step:

1. Find a quiet and isolated table away from other people's eyes, and place the white cotton tablecloth on it.
2. Put the candle in the upper left corner of the table
3. Place the glass of water in the upper right corner.
4. Put the crystal stones or coins in the lower left corner.
5. Place the censer with the incense stick in the lower right corner.
6. Create a circle in the center of the table using the coarse salt. Leave enough space in the circle to place the cards one by one after the consecration ritual.
7. Keep the entire deck of cards outside the coarse salt circle.

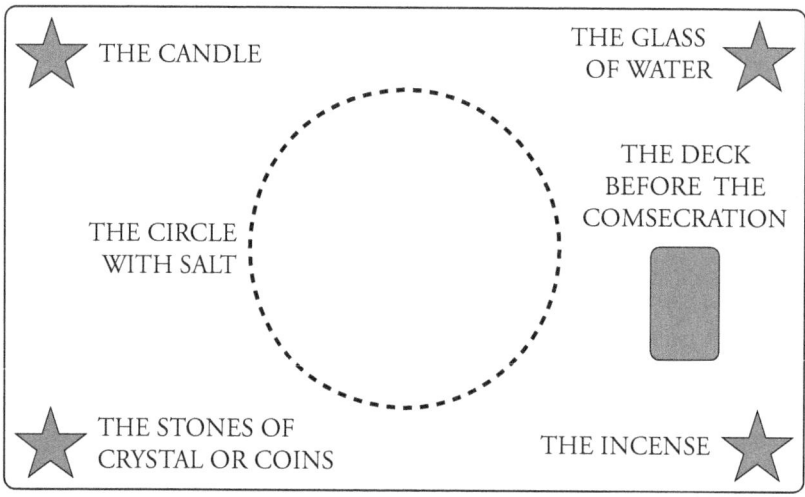

Once the table is prepared for the ritual:

1. Light both the candle and the incense.
2. Take each card one by one and pass it slowly and calmly through the smoke of the incense, front and back, before placing them inside the salt circle. During the consecration, you may say a prayer or a creed that you have composed.

3. After completing the ritual, seal the consecration with the words "And so it is!"
4. Leave everything on the table until the candle burns out completely. Then, dispose of the remaining candle, incense, salt, and glass of water in a newspaper and throw them into a river. The coins or the crystal stones can be saved for the next ritual or kept in a box to protect the deck.

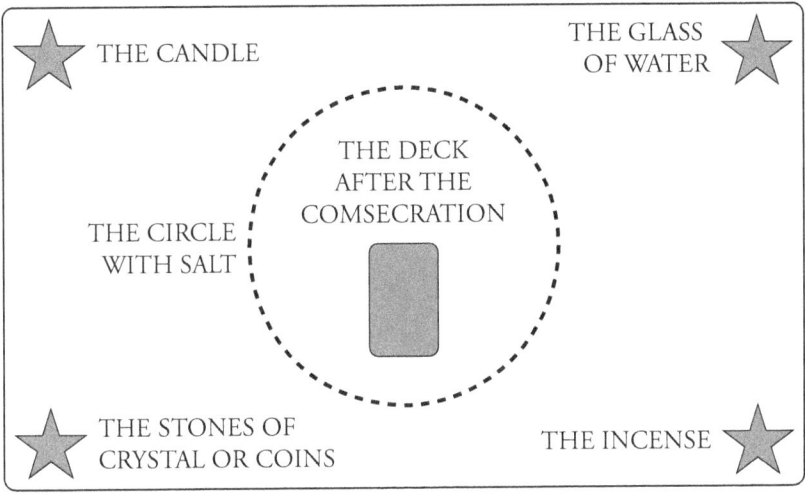

I use to put a few drops of my perfume on my cards.

Take Note:

The consecration can occur any day of the week and at any time unless you follow a religious belief that imposes different rules. This ritual should be repeated whenever you feel it is necessary.

Cleaning the cards

To rid the deck of any negative energies, I recommend performing the same consecration ritual whenever you feel it's necessary.

Put the cards in a plastic bag with talcum powder if they are dirty. Seal the bag and shake it a few times to ensure the talcum powder spreads over each card. Then, open the bag and clean each card individually with a towel or tissue. You'll notice how clean and shiny the cards become.

Protecting the cards (custody)

After the consecration or any consultation, to protect your cards and keep them safe, I suggest keeping your deck safe from other people's hands. You can use a small bag or wrap it in a cloth and place it in a wooden box (this isn't mandatory). To provide further protection, you can include items such as a black tourmaline stone, a picture of yourself, a mandrake root, Chinese camphor, bay leaves, and coarse salt. Feel free to add any other items you believe can serve as protection, as there are no strict rules.

My family has a tradition of making our own deck bag. We sew the small bag for the cards and the cloth where they're placed during the consultations. It's a ritual that I pass on to my students as an "inheritance". I'm honored to be their master and share this tradition with them. Many fortune tellers don't protect their cards and simply keep them in the deck box; it's a personal choice. I don't judge anyone who doesn't follow tradition since everyone is free to do what they want. It doesn't mean they're less capable as fortune tellers if they don't believe in tradition or rituals.

INTRODUCTION

Should the querent touch the cards?

There are many reasons why a fortune teller may choose to touch or not touch their cards and perform consultation rituals, such as: shuffling, cutting, and drawing the cards.

Some fortune tellers believe it's positive to actively involve the querent in these rituals as it allows them to directly project their real reasons for seeking help onto the cards, establishing a dialogue between the querent and the cards. The querent assumes the role of a direct channel with the cards while the fortune teller acts as a spokesperson.

Some fortune tellers prefer that the querent not touch the cards, simply because they want to protect their cards from inexperienced hands that might damage them. In addition, it can be emotionally devastating for the fortune teller to see their cards being handled violently, unsafely, and without proper focus by someone who doesn't know the rituals, is inexperienced, or emotionally overwhelmed due to personal problems. Can you imagine having such an experience?

I've asked myself countless times why I should involve someone in a ritual who probably has no desire to do so. I believe anyone who consults a fortune teller doesn't expect to be asked to perform some tasks, even against their will.

That's why I don't allow them to touch my cards. Since the first time I chose them to work with me, a strong bond has been formed between me and my cards. I treat them with love and protect them from any outside influence. I'm convinced that only the fortune teller should perform the consultation rituals because only they have the agility, practice, and preparation to generate the energy necessary for a balanced reading.

CHAPTER 1:
ORIGINS, CARDS AND SUITS

When we begin the study of any divination deck, it's necessary to know its roots, history, and other related aspects. This knowledge will allow us to understand its true essence and language.

This chapter will cover the following topics:

- Origins of the Petit Lenormand
- The anatomy of the cards
- The suits

A BRIEF HISTORY OF THE ORIGINS OF THE PETIT LENORMAND

Even today, many people attribute the origin of the Petit Lenormand deck, also known in Portugal and Brazil as the gypsy deck, to the famous French fortune teller Marie-Anne Adelaide Le Normand – also known as Mlle. Le Normand or La Sibylle de Salons, or the gypsy people.

Until recently, most fortune tellers, masters, and writers worldwide believed that the numerous existing decks bearing the name of Mlle. Le Normand were authored by her, as there was no evidence to the contrary. However, thanks to researchers and scholars such as Mary K. Greer, Helen Riding, Marcus Katz,

Tali Goodwin, and Andy Boroveshengra, we now have evidence showing that the origins of Petit Lenormand deck are not as magical as the popular narratives suggest. I'll take you on a brief historical tour to understand the deck's origins and introduce you to three key figures who played a significant role in its creation and widespread use. In short, that's all we know so far. I believe there's still much to be discovered!

Lady Charlotte Schreiber

Lady Charlotte Schreiber was born in Uffington, Lincolnshire, England, on May 19, 1812, and passed away on January 15, 1895, at the age of 82, in the Canford Manor estate in Dorset.

From an early age, she showed a keen interest in foreign languages and literature. Lady Schreiber gained recognition as a translator, entrepreneur, and collector of pottery and decks. She left her extensive deck collection to the British Museum when she died.

Even if you don't have the opportunity to visit the museum in person, you can take a virtual tour of the archives on their website: *www.britishmuseum.org*.

The website also provides access to the catalog record for Lady Charlotte Schreibe's deck collection: *www.archive.org*.

Among her deck collection is a German deck called Das Spiel der Hofnung (the Game of Hope), dated 1798/9, which consists of 36 cards symbolically identical to the Petit Lenormand deck.

To continue our story, it's necessary to introduce a second character.

CHAPTER 1: ORIGINS, CARDS AND SUITS

Johann Kaspar Hechtel

He was born in Nuremberg, Bavaria, Germany, on May 1, 1771, and died there on December 20, 1799, a victim of a smallpox epidemic.

In 1798/9, Johann Kaspar Hechtel, an entrepreneur and parlor game creator, developed a deck called Der Spiel der Hofnung (the Game of Hope) in Nuremberg. Years later, in 1846, this game served as a prototype for the Petit Lenormand deck.

Das Spiel der Hofnung [Reg. 1896, 0501.495] (The Game of Hope)
Nürnberg - GPJ Bielin

It was first mentioned by German professors and historians Detlef Hoffmann and Erika Kroppenstedt in a 1972 edition of Wahrsagerkarten (Letters of Divination) titled "Ein Beitrag zur Geschichte des Okkultismus" (A Contribution to the History of Occultism), published by Deutsches Spielkartenmuseum in Bielefeld.

In 1996, scholars and historians Ronald Decker, Thierry Depaulis, and Michael Dummett published the book "A Wicked Pack of Cards, The Origins of the Occult Tarot", in which they also discuss the origins of the Petit Lenormand deck. According to them, «*the cards are hand-illustrated and colored, and each one has two miniature cardboards: one with the German pattern known as the "Ansbach pattern" and the other with a French pattern called the "French suits". The symbols and numbers on these cards correspond precisely to what we will later know as "Petit Lenormand."*»

The deck is preserved at the British Museum in London. For those who are unable to appreciate this beauty in person, they can still enjoy it virtually through the website. This deck also includes an instruction sheet, in German:

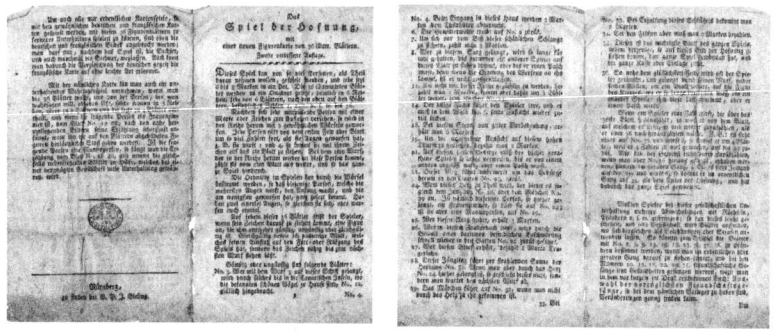

"*Hechtel, JK – the Game of Hope, a pleasant entertainment game, with 36 cards, packed[1]*"

---

1. "Hechtels, JK - das Spiel der Hoffnung, eine angenehme Gesellschaftsunterhaltung, mit 36 illumirten Figurenkarten, gebunden" translated by Alexsander Lepletier

CHAPTER 1: ORIGINS, CARDS AND SUITS

We can find a reference about Das Spiel der Hoffnung in the book "Humoristische Blätter für Kopf und Herz" (Bieling, 1799)

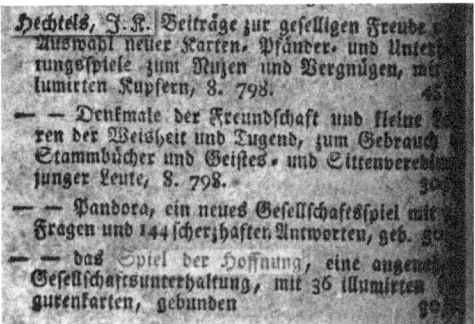

We have the privilege of having the document translated into the Portuguese language on the blog of my dear friend and colleague, Brazilian Alexsander Lepletier (*www.lenormando.blogspot.com*). Based on this translation, now is possible to bring the instructions of the "Game of Hope" in English.

THE GAME OF HOPE
Instruction sheet translation

«This game was designed to be played by any number of people who wish to participate (it reminds me of the Gloria game). Each player has a pawn (or piece), different from their opponents, which they use to move around the board.

The 36 cards are laid out in a square formation with six rows of six cards (forming a 6 by 6 cardboard, arranged in the order of the cards, from 1 to 36). Each player takes a pawn or a piece and rolls the two dice. Players cover a number of cards based on the sum of the two dice rolls, starting with the first. For example, if a player rolls a four and a one, they move their piece to the fifth card. On the next turn, they will move the number of cards from the fifth to the end of the game. The dice can also be used to determine the order of play, with the highest roll playing first and the lowest playing last. In the case of a tie, the players who roll the same name and number of dice can roll again to decide the game.

In each of the 36 sheets where the pawn lies, there's a figure that can be favorable, unfavorable, or neutral. I call those neutral sheets that don't influence the direction of the player's pawn, either forward or backward, but the pawn remains on the sheet until the next round.

The following sheets are favorable or unfavorable.

- No. 3 – The one who throws 3 and gets to The Ship, will be happily taken to the Canary Islands where the well-known beautiful Birds are at home, card no. 12.
- No. 4 – On entry on this House, two marks (money) have to be given to the doorkeeper.
- No. 6 – The Thunderclouds take the player back to no. 2.
- No. 7 – To stay safe from the dangerous bite of this snake, three marks have to be paid.
- No. 8 – The one who gets to this Coffin is considered dead until another player comes to this sheet, or until he rolls a double, for when it his turn to roll the dice he is not excluded.
- No. 11 – So as not be castigated by this Rod, pay two marks; and move forward two sheets to the no. 13, the Lad (Child).
- No. 14 – The cunning Fox leads the player astray who has to find refuge in the Wood at no. 5.
- No. 16 – Arriving at the Star, there are good prospects, and the player receives six marks.
- No. 19 – To enjoy a pleasant view of The Tower, one pays two marks.
- No. 21 – On these steep Alps, the player has to remain until another player arrives to release him or until he has to cast a double.
- No. 22 – Unnoticed, this path leads back to The Garden at no. 20.
- No. 24 – Whoever wins this heart, will immediately offer it either to the Youth at no. 28, or to the Girl, at no. 29.
- No. 25 – Whoever finds this ring, receives three marks.

- No. 26 – Whoever reads in this Grimoire (book of magical knowledge) will by a hex therein be forcefully returned to The Garden in no. 20.
- No. 27 – Whoever receives this Letter has to pay two marks for the bearer.
- No. 28 – This Youth leads to the brilliant Sun of hope in no. 31. However, for those who got here by way of The Heart, no. 24, this does not happen, wait here for the next time.
- No. 29 – The Girl leads on to card 32, unless one arrives here through The Heart (no. 24).
- No. 33 – On reaching this Key, one receives two marks.
- No. 34 – Reaching the fish, one has to pay two marks.
- No. 35 – This is the most important sheet on the whole game and one who lands here is the winner and draws all the cash box or deposit.
- No. 36 – So near to the luckiest field, the player is cheated and, against his will, he has to advance one step too far to the figure of The Cross, where he has to remain until another player lands on this card and takes the burden off him or he throws a double.

If a player rolls a number that takes them beyond the 36 cards, the player must count back as many numbers as he would move after The Cross. For example, if the player stands on 32 and casts 8, they must count back four houses, as they have exceeded 36. They would then stay in house 28.

It's not possible to receive the cash box by counting back an excess of the 36 cards. The only way to get it is through forward movement. For example, if a player stands on 29 and casts a six, they'd land on The Anchor card (number 35) and win.

If players want to add more variety to the game's entertainment, they can include riddles, forfeits, or other activities or penalties, and they'll be able to find sheets to which these can be added. For example, sheets 2, 5, 9, 13, 15, 18, 23, 30, 32, and 36 may be declared as forfeits, and when they're reached in an orderly way, on 10, 12, 17, 29, and 35, they can be required to sing songs of friendship and health-wishing. The book "Selection of the Most Excellent Songs of Friendship", published by the same publisher, offers several suggestions.

To play any common card game, it included the German and French playing cards with these 36-figure cards at the top of the card. It was only necessary to exclude the sixes and the sevens from the game. This also makes it easier to learn to compare German and French cards.

It's also possible to use these same cards to play an entertainment oracle game by shuffling the 36 cards and then having the person seeking the oracle cut them. Then lay out the cards in five rows with four rows of eight cards and the fifth row with the remaining four cards. If you're consulting a woman, start telling a happy story from the cards around sheet 29. If it's for a man, you start from sheet 28 and, again, use the cards surrounding it to tell your story. This game will add a lot of entertainment to a festive gathering.»

This last step, written by Johann Kaspar Hechtel, leaves us with a significant message: "The Game of Hope" deck might be used for divination purposes. He also describes the scheme for arranging the cards on the work table, "5 rows with 4 rows of 8 cards and a fifth row with the remaining 4", known today as Grand Tableau Lenormand or 8x4+4.

In the few lines written by Hechtel, there is another point that gives the first clues about how to interpret these cards in a divination reading: "If the person you're consulting is a woman, one starts from sheet 29 spinning a happy tale from the cards nearby around the figures on display. If it is for a man, the story begins from sheet 28 and, again, uses the cards surrounding it."

I believe that Philippe Lenormand was inspired by Hechtel's writings and, through deep study, worked out the meanings of the 36 cards and their interpretation for the Grand Tableau, locating the card that represents the querent and taking into account the close cards, as these have a greater influence on the querent, than those that are far away.

Mlle. Le Normand

Marie-Anne Adelaide Le Normand claimed she was born in Aleçon, Normandy, France, on May 27, 1772, and passed away on June 25, 1843, in Paris, Île-de-France, in France. However, official documents indicate that she was actually born on September 16, 1768. Her parents, Jean Louis Antoine Le Normand and Marie Anne Le Normand, died young, so she was raised in a convent from age five.

Marie-Anne Le Normand François Dumont (1793)

In 1790, Le Normand settled in Paris, and three years later, she joined Madame Gilbert and then started working as a fortune-teller. In 1797, she opened a bookstore on 5 Rue de Tournon, which was actually a front for a fortune-telling business. Le Normand had many illustrious clients, including Marat, Robespierre, Tsar Alexander I, and Saint-Just – for whom she predicted a violent and tragic death.

She also claimed she had been a confidante and clairvoyant of Empress Josephine and her husband, Napoleon Bonaparte. In 1814, she started a literary career and published several books narrating her career and her interactions with some distinguished personalities of the time. These books and some of her predictions created a public controversy, leading to court action and imprisonment. Her remains are in division three of the Père Lachaise Cemetery in Paris

These are the books written by Mlle. Le Normand:

- Les souvenirs prophétiques d'une sibylle sur les causes secrétes de son arrestation – Paris (1814);
- Anniversaire de la mort de l'impératrice Josephine (1815);
- La sibylle au tombeau de Louis XVI (1816);
- Les oracles sibyllins ou la suite des souvenirs prophétiques - Paris (1817) (528 pages);
- La sibylle au congrès d'Aix-la-Chapelle (1819);

- Mémoires historiques et secrets de l'impératrice Joséphine, MarieRose Tascher-de-la-Pagerie, première épouse de Napoléon Bonaparte - Paris (1820);
- Mémoire justificatif présenté par M.lle Le Normand (1821);
- Cri de l'honneur (1821); Souvenirs de la Belgique - Cent jours d'infortunes où le procès memorable (1822);
- L'ange protecteur de la France au tombeau de Louis XVIII (1824);
- L'ombre immortelle de Catherine II au tombeau d'Alexandre Ier (1826);
- L'ombre de Henri IV au palais d'Orléans (1830);
- Le petit homme rouge au château des Tuileries - Paris (1831);
- Manifeste des dieux sur les affaires de France (1932);
- Arrêt suprême des dieux de l'Olympe en faveur de Mme. la duchesse de Berry et de son fils (1833).

A reference to the deck used by Mlle. Le Normand and her readings can be found in the book *L'Oracle Parfait ou Le Passe-Temps Des Dames Art De Tirer Les Cartes* written by Etteila in 1875.

L'Oracle Parfait ou Le Passe-Temps Des Dames Art De Tirer Les Cartes
M.lle Lenormand, Etteila (1875)

According to this book, Mlle. Le Normand used a standard deck comprising 36 cards with nine cards for each suit: King, Queen, Jack, Ten, Nine, Eight, Seven, Two, and Ace. And that the drawing method used by Mlle Le Normand was a layout of nine cards in four rows, making up of 36 houses (a layout now known as the 9x4 Grand Tableau Lenormand), representing various life areas, emotional states, or events that served as a guide during the reading.

This layout, known today as the Grand Tableau Lenormand of Houses, is widely practiced in Switzerland, Germany, Austria, and France.

1 Projet.	2 Satisfaction.	3 Réussite.	4 Espérance.	5 Hasard.	6 Désir.	7 Injustice.	8 Ingratitude.	9 Association.
10 Perte.	11 Peine.	12 État.	13 Joie.	14 Amour.	15 Prospérité.	16 Mariage.	17 Affliction.	18 Jouissance.
19 Héritage.	20 Trahison.	21 Rival.	22 Présent.	23 Amant.	24 Élévation.	25 Bienfait.	26 Entreprise.	27 Changement.
28 Fin.	29 Récompense.	30 Disgrâce.	31 Bonheur.	32 Fortune.	33 Indifférence.	34 Faveur.	35 Ambition.	36 Indisposition.

The 36 Houses of Mlle Le Normand's Tableau

Although the keywords may seem ambiguous, the book provides few details regarding their meanings. The complete deck of 36 cards is distributed into 36 houses, and the reading is based on observing the color of the playing card inserts in the houses.

These are meaning of the 36 cards:

- **Suit of Hearts:** These cards are positive and announce success, love, and good feelings.
- **Suit of Clubs:** They're considered good omen and predict success, support, loyalty, and friendship.

- **Suit of Diamonds:** They're both positive and negative and usually indicate profits, business opportunities, difficulties, delays, envy, or jealousy.
- **Suit of Spades:** These cards are considered negative omens and herald the arrival of problems of all kinds and mysteries.

Below are a few examples of how certain cards can be interpreted within the houses to help you get an idea of how the system works:

House no. 1 – Project

- Hearts: Happiness and successful projects.
- Clubs: Faithful people work for the success of a project.
- Diamonds: Great difficulty in business due to jealousy.
- Spades: Betrayal leads to bankruptcy

House no. 8 – Ingratitude

- Hearts: The querent will receive justice against ungrateful people.
- Clubs: The querent's honor will be restored with the help of friends.
- Diamonds: Jealousy will be the only cause of the ingratitude.
- Spades: The same ungrateful people will betray the querent.

House no. 23 – The Lover

- Hearts: A lover who's passionate and have a good character.
- Clubs: A Faithful lover with good intentions.
- Diamonds: A Jealous, suspicious, and upset lover
- Spades: A deceitful and vengeful lover.

House no. 28 – The End

- Hearts: The loss of a loved one will increase the querent's fortune.
- Clubs: The loss of a friend that will leave good memories.
- Diamonds: The loss of an opponent.
- Spades: The loss of a dangerous enemy or rival.

The cards touching the card and positioned to the left, right, above, and below will provide details about the central card. For example, if the focus is on the card placed in the 14th house, Love, the card receives the influence of the cards placed in the 5th, 15th, 23rd, and 13th houses. On the other hand, if the focus is on house No. 36, Indisposition, the cards to consider are those in positions No. 27 and No. 35. And so on. According to Etteilla, the 36 cards used by Mlle. Le Normand had the following meanings:

Suit of Hearts
- The King: A good, caring, kind, and thoughtful man.
- The Queen: A good, loving, kind, and thoughtful woman.
- The Jacks: A good, affectionate, kind, and thoughtful young man.
- 10: Happiness, great joy, feast, celebration.
- 9: Love, success, victory, conquest.
- 8: Joy, honor, wealth, advancement, lovely feelings.
- 7: Youth, child, emotional life, a visit.
- 2: The querent.
- Ace: The house, the home, the family, a relative, friendship.

Suit of Clubs
- The King: A loyal, helpful, and prudent friend. Benevolent and protective man.
- The Queen: A loyal, devoted, discreet, and respected friend. Benevolent and protective woman.
- The Jacks: A virtuous young man. A loyal, discreet, respected, and younger friend.
- 10: A large sum of unexpected money.
- 9: A gift.
- 8: Profits, salary.
- 7: A lover, a rival.
- 2: The querent's confidant.
- Aces: Success, abundance, fame.

Suit of Diamonds
- The King: A strange, powerful, jealous, mean, and bad-tempered man.
- The Queen: A strange, powerful, jealous, mean, bad-tempered woman.
- The Jacks: A jealous, unknown young man.
- 10: A trip by land or sea, short or far away.
- 9: News, good or bad, will be announced by the surrounding cards.
- 8: Short trips for leisure or business.
- 7: A foreign child.
- 2: A lover, a father.
- Ace: A letter, a contract.

Suit of Spades
- The King: A brutal, evil, and deceitful man.
- The Queen: A vicious, cruel, and dishonest woman.
- The Jacks: A brutal, mean, and untruthful young man.
- 10: Sadness, emotional pain, and disappointment.
- 9: Rupture, end.
- 8: Afflictions, tears, annoyances, tribulations.
- 7: Falsehood, infidelity, rivalry, inconstancy.
- 2: The Rival.
- Ace: Perseverance, constancy

Another suggestion that Mlle. Le Normand might have used an ordinary deck of playing cards (32 cards) for her consultations is in her book Les Oracles Sibyllins or La Suite des Souvenirs Prophétiques, published in Paris in 1817. In this book, she vaguely mentions her card spreads and provides the meanings of some cards.

After the death of Mlle. Le Normand, her name became associated with several decks for commercial purposes. Precisely, in 1845, a year before the release of the Petit Lenormand deck, the Great Game of Mlle. Lenormand was published by Grimaud, along with five books on topics such as astrology, geomancy, and palmistry. The author used the pseudonym "Mme. la Comtesse de ***" with an address provided by the publisher, "46, Rue Vivienne", which was probably a marketing strategy for commercial reasons.

Due to its apparent complexity, it's less popular and less practiced worldwide. However, I've found a few fortune tellers in Germany, France, and French Switzerland who still practice it. I've been studying this deck in-depth for a few years, and I've seen the predicted events to be accurate in my readings.

Brief presentation of the Grand Jeu de Mlle. Lenormand

The Grand Jeu de Mlle Lenormand deck has 54 cards each card contains eight symbols), two cards representing the querents, and the remaining 52 are divided into five categories:

1. The Golden Fleece, also known as The Conquest of the Golden Fleece, represents worldly affairs, trade, business, and travel. It consists of six cards: 10 of Diamonds, 9 of Diamonds, King of Clubs, 4 of Diamonds, Ace of Clubs, and 9 of Hearts;

2. The Trojan War symbolizes the triumph of the stronger over weaker. The cards in this group reveal the struggles that must be overcome to achieve their goals. It consists of nine cards: 5 of Clubs, 2 of Spades, Jack of Diamonds, 10 of Clubs, 9 of Spades, 6 of Clubs, 6 of Spades, 8 of Spades, and Queen of Diamonds.

3. Hermetic Knowledge is associated with love, relationships, family, friendship, unions, and marriage. It consists of seven cards: 7 of Spades, 3 of Clubs, 4 of Clubs, 8 of Clubs, 6 of Hearts, 7 of Hearts, and 10 of Hearts;

4. The Unpredictable. This group of cards brings unpredictable events that aren't easily foreseen and may either facilitate or hinder project completion. It consists of 19 cards: 2 of Clubs, Jack of Clubs, 7 of Diamonds, 8 of Hearts, 3 of Hearts, 6 of Diamonds, 2 of Hearts, King of Diamonds, Queen of Spades, 3 of Spades, 4 of Spades, Queen of Clubs, 5 of Hearts, 10 of Spades, Ace of Hearts, 2 of Diamonds, Ace of Diamonds, King of Hearts and King of Spades;

5. The Order of Time is represented by the 12 zodiac signs, which stand for the passage of time. This group contains 12 cards: Jack of Hearts, Ace of Spades, 3 of Diamonds, 9 of Clubs, 9 of Hearts, Queen of Hearts, Jack of Spades, 5 of Diamonds, 5 of Spades, 7 of Clubs, 8 of Diamonds, and 4 of Hearts.

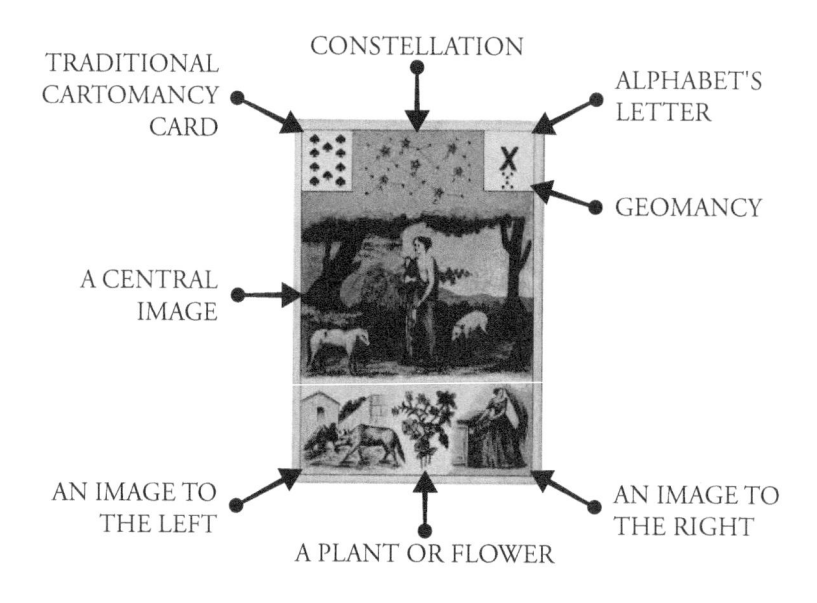

- TRADITIONAL CARTOMANCY CARD
- CONSTELLATION
- ALPHABET'S LETTER
- GEOMANCY
- A CENTRAL IMAGE
- AN IMAGE TO THE LEFT
- A PLANT OR FLOWER
- AN IMAGE TO THE RIGHT

This deck and instructions for using it are available at the British Museum, which can be accessed online: *www.britishmuseum.org*

CHAPTER 1: ORIGINS, CARDS AND SUITS

In 1846, a deck of cards called "Wahrsagerin, die, M.lle Lenormand. Erklärung des Kartenspiels d. berühmten Wahrsagerin Mlle. Lenormand in Paris" – "Divination card game by the famous fortune teller Mlle. Lenormand from Paris" was published, and it was inspired by "Das Spiel der Hofnung" or "The Game of Hope".

The German suits were removed from the prototype deck of the Petit Lenormand, and the French suits were kept to emphasize that the deck was of French origin and had been created by Mlle. Le Normand. From then on, all the decks published worldwide under Mlle. Lenormand's name would bear the French suit.

Wahrsagerin, die, M.lle Lenormand. Erklärung des Kartenspiels d. berühmten Wahrsagerin M.lle Lenormand in Paris - 1846

In 1846, the first instruction booklet was also published, accompanying a deck of cards by Philippe Lenormand, who claimed to be Mlle. Le Normand's nephew and heir. However, it was later revealed that Philippe Lenormand was a fictitious name used for marketing purposes. Nevertheless, the booklet provides practical information for the immediate use of the deck.

Directions for use

"Mlle. Lenormand has left among us so many favorable opinions, and so full a memory of her rare talent, that we believe we render a service to the admirers of her system by publishing these cards, which were found with her after her death. It was with these same cards that she prophesied to the Emperor Napoleon I his greatness, and to many of his princes and great men of France their downfall and their misfortunes. Thousands of noblemen acknowledged her great talent already during her life time, and often confessed that her method was full of truth and exactness.

What makes our publication still more interesting, is the fact that we give the explanation of the cards exactly as Mlle. Lenormand left them. We have also arranged it in such shape, that every lady or gentleman can read his or her fortune without have to obtain the aid of anybody else.

Directions for using the cards

After having shuffled the 36 cards and cut them with the left hand, divide them into five heaps, 4 of them containing each 8 cards, which we place in four rows from left to right, and the last consisting of four cards, in the center under the last row, as presented in this diagram.

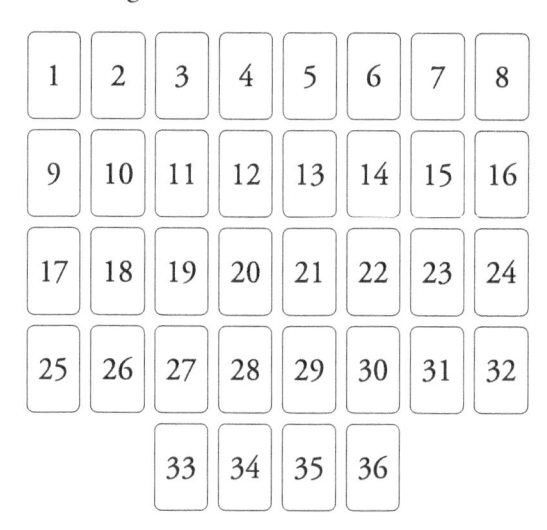

1	2	3	4	5	6	7	8
9	10	11	12	13	14	15	16
17	18	19	20	21	22	23	24
25	26	27	28	29	30	31	32
		33	34	35	36		

The persons who wish to have their fortune told, are represented by number 29 for a lady, and number 28 for a gentleman. The greatest attention must be paid to these cards, numbers 28 and 29. Their position signifies the future happiness of misfortune of the person, all the other cards take their meaning from these, and in such a way, that their position, as it near to or more distant from these, rule the future the destiny.

Signification of the 36 cards

- **No. 1 – The Cavalier:** is a messenger of good fortune if not surrounded by unlucky cards, brings good news, which the Person may expect, either from his own house or from abroad; this will, however, not take place immediately, but some time later.

- **No. 2 – A Clover Leaf:** is also a harbinger of good news; but if surrounded by clouds it indicates great pain; but if No. 2 lies near No. 29 or 28, the pain will be of short duration, and soon change to a happy issue.

- **No. 3 – The Ship:** the Symbol of commerce, signifies great wealth, which will be acquired by trade or inheritance; if near to the Person, it means an early journey.

- **No. 4 – The House:** is a certain sign of success and prosperity in all undertakings; and though the present position of the Person may be disagreeable, yet the future will be bright and happy. If this card lies in the centre of the cards, under the Person, this is a hint to beware of those who surround him or her.

- **No. 5 – A Tree:** if distant from the Person, signifies good health; more trees of different cards together, leave no doubt about the realization of all reasonable wishes.

- **No. 6 – Clouds:** if their clear side is turned towards the Person, are a lucky sign; with the dark side turned to the Person, something disagreeable will soon happen.

- **No. 7 – A Serpent:** is a sign of misfortune, the extent of which depends upon the greater or smaller distance from the Person; it is followed invariably by deceit, infidelity, and sorrow.

- **No. 8 – A Coffin:** very near to the Person, means, without any doubt, dangerous diseases, death, or a total loss of fortune. More distant from the Person, the card is less dangerous.

- **No. 9 – The Bouquet:** means much happiness in every respect.

- **No. 10 – The Scythe:** indicates great danger, which will only be avoided if lucky cards surround it.

- **No. 11 – The Rod:** means quarrels in the family, domestic afflictions, want of peace among married persons; also fever and protracted sickness.

- **No. 12 – The Bird:** means hardships to overcome, but of short duration; distant from the Person, it means the accomplishment of a pleasant journey. 2

- **No. 13 – The Child:** is a sign that the Person moves in good society, and is full of kindness towards everybody.

- **No. 14 – The Fox:** if near, is a sign to mistrust persons with whom you are connected, because some of them try to deceive you; if distant, no danger is to be apprehended.

- **No. 15 – The Bear:** is either a messenger of good fortune, or admonishes us to keep away from company; particularly from that of the envious.

- **No. 16 – The Star:** confirms good luck in all enterprises; but if near clouds, it means a long series of unhappy accidents.

- **No. 17 – The Stork:** indicates a change of abode, which will take place, the sooner the nearer the card lies to the Person.

CHAPTER 1: ORIGINS, CARDS AND SUITS

- **No. 18 – The Dog:** if near the Person, you can consider your friends faithful and sincere; but if very distant and surrounded by clouds, be cautious not to trust those who call themselves your friends.

- **No. 19 – The Tower:** gives the hope of a happy old age; but if surrounded by clouds, it forbodes sickness, and, according to circumstances, even death.

- **No. 20 – The Park:** prognosticates that you will visit a very respectable company; if very near, that you are to form a very intimate friendship, but if distant, it hints to false friends.

- **No. 21 – The Mountains:** near the Person, warn you against a mighty enemy; if distant, you may rely on powerful friends.

- **No. 22 – The Roads:** surrounded by clouds, are signs of disaster; but without this card, and if distant from Person, that you shall find ways and means to avoid the threatening danger.

- **No. 23 – The Mouse:** is a sign of a theft, a loss; when near, it indicates the recovery of the thing lost or stolen; if at a distance, the loss will be irreparable.

- **No. 24 – The Heart:** is a sign of joy leading to union and bliss.

- **No. 25 – The Ring:** if on the right of the Person, prognosticates a rich and happy marriage; when on the left, and distant, a falling out with the object of your affection, and the breaking off of a marriage.

- **No. 26 – The Book:** indicates that you are going to find out a secret; according to its position, you can judge in what manner; great caution, however, is necessary in attempting a solution.

- **No. 27 – The Letter:** without clouds, means luck, which comes to you by distant, favorable news; but if dark clouds are near the Person, you may expect much grief.

- **No. 28. & No. 29 – The Gentleman and The Lady:** The whole pack refers to either of these cards, depending, if the person whose fortune is being told is either a Lady (No. 29) or Gentleman (No. 28).

- **No. 30 – The Lilies:** indicate a happy life; surrounded by clouds, a family grief. If this card is placed above the Person, they indicate the same as being virtuous; if below the Person, the moral principles are doubted.

- **No. 31 – The Sun:** lying near, points to happiness and pleasure, as its beams spread light and warmth; far away, it indicates misfortune and sorrow, as without the Sun's influence nothing can grow.

- **No. 32 – The Moon:** is a sign of great honors, fortune and fame, if the card lies at the side of the Person; if at a distance, it means grief and misery.

- **No. 33 – The Key:** if near, means the certain success of a wish or a plan; if distant, the contrary.

- **No. 34 – The Fishes:** if near the Person, point to the acquisition of large fortune by marine enterprises and to a series of successful undertakings; if distant, they indicate the failure of any speculation, no matter how well projected or planned.

- **No. 35 – The Anchor:** is a sign of a successful enterprise at sea, of great advantage in trade, and of true love; but distant, it means a thorough disappointment in ideas, and inconstancy in love.

- **No. 36 – The Cross:** is always a bad sign; if very near the person, you may hope that the misfortune will not last long.

In accordance with the foregoing explanation, we take the following example of Fortune Telling, the cards being laid for a Lady of which we can give the following auspicious and happy solution:

CHAPTER 1: ORIGINS, CARDS AND SUITS

The Sun, No. 31, which is placed above your head, assures you of a lasting happiness, because the Star, No. 16, which is on your right, shines on you. Through it all your enterprises have been successful, and by it you have been happy in your marriage.

Your husband, No. 28, who is at your right, testifies to your virtue, which is affirmed by the child No. 13, which is at your left. The Lilies and Flowers, which overshadow you in Nos. 30 and 9, are proofs of your good deeds.

Fate also employs the Cavalier, No. 1, to speak to your praise, and give the news of it to your true friends. Your good and benevolent actions, confirmed by the cards Nos. 2, 3, 24, 4, 5, 32, 27, 18, 26, 21, 20, 15 and 34, which surround you, are additional proofs of your future happiness. Your united forces have protected you hitherto in spite of the calumnies which should injure you, which proves, triumphantly, that virtue always overcomes the intrigues of the bad.

Your happiness, however has been troubled for a short while by envious spirits which endeavored to injure you; they are represented by Nos. 14, 12, 35 and 33, which have done everything they could to ruin you, but their calumnies were rebuked by public opinion, which was on your side.

The Tower, No. 19, promises you a happy old age as a recompense for your courage in bearing up under these sights. You have vanquished No. 11, which had sown the seed of discord in your household. No. 17 teels you that you will soon change your place of residence: no. 10, it is true, is a sign of mischief, but you will overcome it by the means of No. 25, aided by The Key, No. 33, which is placed at your feet.

In general, everything disagreeable will remain far from you, because its harbingers, the coffin, the clouds, the terrible serpent and the dangerous cross, represented in Nos. 8, 6, 7 and 36 are far distant from you, and cannot reach you for a long time. Providence has sealed your happiness, and henceforth you will enjoy the recompense of your virtue, in spite of a vicious, corrupted world; always trust in Providence, and she will never forsake you. Thus, your destiny is the best which can be hoped for, and we are glad that it was in our power to solve it for you.

This is the whole science of Mlle. LeNormand; so we deliver her cards to the Public with confidence, convinced that our purpose will have some success, either by confidence or faith in the divination, or as serving as a pleasant pastime. We are satisfied that we have done something for the memory of the famous Sybil by perpetuating the system by which she achieved a celebrity, not confined to the period of her lifetime, but lasting, and to last throughout the ages.

(Signed) PHILIPPE,
Heirs of Mlle. LeNormand.

Mary K. Greer

In 2013, Mary K. Greer, an influential figure in the esoteric world due to her extensive contribution to the discoveries she made based on research and studies of The Petit Lenormand and the Tarot, rediscovers a deck accompanied by a 31-page booklet published in England in 1796, but which had been published in Vienna, Austria, in 1794.

The book "Les Amusements des Allemands; or, The Diversions of The Court of Vienna" and a deck of 32 cards. Each card has a number (from 1 to 32), a printed image of a campaign landscape or a place of daily life, with a dominant image (a snake, a ring, a coffin, an anchor, etc.), and a text with a predictive purpose or advice. The similarities between this deck, The Game of Hope deck, and The Petit Lenormand are extraordinary. For example:

- Card number 1, The Crossroads, corresponds to card number 22, The Crossroads, in both the Petit Lenormand and The Game of Hope decks.
- Card number 9, The Dog, corresponds to card number 18, The Dog, in both the Petit Lenormand and The Game of Hope decks.
- Card number 12, The Clouds, corresponds to card number 6, The Clouds, in both the Petit Lenormand and The Game of Hope decks.
- The Heart, card number 24, is the only card that retains the same card number and name in both decks.

This fact leads us to conclude that Johann Kaspar Hechtel was inspired by the deck "Les Amusements des Allemands, or, The Diversions of The Court of Vienna" when designing "The Game of Hope" deck, except for cards number 16, The Tree, and number 30, The Vipers.

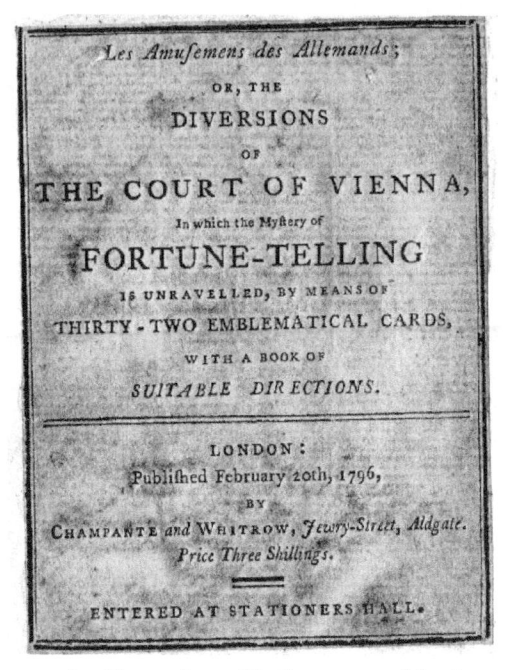

Les Amusements des Allemands; or, The Diversions of the Court of Vienna, in which the Mystery of Fortune-Telling

Mary K. Greer believes that card number 28, The Lion, is represented by card number 15, The Bear, in The Petit Lenormand, as it strongly resembles the coffee grounds: *«The Lion, or a fierce animal»*. The cards' meanings in the "Les Amusements des Allemands" deck, or "The Diversions of The Court of Vienna," correspond to the meanings in the Petit Lenormand.

Let's take card number 23, The Mice, as an example. The text on card no. 21 says: *«21 The Mouse: Keep your eyes open with your servants, for your negligence can turn an honest man into a thief.»*

On page 27 of the booklet that comes with the deck, the text referring to the card The Mouse says: *«Since this animal lives furtively, and it's also an emblem of theft or robbery, if it is clear, it indicates that what has been stolen will be recovered, however, if it appears unclear, do not hope for recovery.»*

CHAPTER 1: ORIGINS, CARDS AND SUITS

Card no. 21 – The Mouse
Le amusements des Allemands; or,
The Deversions of The Court of
Vienna (1794/1796)

Card no. 23 – The Mice
Philippe Lenormand
(1846)

Reading the text reminded me of the coffee grounds technique that my grandmother and a Turkish woman named Latifa taught me. In this technique, all the easily recognizable symbols, clear and positioned near the cup handle, announce what is about to happen in the querent's life. However, if these symbols are not evident or unclear, they indicate that the event may not occur or involves a mystery that can't be identified at the moment.

A second example is The Clouds card, concerning the technique of light and dark clouds, which was already present in 1794 when this beautiful deck was created. Part of the text of card number 12, The Clouds, from the deck "Le amusements des Allemands" states: «*If the clouds are lighter than dark, you can expect a good result; your hopes will be fulfilled; if they are darker, then you will have to abandon your plans and hopes.*»

Card no. 12 – The Clouds
Le amusements des Allemands; or,
The Deversions of The Court of
Vienna (1794/1796)

Card no. 6 – The Clouds
Philippe Lenormand
(1846)

Based on this statement, I can infer that the passage *«if it is clear, it shows that what was stolen will be recovered, but if it appears unclear, do not hope for recovery.»* if the clear clouds are in contact with The Mouse card, the probability of discovering fraud or finding something stolen is higher than if the dark clouds touching The Mice card.

The instruction sheet by Philippe Lenormand in 1846 states: *«23 - The Mouse is a sign of a theft, a loss; when near, it indicates the recovery of the thing lost or stolen; if at a distance, the loss will be irreparable.»*

Based on the factors presented, we must agree that the meanings and reading techniques attributed to the Petit Lenormand deck have ancient roots, probably much older than the dates reported here. The recent discovery confirms that the symbols or emblems in the deck originated in coffee ground divination. It's also believed that Johann Kaspar Hechtel decided to create a deck with 36 cards based on the Schafkorpf Tarock Bayerisches, which was very popular at the time, adding four additional cards to the 32-card deck.

I'm not surprised that the Grand Tableau method, described in the booklet "Les Amusements des Allemands" or "The Diversions of The Court of Vienna", is associated with this deck or other decks from that time.

Le amusements des Allemands; or, The Deversions of The Court of Vienna (1794/1796)

CHAPTER 1: ORIGINS, CARDS AND SUITS

My grandmother used to tell me that the fortune tellers in the previous century worked with large "games" that involved the entire deck in the reading and that the card's interpretation was based on their distance from the card representing the querent or from another card representing a specific life area a concern at the time. Through this structure, known today as the Grand Tableau, I learned to read the cards with any deck.

My grandmother passed on her wisdom to me, first with the "little French cards" (The Petit Lenormand), the traditional deck, and then with the Kipper, the Belline, and Tarot.

These are the 32 cards from the Les Amusements des Allemands deck; or, The Diversions of The Court of Vienne:

In 2015, my dear friend Giordano Berti, an Italian researcher and historian, approached me about collaborating on a new deck called The Sibyl of The Heart. I had in my hands only 40 enigmatic figures designed by a follower of the Rosicrucians, the German theologian Daniel Cramer (January 20, 1568 - October 5, 1637). These emblems, which are part of a series of emblems, were first published in 1617.

My role in creating the Sybil of The Heart deck was to provide each card with a unique identity and a voice based on a divinatory perspective. During the process, Giordano and I discovered that many of these emblems used in the deck contained symbols identical to those found in The Petit Lenormand deck.

For instance, the Affligor emblem features two hands holding a broom and a whip, which are the symbols of the broom and the whip found on card number 11 of The Petit Lenormand. Similarly, the Crucifigor emblem represents The Crucified One, where a large cross with a heart studded with four nails is the predominant symbol. This emblem is also found on card number 36, The Cross.

Affligor emblem    *Card no. 11*   *Crucified emblem* 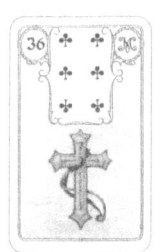   *Card no. 36*
                    The Broom and   *The Cross*
                    The Whip

CHAPTER 1: ORIGINS, CARDS AND SUITS

THE ANATOMY OF THE 36 CARDS

The Petit Lenormand deck is composed of 36 cards, numbered from 1 to 36 and all the cards are illustrated with symbolic figures that are easy to understand.

Each card is associated with a number, a traditional playing card insert, and a symbol.

- **A number:** the number on each card doesn't have a premonitory function. Its only purpose is to identify the card. However, in some countries, such as France and Russia, the numbers on the cards are used to analyze the querent's numerological profile.

- **A traditional French cartomancy card insert:** the 36 cards are divided into four families or suits, each one with nine cards: Ace, King, Queen, Jack, 10, 9, 8, 7 and 6.

- **A Symbolic Image:** Each card also features a central symbol that depicts a symbolic figure (people, objects, animals, plants, celestial bodies, buildings, flowers, among others), and symbols that represent everyday life. It's through these symbols that each card receives its name.

A NUMBER

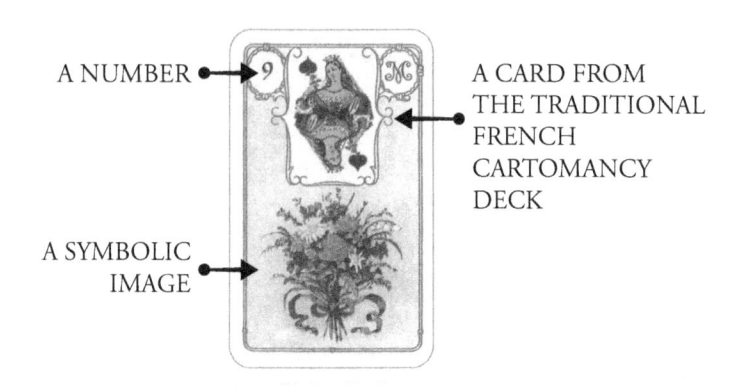

A CARD FROM THE TRADITIONAL FRENCH CARTOMANCY DECK

A SYMBOLIC IMAGE

The 36 cards (number and name)

- No. 1 – The Rider
- No. 2 – The Clover
- No. 3 – The Ship
- No. 4 – The House
- No. 5 – The Tree
- No. 6 – The Clouds
- No. 7 – The Snake
- No. 8 – The Coffin
- No. 9 – The Bouquet
- No. 10 – The Scythe
- No. 11 – The Broom and The Whip
- No. 12 – The Owls
- No. 13 – The Child
- No. 14 – The Fox
- No. 15 – The Bear
- No. 16 – The Stars
- No. 17 – The Stork
- No. 18 – The Dog
- No. 19 – The Tower
- No. 20 – The Garden
- No. 21 – The Mountain
- No. 22 – The Crossroads
- No. 23 – The Mice
- No. 24 – The Heart
- No. 25 – The Ring
- No. 26 – The Book
- No. 27 – The Letter
- No. 28 – The Man
- No. 29 – The Woman
- No. 30 – The Lilies
- No. 31 – The Sun
- No. 32 – The Moon
- No. 33 – The Key
- No. 34 – The Fish
- No. 35 – The Anchor
- No. 36 – The Cross

CHAPTER 1: ORIGINS, CARDS AND SUITS

I recommend that everyone learn to identify the cards by number and name. For example, when referring to The Scythe card, it's essential to know that it corresponds to card no. 10 of the deck. Similarly, when referring to card no. 14, we must know it corresponds to The Fox card.

Why is this lesson important? I believe that all of you visit study rooms or use blogs to find information about the cards, and as you may have noticed, most authors identify the cards by their numbers or names. Moreover, identifying the cards by numbers helps when working with The Houses of the Grand Tableau, where each house is identified by the card that rules it, so the 31st house is ruled by card no. 31, The Sun.

First, to truly understand the Petit Lenormand deck, you must become intimately familiar with it. As we know, the deck used in The Game of Hope served as the prototype for all Petit Lenormand decks. Johann Kaspar Hechtel, for commercial reasons, included both the traditional German deck pattern, the Schafkorpf Tarock Bayerisches, and the traditional French deck design.

GERMAN PLAYING CARD SCHAFKORPF TAROCK BAYERISCHES ◆ ◆ TRADITIONAL FRENCH PLAYING CARD

THE GAME OF HOPE (1779)

Since the first appearance of The Petit Lenormand in 1846, the French design has accompanied the deck. For the same reason, the traditional French deck association has confused the reading for many years.

The contradicting nature of the meanings is significant, causing fortune tellers often prioritize the suits for divination and use the symbols as guidance or advice. In some cases, readers even choose to ignore the suits entirely during a reading.

Let's take the card no. 9, The Bouquet, as an example. It's represented by the Queen of Spades and a branch of flowers as a symbol. The Bouquet is a positive card representing joy, happiness, affection, praise, conquest, etc. On the other hand, the Queen of Spades has a negative meaning, symbolizing a distant, calculating, and potentially adversarial woman. She may bring deceit, manipulation, revenge, and the harshest form of betrayal. This illustrates the contradiction between the card's suit and the symbol it represents.

As you've noted, the contradiction between the suit and the symbol the card represents can be reconciled by studying German design, where the German suit and the symbolism depicted on the card are connected in a single meaning. I believe the symbolic images on each card serve as a mnemonic device for the traditional meanings depicted on the card.

THE GERMAN CARTOMANCY SUITS

When studying the origins of The Petit Lenormand, we learn that the deck has its roots in Nuremberg, Bavaria, in Germany, so it "speaks" German. Starting with this very important point is crucial to understand the deck. Thus, it's essential to focus on studying the traditional German deck in Germany. The first step is to learn how to identify German suits and their corresponding French suits.

In the German suit:
- The Hearts (Rot) correspond to the French suit of Hearts;
- The Leaves (Laud) correspond to the French suit of Spades;

- The Bells (Schellen) correspond to the French suit of Diamonds;
- The Acorns (Eichen) correspond to the French suit of Clubs;

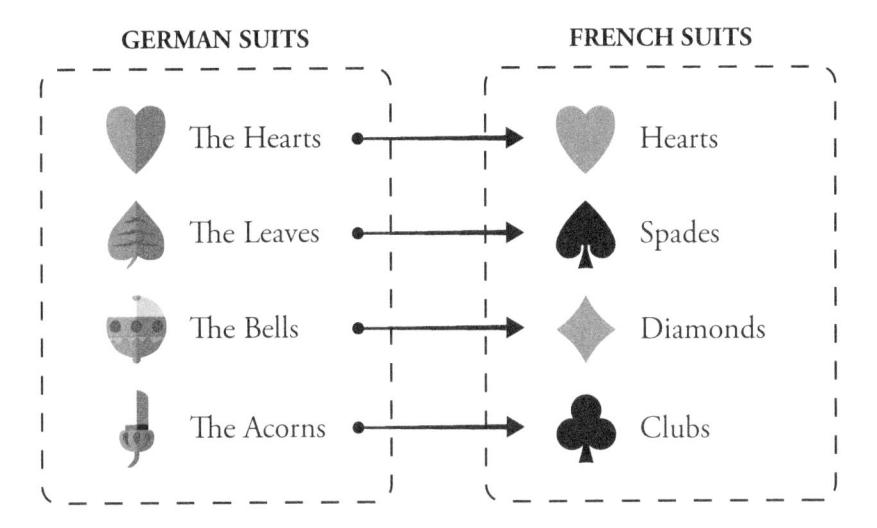

GERMAN SUITS	FRENCH SUITS
The Hearts →	Hearts
The Leaves →	Spades
The Bells →	Diamonds
The Acorns →	Clubs

Those familiar with the traditional French deck probably found weird the order I arranged the suits: hearts, spades, diamonds, and clubs. However, there's a reason for this, which you'll understand when you learn the meanings of each German suit.

As you can see in the following image, in Germany, the suits have different colors, especially the spades suit, which is green, and the diamonds suit, which is orange. In Germany, the suits are known as Vier Farben, translated into "the four colors" in English, and clearly represent the four suits.

It would be fantastic if the makers of The Petit Lenormand decks would consider replacing the French suits with the German ones and if the scholars and masters of the Petit Lenormand deck would begin referring to the suits by their proper names: hearts, leaves, bells, and acorns. This would not only honor the deck but also help to avoid further confusion during the reading. In my courses, I encourage the students to refer to the suits by their real names, hearts, leaves, bells, and acorns, to get them accustomed to the German system from the start of their studies.

FRENCH SUITS

- ♥ Hearts
- ♠ Spades
- ♦ Diamonds
- ♣ Clubs

FRENCH SUIT WITH GERMAN COLORS

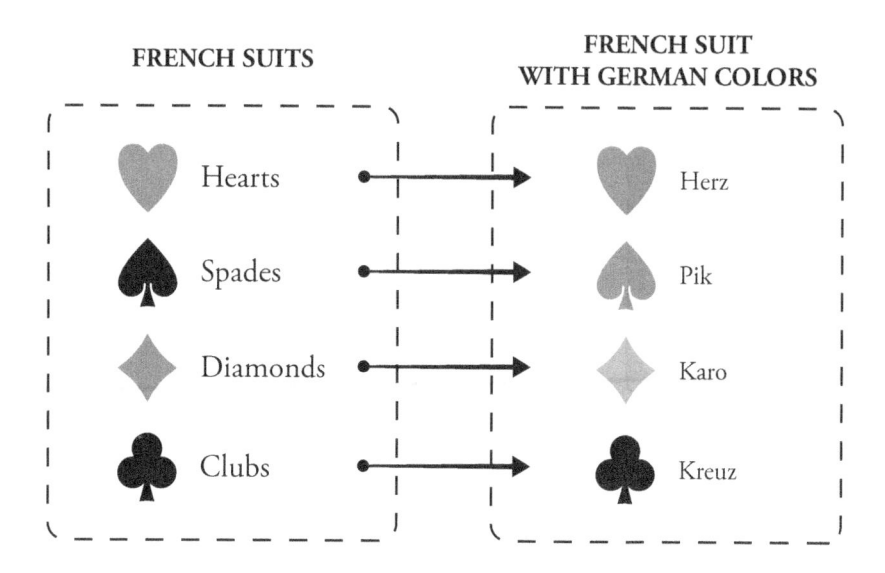

- ♥ Herz
- ♠ Pik
- ♦ Karo
- ♣ Kreuz

SCHAFKOPF TAROCK BAYERISCHES DECK

♥ ROT
(The Hearts)

CHAPTER 1: ORIGINS, CARDS AND SUITS

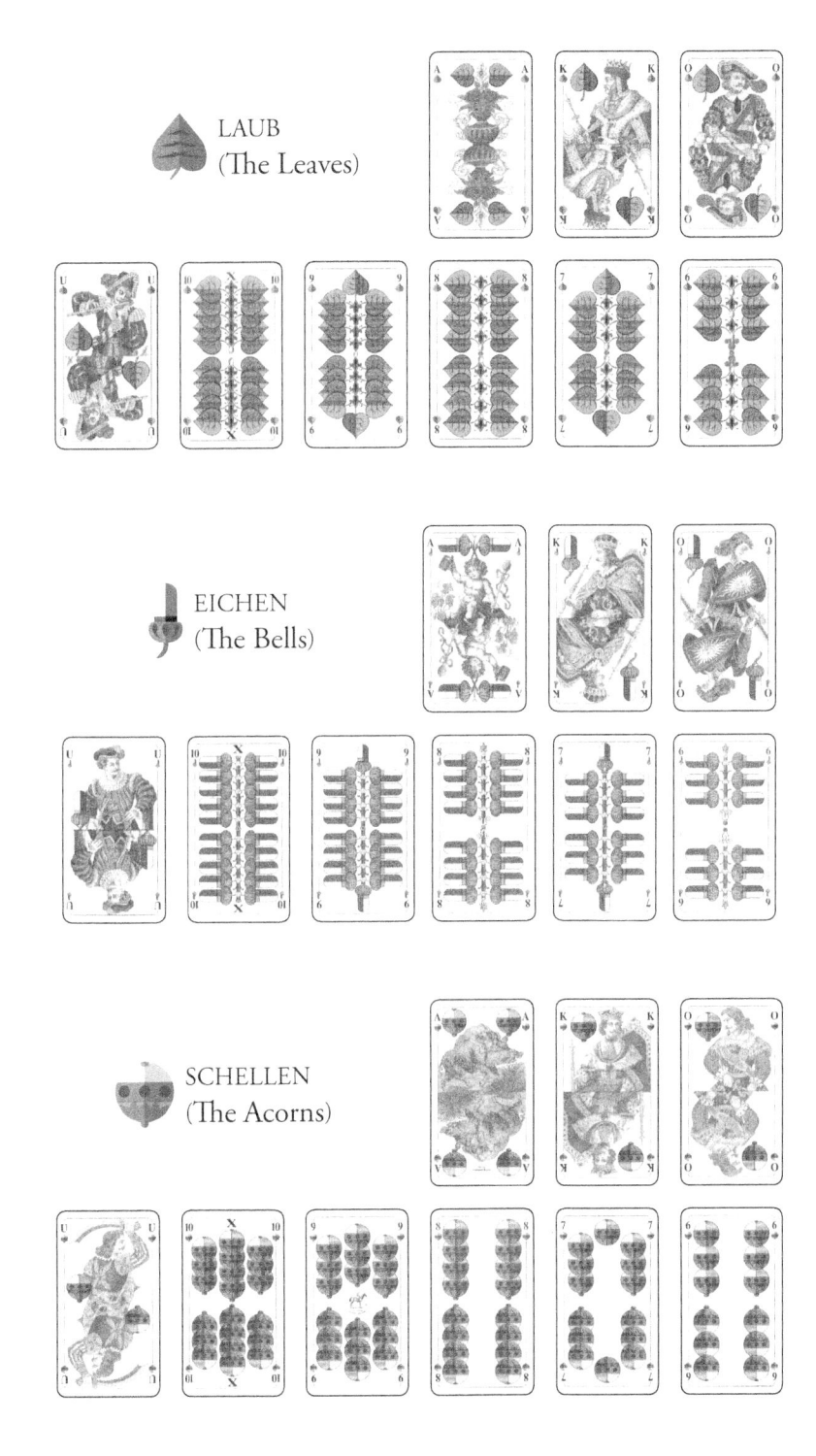

LAUB
(The Leaves)

EICHEN
(The Bells)

SCHELLEN
(The Acorns)

According to German tradition at that time, the four suits corresponded to the four social classes:

- The suits of **Hearts** belonged to the clergy and the church;
- The **Leaves** belonged to the landowners and the peasants;
- The **Bells** belonged to the nobility;
- The **Acorns** belonged to the lower class, to the serfs.

I now propose you place the suits in front of you in the following this order:

The Hearts

This suit represents emotions, feelings, passions, joys, pleasures, good and bad desires, as well as loyalty, honesty, sincerity, trust, support, assistance, and help.

	Ace	The King	The Queen	The Jack

10	9	8	7	6

The Leaves

This suit stands for hopes, travels, communications, contacts, maturity, stability, balance, justice, and it brings happy events.

| Ace | The King | The Queen | The Jack |

| 10 | 9 | 8 | 7 | 6 |

The Bells

This suit represents financial matters, earnings and expenses, business, risks, fortune and misfortune, reward, and the formations.

| Ace | The King | The Queen | The Jack |

| 10 | 9 | 8 | 7 | 6 |

The Acorns

This suit predicts problems, annoyances, diseases, thefts, losses, destruction, betrayals, lies, falsehoods, jealousy, envy, obstacles, delays, pacts, burdens, sorrows, mourning, sufferings, anguish, bitterness, torments, and threats.

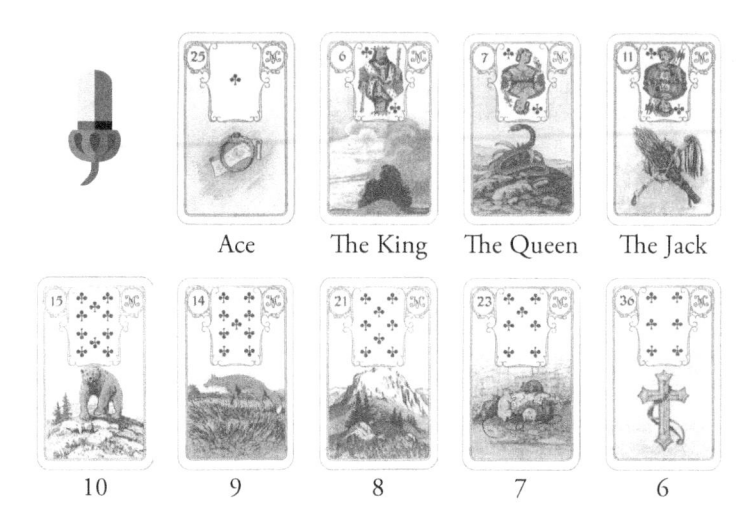

| Ace | The King | The Queen | The Jack |

| 10 | 9 | 8 | 7 | 6 |

As you can see, most of the negative cards belong to the Acorns suit, with some also found in the Bells suit. At this point of your studies, I believe you've already started grasping the energies of the four suits:

- The Hearts – positive;
- The Leaves – positive;
- The Bells – positive and negative;
- The Acorns – negative.

According to the German book "Das Kartenlegen", by Augustus Tora, 1914, the characteristic of a card can be amplified or subdued depending on the suit of the nearby card. Let's take the example of the Jack of Acorns, which stands for a police officer or a court judgment. When this card is paired with another card of the same suit that has a negative connotation, its negative meaning is strengthened, especially when the Jack of Acorn is combined with the card no. 9 of Acorn, which announces a mistake made by the authorities.

Once you've understood the meanings of the four German suits, we can move on to the meanings of the 36 cards in the deck.

2

CHAPTER 2:
THE MEANING OF THE 36 CARDS

Before discussing he meanings of the 36 cards, it's important to clarify three points that have been the subject of much discussion among cartomancy scholars.

- The schools or The Petit Lenormand traditions
- The reversed cards
- Tarot cards similar to some cards in the Petit Lenormand deck

Once these three points are understood, we can start studying the meanings of each card.

Each card is composed of:

1. **Number and name of the card.**

2. **The card suit** – According to German standards, each suit is represented by its name.

3. **A text by Philippe Lenormand (1846)** – All scholars of Petit Lenormand should take into account the true meanings of the deck presented in the instruction sheet. These meanings form the source and basis of the 36-card meanings that exist today. Since this document is essential for a good understanding of the deck, I've concluded that it's helpful to reference it for the study of each card.

4. **What role does the card play in a reading?** In this section, I will provide a summary of the role that each card plays in a reading.

5. **In general** – This position involves exploring the card in detail and analyzing its relationship according to its proximity or distance from the querent's card or other cards.

6. **Traditional keywords** – These are keywords based on Philippe Lenormand's original text .and serve as a synthesis of the card's meaning.

7. **Modern Keywords** – They refer to all those words that have emerged from our experience with the deck.

What are keywords?

Keywords are a group of words that summarize the essence of a specific card. They serve as a memory aid to simplify the reading, especially when building card combinations.

In addition, they're extremely useful for those taking their first steps in the Lenormand study, enabling them to easily recognize the primary meanings of each card without having to memorize the multitude of possible meanings. Keywords help the reader connect naturally to the deck.

To interpret the cards correctly, it's essential to remember that the reading must focus on a specific theme so that the most appropriate keywords can be chosen, making the answer much clearer.

> **Important Note:**
>
> It's common to find certain cards during the learning process, which may cause rejection or difficulty understanding them. I've personally experienced this as well. So, it's crucial to focus on these cards and research and deepen your studies. Keep in mind that every card is an integral part of the reading, and developing a comprehensive understanding of each card will help you become a more skilled card reader

CHAPTER 2: THE MEANING OF THE 36 CARDS

THE SCHOOLS OR THE PETIT LENORMAND TRADITIONS

If you attend or have attended my Lenormand study group on Facebook, you have already had the opportunity to see my texts regarding various Lenormand traditions. I've explained that the Petit Lenormand has multiple "languages" or traditions

Therefore, when someone claims to belong to the European Lenormand tradition, I ask them to specify which tradition they're referring to. In Europe alone, there are numerous traditions, and over the years, certain countries or traditional fortune-telling families have developed their own style based on the tradition of their respective countries, such as Germany, Switzerland, Holland, Belgium, France, and Russia. Each tradition has its unique identity that sets it apart from the others. There are subtle differences between the various Lenormand schools, but it's important to understand that they all have their roots in Philippe Lenormand's traditional method.

In the past, the Brazilian Lenormand school was criticized and rejected by some followers of the other schools. Nevertheless, Brazilian professionals who have a deep understanding of the Gypsy deck have generously shared their knowledge with the whole world through online courses, lectures, events, and providing materials on their blogs that help understand the Gypsy deck in an illustrative way I've had the honor of meeting some of these experts, and I can assure their personal and professional integrity.

The Gypsy deck is strong, as evidenced by a large number of Brazilian fans and its use in many African countries (such as Mozambique, Angola, Cape Verde, Guinea-Bissau), as well as in Madeira, The Azores, and Portugal. In Italy, specifically in Naples, Calabria, and Sicily, I met Italian students who had read the Gypsy Deck. Therefore, don't judge a deck based on negative experiences with unskilled fortune-tellers or prejudice against a particular culture or religion. In this case, all "schools" would have to be judged without exception.

For those curious about the Brazilian Lenormand tradition, I have included some excerpts from the book As Cartas Ciganas e os Orixás (The Gypsy Deck and the Orishas) by Filipi Brasil and Tânia Durão, regarded as the world-renowned experts on the gypsy deck. I want to thank Tânia Durão for providing both the cards and the text.

THE GYPSY CARDS AND THE ORISHAS
by Filipi Brasil and Tânia Durão

The word Orisha was brought to Brazil by enslaved Africans who knew the African pantheon. Orishas represent the force of NATURE and are associated with its various manifestations. There are more than 600 Orishas in Africa, but only 16 are worshipped in Brazil, and 12 are the most worshipped.

In the Yoruba language, Orisha means "the deity that inhabits the head." "Ori" is the word for "head," and "shah" means the "king" or "deity." In esotericism, Orisha means "Light of the Lord" or "Messenger of the Lord." Orishas correspond to the forces of nature, their archetypes, and their characteristics.

They're divine agents that represent the vibrations of the elemental forces of nature. The Orishas are subordinate to Jesus Christ, the ruler of the Earth. However, those who practice the Umbanda religion believe that those who act in the cult of Umbanda are the entities or spiritual guides, also known as *Falangeiros*. These guides are the messengers of the Orishas, who were once incarnate and are spirits of great light and spiritual strength.

The Orishas are responsible for the physical, emotional, and spiritual qualities of their "sons" or "daughters."

CHAPTER 2: THE MEANING OF THE 36 CARDS

Card no. 01 – The Rider / Orisha Exu

In Candomblé, Exu is an Orisha of the African pantheon who is considered to be the "Head Father/Regent of the Ori" - the most human-like and oldest of the Orishas. According to legend, Exu existed in the nothingness and void before the world's creation, so he is everywhere. He serves as a "messenger" between humans and the Orishas and safeguards the doors, temples, *terreiros*[1], houses, and people.

Card no. 01
The Rider
Orisha Exu

Exu is also the executor of karmic justice, and his actions help to open paths and connect the material with the spiritual through a ritual called *descarrego*[2]. He can expand, absorb, and neutralize; as a strong warrior of the law, he is skilled in battle and can use his power to eliminate dark magic. Exu is the closest to the humans and acts quickly because he's the dynamo that connects heaven and earth. Communication is his most remarkable ability, and he's known for transforming principles, particularly human suffering. He stimulates the market and big business.

Card no. 03 – The Ship / Orisha Iemanjá

Iemanjá is regarded as the mother of all and welcomes all her children equally. She's known as the "mother whose children are fish" and is revered as the queen of the sea, a mermaid, the patroness of families and homes, and the archetype of motherhood.

Iemanjá is one of the most well-known and popular Orishas in Brazil. She's revered as the mother of almost all Orishas and is the wife

Card no. 03
The Ship
Orisha Iemanjá

---

1. T/N: "Terreiro" is the sacred place where Candomblé, an African religion, is performed, known as Ilê Axé, and where religious rituals take place.
2. T/N: "Descarrego" (discharge) is a ritual in Umbanda religion where negative energies are removed through spiritual cleansing.

of Oxalá'. Her emissaries are responsible for purifying and discharging (*"descarrego"*) the negative feelings and thoughts in the *"terreiro"*.

They wash away all the evil, disturbances, and wounds, carrying them to the depths of the sea. They also change the energetic currents that surround us. Iemanjá values the power of love and inspires us to awaken our motherly instincts, recognizing that we can generate and create "life. "She helps us to understand that we are co-creators with the divine Father. Iemanjá also encourages us to feel maternal love without becoming too attached so that we can raise our children to be responsible global citizens.

Card no. 05 – The Tree / Orisha Oxóssi

Oxóssi is the son of Iemanjá, the husband of Oxum, and the father of Logun Edé. He is the king of the Ketu nation. Oxóssi is the hunter of a single arrow and is also known for his love of the arts and his diplomatic abilities. He is the great curator and the patron of the *Linha dos Caboclos*[3].

Oxóssi is the Orisha associated with abundance, prosperity, wealth, knowledge expansion, sustenance, food, cunning, and intelligence. He's the lord of the woods, forests, animals, and everything that lives in them. Oxóssi is associated with the earth element, the "soul hunter," and counselor. He corresponds to our need for health, nutrition, vital energy, and physiological balance in constant growth and renewal. He is associated with abundance, richness, and freedom.

Card no. 06 – The Clouds / Orisha Iansã

Iansã learned from Ogum how to use the sword, from Xangô how to manipulate lightning, from Oxóssi how to hunt, and from Obaluaê how to deal with the secrets of death. She's the mistress of the nine oruns (heavens)and is the mother of nine children. The dagger is one of her most important symbols.

---

3. T/N: "Linha dos Caboclos" refers to a group of powerful and benevolent spirits or entities that are associated with indigenous people and the forest.

She represents winds, lightning, hurricanes, cyclones, storms, weather, and also bamboo, movement, passions, and warrior-like qualities. Iansã is also the mistress of the Eguns (disembodied) and the goddess of the passions. She has the strength of the buffalo and the lightness of the butterfly. She's the gentle breeze, the gale, and the devastating hurricane. She's the Orisha of movement, intensity, and change; and embodies the need for displacement, material transformations, technological and intellectual progress, and the fight against injustice.

Card no. 07 – The Snake / Orisha Oxumaré

Oxumaré, the son of Nanã and the brother of Obaluaê, is symbolized by the serpent, which embodies mobility, cycles, skill, flexibility, and infinity. He embodies ambivalence, combining water and earth elements and masculine and feminine qualities. He represents the rotation of the universe and is also associated with the rainbow, luck, wealth, and prosperity.

According to legend, Oludumare (god) once had a problem with his eyes that prevented him from seeing the earth, and he called upon Oxumaré to ascend to heaven and heal him. After he was healed, Oludumare invited Oxumaré to live with him in heaven. Every time a rainbow appears in the sky, it's said that Oxumaré is on earth.

He's the Orisha of agility, prosperity, wealth, fortune, abundance, duality, masculine and feminine, polarities, the whole, and the parts, movement, constant change, the meandering through the paths of life experiences, the integration symbolized by the snake that bites itself in the tail and forms a continuum, the wheel of life.

Card no. 09 – The Bouquet / Orisha Nanã

Nanã is married to Oxalá, and she's the mother of Obaluaê and Oxumaré. As the oldest of the Orishas, she rules over the mature people and protects the elders. Nanã is associated with the lineage of the People of Water and is represented as the archetype of the older woman, the grandmother figure.

She's also known as the Lady of the Portal and the owner of the mangroves, swamps, and mud. She embodies the fusion of rainwater with land, mud, and clay, and represents the ancient memories of our ancestors. Nanã combines the kindness of a grandmother with strict austerity but also with calmness and compassion.

She's the first moment when the water rises from the Earth or stone, and the ruler of the water, the mud, the swamp, and the land in contact with the water. She's the rain, the storm, and the drizzle.

Card no. 09
The Bouquet
Orisha Nanã

Nanã is the guardian of the passage from this life to the next and is the ruler of the mystical portal between dimensions. This orisha reminds us of our spiritual heritage and the moment we were created as souls. Water and clay symbolize her power since water is essential to the origin of life on Earth, and clay or mud symbolizes the moment when the divine Father created us. Nanã leads the disembodied spirits back to the spiritual world and embraces them.

Card no. 10 – The Scythe
Orisha Obaluaê (younger) / Omulu (elder)

Obaluaê/Omulu was born with wounds covering his entire body, and his mother Nanã couldn't cope with his disease and gave him to the sea. Iemanjá then took him as his mother at heart, welcomed and raised him from childhood to adulthood, helping him to heal. She was responsible for his reconciliation with Nanã. To hide his wounds, Iemanjá covered Obaluaê / Omulu's body with straw. Obaluaê means: "Owner of Earth and Life," while Omulu means "Son of the Earth" and is responsible for skin diseases, plagues, and their healing.

In Umbanda, Obaluaê and Omulu are regarded as a single Orisha, but there is an energetic distinction between them. Obaluaê embodies the energy of the youngest and the warrior, while Omulu is the oldest energy and the sorcerer.

This Orisha is associated with the earth element, and its energy is an observer. Obaluaê/Omulu embodies the earth's force and energy and is evoked in rituals for discharging and healing.

He is the Orisha who rules over the planet and is the master of physical and soul healing. He's also the master of magic, responsible for transmutation and changes in the cycles of life. As the ruler of death and life, his domain includes the graveyard and the depths of the sea. Obaluaê/Omulu is the Orisha of transformation and the karmic agent to whom all living beings are subordinate. He governs the "reconstruction of the bodies" in which spirits are reincarnated since each of us has a physical body corresponding to our need for evolutionary readjustment.

*Card no. 10
The Scythe
Orisha
Obaluaê / Omulu*

Thus, all the physical diseases we experience are necessary to strengthen our spirit. Omulu doesn't cause diseases; on the contrary, he takes them away and "returns" them back to the earth. He corresponds to our need to understand karma, renewal, evolution, existential transformations, and transmutations. He represents the unknown and death, the ground to which all bodies return, and which contains not only the essential elements, but also the secret of the cycle of birth and death. Omulu is the Orisha of mercy. He's present in hospital beds and outpatient clinics, and invoking him in times of illness can bring healing, relief, and restoration of health based on merit and in accordance with Divine Law.

Card no. 13 – The Child / Orisha Ibeji

Ibeji is considered a child Orisha. They're depicted as twins, child deities associated with joy, new beginnings, the essence of life, happiness, and unity. They're the children's protectors and symbolize birth and everything new, so they're associated with the river sources, waterholes, purity, germination, and all forms of creation. As twins, they're related to the concept of duality.

In Umbanda, they're syncretized with Saint Cosme and Saint Damian, twin Catholic saints who were doctors and cared for children. In Umbanda tradition, Ibeji is related to "Ibejada," the name given to the children's phalanx in the ritual. Additionally, it's worth noting that a third smaller image, Doun accompanies the Catholic images of Saint Cosme and Saint Damian.

In Umbanda, Ibeji isn't considered the Head Father. In Candomblé, the son of this deity, orisha is considered uncommon. Ibeji is the orisha of happiness, joy, spontaneity, the meaning of life, simplicity, energy, agility, and the will to live. He represents birth, new cycles, flourishing, expansion, the purity of feeling, truth, survival, and continuity.

Card no. 13
The Child
Orisha Ibeji

Card no. 20 – The Garden / Orisha Ossaim

Ossaim is the Orisha who protects the sacred herbs and leaves and their magical mysteries and secrets. He's a sorcerer and is believed to dwell deep in the forests. In Umbanda, it isn't common to worship Ossaim. Ochosi is associated with the leaves and everything related to woods and forests. In Umbanda, the religion practiced in our region, we believe that the Orishas come from the potential of God. Since we're all children of God, we understand that we have the energy of all the Orishas in our crown, some to a greater extent and some to a lesser extent.

So, there are no "quizilas" (disputes) among the orishas, since they all originate from God's unified vibration. Therefore, using an herb that doesn't belong to your Orisha isn't a problem.

Ossaim is the father of the sacred herbs, a discreet, reserved, analytical, patient, suspicious, and mysterious healer.

Card no. 20
The Garden
Orisha Ossaim

He's a sorcerer who knows the secrets of the leaves and enjoys solitude and silence. He's demanding and the owner of *axé*[4].

Card no. 21 – The Mountain / Orisha Xangô

Xangô derives from "Xa", meaning Lord and ruler, and "Ango, meaning lightning, fire, and soul. Therefore, Xangô is the Lord of lightning, fire, thunder, quarries, knowledge, power, and strength. He encourages us to make balanced decisions and is the Orisha of Justice who records judgments, so Ogun and Exu can ensure the law.

Xangô is solid as a rock and has three wives: Obá, Oxum, and Iansã. He's the Orisha of wisdom and prudence who understands the chain of our actions and reactions that create a cause-and-effect relationship for spiritual ascension and karmic balance.

Card no. 22 – The Crossroads / Orisha Ogum

According to some legends, Ogun is believed to be the eldest brother of the Orishas Oxóssi and Exu and the son of Iemanjá. This is one of the explanations for the close relationship between Exu and Ogun. Ogun is the Orishas of the roads and is present in all the kingdoms of the other Orishas. He is a blacksmith, a soldier, a commander, a warrior, and a general in Umbanda, as well as the patron of agriculture and technology. He's skilled in countering magic and breaking demands. When we call upon the energy of Father Ogun, we evoke his values, potential, and virtues. Ogun represents perseverance, tenacity, courage, strength, determination, bravery, and courage. He is also the pioneer, the first step, the impulse, the fulfilling energy, the quest for daily bread, and the victor of demands. Ogum is the executor of the laws. He is the military archetype, the commander, the leader, and the warrior that resides within us. Ogum is the Lord of wars, not bloody battles, but of the internal struggles we fight for our inner transformation. He's the desire, impulse, first step, conquest, claw, victory, and the blood that flows in our veins. He represents the different paths in life.

---

4. T/N: "Axé" is a word from the Afro-Brazilian religion that represents the life force energy and positive vibration.

Card no. 30 – The Lilies / Orisha Oxum

Oxum is Oxalá's daughter and one of Xangô's wives, and she's responsible for promoting fertility, motherhood, and the female uterus.

She also protects newborns and is regarded as the goddess of waterfalls, rivers, and fresh water. In addition, Oxum is also the goddess of beauty and love, compassion, gold, wealth, and prosperity. This orisha is often called upon to protect pregnancy, motherhood, fertility, and for children. Oxum is associated with the water element as a water-related deity and is said to provide love, emotional balance, harmony, satisfaction, and fertility.

Card no. 30
The Lilies
Orisha Oxum

Card no. 31 – The Sun / Orisha Oxalá
(Oxaguian = young and Oxalufan = old)

Oxalá is a word that derives from Portuguese and Arabic, meaning "if God wills" or "God hopes." In the Yoruba language, he is known as Orixalá or Obatalá and is considered the king of the white cloth or the king of creation itself.

Oxalufan is depicted as a wise elder holding a staff and represents Oxalá. In the African religions, Father Oxalá is syncretized with Jesus Christ. In Umbanda, however, this relationship goes beyond syncretism, as we understand Jesus as the Master, one of the greatest avatars of humanity, and a spirit of highly spiritual scope, the spiritual ruler of the Earth.

In this way, Umbanda can be understood as a religion with a Christian influence since it follows the teachings of Jesus, God, and the Orishas. When we see the image of Jesus on our altars, we connect with Oxalá and Jesus. However, the Umbanda religion doesn't worship the image of Jesus crucified or suffering crucified. Instead, Oxalá is regarded as the Father of all orishas, who created the world and bestowed free will upon man. He symbolizes peace and faith and is the Orixá of light, whiteness, ethics, religiosity, spirituality, serenity, and creation.

CHAPTER 2: THE MEANING OF THE 36 CARDS

He represents the cosmic synthesis, the masculine, the beginning and the end, life and death.

Therefore, Father Oxalá is welcomed at the opening and closing of the "Giras de Umbanda". Like the Orisha, mediums wear white uniforms throughout the ritual in honor of Father Oxalá during the spiritual walk. In addition, they're buried in white to symbolize the end of their incarnation cycle.

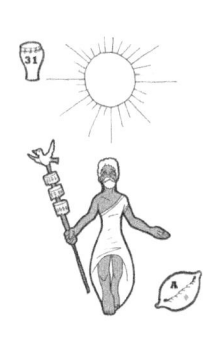

Card no. 31
The Sun
Orisha Oxalá

It's customary for mediums to undergo certain rituals (initiations, baptisms, amakis, consecrations, etc.) for Oxalá when they enter a mediumistic current. These rituals are considered a milestone, representing the individual's birth into religion and the emergence of a neophyte/beginner. Father Oxalá is often the first guide for mediums, especially for those just starting. Some children dedicate Fridays to Father Oxalá as a form of reverence, and they also wear white clothes and eat white meat.

As the Orisha of light and clarity, rituals are typically performed during the daylight hours, before sunset. Oxalá represents strength and patience and helps establish a connection with spirituality, awakening faith and understanding how to reconnect with one's inner Christ.

As Cartas Ciganas e os Orixás – 2nd edition
Authors: Filipi Brasil e Tânia Durão.
Published by: Bonecker

REVERSED CARDS

Traditionally, Lenormand cards aren't read in the reversed position, as Philippe Lenormand's instruction sheet doesn't mention it.

Upright *Reversed*

However, recently, some scholars and card-playing enthusiasts in France and Russia have created reversed meanings for the 36 cards, which has caused great controversy among those who oppose this practice, arguing that a reading based on upright and reversed cards wouldn't provide an accurate prediction.

Nonetheless, I had the opportunity to work side by side with colleagues in Russia and France who used the reversed card technique in their readings, and I was surprised by how accurate the readings were.

My curiosity led me to delve deeper into the reversed meanings and tested some of my readings, resulting in a good experience with satisfactory results.

In 2015, I received a beautiful Russian Lenormand deck called Lenormand Oracle Autumn Whisper from Sofia Kuznetsov, a Russian scholar and tarot expert. Each card in the deck is divided into two scenarios, upright and reversed, as shown in the two cards provided as an example.

Lenormand Oracle Autumn Whisper

Card no. 5
The Tree

Card no. 6
The Clouds

Card 5 – The Tree

In the **upright position**, the card represents a vigorous, strong, and healthy tree. It symbolizes good health, vitality, resistance, and well-being. The bright sky and green field surrounding The Tree radiate life, tranquility, and peace.

In the **reversed position**, the card depicts a depressing, distressing, and melancholic image. The Tree is dry, and the surrounding landscape is gloomy, dark, and lifeless. The card in this position indicates illness, weakness, and depression.

Card 6 – The Clouds

In the **upright position**, the clouds, the main symbol of the card, are clear, and the sky is bright. The author has introduced another vital element that can help to understand this card: a river with clear and calm water. This image conveys a sense of peace and promises a journey without disruptions.

In the **reversed position**, the card indicates a journey through bad weather. The dark and heavy clouds are hovering low over the land. The river is turbulent, overflowing and flooding the adjacent land. In a reading, the card in this position announces the arrival of unexpected and unpleasant events that will surprise the querent or may worsen a significant problem.

As you may have noticed, I don't read reversed cards, but I endorse this method for anyone who wants to learn it. I've never needed to reverse the cards to look for additional meanings. Why is that? In my opinion, every card has its positive and negative side.

In a reading, I consider the card nearby to determine which side it expresses. Let me explain this concept further using the image of card 9, The Bouquet. This card symbolizes deep feelings, emotions, and attitudes in every moment of our lives, whether good or bad.

In good times, it represents a reward for a joyous event, such as a birthday or the birth of a child. It can also mean recognition of a job well done, such as winning a competition, getting a promotion, applauding a dancer, singer, or writer, or for a kind gesture like helping someone in need.

Some combinations:

- The Bouquet + The Ring
    - A celebration of a recurring date or event, such as a birthday or anniversary;
    - An engagement or marriage proposal.

- The Bouquet + The Lilies
    - Ask of forgiveness and apologies;
    - Expressions of noble gestures of loyalty.

- The Bouquet + The Moon
    - Promotion or advancement in career or personal life;
    - Expressions of admiration and respect from admirers or fans;
    - Recognition for talents or achievements.

A bouquet is a comforting presence even in the darkest and saddest moments of our lives, such as visiting a sick relative or acquaintance or attending the funeral of a loved one.

- The Bouquet + The Coffin + The Lilies
    - Funeral wreath;
    - Celebration of a special person's death anniversary;
    - Day of the Dead

CHAPTER 2: THE MEANING OF THE 36 CARDS

COMPARING SIMILAR TAROT CARDS TO THE PETIT LENORMAND

It's important to understand that even if two different decks have cards with identical names or symbols, it doesn't necessarily mean they have the same divinatory meaning. Tarot readers may apply their meanings to some Lenormand cards with similar names. This is especially true for the following cards: The Stars, The Tower, The Sun, and The Moon.

	THE STARS	THE TOWER	THE SUN	THE MOON
PETIT LENORMAND				
TAROT				

While the meanings of The Stars and The Sun are almost identical in both decks, there are notable differences in The Tower and The Moon. When I compare these cards, I won't delve into their meanings, but I just want to emphasize their differences.

The Tower
Card no.16, **The Tower of the Tarot**, depicts a dramatic scene where a tower is struck by lightning, causing its destruction. It's a highly negative card, representing sudden changes, unexpected and traumatic events, plans collapsing, pain, separation, and so on.

On the other hand, **The Tower card, no. 19, in Lenormand** has a different interpretation. According to tradition: *"... The Tower gives the hope of a happy old age; but if surrounded by clouds, it forbodes sickness, and, according to circumstances, even death".*

The Tower in Lenormand generally stands for security, seriousness, integrity, stability, authority, career, and longevity. However, if The Tower is near unfavorable cards, it's a harbinger of misfortune and death.

The Moon

Card no. 18 of the Tarot, The Moon, depicts a moon with a profile of a human face from which rays emanate over two dogs or wolves howling at The Moon as if worshipping it. A crab emerges from the water and also seems hypnotized by it. The Moon represents the supernatural world, mystery, enemies and hidden dangers, illusion, and betrayal. My grandmother used to call it "the black soul" because The Moon's influence on people's minds and souls is so contradictory and obscure.

About **the card 32, The Moon of Lenormand**, tradition says: *"... The Moon is a sign of great honors, fortune and fame, if the card lies at the side of the Person; if at a distance, it means grief and misery."*

As you can see, the differences between The Tower and The Moon in both decks are significant. It's necessary to understand the true language of each deck to ensure accurate interpretations. So don't confuse the meanings of one deck with those of the other.

THE MEANING OF THE 36 CARDS

Card no. 1
THE RIDER
9 of Hearts

"No. 1 – The Cavalier is a messenger of good fortune – if not surrounded by unlucky cards, brings good news, which the Person may expect, either from his own house or from abroad; this will, however, not take place immediately, but some time later."

Philippe Lenormand, 1846

What's the role of the card in a reading?

The Rider brings movement, news, messages, ideas, or a visitor coming to you. This card also brings determination and boldness to set things in motion.

General meaning:

When The Rider appears in a reading, it indicates that new experiences are on the horizon. The closer this card is to the querent's card, the sooner this event will take place, and it may also speed up the nearby cards.

The Rider stands for incoming information, either verbal or written. This information can come through various means of communication. With The Letter card, the news is coming by mail or other written means, such as newspapers, magazines, notes, postcards, etc. With The Owls card, by phone, mobile, fax, e-mail, or television. To better understand how the information will reach its destination, check out the cards flanking The Rider before and after.

When reading the Grand Tableau, if The Rider is the last card in a line, the cards to its left, in front of the horse's gaze, show where it's heading. Thus, the cards in this position represent the recipient or the place where The Rider is going, if there's something to deliver. If The Clouds card is in this position, it suggests that the "baggage" The Rider is carrying may not be the best. It'll surely bring something unpleasant that will annoy you or indicate car or motorcycle damage. With The Coffin, it could mean that the message won't reach its destination or that it will cause significant pain. The cards to the right of or behind The Rider will give you information about the "sender" and the purpose of the message. They'll also provide insight into the reasons for this trip, visit, or meeting.

For instance, The Rider:
+ The Coffin: bad news;
+ The Child: a visit of a child, pregnancy, new beginnings;
+ The Stars: new inspirations and ideas;
+ The Stork: the return of someone in the querent's life or a significant change;
+ The Lilies: visit of the elderly, a peaceful moment.

Traditional keywords:

News, novelty.

Modern keywords:

An agile mind, ideas, new plans, messages, something new, approaching something or someone, moving or arriving in the querent's life; a visitor, a guest, means of communication, novelty, news (phone calls, mail, telegram, fax), exchange of important information (data), proposal, date, meeting, something transmitted, delivery, commission, feedback, update, displacement, movement, advancement, action, progress, development, note, task to be performed, go ahead, advance, sport; a foreigner or outsider; a vehicle (car, motorcycle, bicycle); transport animals.

Card no. 2
THE CLOVER
6 of Bells

"No. 2 – A Clover Leaf is also a harbinger of good news; but if surrounded by clouds it indicates great pain; but if No. 2 lies near No. 29 or 28, the pain will be of short duration, and soon change to a happy issue."

Philippe Lenormand, 1846

"Each leaf symbolizes a different characteristic of luck: the first is for hope, the second for faith, the third for love, and obviously, the fourth is for fortune."

A Celtic quotation

What's the role of the card in a reading?
It means new opportunities can encourage, motivate, and bring hope to a previously hopeless situation. It also means luck and fortune.

General meaning:
The Clover is a symbol of good fortune, and when it appears in a reading, it instills a sense of hope that inspires action. The possibilities offered by this card have a beneficial influence that infuses energy, vitality, courage, and self-confidence to move forward to pursue projects or endeavors. The luck this card brings comes up unexpectedly and randomly, opening up new opportunities you didn't expect. The Clover represents good luck that works in our

favor by providing opportunities to achieve our desires, bridging hope and fulfillment. This card offers what is necessary to move forward and should be seized as a brief moment of happiness.

It's essential to pay attention to its position, whether near or far from the querent's card. When The Clover touches the querent's card, it brings good fortune and protection. This card also describes the end of a difficult period and the closing of troubling situations. If The Clover is far from the querent's card, it can bring disillusionment, disappointment, and a lack of resources to carry out their projects, or else, it may indicate that it'll take some time to accomplish them.

Regardless of its proximity to the significator card, if The Clover touches The Clouds or other unfavorable cards, such as The Scythe or The Coffin, it predicts unfortunate situations, inconveniences, serious concerns, disappointments, sorrow, and sadness in the querent's life. For an accurate interpretation, it's essential to consider the meaning of the cards next to it.

Important Note:

The Clover can lessen the impact of the unfavorable cards surrounding it, alleviate difficulties (even briefly), and enable the progress of an issue.

Traditional keywords:

Good luck, fortune

Modern keywords:

Pleasant surprise, joy, happy event, satisfaction, improvement, favorable circumstances, fortunate encounter, hope, chance, unexpected help, support, surprising, sudden, something important, trustworthy, opportunity, second chance, optimism, something that gets going, impetus, encouragement, relief, small, little, something special or rare, exclusive, offer, bonus, early, brief, quick, carefree, fun, short-term, lottery, gambling, risky, games and entertainment, lucky charm, superstition, vegetables.

Card no. 3
THE SHIP
10 of Leaves

"No. 3 – The Ship, the Symbol of commerce, signifies great wealth, which will be acquired by trade or inheritance; if near to the Person, it means an early journey."

Philippe Lenormand, 1846

What's the role of the card in a reading?

It announces movement, new directions, and also travel and business.

General meaning:

When The Ship card shows up in a reading, it indicates a significant change in the querent's life or the area being investigated. This change may involve something coming into or leaving the querent's life, and the answer can be found in the flanking cards.

The Ship card brings news of great importance, including an upcoming trip to faraway places (which can also be a psychical or spiritual journey), such as a cruise or a visit to culturally different locations. The cards touching The Ship will reveal the nature of the trip. For example, if it's next to The Garden card, it suggests a vacation trip, while if it's next to The Tree, it may denote a health-related trip.

However, before determining whether these journeys are favorable, I recommend you look at the nearby cards. When The Ship is next to The Fish, it predicts financial gain through inheritance or business with distant countries, including via the

Internet.

This card may also represent a journey into the depths of one's soul or a sense of nostalgia or longing for someone that has passed away. In such cases, the querent might experience intense emotions that can make them melancholy, sad, or even depressed.

If The Ship is far from the querent's card, the events depicted by the surrounding cards will come about slowly and take longer. The trip will take time and could even be delayed. It's important to understand that The Ship card represents a strong desire for transformation, which could lead to a new direction, and considerable change in the querent's mental, psychological, or physical state, which will be gradual and slow. When The Ship is combined with The Coffin card, it can announce a profound transformation.

For a long time, The Ship card kept showing up in a querent's reading, which caught my attention. When The Ship appeared with The Coffin, I interpreted it as the end of the querent's transformation, he confirmed that he had undergone gender reassignment surgery, and although it had been a long and challenging journey at times, he had finally achieved his goal. The Ship and The Coffin combination indicated a profound and radical change, but it was finally completed. Sometimes, this card can also represent events or issues far from the querent.

In a reading, The Ship may also suggest that the querent is expecting something in their life.

The Ship
- + The Owls: waiting for a call or talking to someone;
- + The Child: expecting a child; waiting for the right time to start a new venture;
- + The Heart: waiting for true love.

The Ship card can also represent a sense of longing and nostalgia for something or someone. The card in front of it may provide insight into it.

The Ship
+ The House: homesick;
+ The Ring: missing a partner;
+ The Anchor: missing the work.

The Ship also indicates a transition; for this reason, it's common to find it alongside other cards in a reading announcing someone's death.

Traditional keywords:
Trade, import and export, travel.

Modern keywords:
Buying and selling, journey (physical, mental or spiritual), long-distance commute, foreign country, overseas, international, other cultures (beliefs, culture, languages, tastes), tourism, contact with distant places (including via the internet), emigration, new horizons, new visions, new experiences, directions and perspectives, a different direction, change, interchange, exchange, exploration, curiosity, expansion, expedition, transaction, transfer (property, etc.),
action, progress, slow but continuous movement, gradual development, gestation, maternal womb, longing, nostalgia, desires for growth, detachment, departure, absence, retreat, abandonment, separation, inheritance, soul, trespass; large (heavy) vehicles, public transportation (train, bus, subway, boat, ship, hoy), transportation equipment; water, river, lake, sea, ocean.

Card no. 4
THE HOUSE
King of Hearts

"No. 4 – The House is a certain sign of success and prosperity in all undertakings; and though the present position of the Person may be disagreeable, yet the future will be bright and happy. If this card lies in the centre of the cards, under the Person, this is a hint to beware of those who surround him or her."

Philippe Lenormand, 1846

What's the role of the card in a reading?

It brings news about the querent's home and information about the environment where they live or work, as well as the family or people they live with.

General meaning:

The House card symbolizes our "inner self" and reflects our soul. Our home is where we feel most like ourselves, finding comfort and peace away from the chaos of everyday life. And it's in The House where we keep our most intimate secrets, and it's where we struggle with ourselves to find balance and stability in our soul and life.

When The House shows up as the first card in a reading, it indicates that the querent's domestic affairs are of primary concern, including everything related to it, such as household chores, family, neighbors, furniture, appliances, rent payment, and more. This card represents a situation that lasts over time and suggests a deep connection to a place or family. It can also indicate that something significant is happening within the house or that the house itself plays an important role in the querent's life. Moving to another country or house should be considered if The Ship or The Storks cards are nearby.

The cards surrounding The House can also provide insight into how the querent interacts with those around them and if the people in their home can be trusted. For example, if The House (especially accompanied by The Lilies) is close to the querent's card, it reveals a strong family connection. It also reveals details about the querent's house and neighborhood.

On the other hand, If The House is surrounded or touches cards that represent falsehood and betrayal, such as The Mice, The Fox, or The Snake, it means that the querent should be cautious of the people they receive at home, particularly a family member that may harbor negative feelings like anger, jealousy, or envy, or someone who is betraying the querent's trust. It may also indicate various problems brought on by neighbors or guests.

Traditional keywords:
House.

Modern keywords:
Homeownership (house, apartment, lodging, dwelling, farm, country house, company headquarters), a small building, family, values, tradition, neighbors, relatives, tenant, team, household management, home, personal life, intimate environment, personal matters, address, base, between four walls, hospitality, habits, routines, website, blog, Facebook page, protection, security, stability, trust, comfort zone, maintenance, support, sponsorship, real estate market, the body.

Card no. 5
THE TREE
7 of Hearts

"No. 5 – A TREE, if distant from the Person, signifies good health; more trees of different cards together, leave no doubt about the realization of all reasonable wishes.

Philippe Lenormand, 1846

"Trees are indispensable: they help and accompany us throughout life and remain with us even after death with the four woods of the coffin."

Alfonso Burgio
Dizionario delle superstizioni - Hermes Edizioni

What's the role of the card in a reading?
The Tree provides information about life and health.

General meaning:
The Tree is a symbol of life and represents the health of the significator card in contact with it. For example, if it appears with The Ring, it may suggest that the relationship isn't healthy and requires the querent's healing and attention. The cause might be attributed to factors such as routine or external interference.

The surrounding cards can provide further clarification. In a reading, the cards surrounding The Tree bring information about the querent's overall health and well-being. If The Tree lies close to the querent's card and is surrounded by unfavorable cards like The Clouds, The Coffin, The Scythe, The Broom and The Whip,

The Mice, and The Cross, it predicts malaise or a severe and prolonged disease. Therefore, it's crucial to look at the neighboring cards for more information.

If The Tree is far from the querent's card, it indicates good health, particularly if it's positioned in the past. When it falls in the future, even if it's distant from the querent's card, it's still necessary to observe the flanking cards as they'll provide information about the future state of health.

Traditional keywords:

Health, well-being.

Modern keywords:

Peace, calmness, tranquility, stability, life, life condition, life path, lifetime, inner resources, resilience, rooted situation, strictness, inflexibility, monotony, boredom, laziness, slow, long-term, growth, development, progress, maturity, past, origin, family tree, traditions, conservatism, ancestry, generation, patience, silence, reliability, firmness, nature, medicinal plants, medicine, nutrition, fruit.

Card no. 6
THE CLOUDS
King of Acorn

"No. 6 – CLOUDS, if their clear side is turned towards the Person, are a lucky sign; with the dark side turned to the Person, something disagreeable will soon happen."

Philippe Lenormand, 1846

What's the role of the card in a reading?
The Clouds announces troubles, annoyances, and short-term chaos.

General meaning:
Philippe Lenormand teaches us that when The Clouds card appears in a reading, it's essential to consider two aspects: light and dark clouds. The closer the dark side is to the querent's card, the more challenging to handle the predicted events. On the other hand, the cards near the light clouds will receive brightness and positivity.

The Clouds card may be compared to a weather thermometer. If we see light and clear clouds, it announces a beautiful journey ahead. However, if the clouds are dark, it predicts bad weather conditions. In a broader context, The Clouds card symbolizes the unexpected setbacks and worries in the querent's life.

It announces an unclear and ambiguous situation that makes it difficult to understand reality. This card brings vague and imprecise information about a subject, event, or situation that may be hiding a trap. The Clouds can also stand for emotional changes and mental instability, which might cause the querent to lose focus and direction towards their goals.

When accompanied or surrounded by unfavorable cards, it can exacerbate the emotional and mental state, leading to obsessive, harmful, and destructive behavior, such as excessive use of medication, drugs, and alcohol. It's a time of emotional vulnerability, destabilization, depression, anxiety, uncertainty, and frustration.

The Clouds card, when paired with The Lilies, may indicate sexual insecurity or someone hiding their true sexual orientation. The repetition of this combination may suggest a lack of peace and tranquility in one's life or heralds a family betrayal. External factors may be causing confusion and chaos in the querent's life, compelling them to put off achieving or resolving their goals. Even if it's a temporary setback, it can cause significant frustration and unhappiness.

Other cards, such as The Snake, The Broom and The Whip, or The Book, can confirm that there are secret enemies or magical forces. In such cases, The Clouds advise to be careful and keep calm during this period. It's best to wait a few days before moving or taking action.

Important Note:
When The Clouds card is the last card in a line, it means that the situation being analyzed is changing and that new events or old issues will certainly resurface with relevance in the current situation. It also announces that the matter is ongoing and that the querent has no control over the problem under investigation.

Traditional keywords:
Problems, annoyances.

Modern keywords:

Annoyances, worries, obstacles, difficulties, chaos, confusion, delays, crisis, threat, abuse, uncertainty, indecision, changeable situation or issue, unstable, unreliable, misfortune, anxiety, obscure, hidden, invisible, appearance, illusion, delusion, contradiction, pretense, secrets, hidden, camouflage, unclear situation or issue, lack of transparency, misunderstandings, imprecision, unfounded accusations, impediment, hindrance, postponement, drama, disorder, anger, irritation, tension, melancholy, chemical, toxic, vapor, smoke, dust, gas, dim, shadow, opaque, pollution, dark, sky, atmosphere, fog, storm, thunderstorm, rain, wind, bad weather (adapt to the season at the time of reading).

Card no. 7
THE SNAKE
Queen of Acorns

"No. 7 – A SERPENT is a sign of misfortune, the extent of which depends upon the greater or smaller distance from the Person; it is followed invariably by deceit, infidelity, and sorrow.

Philippe Lenormand, 1846

What's the role of the card in a reading?

It warns you to be aware of events, situations and people.

General meaning:

When The Snake card appears in a reading, we need to be extremely cautious. This card stands for betrayal, deception, and manipulation of events by others, which can destroy the querent's reputation and life.

So, the querent must be vigilant and pay close attention to their behavior and what is commented about them. The Snake indicates that someone may be plotting and manipulating events in intricate details to lure the naive querent into betraying themselves. Evidence of this "weakness", such as recorded conversations, writings, or footage, will be made public or used for blackmail to damage the victim's reputation.

In certain situations, this card advises using the cunning and strategic of a snake to overcome any obstacles impeding the successful completion of a project. It may not be necessary to follow the original path strictly.

Sometimes unexpected situations arise that force us to take alternative routes.

The Snake card is a warning, especially if it's close to the querent's card. The cards surrounding it will give more information about the type of danger the person will face and which life area will be affected.

When The Snake is near challenging cards, such as The Broom and The Whip and The Clouds (as previously confirmed), it might indicate the influence of a curse or magic on the querent. If it's next to the partner's card, or even with The Ring, it may announce the presence of a rival or lover; its proximity to the querent only indicates that danger is imminent due to the negative energy it brings.

Therefore, even when The Snake is far from the querent, it's advisable to examine the cards surrounding it carefully.

Traditional keywords:

Deceit, betrayal.

Modern keywords:

Envy, jealousy, flattery, hidden threat, danger, evil, sin, diabolical mind, hypocrisy, seduction, adulation, manipulation, slander, intrigue, perfidy, defamation, dishonesty, malice, enmity, desire to harm by lying, intentional lies (pathological liar), harassment, complications, serious problems, complex situation, poison, revenge, don't get straight to the point, twists and turns, detour, indirect, taunting, deception, bad advice, occult forces, curse, sorceress, magic, devil, , enemy, rival, lover, hypnosis, crawling, reptiles; wisdom, intelligence, cunning, strength of mind and healing.

Card no. 8
THE COFFIN
9 of Bells

"No. 8 – A COFFIN, very near to the Person, means, without any doubt, dangerous diseases, death, or a total loss of fortune. More distant from the Person, the card is less dangerous."

Philippe Lenormand, 1846

"I carry dead people"

Donald "Pee Wee" Gaskins
Serial Killer

What's the role of the card in a reading?
The Coffin signifies the end of something or the definitive loss of something or someone. It also means a significant, traumatic, and devastating change.

General meaning:
The Coffin is a vehicle for profound change, often shocking and hard to bear. It announces the end, the outcome, and the detachment of something useless, harmful, or irretrievable. Therefore, when this card comes up, it suggests it's time to let go of anything that is no longer serving you, even if it's difficult or painful. This includes old habits, beliefs, behaviors, or thought patterns holding you back from being happy.

The Coffin card encourages you to make an effort to face the situation bravely and accept the reality of the situation, no matter how challenging and painful it may be in the moment. The significator card nearby points out the life area ending or undergoing significant change. For instance, if The Coffin card is next to The Anchor, it may indicate the end of a career, unemployment, or retirement. But the same combination can also represent completing a task or duty.

On the other hand, if a significator card is close to The Coffin, it may identify the life area that needs to be updated and renewed. Sometimes it warns against something that should remain buried, unspoken, forgotten, or not experienced again.

According to tradition, if The Coffin is near the querent or a significator card, it predicts loss, suffering, disease, or even death. It also indicates that the querent is depressed or going through a severe life challenge. If The Tree and The Clouds are nearby, it means a serious health issue. However, if The Coffin is far from the querent, its impact is less intense, and it doesn't necessarily represent physical death but rather the end of a cycle that brings renewal.

To represent physical death, The Coffin card must be combined with other cards, such as The Ship, The Tree, The Tower, The Lilies, and The Cross. We'll delve deeper into this later when we study the group of negative cards.

Those who participated in my Facebook study group may recall a consultation I did in early January 2013 when my older brother was hospitalized in Lisbon, Portugal, in a critical situation.

So I inquired the cards about his health evolution, and in the deck cutting, I got The Tree card, which represents life, it still also expansion and growth, but when paired with The Coffin card, it conveyed a message of grief and indicated that his condition was very serious.

Then, I gathered the two piles from the deck cutting and fanned out the deck and chose three cards:

- The first card: The Crossroads, which represented the doctors' various attempts to save my brother's life, as well as the passage from this life to the next;
- The second card: The Cross, which symbolizes his pains and sufferings;
- The third card: The Coffin, in a health theme, it indicated a serious and incurable disease.

When I don't use a positional method, I start reading from the first card drawn and combine it with the other cards. Additionally, I have a habit of "mirroring" the cards, a technique I use in any 3, 5, or 7 card line, and also in the Grand Tableau.

- The Crossroads + The Cross: several exams and treatments.
- The Crossroads + The Coffin: futile attempts to save my brother's life, and a decision to let him go. It also suggests two weeks until the end.
- The Cross + The Coffin: slow and painful end, disease worsening until death.

Considering these cards, the prognosis was unfavorable. Ten days after this consultation, on January 14, 2013, at 2 p.m., my brother passed away at Cuf Hospital in Lisbon, Portugal. Rest in peace, my dear brother.

Important Note:

When The Coffin is the first card in the reading, it announces that things from the querent's past are still present or are returning to their life. Another point to consider regarding The Coffin is its position concerning the other cards. It may also bring something good, such as the end of a disease, suffering, or an unhappy situation. This argument will be further detailed in the chapter on Code Reading.

Traditional keywords:

End, disease.

Modern keywords:

Death, mourning, end of a phase (positive or negative), definitive loss, conclusion, cessation, closure, finishing, completion, cancellation, detachment, release, lack, absence, disappearance, no prospects, depleted resources, forgetfulness, exhausted, tiredness, emptiness, exhaustion, radical and inevitable change, trials, traumatic experience, shock, anguish, pain, suffering, despair, illness (bedridden), discouragement, depression, fear, hurts, a painful separation, divorce, rupture, ruin, decay, (material) damage, debts, dismissal, suspension, something that doesn't work, an issue that doesn't develop, denial, refusal, a farewell, fear, shock, trauma, nightmare, something evil, incubation, stopped, stagnation, passivity, imprisonment, forced isolation, loneliness, widowhood, retirement; the past (memories), secret, hide, closed, dark, bed, uterus, incubator, fast, tunnel.

Card no. 9
THE BOUQUET
Queen of Leaves

"No. 9 – The Bouquet means much happiness in every aspect of the querent's life."

Philippe Lenormand, 1846

What's the role of the card in a reading?

When this card appears in a reading, it announces that a significant event is about to occur, such as passing an exam, recovering from a disease, being recognized for artistic work, a birthday, a visit, and so on.

General meaning:

The Bouquet card expresses emotions, affection, and respect. This card denotes a special event that inspires enthusiasm and confidence to move forward, such as an invitation to a wedding, birthday, movie, and it also indicates a proposal, gift, or gesture of gratitude.

The Bouquet symbolizes beauty, joy, pleasure, and fulfillment in the querent's life. When a bouquet is gifted, it brings joy to a room or the top of a desk as well as to the person who receives it. It's a gesture that expresses kindness and affection for another person. It symbolizes something that comes from the heart. It also represents the need to present oneself in a certain way in front of certain people or situations.

When it shows up next to the querent's card, The Bouquet stands for wealth, jewels, happiness, and success. However, when it touches the dark side of The Clouds, it indicates weakened or dying feelings or the ambiguity of kind and friendly people. When paired with The Moon card, you'll receive a reward and recognition for a job well done, like receiving applause. Along with The Book, it announces academic achievements.

Important Note:
During my cancer disease, in my readings to know the progress of the treatment, I could notice that whenever The Bouquet card showed up after any card, especially after unfavorable cards, the outcome of the cure was favorable. So, when The Bouquet is placed after an unfavorable card, it announces the overcoming of a difficult moment or a minor victory.

Traditional keyword:
Happiness.

Modern keywords:
Surprise, joyful events, pleasant experience, stage successfully reached reward, promotion, award, recognition, admiration, pleasure, appreciation, acknowledgment, gratitude, relief, recovery, an attempt at reconciliation, gift, affection, present, gesture, praise, greeting, apology, diplomacy, formality, showing affection, pampering, courtesy, friendship, kindness, politeness, manners, etiquette, elegance, charm, beauty, vanity, aesthetics, fashion, decoration, invitation (celebration, birthday, dinner, concert, movie, etc.), visit, entertainment, recreation, talent, hobby, favorable circumstances, positive response, achievement, proposal, sponsorship, service, creativity, art, exhibitions, flowers, manual or artistic work, artistic talent, herbs, short-term.

Card no. 10
THE SCYTHE
Jack of Bells

"No. 10 – The Scythe indicates great danger, which will only be avoided if lucky cards surround it."

Philippe Lenormand, 1846

What's the role of the card in a reading?

The Scythe indicates a cut, for better or worse.

General meaning:

The Scythe card symbolizes cutting, separating, or harvesting something. When it appears in a reading, it can cause fear and anxiety for the querent. However, it's necessary to reassure them by explaining that it doesn't always indicate tragic events.

This card can also represent liberation or relief from oppressive people or situations that may hinder personal growth and development. The Scythe can denote the end of an argument or abuse when combined with The Broom and The Whip. When paired with The Mountain, it may announce the release of a stagnant situation.

If it's close to the querent's card, it serves as a warning of imminent danger or may indicate the presence of a dangerous, violent, and sharp-tongued person.

Therefore, it's recommended to pay close attention to the cards surrounding it; if they're favorable, they can lessen the negative energy that The Scythe brings.

Traditional keywords:

Danger, rupture

Modern keywords:

A warning, danger alert, danger of accidents, risk, injury, wound, shock, trauma, panic, horror, violence, aggression, cruelty, coldness, rejection, cut, division, eliminate, necessary rupture, separation, breakup, interruption, cancellation, cessation, decisive action, position taking, irrevocable decision, execution, final verdict, sentence, unexpected, unforeseen, suddenly, quickly, unexpected twist, penetration, rape, adultery, criminality, spark, tools, weapons, harvest time, vintage, pain, fever, misfortune, surgery, scar, tattoo.

Card no. 11
The Broom and The Whip
Jack of Acorns

"No. 11 – The Rod means quarrels in the family, domestic afflictions, want of peace among married persons; also fever and protracted sickness."

Philippe Lenormand, 1846

What's the role of the card in a reading?

The Broom and The Whip card represents divergences, conflicts, hostilities, adversities, punishment, imposition of rules (for better or worse), abuse, and accusation. It can also stand for the law; and brings cleansing, removal, and purification.

General meaning:

When The Broom and The Whip card falls close to the querent's card, it predicts disagreements and serious verbal confrontations that can last a long time. When paired with The Clouds card, it may indicate psychological or physical abuse. If The Scythe is in this group of cards, it can denote physical aggression. When combined with The House card, it forecasts family conflicts. If paired with The Tower, it indicates legal problems or military issues.

Along with The Garden card, it might denote a mass protest, an uprising, or a revolt involving many people. With The Ring card, it means discord or abuse within the relationship, but it may also indicate that the querent is involved in two relationships at the same time.

Combined with The Anchor, it may indicate two jobs or work-related disagreements. If The Broom and The Whip card is surrounded or accompanied by positive cards, its negative impact is reduced. For example, if paired with The Clover card, it indicates minor conflicts, discords, or disagreements. However, its negative omen is heightened if it's near unfavorable cards.

Therefore, it's necessary to carefully examine the surrounding cards, regardless of their distance from the querent's card.

Traditional keywords:

Divergence, affliction, illness.

Modern keywords:

Dispute, discord, polemic, discussion, arguments, conversations, debate, verbal or physical aggression, shouting, raising voice, complaints, quarrels, lawsuits, complaint, fine, cause, contention, controversy, criticism, confrontations, conflicts, disagreements, anger, abuse, beating, torture, punishment, penitence, torment, struggle, battle, repetitive, repetition of something, negotiation, writing, separation, magic, regulation, discipline, imposition, impose, dominate, submit, power, authority; legal affairs, law-related issues, sport, physical activity, competition, training, instructor; stimulation, sadism; sign language, mime, witchcraft, number 2.

Card no. 12
THE OWLS
7 of Bells

"No. 12 – The Bird means hardships to overcome, but of short duration; distant from the Person, it means the accomplishment of a pleasant journey."

Philippe Lenormand, 1846

What's the role of the card in a reading?
The Owls card brings minor everyday upsets, as well as news or spoken information.

General meaning:
The Owls card primarily means minor annoyances, worries, upsets, and everyday stresses. These events will likely have no consequences if it shows up close to a positive card.

However, the situation may become complicated if negative cards surround The Owls. In addition, The Owls card is associated with oral communication, such as conversations, dialogues, and the exchange of opinions or information.

The content of this communication will be indicated by the cards surrounding it. For example, The Stars card stands for the Internet and modern technology and communication via the Internet (Messenger, WhatsApp, Skype, etc.). If The Bouquet card accompanies The Owls along with The Stars, it indicates that praise or a message will be received through a video call or conversation, which will cause joy.

This same combination also announces a friendship invitation or a virtual flirt. When paired with The Tree card, it can indicate worries or phone calls concerning health issues. If The Letter card is nearby, it denotes a written message, while if The Clouds accompany it, it predicts the arrival of bad news or a stressful time. Along with The Lilies, it might indicate an erotic phone call or a call with the family that could result in upsets, especially if The House or The Tree card is also present.

On the other hand, The Owls cards combined with The Snake card may indicate slander, gossip, or malicious rumors aimed at damaging a person's reputation. This combination also suggests the presence of a fortune teller (with The Book card), an astrologer (with The Stars card), or practices related to witchcraft and curses.

The Owls can also mean the arrival of news and information through advertising or word of mouth, which will likely receive a significant response. Sometimes, The Owls card also reveals a desire for independence, freedom, or personal space, leading to avoiding responsibilities.

When this card is far from the querent's card, it announces a short trip or a long-awaited communication will be delayed. In my experience, The Owls card represents a short trip or journey, especially when it falls near a card representing the querent or another person; it also announces that the querent will move to a nearby place. Another detail I have noticed in my readings is that these trips tend to be made by plane or helicopter.

Traditional keywords:

Small problems, temporary everyday difficulties.

Modern keywords:

Sadness, upsets, bitterness, stress, anxiety, agitation or discomfort (of short-term), disagreements, caution, vigilance, oral communication (news), information exchange, conversations (lecture, speech, comments, gossip, whispers, slander), contact, meeting, date, interview, colloquium, negotiation, sale, phone call, chat (WhatsApp, Skype, etc.), social networks (Facebook,

Instagram, forum, etc.), telecommunications (TV, radio), voices, sound, music, concert, announcement, advertising, rush, come and go, brief displacement, (excursion, tourism, commuting or everyday chores), flirting, thoughts, number two, elderly couple, minor events, clairvoyance, visions, magic, sorcery.

Card no. 13
THE CHILD
Jack of Leaves

"No. 13 – The Child is a sign that the Person moves in good society, and is full of kindness towards everybody.

Philippe Lenormand, 1846

What's the role of the card in a reading?

The Child card brings news about a child or teenager. It stands for a new fact or something never experienced before, a new beginning, a new phase of life.

General meaning:

When The Child card falls close to the querent, it heralds the arrival of new circumstances that will allow you to rebuild your own life. When paired with The Heart card, it may represent a new romantic relationship. Along with The Ship card, it indicates that the person has a foreign background or currently lives geographically far away from the querent.

If The Child card is accompanied by The Storks, it indicates a birth in the family or a desire for parenthood. And if The Storks card is paired with The Owls, it can predict the birth of twins but may also indicate a nervous and stressed child. When The Child card is next to the querent's card, along with The Clouds, it announces the beginning of something related to a child (such as a child or teenager) that causes disorientation, worries, or problems. It could also indicate that the querent is a spoiled person with tantrums.

Combined with The Fish card, this card denotes small investments that will bear fruit in the future. If it falls in the past line, far from the querent's card, and is accompanied by The Clouds and The Mountain, it implies that the querent had a difficult childhood. More details about the past can be obtained from the surrounding cards.

Additionally, The Child card may suggest that the querent is a kind-hearted person who is sometimes overly trusting and naive. If it's far from the querent, it could indicate that a child is away or that the querent has a strained relationship with their children (if they have any) or with someone younger.

Traditional keywords:

Kindness, trust.

Modern keywords:

A new beginning (projects, life), first steps, starting from scratch, a fresh start, an initial phase, debut, a pleasant surprise, growth, evolution, immaturity, innocence, naivety, vulnerability, sensitivity, frailty, inexperience, immaturity, carefree, relax, play, fun, kindness, trust, tenderness, joy, animation, small, littleness, partial, short term, temporary, small size, birth, childhood, a child or an adolescent, dependence, obedience; childhood diseases.

Card no. 14
THE FOX
9 of Archons

"No. 14 – The Fox, if near, is a sign to mistrust persons with whom you are connected, because some of them try to deceive you; if distant, no danger is to be apprehended."

Philippe Lenormand, 1846

What's the role of the card in a reading?
The Fox card indicates that something is wrong.

General meaning:
The Fox card warns to be cautious of malicious people or situations involving lies and deceit. It represents cunning, trickery, and strategy to overcome adversity. The querent may be at risk of falling into a well-planned trap, and this card advises them to be more careful in the life area represented by the cards in the direction indicated by the fox's snout.

For example, when combined with the following cards:
- The House: something is wrong with neighbors or family members;
- The Tree: something is wrong with the health;
- The Child: something is wrong with the children or a project that has just started;
- The Ring: something is wrong with a contract or partnership;

- The Letter: something is wrong with emails, mail, invoices, or receipts;
- The Anchor: something is wrong at work, etc.

When surrounded by positive cards, The Fox symbolizes creativity, intelligence, and wisdom that benefit oneself or others. However, if it lies close to the querent's card or a significator card, it indicates that the person is likely experiencing deceit of the worst kind. Someone is conspiring, lying, or deceiving the querent. It can sometimes even represent self-sabotage or sabotage against another person. The Fox card advises you to open your eyes, be aware of reality and let go of fantasies. It's a call to face reality and adapt to life's circumstances. It recommends you investigate a situation thoroughly before making a decision. Nevertheless, it poses no danger if it's far from the querent's card or a significator card.

Traditional keywords:

Danger, mistrust, deceit, fraud.

Modern keywords:

Lie, threat, alertness, "dirty game", tricks, traps, sabotage, simulation, camouflage, disguise, invisibility, stalking, spying, peek, hiding, bluffing, stealing, premeditated attack, taking advantage of a situation, waiting for a good opportunity, calculation, strategy, manipulation of facts, conspiracy, unrealistic goals, counterfeiting, falsification, false witness, negative thing or person, distortion, mistrust, suspicion, wrong decision, seduction, cunning, agility, crafty, insight, intelligence, quick thinking, wisdom, description, patience, persistence, agility, adaptability, integration, independence, intuition and instinct, strong survival spirit; independent, autonomous; false prophet, investigation; wild or stray animals.

Card no. 15
THE BEAR

10 of Archons

"No. 15 – The Bear is either a messenger of good fortune, or admonishes us to keep away from company; particularly from that of the envious."

Philippe Lenormand, 1846

What's the role of the card in a reading?
The Bear card provides information about the querent's possessions, savings, and assets.

General meaning:
Card number 15 depicts a bear atop a mountain, symbolizing authority and power. Its left paw is slightly raised in a defensive attitude or as a warning of caution to those who invade its territory.

This card represents good results achieved through well-defined actions or projects, perseverance, and determination. The Bear card is a symbol of energy, vitality, strength, endurance, and intelligence used wisely and constructively.

It explicitly refers to the presence of a particular person in the querent's life, such as a mother, father, boss, friend, or influential figure, who provides support or protection during difficult times.

Have you ever watched the movie The Golden Compass? If not, it's a pity! This movie beautifully portrays a bear's primal instinct and physical abilities when it needs to defend its loved ones from harm.

If The Bear is near the querent's card, it indicates they will receive protection and support from a parent or someone with influence.

However, when accompanied by The Clouds card, it forecasts envy and ambiguity from those close to the querent, so it's necessary to keep silent and act with prudence and vigilance. This combination may also suggest an incompetent authority figure and abuse of power.

On the other hand, if combined with The Lilies card, it implies strong family ties and that the family significantly influences the querent's life. If The Bear is surrounded by or close to unfavorable cards, it indicates jealousy, aggression, or possessiveness.

Traditional keywords:

Strength, power.

Modern keywords:

Personal finance, savings, accumulating assets, prosperity, profit, stock market, possessions, endurance, stability, hibernation, fat, nutrition, food; stability, honesty, trust, authority, personal power, strength of mind, courage, perseverance; resources, dominance, experience, competence, protection, control, taking charge, guardianship; guru, shaman, therapist, spiritual guide, leadership, sponsor, influential person, fidelity, security but also envy, jealousy and possessiveness.

Card no. 16
THE STARS
6 of Hearts

"No. 16 – The Star confirms good luck in all enterprises; but if near clouds, it means a long series of unhappy accident."

Philippe Lenormand, 1846

What's the role of the card in a reading?

The Stars card refers to guidance and new projects. It adds transparency, clarity, and improvement to any situation.

General meaning:

When the Star card is next to the querent's card, it represents a mystical person, such as a fortune teller, astrologer, psychic (if accompanied by The Moon), or the gift of clairvoyance. If this card touches The Clover, it announces a period of fortune and good luck, but only for a short time, and the querent should seize the moment. However, If The Stars card is near The Coffin, it predicts the end of an ideal or a dream.

When The Storks card is nearby, it indicates it's a good time for a change. If it's paired with The Anchor, it suggests professional success. When The Garden accompanies The Stars card, it means that the querent should showcase their talents to the public as they will likely be well received.

However, this card combination may also denote substance abuse, such as alcohol or drug abuse, especially if The Fish card is also in the group of surrounding cards.

If The Stars card falls in the querent's house (see the Grand Tableau of Houses), it shows that the querent is confident, optimistic, and capable of creating their own opportunities.

Traditional keywords:

Luck, success.

Modern keywords:

Success, hope, expectations, motivation, optimism, encouragement, protection, clarity (truth revelation), a new beginning, idea, enlightenment, inspiration, a true vocation, talent, potential, art, music, fashion, creativity, new projects, goals (pursuing higher goals), wish fulfilled, common sense, fame, reputation, popularity, abundance, expansion, progress, development process, direction, guidance, guide, northern, strategy, chart, esotericism, occult sciences (combined with The Book), astrology, clairvoyance, intuition (well-developed senses), spirituality; universe, astronomy (combined with The Moon), innovation, science, technology, internet; many (number or things), beauty, fascination, skin, cells, cold, night, winter, snow, ice; Religion: Jewish, Wicca, Islamic (combined with The Moon).

Card no. 17
THE STORKS
Queen of Hearts

"No. 17 – The Stork indicates a change of abode, which will take place, the sooner the nearer the card lies to the Person."

Philippe Lenormand, 1846

What's the role of the card in a reading?

When The Storks card appears in a reading, it announces an upcoming change or transformation. This card represents the desire for change and progress.

General meaning:

The Storks card stands for a transformation and a change in one's position or situation, as well as a movement that breaks away from routine or habits, such as food, aesthetics, behavior, attitude, ideas, or opinions. This card is commonly regarded as a symbol of renewal, new beginnings, and longevity.

It also implies the need for prudence and vigilance to avoid falling into monotony. Change can bring both negative and positive outcomes. By analyzing the surrounding cards, we can determine which area of the querent's life is undergoing transformation.

The Storks card indicates an existential renewal that has been carefully considered over time and carried out with confidence and certainty. Change and movement are the defining characteristics of this card. Further details on the subject can be found by examining the nearby cards.

For instance:
- The Ship: business travel, emigration, or moving abroad;
- The House: moving house or improving one's home or workplace.
- The Tree: a change in one's lifestyle and health conditions;
- The Broom and The Whip: new laws and rules;
- The Owls: a change of mind;
- The Garden: a change in social life;
- The Heart: changes in emotions and feelings;
- The Ring: changes in marriage or contractual agreement;
- The Fish: changes in financial situation.
- The Anchor: a change in career or job.

This card announces significant changes in activities, projects, routines, plans, or life. The cards on its right will confirm whether these changes will be positive or negative. The Stork also reveals the desire to run away, to escape from the current reality and seek a new situation in another place, discovering new rhythms that life has to offer. Fulfilling this desire to dynamize, renew, rebuild, and change requires determination to implement a plan.

For those hoping to have a child, this card brings joy because it announces an upcoming pregnancy, a birth in the family, or an adoption (with The Ring).

When The Storks card is nearby or touches the querent's card, it indicates that something is about to change. If surrounded by favorable cards, the querent may focus on the present, rebuilding their life, or even experiencing a moment of significant transformation. When it's near The Rider or The Ship card, for example, it announces a forthcoming trip or the arrival of someone from the past. However, when surrounded by negative cards, such as The Clouds or The Coffin, it predicts drastic or unnecessary changes, nervousness, doubts, and even inactivity, boredom, or laziness.

The Stork card may denote personal changes that the querent is currently undergoing in various areas of their life, including psychological, emotional, or physical.

If The Storks card is far from the querent's card, it predicts a postponed or canceled trip or move. This delay or cancellation may be prolonged if accompanied by one of the following cards: The Tower, The Mountain, The Lilies, or The Anchor.

Traditional keywords:

Changes in general.

Modern keywords:

Movement, arrival, return or departure, constant coming and going, travel (by plane), displacement, change (idea or direction), transfer, transaction, update, reorganization, renewal, shift, conversion, variation, modification, alteration; something new, new experience, progress, evolving, improvement; delivery; fecundity, fertility, pregnancy, childbirth (if The Child is the next card); adaptation, flexibility, patience; emigration.

Card No. 18
THE DOG
10 of Hearts

"No. 18 – The Dog, if near the Person, you can consider your friends faithful and sincere; but if very distant and surrounded by clouds, be cautious not to trust those who call themselves your friends."

Philippe Lenormand, 1846

What's the role of the card in a reading?

The Dog card symbolizes trust, seriousness, loyalty, and obedience and indicates long-term reliability. This card brings news about friends, colleagues, or others close to the querent. The Dog card can also represent pets.

General meaning:

When The Dog falls close to the querent's card, it represents a friend or suggests that the querent is reliable and friendly. It also refers to someone with whom the querent has a mutually respectful relationship. It means that the querent is surrounded by loyal friends on whom the querent can count during difficult times.

However, if The Clouds card pairs The Dog, it may announce the presence of untrustworthy, disappointing, and misunderstanding friends. In addition, if The Ring is close to The Snake card, it might foretell infidelity and betrayal in the relationship.

When The Dog is close to The Rider card, it indicates that the querent received news from a friend. However, if it's far from the querent and surrounded by negative cards, it can denote potential infidelity or betrayal by friends.

Traditional keywords:
Friendship, loyalty, sincerity.

Modern keywords:
Loyalty, trust, truth, values and principles, respect, obedience, security, submission, emotional attachment, support, help, sustenance, adoption, companionship, fellowship, teamwork, instinct, disciple, follower, pet, protection.

Card no. 19

THE TOWER

6 of Leaves

"No. 19 – The Tower gives the hope of a happy old age; but if surrounded by clouds, it forbodes sickness, and, according to circumstances, even death."

Philippe Lenormand, 1846

What's the role of the card in a reading?

The Tower card represents authority, government, and institutions. It often denotes a sense of detachment from the outside world and isolation within oneself. It also brings boundaries, a desire for distance, and high ambitions.

General meaning:

When The Tower card touches the querent's card, it describes a lonely or single person. Along with favorable cards, it predicts longevity and resistance to overcome the storms of life. It may announce reform if The Anchor card is nearby.

When The Tower shows up to the right of the querent's card, it might announce isolation or escape from a problem. When surrounded by unfavorable cards, such as The Mice or The Coffin, it foretells the possibility of hospitalization for medical examinations or sickness. If paired with The Clouds, it indicates severe health problems. With The Broom and The Whip, it means serious problems with the authorities, borders, and customs (such as an embassy, consulate, or government agency), especially when accompanied by The Mountain.

Important Note:

When positioned as the last card in a line, The Tower can also stand for a situation that remains unchanged for a long time. The separation represented by The Tower doesn't always imply an actual breakup, so it's essential to pay close attention to the surrounding cards to get an accurate picture of the situation.

For example:

- The Ring + The Tower predicts a partner's departure, which can have several causes, such as:
    - The Coffin: disease or even death (if confirmed by other cards)
    - The Book: the partner is studying or researching. It may also indicate a partner is considering a potential separation, resulting in distancing and detachment.
    - And so on.

The Tower can also signify constraints or limitations in a relationship or life (debts, external or internal factors, etc.) that promote social isolation.

Traditional keywords:

Longevity.

Modern keywords:

State, government, institutions (hospitals, government or monarchy palaces, banks, schools, departments, public offices, administrative offices, embassies, consulates, courts, military headquarters, etc.), authority, the law, legal matter (if it's accompanied by the Broom and Whip), conventions, bureaucracy, hierarchy, career, ambition, restriction, limitation, boundary, unauthorized space, reserved space, separation, divorce, distance, solitude, isolation (necessary), rest and reflection period, departure, retreat, withdrawal, rigidity, self-sufficient, independent, what is old, elderly, erect, straight, fixed, hardness, tall, strength, constancy, endurance, persistence, inflexibility, belonging to the upper class, ego, high self-esteem, ambition, protection, tall buildings, buildings, towers, palaces, castles, and archeological sites.

Card no. 20
THE GARDEN
8 of Leaves

"No. 20 – The Park prognosticates that you will visit a very respectable company; if very near, that you are to form a very intimate friendship, but if distant, it hints to false friends."

Philippe Lenormand, 1846

What's the role of the card in a reading?

The Garden card provides insight into one's social life, including social media platforms. It can also reveal information about events, gatherings, and groups (classes). This card is also associated with the public and customers.

General meaning:

The Garden card represents the querent's social circle, experiences, integration, and connection with the outside world. It symbolizes the space where the querent's dreams and goals come true.

In addition, it may indicate the desire to escape the daily hustle and bustle and find peace in a quiet and natural environment. This card foretells a period of inspiration and creativity if it's near the querent's card. If paired with The Dog card, it means the arrival of new friends, while The Anchor card indicates the arrival of new clients. When The Garden is paired with The Tower, it announces that the querent will meet influential people who can help them in the future. With The Heart card, it means that the querent enjoys being in the public eye and is loved by others.

However, if surrounded by unfavorable cards, it might denote slander or public defamation. If The Garden is far from the querent's card and surrounded by negative cards, it predicts bad company, people pretending to be friends, or lack of inspiration. Pay attention to the cards that touch The Garden; they will provide further clues about the querent's social life.

Traditional keyword:
Social life.

Modern keywords:
External space, population, people, public, crowd, group, political party, public performance, socialization, social communication, social network (Facebook), forum, internet, date, meeting, event (demonstrations, celebrations, rallies, seminar, festival, concert, parties, exhibition), free time, fun, entertainment, audience, party, audience, vacation, outdoors, advertising, marketing, public communication, openness, growth and development, third-party help, ground, nature, artistic talent, public places (public park, stadium, bars, clubs, restaurants, shopping centers, hotels, etc.), community, environment.

Card no. 21
THE MOUNTAIN
8 of Acorns

"No. 21 – The Mountains, near the Person, warn you against a mighty enemy; if distant, you may rely on powerful friends."

Philippe Lenormand, 1846

What's the role of the card in a reading?

The Mountain card indicates serious problems, difficulties, obstacles, and blockages.

General meaning:

When The Mountain card appears in a reading, it announces a huge obstacle impeding a project's progress, causing delays, frustrations, exhaustion, oppression, and anxiety.

This card predicts challenges that can only be overcome with discipline, rigor, perseverance, effort, commitment, and sacrifice. It's necessary to think and act carefully and without prey.

If The Mountain appears near the querent's card, it means a significant obstacle, which could be an opponent, a powerful enemy, or a severe problem. Likewise, The Owls or the Path card nearby denotes two enemies who will create serious problems for the querent, leading to opposition towards the positive evolution of an issue.

The querent's project is likely to stall and make no progress. The adjacent cards will tell the reasons and potential solutions to the problem.

For instance, if The Dog card is placed before The Mountain, it indicates that a friend is hindering the querent from achieving their goals. However, if The Dog comes after The Mountain, it suggests that a friend will help resolve a challenging issue.

When it's far from the querent's card, it doesn't pose a threat, implying that the path to achieving goals is free from hindrances, with the help and support of powerful friends.

Traditional keywords:

Enemy, opposition.

Modern keywords:

A complex problem, a hostile situation, serious difficulties, obstacles, blockage, hindrance, boundary, border, limits, restrictions, inaccessible, frontier, block post, distance, away, something that is far away from reaching, objection, opposition, resistance, no developments at the moment, delay, inactivity, immobility, stagnation, oppression, heaviness, heavy, ascent, effort, resistance, rough surface, hard, cold, ice; powerful enemies, adversary, opponent, loneliness, isolated, altitude, hills, mountains.

Card no. 22
THE CROSSROADS
Queen of Bells

"No. 22 – The Roads, surrounded by clouds, are signs of disaster; but without this card, and if distant from Person, that you shall find ways and means to avoid the threatening danger."

Philippe Lenormand, 1846

What's the role of the card in a reading?

The Crossroads card represents choices and alternatives.

General meaning:

The querent is at a crossroads, compelled to make a crucial choice that will determine their future. If favorable cards influence The Crossroads, it suggests a decision is made according to one's own free will and without any coercion or pressure. But, when unfavorable cards accompany it, it's necessary to proceed with extreme caution since it's possible that the querent's life or the subject under investigation may be impeding a new direction.

The querent is at a crossroads, compelled to make a crucial choice that will determine their future. Favorable cards influencing The Crossroads card suggest that a decision is made according to one's free will and without coercion or pressure. On the other hand, when unfavorable cards touch it, it's necessary to proceed with extreme caution since the querent's life or the subject under investigation may be impeding a new direction.

When The Crossroads card appears next to the querent's card, it announces that a conflict or situation will arise requiring a decision. In this case, it's essential to look at the surrounding cards for further information. For example, if The Anchor card is nearby, it suggests that the querent will make a definitive choice or decision.

With The Coffin card, it denotes that the dilemma will come to an end. However, when The Crossroads card is accompanied by The Clouds, it predicts misfortune or that it's not the right time to make a decision; emotional or psychological pressure may be created by the crisis of the moment. If paired with The Fox card, it indicates that someone may be manipulating the querent in order to force a decision. Be cautious. If The Ship is nearby and next to The Clouds card, it signals a journey through misty or stormy conditions, where accidents or harassment may take place.

If it's far from the querent's card and free from the influence of negative cards, it indicates that a favorable decision will be made regarding the subject being investigated or that the querent will have the time to control the situation by taking some positive measures and actions.

Traditional keywords:
Choice.

Modern keywords:
Decision-making, option, alternative, possibility, other points of view, different definitions, ambiguity, doubt, uncertainties, instability, dilemma, a proposal under evaluation, an indeterminate issue, plans, turning point, change of direction or idea, indecision, research, search, hesitation, outstanding issues, dispersion, send to more people, sharing, election, selection, free will, freedom of choice, temporary break up, desertion, escape, wander, adventure, aimless, travel, displacement, walking or cycling, hiking, road, a geographic map, route, explore, avoid meeting someone, polygamy, infidelity, the number two of something; new treatment methods

Card no. 23
THE MICE
7 of Acorns

"No. 23 – The Mice is a sign of a theft, a loss; when near, it indicates the recovery of the thing lost or stolen; if at a distance, the loss will be irreparable."

Philippe Lenormand, 1846

What's the role of the card in a reading?

The Mice card brings loss, decay, and disease.

General meaning:

The Mice card signifies the problems that cause distress, negative thoughts, anguish, and anxiety. It also represents the cunningness and persistence required to achieve one's goals.

The Mice are harbingers of severe problems and ruin. This card may mean rush and haste, looking for solutions to problems in a thousand directions, some of which will lead nowhere. According to tradition, if The Mice card is nearby or touching the querent's card, it means recovering lost or stolen items. However, if it's far from the querent, those items may never be found or retrieved.

In my experience with Philippe Lenormand's Method, the Near/Far Technique, particularly with this card, I have learned that, as with any other card in a reading, it's not recommended to adhere to this rule strictly. When The Mice card is close to the querent's card, it means that the person is currently suffering a loss, which may be caused by various factors, such as energy, health, money, or employment. The flanking cards will provide more details.

The Mice card is a warning about the possibility of theft and loss of people or possessions. When accompanied by The Rider or The Storks cards, it brings back something lost or stolen, as well as missing people.

Therefore, or all that has been described above, it's crucial to check the cards surrounding The Mice, whether the Near/Far Technique is applied or not.

It's also important to remember that in Petit Lenormand, the cards are never interpreted individually but in combination with those near them. Keep this detail in mind! When The Mice is the first card in a reading, it represents anxiety, worry, and stress. Something is "gnawing" and upsetting the querent emotionally and mentally. The causes of this condition can be found in the surrounding cards:

- The Child: a son/a daughter
- The Ring: relationship, marriage;
- The Fish: money
    o The Fish + The Mice + The Ring: payment of a bill
    o The Fish + The Mice: debts.

Traditional keywords:
Theft, loss

Modern keywords:
Gradual or partial loss, risk of assault, betrayal, infidelity, distrust, lessen, reduction (work, money, health, illness, kilos, etc.), fading out, running out, disappearing, lack (of self-esteem), second-hand, low-value goods, damage, material, injury, ruin, decay, poverty, destruction, greed, abandonment, deprivation, waste, disease (nervous system, stomach, infectious disease), corruption, marginalization, plagiarism, misappropriation, blackmail, deception, serious concerns, difficult circumstances, unpleasant surprises, annoyances, dissatisfaction, fear, stress, dirty, filthy,

disgusting, rubbish, dump, debris, manure, feces, putrefaction, stinky, nasty, spam, vandalism, defect, impure, dependence, vices, bad habits, weakening, ignorance, offenses, hypocrisy, bad manners, bad-words, disrespect, contempt, repulsion, reject, hunger, enemy presence, envy, jealousy, negative energy, witchcraft, evil eye, rodents.

Card no. 24
THE HEART
Jack of Hearts

"No. 24 – The Heart is a sign of joy leading to union and bliss."

Philippe Lenormand, 1846

What's the role of the card in a reading?

The Heart card expresses positive and negative feelings and emotions, such as love, passion, generosity, sensitivity, charity, hatred, resentment, etc.

General meaning:

The Heart card symbolizes love, but whether it's positive or negative depends on the surrounding cards. This card deals with all issues of the heart and everything that inspire people to fall in love or feel enthusiastic.

It represents the natural way of acting (expression, talent, vocation) when doing something enjoyable, such as cooking, eating, drinking, reading, writing, traveling, practicing sport, engaging in art, music, communicating, working, teaching, studying, loving, dancing, making love, raising children, or building a home and family.

The Heart card represents both the external and internal beauty of a person. Its true meaning is revealed through the surrounding cards. When The Heart card lands close to the querent's card, it announces happiness, romanticism, support, and love. It also indicates that the querent loves themselves and cares for those in need. It also suggests something or someone will make the querent's heart flutter.

But be careful! If unfavorable cards influence The Heart card, it reveals negative feelings and emotions, such as hatred, envy, jealousy, and revenge, as well as unhealthy and destructive ties or attraction to evil.

When The Heart is combined with The Ring and The Cross, it suggests that a love story is being lived with pain or as a burden.

Traditional keywords:

Joy, love

Modern keywords:

Intimate feeling, intense emotions, affections, desire, passion, attraction, seduction, sensuality, pleasure, love of things, happiness, romance, enthusiasm, preferred, sharing, affinity, donation, compassion, charity, sensitivity, tenderness, affection, human warmth, intimacy, availability, sympathy, protection, attachment, forgiveness, kindness, sincerity, honesty, loyalty, help, support, taste, candy, art, music, dessert, happy circumstances, vanity, obsession.

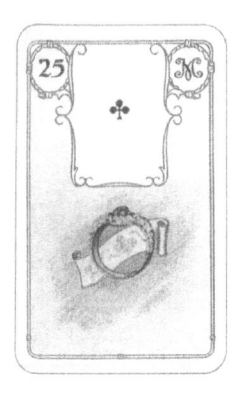

CARD NO. 25
THE RING

ACE OF ACORNS

"No. 25 – The Ring, if on the right of the Person, prognosticates a rich and happy marriage; when on the left, and distant, a falling out with the object of your affection, and the breaking off of a marriage."

Philippe Lenormand, 1846

What's the role of the card in a reading?

The Ring card represents the formalization of a situation or union to ensure the security of all parties involved, including a commitment, a contract, a signature, a pact, an oath, an engagement, a marriage, and ethics. However, it also brings obligations and responsibilities that must be fulfilled.

General meaning:

The Ring generally represents a sense of duty, respect for laws and morals, as well as the exposure of all that is fair and right. This card stands for a legal declaration, a contract, a condition, or a situation that has finally become legitimate. The Ring suggests a bond with a lifelong commitment that can be either enjoyable or burdensome. This card requires you to adhere to strict boundaries of absolute legality, whether cultural, legal, or religious context. It demands a self-compromise to bring order to one's life.

In some cases, The Ring points out that the querent needs discipline to reorganize their life without forgetting their moral and social values. It's essential to follow the rules for every planned action during this time since order, discipline, and commitment are the motto of this card and are vital for success.

All kinds of written or verbal contracts, including those for buying and selling property (house, car, etc.), work, credit, joying a group or course, dating, engagement, and marriage, are represented in this card. According to tradition, when The Ring appears close to the querent's card, it's important to note whether it's placed on the right or left side.

If it's on the right, it predicts a happy relationship, and for single people, it may indicate a relationship with someone with a good financial situation. However, if it's on the left, it augurs litigation, disputes, or the end of a relationship.

Therefore, whether using the Near/Far Technique or any other reading technique, it's necessary to check the cards surrounding the significator card, in this case, The Ring. This observation will provide more information about the type of relationship being experienced. This is my personal reading of The Ring card using the Near/Far Technique:

- If The Ring appears in the <u>future line</u> and <u>near the querent's card</u>, it announces an upcoming relationship; the surrounding cards will provide information about the nature of the relationship.

- If The Ring is in the <u>future line</u> but <u>far from the querent's card</u>, it indicates that a relationship will only be possible in a distant future or that an existing relationship will cool down. The Scythe combined with The Ring augurs a divorce or the breaking of an agreement or contract. It may also indicate a severe shock or upheaval for the querent. The surrounding cards will give more details.

- If The Ring is <u>above the querent's card</u>, it means a strong desire for a serious relationship or commitment. But if The Clouds card is paired with The Ring, it suggests that a specific relationship is causing the querent's primary concern.

- If The Ring falls in the <u>past line</u> and is <u>near the querent's card</u>, it represents a commitment, a relationship, or an obligation that has affected the current situation, leading to attachment and dependence.

- When The Ring is placed in the <u>past line</u> but <u>far from the querent's card</u>, it may refer to a previous relationship, such as a marriage, engagement, or partnership, which has left a lasting impression. For example, The Scythe card combined with The Ring could foretell the possibility of a divorce or separation.

- If The Ring card <u>is next to the card representing one of the partners</u>, the surrounding cards may refer to the partner's problems.

Traditional keywords:

Marriage, relationship

Modern keywords:

An agreement, promise, oath, pact, treaty, confirm, commitment, pledge, contract, signature, mutual, linking, bond, connection, obligation, duty, responsibility, guarantee, seriousness, legal relationship, unite, merger, society, branch, affiliation, vote, nomination, regulate, continuity, repetition, monthly, income, rental, being connected to something, chronic, circle, repetition cycle, ritual, ceremony, routine, dogma, proposal, ethics, order, discipline, goals, well-accurate, preservation, official documents, traditional, surname, nickname, delegate, durability, recurring event.

Card no. 26
THE BOOK
10 of Bells

"No. 26 – The Book indicates that you are going to find out a secret; according to its position, you can judge in what manner; great caution, however, is necessary in attempting a solution."

Philippe Lenormand, 1846

What's the role of the card in a reading?
The Book card indicates something unknown and confidential that requires investigation and deep exploration. It also provides information related to education, such as school, studies, qualification, and intellect like culture and intelligence. It represents the unknown, a mystery, something hidden, or a secret.

General meaning:
If The Book card appears near the querent's car, it suggests that the querent is secretive, reserved, and may be hiding a secret. When combined with The Clouds card, this card denotes restlessness due to dangerous secrets or a lack of concentration in studies. If The Scythe shows up before The Book, it indicates that a secret will be revealed or an important document containing crucial information will be discovered.

Pay attention to the position of The Book card in relation to the querent's card: if it's placed behind the card, it represents an unknown person or someone who doesn't want to reveal their identity.

On the other hand, if The Book card is in front of the cards no. 28 and 29, the querent's cards, it represents a known person who will confess or reveal an important secret or information.

It can also mean someone the querent deals with regarding paperwork, documents, or a will.

The closer The Book is to the querent's card, the more important the secret or information is. The surrounding cards will provide additional details.

Traditional keywords:

Secrets, mysteries.

Modern keywords:

Hidden, occult, unknown, knowledge, school, study, instruction, qualification, course, learning, possession of knowledge, education, mind, memory, culture, intelligence, journal, books, documents, papers, material (letters, esoteric products), information, testament, silence, confidential, reserved, not accessible to all, intimacy, privacy, secrecy, taboo, investigation, inquiry, search, code, decipher, discovery, revelation, project, personal data, computer memory, archive, file, books, test, exam, capacity, competence, unofficial, not known yet, puzzles, riddle, occultism, esotericism, deck of cards, literary activity, scholarship, the mind, the brain, future.

Card no. 27
THE LETTER
7 of Leaves

"No. 27 – The Letter, without clouds, means luck, which comes to you by distant, favorable news; but if dark clouds are near the Person, you may expect much grief.

Philippe Lenormand, 1846

What's the role of the card in a reading?

The Letter card represents written information, such as documents, newspapers, mail, email, inbox, fax, chat, and blog.

General meaning:

The Letter card symbolizes messengers of news or information. It represents the arrival of written news and information related to the subject of the reading.

If The Letter is close to the querent's card, it suggests that the querent will receive a written message. However, when The Letter card touches the dark side of The Clouds, it indicates that incoming news may cause the querent great worry and annoyance.

I've learned through my experience not to overlook the surrounding cards as they will provide insight into the message that the querent is about to receive or send.

For example, with:
- The House: news related to the house itself, registering a property, subscribing on a forum or blog, or receiving an email.

- The Tree: medical prescription; medical report, or making an appointment with a doctor;
- The Coffin: news about one's death; rejection of an application;
- The Broom and The Whip: a complaint or grievance form; a traffic ticket; a notice or an email that will cause conflict.
- The Fox: fake news or misleading information;
- The Book: a confidential message; the result of a medical examination, a certificate or diploma, or ordering a book or a deck of cards;
- The Fish: messages related to finances, any paperwork related to money, such as proof of a transfer or deposit, bills with payment instructions;
- The Anchor: work mail or a message of hope.

Traditional keywords

News, information

Modern keywords:

Mail, written correspondence, written media (text message, e-mail, fax, letter), newsletter, information, papers, disclosure, response, reminder, result, notice, warning, a clue, a sign, bureaucracy, form, document, folder, an image, a photograph, a certificate, a license plate, an inscription, mediation, marketing, announcement, article (blog), contact, correspondent, apps (WhatsApp, etc.), superficiality, frivolity.

CARD NO. 28
THE MAN

ACE OF HEARTS

CARD NO. 29
THE WOMAN

ACE OF LEAVES

"No. 28. & No. 29 – The Gentleman and The Lady The whole pack refers to either of these cards, depending, if the person whose fortune is being told is either a Lady (No. 29) or Gentleman (No. 28)."

Philippe Lenormand, 1846

General meaning:

The Man and The Woman cards play the role of physically represent the querent. Before starting a reading, it's essential to assign an identity to each of these querent's cards: The Man and The Woman. If a male querent requests the reading, The Man card portrays him. For a female querent, The Woman card represents her.

In a relationship reading, the other querent's card will represent that person of significance. For example, if a man requests the reading, the card that represents him will be The Man and The Woman card will portray a woman of significant importance to the querent, who could be his bride, girlfriend, wife, lover, colleague, aunt, sister, mother, or anyone else relevant to the question. Similarly, if a woman requests a reading, The Woman card will represent her, and The Man card will represent her husband, fiancé, boyfriend, lover, colleague, father, uncle, brother, male cousin, etc. In a reading without a card representing someone in particular, it's necessary to pay attention to the cards that touch it, as they will provide relevant information about that person.

In fact, the surrounding cards identify the marital status (married, divorced, widowed; age (young or adult), the nature of the relationship with the querent (like father, mother, stepfather, stepmother, godfather, godmother, brother, sister, cousin, uncle, grandmother, boss, colleague, etc.), physical characteristics (tall, short, thin, fat, blond, etc.;) and personality traits (honest, disloyal, liar, intelligent, ignorant, polite, etc.) of this man or woman.

What to do when you need to read for someone of the same gender as the querent? If your card deck has separate cards for male and female genders, assign one of them to stand for people of the querent's same gender. In other words:

- If a male querent seeks a reading for his brother, uncle, colleague, or even his partner, The Woman card will represent him.

- If our female querent seeks a reading for her female friend or colleague, sister, or partner, The Man card will represent her.

Important Note:

The querent's cards are essential, particularly in a Grand Tableau reading, where the near/far technique is extensively employed. The reading starts from the querent's card, and the interpretation is based on the distances - very near/near and very far/far - from the other cards.

Additional information regarding querent's cards will be covered in Chapter 3 as we study the significator cards.

Card no. 30
THE LILIES
King of Leaves

"No. 30 – The Lilies indicate a happy life; surrounded by clouds, a family grief. If this card is placed above the Person, they indicate the same as being virtuous; if below the Person, the moral principles are doubted."

Philippe Lenormand, 1846

What's the role of the card in a reading?

The Lilies card is the symbol of chastity, innocence, and purity. It brings harmony and peace to the querent's life.

General meaning:

If The Lilies card shows up next to the querent's card, it describes a person with virtuous qualities, experience, and good character. However, if The Clouds card touches The Lilies and the querent's card, it suggests that the person described has evil intentions or is of bad character. When The Coffin appears with The Lilies, it may announce a death in the family, while with The Tree indicates a long recovery from a disease. When paired with The Dog card, the querent will receive support and assistance from a very influential person.

According to tradition, when The Lilies card falls below the querent's card, it's said to be a sign of unhappiness and problems. Nevertheless, in my readings, when The Lilies card lands in this position, the querent may not value or respect moral, traditional, personal, or social principles.

Traditional keywords:
Harmony, family, sex.

Modern keywords:
Peace, calmness, pacification, reconciliation, tranquility, relaxation, peace of mind, meditation, yoga, tradition, old generation, vintage, morality, nobility, experience, maturity, mentoring, support, help, honesty, seriousness, respect, integrity, honor, virtue, virginity, seniors, retirement, products aged over time (wine, cheese, preserves), freezing, delays, winter, old-age diseases, sexuality.

Card no. 31
THE SUN
Ace of Bells

"No. 31 – The Sun, lying near, points to happiness and pleasure, as its beams spread light and warmth; far away, it indicates misfortune and sorrow, as without the Sun's influence nothing can grow."

Philippe Lenormand, 1846

What's the role of the card in a reading?

The Sun card represents enlightenment, willpower, vitality, and optimism, bringing significant successes, victories, joy, and happiness.

General meaning:

It's always reassuring when the Sun card shows up in a reading. It heralds a period of productivity, achievements, and progress in the areas that matter to the querent, so they should seize the opportunity and show their best.

The Sun represents a period of personal growth ensuring that the querent's goals will be achieved. It also means that secrets will be revealed, the truth will triumph, and the problems will finally find a solution. The Sun card always points to a favorable situation, a happy and fruitful time. It confirms that the querent is on the right path in their life journey. When The Sun is in the vicinity or close to the querent's card, it's reassuring that they are doing the right thing.

This card denotes that the querent is under the influence of positive energies and will experience a period of complete serenity and peace. They'll feel confident and capable enough to overcome adversity with determination and success; it's essential to check the surrounding cards to identify which life will be most impacted. In combination with the card Pisces, it predicts business success and a good salary.

However, if The Sun is far from the querent's card, it can indicate discouragement and discomfort. The querent may feel drained and lacking vitality and courage to face life's challenges, which will be identified in the surrounding cards. Disappointments are to be expected.

Important Note:

The Sun card can lessen the negativity of the cards to its left, such as The Coffin or The Mountain. If The Sun is the last card in a line, it guarantees the success of the situation under investigation.

Traditional keyword:

Happiness.

Modern keywords:

Success, victory, success, achievement, great fortune, luck, truth, affirmation, positive outcome (YES), solution, overcoming, energy, vitality, revitalization, well-being, gain, positivity, optimism, enthusiasm, satisfaction, confidence, security, light, clarity, abundance, expansion, progression, personal evolution, growth, development, constructive attitude, career advancement, creativity, objectivity, determination, certainty, a strong and charismatic personality, vitamin D, summer, hot, heat, fire, burn.

Card no. 32
THE MOON
8 of Hearts

"No. 32 – The Moon is a sign of great honors, fortune and fame, if the card lies at the side of the Person; if at a distance, it means grief and misery."

Philippe Lenormand, 1846

What's the role of the card in a reading?

The Moon card stands for qualities such as honor, glory, recognition, and status.

General meaning:

The Moon predicts a period of fame (for better or for worse), glory, and popularity. It expresses one's talent and creativity. This card predicts a time of recognition, achievement, and deserved success in various areas, such as work, business, studies, or education. It also shows how much the querent is admired and respected in their surroundings. The Moon also refers to a retrospective evaluation of the querent's past actions and attitudes, which will be projected and judged accordingly. Those who have worked hard and honestly will be rewarded with glory and fame. When close to the querent's card, it foretells memorable events and significant recognition and admiration from others.

The Moon
- The Ship: travel, romantic vacation;

- The Ship + The Stars: international fame and recognition;
- The Snake: the querent's reputation is harmed by lies and slander;
- The Stars: intuition and foresight in dreams, as well as recognition and fame;
- The Garden: public recognition;
- The Keys: success is guaranteed;
- The Anchor: success and recognition at work, but also working the night shift.

When The Moon falls far from the querent, it indicates they may not receive the recognition or rewards they deserve for their work. When it touches The Clouds card, for a woman, it may denote a delay in her menstrual cycle.

Traditional keywords:
Honor, success, recognition, fame.

Modern keywords:
Notoriety, popularity, admiration, accolade, reputation, being the focus of attention (for better or worse), prestige, celebrity (with The Stars), the soul, emotional world, sensitivity, sensation, intuition, intuitive capacity, sleep, dreams, fantasy; creativity, art, romance.

Card no. 33
THE KEY

8 of Bells

"No. 33 – The Key, if near, means the certain success of a wish or a plan; if distant, the contrary."

Philippe Lenormand 1846

What's the role of the card in a reading?
The Key card has a specific purpose: to open and lock something. When it appears in a reading, it assures that the person is acting according to their own will or they have the power to change the circumstances of a situation.

General meaning:
The Key card represents free will in deciding and also opening or closing situations (for better or worse). It brings certainty, solutions, and answers to problems. The Key is associated with the symbolism of the door of a riddle that was opened and revealed. In this sense, it initiates something new when transitioning from one plane of life to another.

The Key card has the ability to solve an enigma, bringing order and clarity to a confusing situation. When we usually say, "I found The Key", we often mean we've finally found a solution or answer to a mental or experiential problem.

In a Grand Tableau reading, when The Key lands next to the querent's card, it announces that their wishes will be fulfilled, and their question will receive a positive answer.

Combined with The Clouds card, it suggests uncertainties or a problem to be solved and that the querent may feel disappointed or that their initiatives and decisions aren't fair.

When The Key is far from the querent's card, it indicates that the solution to a particular problem hasn't been found yet, or the querent lacks the necessary means to achieve their goals.

Traditional keywords:
Success, certainty.

Modern keywords:
Security, solution, answer, solving something, opening or closing something, enter, access to an area (computer, log in, location), discoveries, revelations, hiding or revealing something, desired change, putting into practice, new ideas, a stroke of inspiration, intuition, understanding something, reliable, self-confidence, a new beginning, initiation, prevent, stepping forward, moving to a new phase, free will, autonomy, independence, emancipation, graduation, promotion, achieving a goal, penetration, musical note, instrument, mobile phone, connection, decode, code, keywords, recognition code, combinations, computing, method, system, innovation.

Card no. 34
THE FISH
King of Bells

"No. 34 – The Fishes, if near the Person, point to the acquisition of large fortune by marine enterprises and to a series of successful undertakings; if distant, they indicate the failure of any speculation, no matter how well projected or planned."

Philippe Lenormand, 1846

What's the role of the card in a reading?
The Fish card stands for Information related to money, financial issues, investments, business, and material possessions.

General meaning:
The Fish card symbolizes abundance and material wealth. In the traditional method, if The Fish card is close to the querent's card, it predicts financial prosperity and happiness, while if it's far away, it may indicate financial bankruptcy and heartbreak.

My experience with The Fish using the traditional method has shown me that if it's near the querent's card, it suggests good news and financial success. This is a favorable time to negotiate a raise or make investments. The surrounding cards will provide insights into the sources of income or economic improvement.

If The Fish is above the querent's card, they're working on important projects to improve their financial situation.

However, if The Clouds card is nearby, it predicts financial problems.

When The Fish card falls below the querent's card and next to The Mice card, it indicates debts and financial constraints. If it appears next to The Coffin, it may denote poverty. If it's in the past line but distant from the querent's card, it may suggest they experienced a significant financial collapse or came from a humble background. Sometimes, it may suggest debts incurred due to poor financial management.

When The Fish is positioned in the future line but far from the querent's card, the financial stability may require significant sacrifices. The surrounding cards will provide additional information about the financial future.

When The Fish card falls next to another card, it reveals what the querent values and prioritizes in life. For instance, if it's paired with The Dog card, it indicates that honesty and loyalty are crucial to them; with The Heart card, empathy, compassion, and solidarity toward others are their engine; and with The Lilies card, the person values ethics, moral rules, and the family, or even sexual experience, as The Lilies also represent sex.

Traditional keywords:

Prosperity, abundance.

Modern keywords:

Wealth, finance, money, currency, profit, salary, cash, investment, a gift or inheritance, material value, business, commerce, conquest, expansion, enlargement, fertility, reproduction, contacts, freedom, independence, autonomous work, movement, flow, large family, food, liquid substance, liquid (drinks), fat (oil), water, rain, tears, soul.

Card no. 35
THE ANCHOR
9 of Leaves

"No. 35 – The Anchor is a sign of a successful enterprise at sea, of great advantage in trade, and of true love; but distant, it means a thorough disappointment in ideas, and inconstancy in love."

Philippe Lenormand, 1846

What's the role of the card in a reading?

The Anchor card represents hope, stability, balance, security, determination, and perseverance to achieve one's goals.

General meaning:

The Anchor card provides information related to work issues, such as guidance and professional qualifications. If it's close to the querent's card and is accompanied by The Rider, The Ship, or The Storks card, it announces a change in the professional field.

Along with The Ring, it stands for fidelity and ensures a long-term stable job or marital relationship, even if no feelings are involved. When The Mice card is nearby in a professional question, it suggests a reduction in work (the surrounding cards will give more details). When appearing in a distant position, it predicts adverse events and potential infidelity by the person of interest, offering false hope.

Sometimes, when The Anchor is near or surrounded by unfavorable or stop cards, it indicates that the querent is creating their own obstacles, blocking their evolution, or hindering their growth and progress in life. In contrast to The Mountain card, where the blockage comes from the outside, The Anchor card denotes that the blockage is internal.

Traditional keywords:

Business success, security, hope.

Modern keywords:

Balance, stability, steady, work, profession, occupation, commitment, perseverance, determination, goals, constancy, persistence, grounded, bond, security, safe, fidelity, reliable, ethics, solid foundation, fixed, attachment, not letting go and leave it as it is, conservatism, devotion to one's ideals, addiction, dependability, long-term project, customary, no change, possessiveness, formation.

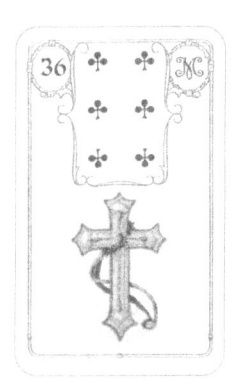

Card no. 36
THE CROSS
6 of Acorns

"No. 36 – The Cross is always a bad sign; if very near the person, you may hope that the misfortune will not last long."

Philippe Lenormand, 1846

What's the role of the card in a reading?
Based on its position, The Cross card shows which area of the querent's life will feel the pressure of responsibility and duty.

General meaning:
The Cross card denotes significant responsibilities in one's life or a person guided by faith and not exempt from suffering and enormous sacrifices. It also represents values and ideologies.

This card announces that the querent will endure adversity and the journey will be arduous with moments of discouragement and pain. In order to accomplish this mission, it's necessary a great deal of courage, strength, and faith, as without these ingredients, they won't succeed.

When The Cross is close to the querent's card, it foretells hardship and tests that will require sacrifice and renunciation to overcome. Combined with The Clouds and The Stars card, it may identify the presence of a fanatical person or a difficult situation from which the querent will need help to escape. If it appears with The Coffin, it predicts the worsening of the disease and the possibility of the patient's death.

When paired with The Ring, it signals that the relationship is going through a severe crisis; the surrounding cards can provide further details on the circumstances.

According to tradition, the pain or distress will be brief when The Cross card is near the querent's card. However, I haven't personally confirmed this situation. In some of my readings, I've noted enormous suffering, tribulations, pain, and a sacrifice to fulfill or endure certain events and conditions described by the surrounding cards.

In a reading with the Grand Tableau, if The Cross falls in the 1st house, it indicates that the querent's life is challenging and that they're aware of their burden. For a time, life is marked by struggles, serious problems, and concerns. The surrounding cards will provide more information. For instance, if The Fish card is next to The Cross card, it implies financial failures, debts, and unpaid bills. It could denote that the querent is paying for past mistakes, which is why The Cross card frequently appears in a reading for someone in prison.

Traditional keywords:

Misfortune, suffering, sacrifice.

Modern keywords:

Pain, trial, test, a burden, something fateful, distressing, despair, tribulation, hardship, affliction, grief, challenge, difficult path, life lessons, sadness, crying, tears, guilty conscience, guilt, sentence, serving a sentence, remorse, regret, something decisive, a fatal situation, inevitable, burden, difficult task, an act of faith, prayer, belief, vocation, devotion, mission, ideology, dogma, mystification.

2

CHAPTER 3:
POLARITY AND SIGNIFICATOR CARD

In the second phase of the study (Chapter 2), I introduced you to the meanings of the 36 cards. You've learned to understand each card's essence before delving deeper into the study.

Now, you know that The Bouquet card announces joyful events in a reading, representing beauty, invitations, and gratitude. When The Fox card appears, you'll know that something isn't quite right with the person or situation related to the nearby cards. It's a sign that you need to be cautious and pay close attention to what you hear, think, and do.

In Chapter 3, we'll deepen into the study of the 36 cards and learn to recognize their polarity (positive, negative, and neutral), the significator cards (theme cards), and the cards in the different life areas (love, money, work, health, etc.).

THE POLARITIES OF THE 36 CARDS

Each card's polarities reveal its true nature: positive, negative, or neutral.

Positive cards:

The positive cards are favorable cards as they represent stability, balance, clarity, harmony, peace, joy, victories, and success in achieving personal goals. They bring hope and strength in times of adversity. They predict favorable changes, growth, development, and a healthy and peaceful life.

- The cards with a positive value are The Clover, The Bouquet, The Child, The Stars, The Dog, The Heart, The Lilies, The Sun, and The Moon.

Negative cards:

The negative cards indicate serious situations that will negatively disturb the querent's life, such as exhaustion, rupture, a harsh and cruel reality, physical death, or the end of a stable situation. Additionally, these cards may represent delays and blockages in accomplishing a specific event, particularly when they are close to other cards in the reading. The negative cards prevent the favorable development of a situation and identify limitations in actions, which can push the querent away from their goals and answer negatively to a question. All of these events can leave a person emotionally, psychologically, and physically vulnerable.

- The cards with a negative value are The Clouds, The Snake, The Coffin, The Scythe, The Broom and The Whip, The Fox, The Mountain, The Mice, and The Cross.

Neutral cards:

The neutral cards don't provide enough information about the situation or the person under investigation. Instead, they express uncertainty and doubt or depend on another card to express themselves.

- The cards with neutral value are The Rider, The Ship, The House, The Tree, The Owls/Birds, The Bear, The Storks, The Tower, The Garden, The Crossroads, The Ring, The Book, The Letter, The Man, The Woman, The Keys, The Fish, and The Anchor.

Important Note:

My grandmother taught me that the card's polarity can be positive, negative, and neutral. She emphasized that each card is subordinated to others in order to reveal its true message. *"It's similar to a person's personality"*, she said, *"where both light and dark sides exist and are revealed through closely observing the surrounding cards."*

THE SIGNIFICATOR CARD

A significator card holds great importance in the reading. Its position in the spread, along with the surrounding cards, helps us determine which events and opportunities are affecting or will affect the querent's life, especially when working with the Grand Tableau. Therefore, they serve like a compass, keeping the reading balanced and objective.

The significator cards are divided into two groups:

- **Group 1: Significator card for People**

    The function of a significator card is to physically identify the querent, a particular person or an animal in a reading.

- **Group 2: Significator card – Theme**

    The function of a theme significator card is to provide information to a particular subject or area of life: emotion, relationship, work, money, health, etc.

Choosing a significator card

All 36 cards in the deck can represent a person, an emotional state, a situation, an object, or an aspect of human life. But only a few cards stand out in this representation, such as:

The theme card that represents:

- The querent: The Man and The Woman
- Love: The Heart
- Relationship: The Ring
- Family: The Lilies
- Real estate issues or the one's own house: The House
- Work: The Anchor
- Study: The Book
- Finance: The Fish
- Friendship: The Dog
- News: The Letter
- Travels: The Ship
- Law or bureaucratic issues: The Tower
- Religion: The Cross
- Spirituality: The Stars
- Health: The Tree
- Disease: The Coffin

We'll go over some of the significator cards in detail to gain a better understand of their role in the reading.

Group 1:
Significator Cards to identify People

When someone comes to us with a problem affecting them, it's important to identify the people who may be influencing their life at that moment and those who can help them.

Identifying people in the Petit Lenormand deck follows these three points:

- The two querent's cards: The Man and The Woman;
- The 34 cards
- The 12 court cards

The points 2 and 3 represent people the querent knows or are directly involved in the investigated issue.

The Two Querent's Cards:
The Man and The Woman

As you've noticed, the Lenormand deck differs from other card decks, such as Tarot, Italian Sibyl, or ordinary playing cards, in terms of choosing a card to represent the querent in the reading.

Unlike those decks, Lenormand doesn't require knowledge of major arcana, court cards, or astrology. The Petit Lenormand deck already includes two cards whose only function is to represent the querent in the reading. These cards are The Man card and The Woman card.

In Philippe Lenormand's instruction sheet, written in 1846, three sentences provide the first instruction on how to use the two cards that represent the querent and their role in the reading.

The first sentence says:
"The whole pack refers to either of these cards, depending, if the person whose fortune is being told is either a Lady (No. 29) or Gentleman (No. 28).

The second sentence says:
"The greatest attention must be paid to these cards No. 28 and 29. Their position signifies the future (in distribution) happiness or misfortune of the person; all other cards take their meaning from these, and in such a way, that their position, as it is near or more distant from these, rules the destiny."

The third sentence says:
"The whole pack refers to either of these cards, depending, if the person whose fortune is being told is either a Lady (No. 29) or Gentleman (No. 28).

Therefore, the cards "The Man" and "The Woman" play a single role, that of physically representing the querent in the reading. If a male person requests the reading, The Man card represents the querent himself. If it's requested by a female, The Woman card represents the querent herself.

According to Philippe Lenormand, these two cards are the central point in interpretation, particularly when using the Great Tableau method, where the position of the querent's card in the tableau is the starting point for interpretation.

We'll discuss it in more detail in Chapter 7, where we'll examine the Grand Tableau. Let's first concentrate on the recognition of persons in the cards.

The Two Cards Representing the Querents in a Relationship Reading

If the reading is about a relationship, the other querent's card will represent the other person involved.

For example, if a man requests the reading, The Man card will represent him, so The Woman card will stand for an important woman to the querent, such as a bride, girlfriend, wife, mistress, colleague, aunt, sister, mother, or another woman, depending on the question.

On the other hand, if a woman asks for a reading, The Woman card will represent her, while The Man card will represent her husband, fiancé, boyfriend, lover, colleague, father, uncle, brother, cousin, and so on.

Before the reading, it's important to "baptize" the other querent's card with that person's name. For instance, let's say I want to know about my professional relationship with a coworker. I baptize The Woman card with my name, Odete, because it will physically represent me in the reading. In turn, I baptize The Man card with my colleague's name.

The term "baptize" the querent's card and theme card was first introduced by American fortune teller Sylvie Steinbach, author of the English-language book, The Secret of the Lenormand Oracle (2007). This technique is used to physically identify the querent and another person in the reading. Sylvie belongs to the French Lenormand "school".

How to investigate someone of the same sex as the querent?

If your deck has only one card to represent the male querent and one to represent the female querent (as in the Blue Owl Lenormand deck), assign one of the two cards the same gender as the querent.

In other words, if the male querent requests a reading for his brother, uncle, colleague, or partner, he'll be represented by

The Woman card. If a female querent asks for a reading for her friend, sister, colleague, or partner, she'll be represented by The Man card.

For those with experience in computer graphics, it's possible to create their own extra cards. However, when doing so, it's important to observe three points:

- Turn the card so that the two characters "face" each other;
- Change the card suit. For example, The Man card is the Ace of Hearts, but when creating an extra card of the same gender, we will use the Ace of Leaves suit;
- Modify the card number. The Man card is represented by the number 28, so for the extra card that will replace The Woman card, number 29, it's natural to assign the number 29 for the extra card.

Therefore, we'll get our extra cards. See the result below.

MALE QUERENT

Card no. 28: The Querent

Card no. 29: The other person

FEMALE QUERENT

Card no. 28: The other person

Card no. 29: The Querent

Some decks on the market are created by authors or fortune tellers that include two or more extra querent's cards. I recommend some of them:

- Gilded Revirie Lenormand by Ciro Marchetti
- Lilac Dondorf Lenormand (I have it and work with it in the Grand Tableau)
- The Game of Hope

When the other card isn't "baptized"

When the other card in reading doesn't represent a specific person, it's necessary to pay attention to the cards touching it, as they will provide valuable information about that person.

In fact, the surrounding cards offer insights into several aspects of the person's life, such as marital status (married, divorced, or widowed), age (young or adult), and the nature of their relationship with the querent (father, mother, stepparents, godfather, godmother, siblings, cousins, uncles, grandparents, boss, mistress, or colleague.

These cards also give clues about their physical appearance (tall, short, thin, fat, blond, etc.) and their personality (honest, disloyal, liar, intelligent, rude, polite, firm, etc.) of this Man or Woman.

THE 34 CARDS:
THE OTHER PEOPLE'S CARDS

As previously studied, the Lenormand deck consists of 36 cards, but two of them only have the function of representing the querent in a reading.

Let's now turn our attention to the remaining 34 cards (symbols), some of which can also represent specific people such as family members, such as the father, mother, son, daughter, father-in-law, son-in-law, daughter-in-law, grandparents, cousins, etc., friend, colleagues, enemies, rivals, adversaries, or professionals like lawyers, judge, and doctors. In addition, they can provide details about a person's profile.

The cards surrounding the card representing the querent give information about their current state and can also describe them regarding their marital status, physical appearance, personality, beliefs, health, profession, and finances.

In later chapters, I'll present a method and an illustrative example to help you identify and describe people during a reading.

People in the 34 Cards

Card no. 1: The Rider

The Rider card represents a son, daughter, lover, acquaintance, guest, traveler, stranger, messenger, foreign person, new employee, mailman (if accompanied by The Letter card), taxi driver, conductor, pilot, train driver, representative, waiter, mediator, customer, supplier, jockey, coachman, military, bullfighter, cowboy, Texan, Indian, athlete, professional athlete, scout, guide, or someone about to enter the querent's life.

Sometimes it can also refer to someone who is working or living abroad.

For example, I live near the Italian border and use this card to represent the emigrants who come daily to Switzerland. But it can also indicate someone who travels long distances like commuting from another city (although not as far as depicted by The Ship card), for business or travel (daily back and forth) purposes.

Card no. 2: The Clover

The Clover card indicates someone who appears unexpectedly to help the querent. This person may not be someone with whom the querent interacts frequently, and they may be even a stranger, yet they bring ideas or solutions to a complex problem. The Clover may also be related to a gambler.

Card no. 3: The Ship

The Ship card represents someone from overseas. I've noticed that this card often describes someone with dark skin or brunette. As a single card, The Ship can only identify a foreign person or someone with foreign origins. If The Ship is next to The Tree card, it identifies someone with foreign ancestry, nothing more.

The surrounding cards can provide more details about the person's origins.

For example, with:
- The Sun: from a tropical, exotic, or southern country;
- The Stars: Nordic origin;
- The Lilies: from a cold country;
- The Fish: Mediterranean origin or being connected with the ocean, sea, and beach. I've already tried this combination for tourists, too.

It's also possible to identify the person's skin color, with:
- The Coffin: a dark-skinned person.
- The Sun: a brunette person.
- The Lilies: a white person with a very light complexion. And so on.

In addition, The Ship card represents foreigners, ethnics, emigrants, sailors, traders, and those who live far away.

Card no. 4: The House

The House card stands for someone connected to the family, such as relatives, neighbors, or a close friend (especially if The Dog card is nearby). It can also symbolize a housewife, caretakers, doorkeepers, homeowners (with The Bear card), and real estate agents.

Card no. 5: The Tree

The Tree card indicates people associated with health and well-being, including patients, environmentalists, and healthcare personnel like doctors, nurses, and assistants. It can also symbolize a connection with one's ancestors.

Card no. 6: The Clouds

The Clouds car denote a drug addict, workers, and spirits.

Card no. 7: The Snake

The Snake card represents a hidden enemy, adversary, two-faced person, or a lover like a boyfriend, girlfriend, wife, or husband (when not represented by a court card in the reading). It can also stand for professionals such as psychologists and healers.

The Snake

- + The Coffin: an occultist or someone adept at magic;
- + The Owls: a witch, sorceress, or healer;
- + The Owls + The Stars: a clairvoyant;
- + The Owls + The Coffin: a psychic;
- + The Stars: an astrologer;
- + The Book: a lover, a hidden enemy.

Card no. 8: The Coffin

The Coffin card stands for someone who is sick or a disease-prone. It can also refer to a victim of a natural disaster, including accidents, earthquakes, or landslides. In addition, it may denote a deceased or missing person, a corpse. A widow, single, or orphan. It's also associated with archaeologists or funeral staff.

Card no. 9: The Bouquet

The Bouquet card refers to a friend, sister, daughter, or niece. It may also represent beauticians, hairdressers, stylists, models, artists, and someone who cares for the querent with love and affection, an admirer, or someone interested in the querent.

Card no. 10: The Scythe

The Scythe card indicates a divorced person, critics, surgeons, dentists, tattoo artists, or farmers. It also indicates workers involved in harvesting crops like grapes, fruits, vegetables, and olives. It can also denote hairdressers, barbers, dressmakers, tailors, and embroiderers. It can describe victims of accidents or war, as well as aggressors, killers, murderers, mercenaries, or soldiers.

- The Scythe + The Ring: a divorced person.

Card no. 11: The Broom and The Whip

The Broom and The Whip card denotes aggressors, defendants, dictators, militaries, law enforcement officers, lawyers, referees, instructors, coaches, activists, and cleaning personnel.

Card no. 12: The Owls

Sometimes The Owls card can represent a couple, twins, or a small group of people. It can stand for witches, fortune-tellers, and occultists. Telephone operators, receptionists, mediators, announcers, television or product presenters, and dealers. Informants, lecturers, or auctioneers.

The Owls

+ The Children: two sons/daughters/children, or twins;
+ The Lilies: an elderly couple.

Card no. 13: The Child

The Child card represents a baby, child, young, or adolescent (with The Rider card), children, nephews, grandchildren, or the family's youngest member. It also denotes beginners, students, kindergarten and elementary school teachers, or babysitters.

The Child

+ The Tree: a biological child;
+ The Tower: the only child;
+ The Ring: an adopted child;
+ The Book: a student, apprentice, an illegitimate child, an unknown child.

Card no. 14: The Fox

The Fox card indicates someone who may be a suspect, deceiver, false prophet, charlatan, thief, forger, spy, stalker, criminal, mobster, murderer, serial killer, and hunter. The Fox is "the devil's advocate." It also denotes gamblers, actors, actresses, salesclerks, politicians, engineers, detectives, undercover police officers, and experts.

When surrounded by favorable cards, The Fox can represent someone who will help the querent to solve an important issue, but it's important not to mistake them for a friend, as that person may only act in their own interests.

Card no. 15: The Bear

The Bear card represents the parents, masters, business people, bosses, directors, CEOs, managers, and owners.

It can indicate someone who has a position of power and enforces the law, like police officers, magistrates, or military personnel (if combined with The Broom and The Whip or The Tower), a patriot. The Bear card also denotes a lover or someone engaged in a serious relationship, such as a fiancé, fiancée, a spouse, as well as an older person. It can also represent professionals in the field of food, such as nutritionists or cooks.

The Bear
- + The House: a landlord;
- + The Tree: a mother;
- + The Broom and The Whip: a referee, police officer, or lawyer;
- + The Tower: the father, lawyer, governor, head of state, and elderly;
- + The Tower + The Cross: The Pope, a priest;
- + The Mountain: a prosecuting attorney;
- + The Heart: a lover;
- + The Book: a teacher, instructor, school principal, accountant, and jurist;
- + The Lilies: the grandmother, the head of the family, tutor, mentor, and judge.

Card no. 16: The Stars

The Star card denotes clairvoyants, psychics, prophets, astrologers, astronomers, and scientists. It's also associated with artists and celebrities from various fields, such as television, movies, theater, shows, fashion, music, and art.

Card no. 17: The Storks

The Storks card stands for those associated with migration, nomadic lifestyles, midwives, obstetricians, providers, and transporters.

Card no. 18: The Dog

The Dog card symbolizes a close friend, a fellow, a partner, siblings, an adopted child, a tenant, a colleague, and healthcare professionals like nurses, doctors, and assistants. It refers to someone you have a close relationship with, a supporter, patrons, or helpers.

It denotes guards or police personnel, and when paired with The Mountain, it indicates a border guard or a jail officer. The Dog also represents a pet.

The Dog

+ The House: a family friend, a neighbor, a tenant;
+ The Tree: a longtime friend, a nursing assistant, a nurse;
+ The Bear: an older friend, lawyer, protector;
+ The Stork: the guardian angel;
+ The Letter: a pen pal or online friendship.

Card no. 19: The Tower

The Tower card indicate people in positions of authority or power, such as politicians (council members, mayors, and deputies), republic presidents, governors, and senators. It also refers to leadership figures like administrators, CEOs, and directors, or those who work in the legal system, such as police officers, judges, and lawyers.

When paired with The Bear card, it can represent federal public employees, inspectors, businesspeople, and high-ranking military officers (including a general, major, or captain).

Combined with The Book card, it suggests a university professor, intellectual, thinker, or psychologist, while pairing with The Tree card indicates a medical specialist.

Card no. 20: The Garden

The Garden car represents the public, citizens, population, customers, voters, group, team, fans, staff, event organizers, gangs, gardeners, acquaintances, and actors.

Card no. 21: The Mountain

The Mountain card denotes prosecutors, attorneys, or adversaries. It may also refer to an employee impeding the development of a task and also managers or supervisors. This card can be associated with disabilities or handicaps. Prisoners, enslaved people, or hermits can be represented by The Mountain, including geologists, mountain climbers, skiers, border guards, or unemployed people.

Card no. 22: The Crossroads

The Crossroads card indicates pedestrians, explorers, street vendors, homeless, gypsies, or separated people.

Card no. 23: The Mice

The Mice card stands for beggars, pickpockets, kidnappers, vandals, infiltrators, hackers, drug dealers, smugglers, clandestine, as well as missing people or fugitives. It also describes someone who lives at the expense of others, such as a pimp. The Mice may describe an idle or unproductive person.

Card no. 24: The Heart

The Heart card depicts a significant person in the querent's life, often someone they deeply love or admire. This person is familiar with the querent and has good intentions.

The Heart
- + The Garden: fans;
- + The Book: a lover.

Card no. 25: The Ring

The Ring card represents everyone you have a connection with or those you've developed a bond with through cooperation or union, such as your spouse, fiancé/fiancée, boyfriend/girlfriend, partner, employee, or colleague. It indicates debtors, collectors, landlords, etc., and members of an organization, cooperatives, clubs, teams, clans, and so on. The Ring also denotes in-laws, such as brothers/sisters-in-law, father/mother-in-law, godparents, or adopted children.

Card no. 26: The Book

The Book card indicates writers, editors, booksellers, librarians, advisors, counselors, teachers, educators, instructors, students, researchers, explorers, historians, and archivists.

The Book card includes classmates, schoolmates, but also strangers, and people you don't know well or want to keep anonymous and a secret admire. If it falls after the querent's card, it suggests an unknown person.

Card no. 27: The Letter

The Letter card denotes social media contacts, intermediaries, informants, mail carriers, secretaries, or correspondents.

Card no. 30: The Lilies

The Lilies card depicts an older person in the querent's life, such as grandparents, great-grandparents, uncles, in-laws, father or mother. It represents a figure of authority and guidance who offers support and protection and looks out for their best interest, such as a social worker, counselor, mediator, sponsor, godfather, mentor, or doctor. It can also refer to legal professionals like prosecutors, lawyers, judges, or magistrates. This card can stand for a family member or a distant relative, if it comes with The Ship card.

- The Lilies + The Tree: a specialist doctor or nursing staff, a mentor, guru, or holistic therapist.

Card no. 31: The Sun

Mostly, The Sun card refers to a leader and someone particularly prominent or well-known. It also denotes Reiki practitioners or electricians.

Card no. 32: The Moon

The Moon card stands for a poet, celebrity, or extremely well-known and popular person. It can also denote a night guard.

Card no. 33: The Keys

The Key card represents a significant person in the querent's life. It also indicates an insurer, jailer, and locksmith, as well as interpreters, computer programmers, and technicians.

Card no. 34: The Fish

The Fish card depicts a mature and influential person who has achieved wealth step by step with commitment and intelligence. It can represent someone who frequently travels for business. It stands for bank clerks, shareholders, businesspeople, traders, internet sellers, fishermen, or swimmers.

Card no. 35: The Anchor

If The Anchor Card surrounds the querent's card, it represents a colleague, boss, superior, or partner.

Card no. 36: The Cross

The Cross card indicates a priest, religious, or missionary. It can depict a defendant or convicted person, as well as someone who is sick or in need of care and support in various aspects of life.

The Theme Card according to Personality, Character, and Behavior

Card no. 1: The Rider

The Rider indicates a determined and courageous person who is active, energetic, independent, clever, and full of life. This person has plenty of ideas and initiatives, is always up to new adventures, and loves traveling. They're open-minded and adapt well to new situations. The Rider is also law-abiding, whether it's following social rules or their principles. They're driven by impulse and intuition, acting in their interest and seizing opportunities, even if it means taking risks to ensure survival. It's someone focused on the future with clear goals they confidently pursue. They handle professional and personal interactions with diplomacy, always being direct and honest without any pretexts or hidden motives.

Card no. 2: The Clover

The person represented by this card is highly desirable and admired. They have a cheerful, optimistic personality and a positive outlook on life. This person has unique qualities, such as putting themselves at the service of others, opening doors, motivating others to move forward with project implementation. This person inspires confidence and is always available without any ulterior motives. He or she is fortunate and generous but shy and modest. It's someone who knows how to size life's small opportunities and use them to accomplish great things. When faced with a problem, they always keep an optimistic attitude and aren't afraid to take risks.

Card no. 3: The Ship

The Ship card represents an open-minded and curious person, always seeking new challenges and goals. It's someone who loves traveling, getting in touch with different cultures and places that contribute to their personal and spiritual growth.

They have an adventurous spirit and enjoy exploring places that give them moments of freedom and add something new to their life experience. These "journeys" of internal or external explorations may lead the querent to change how they see, feel, and live their lifestyle in terms of culture, food, religion, music, and even fashion. At the present phase of their life, the querent focuses on the future. They're "on the high seas" and experience storms and calm tides in the "transition" between dream, project, construction, and achievement. They'll live storms and calm tides. Sometimes they may become emotional and nostalgic.

Card no. 4: The House

The House card represents a pleasant, friendly, welcoming, reliable, helpful, and responsible person. They're a homebody with sedentary personality who loves the comfort they find at home. This person enjoys spending time with loved ones or in an environment where they can freely express themselves and feel "at home."

They're deeply connected to their roots, homeland, and family and feel compelled to preserve their cultural and religious traditions. These values are worth fighting for in order to keep them alive in their family and life.

No matter what situation this person is experiencing at the time of reading, they need to feel comfortable and secure in order to keep good mental and emotional balance.

Card no. 5: The Tree

The Tree card usually depicts a strong and resilient person facing adversity. They're usually calm, patient, and welcoming, but tend to be lazy and even boring.

Card no. 6: The Clouds

This card stands for a person with an easily irritable personality and who is prone to constant changes in mood. Worries, unfounded and trivial fears, or the current situation frequently influence their mental state and emotions. They're unstable, unreliable, and change their mind quickly. They can't handle criticism and has a distorted view of life.

This person may walk around with their head in the clouds and get easily distracted when accomplishing important responsibilities, making them untrustworthy.

The presence of an obscure, ambiguous, impenetrable side is confirmed if the dark part of The Clouds card touches the card representing the querent.

They may become obsessed with beliefs or ideas to the point of fanaticism. The surrounding cards will provide additional details about the situation.

Card no. 7: The Snake

The Snake identifies a person who is magnetic, captivating, and seductive, as well as attractive, diplomatic, clever, intelligent, calculating, false, liar, hostile, hypocritical, treacherous, poisonous, and dangerous. They're obstinate, vindictive, self-confident, and may even wish the querent's misfortune. When driven by envy and jealousy, they act cold-blood, damaging their rival's reputation with lies and slander. According to the German school, the Queen of Acorns represents a bitter and sour woman who can complicate or is already complicating the querent's life. But, on the other hand, she is wise, experienced, and smart, and nothing will ever surprise her.

Card no. 8: The Coffin

The Coffin depicts someone who is sad, exhausted, depressed, and melancholic. They may also feel unhappy, dissatisfied, empty, and lonely. This person tends to close off with their torments and anxieties. They feel stuck with no life prospects and have a gloomy view of the situation and a pessimistic attitude toward life. Sometimes The Coffin denotes a lonely person who is going through a period of deep pain. The surrounding cards will reveal their motivations. They're seen as mysterious and impenetrable.

Card no. 9: The Bouquet

The Bouquet card denotes someone who is elegant, kind, charming, pleasant, cordial, polite, optimistic, as well as sensitive, fascinating, sensual, beautiful, friendly, and happy. This person has a keen sense of timing and diplomacy when necessary. No matter what challenges they may be currently dealing with; they handle them politely and tactfully. They're also a delightful company.

Card no. 10: The Scythe

This is how others perceive the person represented by The Scythe card: unpredictable, aggressive, violent, and sharp-tongued. But this is how they really are: determined, radical, and self-confident, who act at the right time and don't back down from their decisions.

Card no. 11: The Broom and The Whip

The person depicted by this card is bossy, authoritarian, arrogant but also conflicting, contradictory, aggressive, and anxious. These traits make it impossible to live with them.

Card no. 12: The Owls

This interpretation is very personal. But, traditionally, the meaning of card No. 12 in the Petit Lenormand is The Birds.

- <u>The Owls</u>: This card represents someone who is wise, calm, reserved, quiet, and highly knowledgeable and who pays close attention to details.

- <u>The Birds</u>: This card denotes someone who is restless, hurried, anxious, and hassles. They may also be shy and fearful with great physical energy, remarkable ferocity, and courage when defending their territory and own food. They tend to be very talkative and might overlook important details.

Card no. 13: The Child

The Child card describes someone who is naïve, childish, inexperienced, immature, vulnerable, spontaneous, playful, smiling, excited, and curious. They're unpredictable, absent-minded, and don't take life's problems seriously or responsibly.

Card no. 14: The Fox

Focus and determination are the mottoes of the person portrayed by The Fox card. They're adaptable and practical, with a sharp mind that enables them to achieve their goals. This person knows how to masterfully avoid obstacles by employing all their intelligence, cunning, creativity, skill, and ingenuity to escape life's traps or complications.

They're methodical, strategic, patient, and opportunistic, waiting for the right time to seduce their victim before revealing their true intention, attacking and "killing" without mercy or remorse.

This person is a master of ingenuity, able to use whatever means are at their disposal or even create them to achieve their goals.

Survival is the driving force that makes them fierce hunter and predator, yet agile and who uses all their charm to get what they want. They're strong, courageous, determined as well as intelligent, analytical, and resistant. It's someone who is tough and trusts in their intuition, which they use whenever coping with challenging situations.

They don't follow the crowd or others' pace, they're highly individualistic and sets them apart from others. They act independently and aren't influenced by anyone, keeping complete control over themselves.

If The Fox card is surrounded by or touches unfavorable cards, such as The Mice or The Snake, it suggests that this person is using illegal methods to achieve their goals. As skilled manipulators, they exploit the other's weaknesses to their advantage. These people talk about everything but are shallow on many subjects because they just know enough to benefit themselves, using their charm to deceive and get what they want.

The Fox is incapable of being loyal, dislikes being told what to do, and often prioritizes appearances. They prefer to remain unnoticed, quickly escape from uncomfortable situations, and watch from a safe distance, waiting for the right moment to strike again.

Card no. 15: The Bear

The Bear stands for someone with a strong, courageous, and protective personality. They're often viewed as mature, with paternal or maternal traits. However, sometimes they can be perceived as rude, cold, possessive, and jealous. This person moves slowly but decisively. The Bear may depict a conservative person who defends the law and country.

Card no. 16: The Stars

The Stars card represents someone who is calm, positive, intelligent, and clear in their purposes. They are spiritual and has artistical talents. An esoteric.

Card no. 17: The Storks

The Stork card depicts a person with a kind, pleasant, amiable, loving, affectionate, and faithful nature. They also have confident, responsible, and upright behavior. Being active and flexible, they eagerly welcome changes and are adaptable to life's circumstances. This person has a nomadic spirit and dislike doing the same thing every day. This card may indicate that this person has to travel frequently. They're humble and shy, don't seek fame, and are pure in mind and body.

Even considering all the qualities mentioned above, it's essential to keep in mind that The Stork is associated with change. For this reason, it's recommended to closely look at the surrounding cards to understand better what kind of change is coming. For example, if the querent is experiencing an emotional and psychological crisis or going through an insecure and sad phase, this card announces that things will get better. Otherwise, if they're in an emotional and psychological state of joy, optimism, confidence, and generosity, this card could announce an unfavorable change.

Card no. 18: The Dog

The Dog card is associated with an individual who is loyal and balanced and values trustworthiness in their relationships with friends and lovers. This person is honest and enthusiastic, and it's impossible to resist their charm. Reliable and amiable, you can count on them unconditionally. The Dog depicts someone who is direct and firm in their convictions and trusts their intuition when choosing friendship. They're popular and loved by their social circle and friends and have a sincere, approachable, and adaptable character. However, they may tend to seek approval from others. The Dog is easygoing and laid-back.

Card no. 19: The Tower

The Tower card represents a traditionalist and conservative person who doesn't like change and prefers to keep things exactly as they are. This person is often seen as stuck and unable to forget the past. The Tower is often portrayed as an older person as it denotes discipline, correction, and a mature attitude. While it can indicate traits such as tenacity, resilience, strength, and determination, it can also mean rigidity, prepotency, coldness, pride, arrogance, insensitivity, selfishness, and authority. This card represents someone who values stability and is known for their regular habits.

Card no. 20: The Garden

The Garden card indicates someone who enjoys making a good impression of themselves and needs to be recognized and noticed by others, and seeks to be the center of attention. This person seeks appreciation and praise from others and loves sharing their interests with those around them.

Card no. 21: The Mountain

The person depicted by The Mountain card is cold, rigid, and relentless, but with a strong sense of responsibility and takes their duties seriously. They're strict, controlling, and can be arrogant and unfriendly. They're impulsive, love a challenge and take a risk, have a strong character, and doesn't care for other people's opinion. This person doesn't follow orders but instead imposes their own and expects to be obeyed. They have the patience and courage to take on long-term projects. It's someone who has control of their emotions and hates wasting time. This tough, precise, prudent, and calculating behavior requires balance in everything they do in order to avoid future problems. Although they can be intimidating, they're also captivating. They enjoy solitude, mountains, and quiet places.

Card no. 22: Crossroads

The querent represented by The Crossroads card is confused and disoriented, without clear points of reference. This person is evasive and still doesn't know what they want, and tends to overthink and feels restless, as they have a lot on their mind. This card indicates that the querent struggles to focus or make objective decisions, especially regarding important choices and projects.

Card no. 23: The Mice

The Mice card represents someone who feels extremely stressed and worried about their current life situation (the surrounding cards will provide more information about the problem).

This person is unable to find a way out of their suffering and may feel angry or guilty. As a result, they avoid difficult situations or responsibilities and try to find the easiest way to solve problems. They can be rude, complicated, fearful, shy, ignorant, and have low self-esteem.

Card no. 24: The Heart

The Heart card represents someone who is honest, loyal, generous, affectionate, loving, sweet, pleasant, happy, and cheerful. This person is highly emotional, sensitive, and trusts their feelings. They're warm, welcoming, attentive, understanding, and humane.

Their personality is harmonious, graceful, and captivating. This person spreads love wherever they go. They're motivated by love, passion, and desire.

The Heart card also denotes someone who loves having harmonious relationships, which makes them really happy. They value and love themselves, but with negative cards nearby, they may express intense feelings, such as bitterness, jealousy, anger, aggressiveness, obsession, lust, and eroticism.

Card no. 25: The Ring

The person represented by The Ring card is upright, responsible, and committed to keeping their promises. This card also depicts someone who obeys imposed rules and respects authority, but can be inflexible, moralistic, and strict.

Card no. 26: The Book

The Book stands for an intellectual, educated, intelligent person with a closed and enigmatic personality. This individual either has a lot of secrets or reveals very little. They're low-key and reserved, yet they're analytical and have a keen sense of observation.

This is someone with the characteristics of a teacher, being well-informed and methodical in their explanations and conversations. In addition, they're curious and always eager to learn new things.

Card no. 27: The Letter

The person portrayed by The Letter card is communicative, well-informed, and sociable, but can sometimes be superficial, fickle, and changeable. It's someone who usually has many social connections, both online and offline, and who feels more comfortable expressing themselves in writing rather than verbally.

Card no. 30: The Lilies

The Lilies card indicates someone who has left vices or ambition and has chosen to live a quiet life, in peace and harmony with their family, respecting the essential values. This person is diplomatic, peaceful, and has a strong sense of humanity. They're patient, harmonious, mature, and well-prepared, possessing a noble and kind soul. It's a well-intentioned person.

Card no. 31: The Sun

The Sun depicts someone who loves and respects life. They're open-minded, optimistic, balanced, and accomplished. This person has a gift for brightening everything and everyone around them. Cheerful, smiling, charismatic, sincere, loyal, and upright, this person manages to achieve their goals thanks to their self-confidence and belief in their abilities. While they enjoy shining, being the center of attention, and basking in admiration, they can become selfish, authoritarian, arrogant, and overbearing if they don't receive the attention they crave.

However, this person has the courage and willpower to face any adversity life throws their way. Hardly anyone can diminish their self-assurance. Their ambition to achieve fame and success is evident, but they also have a big heart, and their generosity can make a lasting impact on those they meet.

Card no. 32: The Moon

The Moon card describes someone who's a night owl, romantic, and a daydreamer. They're intuitive, sensitive, and moody, but they're also attractive and endearing.

Card no. 33: The Key

The Key card depicts someone who is in control of their own life. They're open-minded, agile, self-confident, independent, and reliable.

Card no. 34: The Fish

The querent values money, is ambitious, and very attached to material possessions and luxury, but also patient and hardworking. This person only makes contacts that will benefit them. They're an entrepreneur who enjoys being successful and love traveling. Monotony and the company of those who don't have big goals or success don't appeal to them; that's why some people might see them as greedy. The Fish card represents a successful business person who has acquired vast financial wealth.

Card no. 35: The Anchor

The Anchor card stands for someone with both feet on the ground, conservative and faithful, but who may also be overly dependent on their routine and others.

Card no. 36: The Cross

The Cross card represents a religious and faithful person with strong beliefs that will help them to endure the current hardship or the upcoming difficult times. Serious and disciplined, this person always supports and helps those in need. However, this card can also imply that this person feels exhausted, depressed, sorrowful, and in pain.

The Court Card Figures

The deck has 12 court cards, including Kings, Queens, and Jacks. These cards represent actual people who will play a decisive role in the querent's life or the situation being explored. Not all fortune tellers agree on whether the court cards always represent people in a reading; this isn't a universal rule. Personally, I take them into account when they're near the querent's card or a theme card.

The Kings

The Kings represent mature, capable, experienced, and responsible men, with their specific attributes varying depending on the suit they belong to. They often hold positions of leadership and authority in the querent's life.

Therefore, consider:

- King of Hearts: A patriarch, father, husband godfather, next of kin (such as an uncle or grandfather), friend, leader, ambassador, religious figure, clergy, counselor, artist, therapist.
- King of Leaves: A powerful man, superior, boss, relative (such as uncle or grandfather), or an old friend;
- King of Bells: A foreigner, partner, colleague, entrepreneur, CEO, politician, bank clerk, financier, sponsor, tradesman, businessman, distant relatives, or in-laws (brother-in-law, father-in-law, etc.).
- King of Acorns: The stepfather, ex-husband/partner, a man from the past, or a military or police officer, legal querent (as a lawyer), or wizard.

The Queens

The Queens represent mature, competent, experienced, and responsible women, with their specific attributes varying depending on the suit they represent. They often hold positions of leadership and authority in the querent's life.

Therefore, consider:
- Queen of Hearts: A maternal figure, such as a mother, wife, godmother, or a close relative (like an aunt). They also represent female friends, psychics (fortune tellers), and healthcare professionals like obstetricians, gynecologists, pediatricians, and therapists.
- Queen of Leaves: A female relative (aunt, grandmother), female friend, colleague, fiancée, or girlfriend.
- Queen of Bells: A foreign woman, entrepreneur, partner, female colleague, businesswoman, and distant relative or in-laws (sister-in-law, mother-in-law).
- Queen of Acorns: A widow, divorced woman, ex-wife/partner, rival, lover, mother-in-law, stepmother, lawyer, delegate, military or police officer, legal consultant, witch, or sorceress.

The Jacks

The Jacks stand for young men and women who lack life experience. They tend to be naïve, impulsive, sensitive, and immature, but they're also adventurous and full of energy, with their specific attributes varying depending on the suit they belong to.

Therefore, consider:
- Jack of Hearts: a lover, suitor, godson, friend, or young artist;
- Jack of Leaves: a son, daughter, adolescent, or young blood relative, such as a sibling, grandchild, niece, nephew, or cousin;
- Jack of Bells: a young relative (but not necessarily by blood), collaborator, apprentice, worker, employee, or young colleague;
- Jack of Acorns: a young rival, servant, employee, or assistant in fields like justice, law enforcement, or military.

The Suit of Hearts

The Suit of Hearts is associated with emotions, sensitivity, cheerfulness, happiness, and a sunny disposition. People represented by this suit are usually caring, kind, friendly, and protective. They follow their instincts, and their ethical code is based on sincerity, loyalty, and honesty. They devote their lives to love and fulfilling their deepest desires. They can give valuable advice and help the querent to solve their problems selflessly. They're also great listeners.

The Suit of Leaves

The Suit of Leaves denotes a person who is mature, experienced, responsible, kind and has strong ethical and moral values.

The Suit of Bells

The Suit of Bells represents people who are intelligent, practical, focused, practical, and achievers. They focus on creating their own sense of security and work hard to reach their goals. They are independent, and when the time comes to leave, they cut ties and move forward. This determined nature can lead people to believe they're selfish, materialistic, insensitive, or cold.

The Suit of Acorns

The Suit of Acorns describes people who are often unpleasant and disturbing, and who only think of themselves. They tend to be ambiguous, confused, restless, and vengeful. They usually are arrogant and try to impose their own will on others. They're impulsive, unreasonable, and harsh critics who enjoy good gossip. They cause disturbances and harm the lives of others. They can be frightening and scary as enemies. However, they can sometimes act as purifying agents.

When considering to include the court cards in a reading, keep the following considerations in mind:

1. The court card's symbol shouldn't be considered during the reading.

2. The court cards represent a person who has an influence on the querent's life. They identify people involved in a particular situation relating to the life area defined by the theme card;

3. The person's identity.

Therefore, if you consider the Queen of Hearts as representing a person, she would be a woman who is very close to the querent, such as a mother, wife, or relative. In this case, we disregard the other meanings associated with The Stork card's symbol, such as mobility, changes, pregnancy, or birth.

The card next to the court card figure indicates the area of the querent's life it belongs to and provides detailed information about that specific person.

For example:
- The Queen of Acorns, combined with The House card, identifies a mature woman who is part of the querent's personal relationships, like a relative or neighbor. However, this woman may act dishonestly or maliciously towards the querent;
- The King of Leaves, when paired with The Tower card, represents a man involved in legal matters, such as a lawyer or police officer. It can also indicate bureaucracy, institutions, or even a boss figure;
- The King of Leaves, in combination with The Tree, symbolizes a doctor or a specialist who will intervene in a health problem.

Important Note:
When a court card touches the querent's card, it indicates that the person represented by the court card is influencing the querent's life, either for better or worse, depending on the surrounding card suits. It could also suggest that the person plays an important role in the querent's life. Observe if the court card is placed in the past, present, or future line.

Group 2: Significator Cards or Theme Cards

Significator Cards for Love, Feelings, Emotions, and Relationships

In a reading, it's important to understand the difference between The Heart card and The Ring card.

- The Heart card represents feelings of love and passion towards something or someone, whether positive or negative.
- The Ring card is the theme card that represents an official relationship or a commitment that doesn't necessarily involve any emotional attachment. Therefore, this card symbolizes all types of relationships, and the surrounding cards will reveal more about the nature of the relationship.

Card no. 24
The Heart

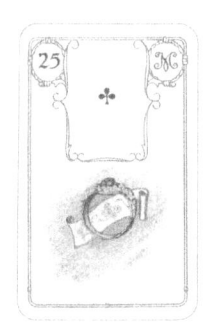

Card no. 25
The Ring

When The Heart and The Ring cards appear together, they usually indicate a romantic relationship and the nearby cards will provide additional information about the characteristics of the relationship.

The Card Meanings for Love and Relationship

Card no. 1: The Rider

For those who are eager to experience a passionate and intense relationship, The Rider card indicates the approach of a person with whom they will live an unforgettable passion. This card always represents serious and deep feelings, which can often be misinterpreted due to frequent absences due to work, studies, or family commitments.

- The Rider + The Heart: It predicts the fast arrival of a new love. This person can arrive through frequent travels, mutual hangout places, and online contacts like email, chat, Skype, WhatsApp, and others.

Card no. 2: The Clover

The Clover card indicates a relationship that comes up instantly as a new opportunity but with some risk. A new love arrives suddenly, bringing renewed hope to their romantic life. However, this newfound happiness may be short-lived, so The Clover advises seizing the opportunity. It also means that after a hard time for the couple, there may be an attempt at reconciliation.

Card no. 3: The Ship

In a love reading, The Ship card announces a change that is taking place within a relationship. It's necessary to pay attention to the position of this card concerning any relationship reading since it may suggest that the couple or the people involved are physically or emotionally distant. The card in front of The Ship will provide more information.

The Ship

+ The Rider: the arrival of someone from a distant place; most likely through the internet, indicating a potential long-distance relationship; the desire to experience a great love;

- + The Ring: an enduring relationship or marriage with a foreigner; a marriage or a stable relationship with someone who lives far from the querent; slowly becoming involved in the relationship; a desire for a romantic relationship or marriage;
- + The Fish: the querent is looking for a partner with a good financial situation for a long-lasting relationship; casual relationships.

Card no. 4: The House

The House card represents long-term relationships. I've noted that in a romantic context, this card can suggest that the querent will meet someone in their neighborhood or the current city, particularly when combined with The Heart and The Rider cards.

Card no. 5: The Tree

The Tree card is often associated with a long-term relationship, which can be either romantic or friendship, depending on the surrounding cards. It can also indicate a secret love affair.

Card no. 6: The Clouds

The Clouds card indicates a crisis in a relationship or with a close person. Sometimes, it may suggest that the querent is in a relationship with lots of misunderstandings, ambiguities, and uncertainties, where the lack of clarity leads to heated arguments or bad moods.

The Clouds
- + The Heart: emotional abuse;
- + The Ring: the couple is experiencing a lack of clarity and understanding in their relationship; causing annoyances, troubles, and disappointment .

Card no. 7: The Snake

When The Snake card appears in a reading for a couple, it represents either a rival or a lover. Additionally, it indicates that the relationship is going through a crisis caused by lying and betrayal, which can be attributed to various factors, not only to an extramarital affair such as vices (smoking secretly), secrets, or family issues. In my experience, The Snake is often associated with complicated and destructive relationships and suggests that the partner doesn't reciprocate the other's feelings. So, check out the card that The Snake touches, as it indicates the source of the betrayal.

The Snake
- + The House: a treacherous relative;
- + The Dog: an unfaithful and deceitful friend;
- + The Heart: a lover; a love affair;
- + The Ring: a rival or a competitor; it can also represent a relationship based on sex;
- + The Book: a secret lover. It may represent someone who is attracted to people of the same gender.

Card no. 8: The Coffin

The Coffin card predicts the end of a relationship, and the surrounding cards will reveal the reason for this end. It suggests that the querent is in a dead-end relationship, marked by pain and the lack of stimulation or excitement. They may feel stuck with someone they're not happy with or is still holding onto an old relationship that is preventing them from moving on and experiencing new feelings and relationships.

Card no. 9: The Bouquet

The Bouquet card indicates, in general, special moments in love and relationships. The querent will feel loved, respected, and admired. The Bouquet denotes the beginning of a relationship or a particular interest in someone who makes them happy. If the marriage is going through a crisis or even a breakup, this card predicts an attempt at reconciliation or that the partner cares about the loved person. The Bouquet also means dating or flirting and often appears in a reading when someone is interested in the querent.

- The Bouquet + The Heart + The Ring: engagement or wedding celebration.

Card no. 10: The Scythe

The Scythe card is a warning that the relationship is in danger and can end abruptly.

The Scythe

- + The Heart: Someone will hurt the feelings of a loved one or break their heart.
- + The Ring: Violence in marriage or union; a breakup or separation.

Card no. 11: The Broom and The Whip

The Broom and The Whip augurs conflicts between couples or close people.

Card no. 12: The Owls

The Owls card represents tender feelings, the need for protection, and love. In a relationship reading, it might stand for a summer love. The Owls card can also indicate a flirting or fickle feelings and short-lived worries or agitation. It also includes several online lovers and interests, such as those found on Facebook. When paired with The Ring, it may denote a form of sexual activity where couples switch partners.

Card no. 13: The Child

The Child card symbolizes new and fresh feelings; love for children, the start of a relationship, and also pure, honest, and sincere love like a precious jewel.

The Child

- + The Heart: a new love, pure feelings;
- + The Ring: a fresh start in a relationship, a new relationship.

Card no. 14: The Fox

The Fox card is a sign of betrayal, infidelity, lies, and deception in a relationship. It represents superficial feelings and relationships as well.

- The Fox + The Heart: someone who hides their feelings well.

Card no. 15: The Bear

The Bear card represents love and protection, which can sometimes be exaggerated, resulting in possessiveness and obsessive jealousy. It also indicates a trustworthy partner, a romantic relationship, or a crush on someone older.

Card no. 16: The Stars

The Star card represents intense or fortunate love, indicating someone who openly expresses their feelings.

Card no. 17: The Stork

In a love reading, The Storks card denotes that the querent may expect to meet or reunite with someone from their past. They'll have mutual feelings, and there are plenty of harmony, solidarity, and complicity. This person can't stand a monotonous relationship and seeks something new, such as communication, libido, or needs more autonomy in their actions. For singles, their current status will soon change as a new love is coming.

Card no. 18: The Dog

The Dog card symbolizes tenderness and affection between family and friends. A friendship may turn into love. A platonic love. It describes a faithful, kind, and serious partner. The relationship is based on mutual trust and respect.

Card no. 19: The Tower

The Tower card may indicate an oppressive and restrictive relationship. It describes a partner who doesn't express their feelings properly and is unlikely to compromise, causing tension and coldness. The Tower also suggests isolation and a lack of communication between the partners or the need for their own space.

Card no. 20: The Garden

The Garden card refers to a partner chosen through social connection, such as a friend, customer, or someone who met at public events. It denotes a large and harmonious family, but sometimes it may also suggest an open relationship.

Card no. 21: The Mountain

The Mountain card suggests that establishing a relationship with someone (Mountain) may take time. Therefore, this card denotes a blocked or frivolous relationship. The surrounding cards will provide more details about the situation under analysis.

Card no. 22: The Crossroads

The Crossroad card indicates a relationship in which the querent can't find a way out and the inability to decide between two relationships. This card offers no security or guarantees. The Crossroads card may announce an extramarital affair; the querent is either a committed person but maintains an affair or is involved with a committed person. It's possible the presence of a parallel relationship, adultery, or bigamy. It also predicts a broke up or separation.

- The Crossroads + The Owls + The Ring: a decision to maintain a parallel relationship. The Crossroads card stands for a choice, a decision, The Owls card represents the number two, and The Ring card symbolizes the relationship.

Card no. 23: The Mice

The Mice card reveals unrequited feelings and disappointments. It may also indicate a careless extramarital affair or unfulfilled promises. This card may also describe a dangerous partner.

- The Mice + The Heart: love that has lost its spark and is no longer interesting.

Card no. 24: The Heart

The Heart is the theme card for feelings and emotions. When reading the Grand Tableau, it's essential to pay close attention to the cards that touch The Heart, as they provide valuable insight into the querent's emotional state or the person they're in love with. The Heart also indicates mutual feelings, compatibility, and a deep connection between the couple. The person loves unconditionally and is entirely devoted to their loved one. Love and harmony prevail among family members and friends. It's possible a future date with someone the querent will fall in love with.

The Heart
- + The Rider: the querent's thought is focused on the person they're in love with; a new lover;
- + The Fox: self-deception, illusion; infidelity; falsehood;
- + The Storks: changes in feelings;
- + The Mountain: difficulties in expressing one's feelings;
- + The Ring: an emotional bond;
- + The Book: a secret or platonic love;
- + The Anchor: a strong emotional bond or dependency.

Card no. 25: The Ring

The Ring card represents a formalized relationship and follows the traditional courtship, including dating, engagement, and marriage. This card also indicates loyalty and fidelity.

The Ring
- + The Ship: the couple is moving away (the card to the right of The Ship will give more details on the relationship's fate); the relationship is transforming or changing, with one or both partners desiring to move away from the relationship; or a long-distance romance;
- + The Tree: a stable and long-lasting relationship but that is boring and unexciting.
- + The Fox: infidelity
- + The Tower: a limiting relationship; a broke up or divorce;
- + The Garden: an open relationship.
- + The Crossroads: evaluating a relationship. A decision must be made about a relationship. For example, in one of my readings where a male querent was involved in an extramarital affair and was unsure about the future of the situation, this combination came up: The Ring + The Crossroad;

- + The House: the querent, who was in a parallel relationship, chose the family;
- + The Heart: a loving bond and relationship; the couple shares a deep level of understanding and complicity, and one partner is fully devoted to the other.
- + The Heart + The Clover: a short-term romance or a flirt.

Card no. 26: The Book

The Book card denotes a relationship kept secret or hidden from the family. One of the partners is hiding something.

Card no. 27: The Letter

The Letter card announces a significant novelty in the emotional aspect. The querent may receive a written proposal or statement. The surrounding cards will provide information about the sender's identity. It may indicate a correspondence-based relationship through letters, emails, chats, or social media like Facebook, WhatsApp, etc.. It also suggests a superficial relationship.

- The Letter + The Heart: A proposal or a love declaration.

Card no. 30: The Lilies

The querent enjoys a harmonious relationship with their family and between themselves. It represents a mature relationship; it may not involve sexual intimacy. In case of crisis or break up, The Lilies ensure reconciliation.

Card no. 31: The Sun

The Sun card symbolizes a harmonious and happy family or relationship filled with affection, warmth, and comfort., The Sun indicates the strengthening of a relationship or the possibility of reconciliation if the relationship faces any crisis or separation. In addition, this card implies an intense and passionate relationship with a strong sexual connection. For the singles, a significant date may be on the horizon.

Card no. 32: The Moon

The Moon card stands for romance, sentimentality, passion, or a memorable and romantic date.

Card no. 33: The Key

The Key card indicates that the person feels ready and available to love or enter a relationship. This person is protective and enjoys providing security for their loved ones. The partners love each other.

Card no. 34: The Fish

The Fish card represents someone hard to catch and who isn't ready for a committed relationship. They may be seeking a casual, short-term relationship or a flirt. Most of the time, the relationships are motivated by convenience or personal interests.

Card no. 35: The Anchor

The Anchor card indicates a stable and secure love but with some co-dependency or even obsession. It may denote the person is in love or in a romantic relationship with a colleague at work.

Card no. 36: The Cross

The Cross card denotes emotional anguish and distress. Love that brings lots of suffering and crisis.

To clarify:

- When The Tree, The Dog, The Tower, or The Anchor appears next to The Ring card, they indicate an enduring and long-term relationship;
- If The Ring card shows up next to the querent's card or with any other court cards representing a person, it announces a committed or married person;
- Card that represents emotions: The Heart;

- Cards that express <u>emotion</u> and <u>feelings</u>: The Clover, The Bouquet, The Heart, The Sun, and The Moon;
- Cards that represent <u>happiness, joy, and satisfaction</u>: The Clover, The Bouquet, The Sun that means great happiness and pleasure;
- Cards that represent <u>unhappiness, sadness, and grief</u>: The Coffin and The Cross;
- Cards that represent <u>anxiety, nervousness, and stress</u>: The Clouds, The Owls, and The Mice.
- Cards that represent <u>the end of a relationship</u>: The Coffin announces a definite separation in a relationship. When The Coffin and The Tower cards fall next to The Ring card, they predict a divorce. The Scythe and The Crossroads next to The Ring predict a break up;
- Cards that represent a <u>reconciliation</u>: The Bouquet and The Lilies both announce a reconciliation when accompanied by Ther Rider and The Storks, which are the cards that take and bring something;
- Card that represents <u>fidelity, honesty, and loyalty</u>: The Dog
- Cards that represent <u>betrayal and infidelity</u>: The Clouds, The Snake, The Fox, The Mice, and The Book Cards that represent extramarital affair, a lover, with the following combination.
    - The Clouds + The Ring
    - The Snake + The Ring
    - The Snake + The Heart
    - The Ring + The Book
- Cards that represent <u>troubles in a relationship</u>: The Clouds, The Snake, The Broom and The Whip, and The Mountain.

Theme Cards for Communication and News

After all, what is communication?
To put it simply, communication is the act of communicating information that is significant to us, such as thoughts, ideas, humor, concepts, and so on. Since the beginning of life, all living beings on Earth, including plants, animals, and humans, have been able to communicate and understand each other. Throughout history, different communities have developed their own distinct languages and communication methods that set them apart. For example, some cultures use tattoos, dances, traditional practices, clothing, and even gods to express themselves. Therefore, communication can be expressed in different ways, such as:

- Words
- Gestures,
- Mimes
- Writing (symbols, drawings, paintings).

Some cards are better suited to represent communication and news than others. During a reading, it's essential to understand the meaning of these cards regarding communication and news. But which cards are they? I'll list them here in numerical order in the deck: The Rider, The Owls, and The Letter.

Card no. 1: The Rider

The Rider card can represent a means of transportation or delivery that serves as a "vehicle" for transmitting news or information from one person to another, such as a computer, postal service, FedEx, courier, or even a person. This card indicates that something is on its way, probably a newsbearer. The surrounding cards will provide more details about the nature and content of the incoming communication.

The Rider

- + The House: News from home or a property.
- + The Tree + The Lilies: News from family.
- + The Clouds: Unclear messages, information, or communication.
- + The Snake: News about betrayal.
- + The Scythe: A telegram.
- + The Broom and The Whip: A request or the arrival of a written message.
- + The Owls: Telephone or Skype communication; video conferencing.
- + The Letter: Written communication, email, chat, or a letter. It may also indicate a notification or an important announcement.

Card no. 12: The Owls

The Owls card represents social communication in all forms, including verbal communication and news spread through various media, such as radio, TV, newspaper, magazine, and music. This card stands for information exchange through conversations, chats, gossip, obtaining or disseminating information, interviews, and meetings. The Owls can also include phone calls, such as cell phone, WhatsApp, Messenger, or Skype, as well as any form of noise, voice, or singing.

The Owls

- + The Ship: Foreign language or accent and telepathic connection;
- + The House: speaking a dialect
- + The Tree: vernacular language;
- + The Snake: anonymous phone calls. Using conversations to cause harm and spread slander, defamation, and lies. This card depicts people who know how to manipulate others using persuasive language;

- The Coffin: communication with the dead. They frequently talk about the past or people who are missing or deceased. The ending of a conversation. There's no contact. Stopping talking to someone
- The Coffin + The Mountain: dumbness;
- The Bouquet + The Fox: a tendency to flatter to please or make a good impression;
- The Broom and The Whip: it indicates a speech impediment (stuttering) or a high, authoritarian, authoritative tone. Most of the time, this card refers to aggressive communication (shouting, criticizing). It also describes someone who expresses themselves in an authoritarian, despotic, intimidating (threatening), or insulting way;
- The Fox: the way of communicating isn't appropriate. It describes someone who doesn't speak the language well or who imitates the way others talk (an actor or a known person). Flattery;
- The Stars: Clear communication. It stands for a telephone, cell phone, or television;
- The Tower: someone who tends to talk to themselves.
- The Garden: Publishing an advertisement in the media so that the information reaches the general public. Social media. "Washing dirty linen" in public. The person tends to talk to everyone everywhere;
- The Mountain: blocked communication. It may also indicate communication problems, such as a telephone or cell phone that doesn't work or that WhatsApp, Skype, or email are unavailable;
- The Mice: swear-words; speaking impediment.
- The Heart: soothing words that calm down and comfort. Speaking how they feel. A spontaneous person.
- The Book: an interpreter or translator. Confidential conversation;
- The Book + The Mountain: learning disorder;

- + The Letter: communication through chat or Skype. Two or several messages or emails. Message exchange. Talking about the news;
- + The Man: strong, grave, masculine voice;
- + The Woman: sweet, gentle, feminine voice;
- + The Cross: a prayer, a church choir. Singing mass.

And also,
- The Broom and The Whip + The Owls: telephone or recorded threats, verbal abuse;
- The Scythe + The Owls: interrupted communication; brief and objective speech; telephone line cut off.

Card no. 27: The Letter

The Letter card represents all kinds of written communication, including postal correspondence, emails, text messages, faxes, magazines, newspapers, advertisements, and marketing.

The Letter
- + The Ship: international mail, news that comes from afar;
- + The Coffin: a condolence note, an answer that won't arrive, end of contact;
- + The Bouquet: an invitation, a pleasant note;
- + The Broom and The Whip: legal mail or communications from authorities that will cause discussions, litigation, fines, or complaints. Anger and rage in an email, message, or letter; threats in a chat or written message;
- + The Broom and The Whip + The Fox: forged signature or handwriting;
- + The Owls: contact via chat, registered message;
- + The Fox: misspelling; a false letter;

- + The Stars: communication via the internet (social media);
- + The Tower: news about a breakup. Correspondence from an institution (state, governmental, or corporation);
- + The Tower + The Owls: mail from a telephone company;
- + The Garden: public communication, news sent to a lot of people, social media.
- + The Mice: spam;
- + The Book: confidential news or messages; personal or confidential mail;
- + The Book + The Broom and The Whip: a tendency to correct the way other people speak;
- + The Book + The Owls: call log;
- + The Fish: bank statement; talking about money.

Important Note:

Obviously, none of these three cards is considered individually in a "reading". It's necessary to observe the cards that lie next to them (The Rider, The Owls, and The Letter) because they will confirm not only that it's a real message but also the content of the message.

CHAPTER 3: POLARITY AND SIGNIFICATOR CARD

THEME CARDS FOR WORK

Card no. 35: The Anchor
The Anchor card symbolizes solidness, stability, and security. It's often chosen as a significator (or theme) card to represent the main and steady job with a formal contract that ensures a consistent income.

Card no. 14: The Fox
One of the meanings of The Fox card is survival.
In my readings, I use this card as a significator when the querent already has a steady job but needs to take additional work to supplement their income. It may include cleaning, babysitting, caring for an elderly person, or card readings.

Card no. 19: The Tower and Card no. 32: The Moon
These two cards are associated with the career. The Moon often relates to professional reputation.

 The cards surrounding or touching the significator card describe professional circumstances, such as successes, failures, promotions, changes, and careers.

THEME CARD MEANINGS FOR WORK

Card no. 1: The Rider
The Rider represents a motivated person focused on professional growth who seeks to establish contacts and connections to expand and implement their ideas and projects. This person is open-minded, communicative, and adaptable to different situations. Moreover, they excel as mediators between customers and the company and execute tasks efficiently.

The Rider also indicates new opportunities brought by the media or an outsider and may denote a likely favorable response to a job application. When this card shows up for those who are currently unemployed, it announces significant professional news and advises them to go on and actively look for a job. It also predicts progress or the arrival of new professional tasks, often requiring movement or travel. However, it also means excessive spending.

The Ride
- + The Bouquet: a job offer;
- + The Bouquet + The Ring + The Anchor: professional cooperation proposal;
- + The Broom and The Whip: a professional athlete
- + The Anchor: reliable news about a job or a new job assignment,

Card no. 2: The Clover

The Clover suggests an opportunity for an extra or temporary job or a promotion that could bring relief during a difficult time. It indicates small but satisfying successes in the professional area and a period of good fortune for the querent. In addition, there's a possibility that someone may come to the querent's help and offer them an excellent and fortunate professional opportunity. If you're looking for a job, The Clover near The Anchor card announces an offer for a temporary position.

Card no. 3: The Ship

The Ship card means the opening of new professional horizons and the discovery of new people, things, and places. In today's world, the internet is a navigational tool to launch products, receive news, find new jobs, make partner contacts, and so on. When this card appears in a reading about a professional situation, and the querent is already employed, it announces that changes are coming to the company or workplace. It also implies that the querent has to commute a long distance to get to work.

If the person is currently unemployed and is seeking a job, this card indicates that it may take some time for a job opportunity to come up. Additionally, it suggests that a negotiation or project implementation will develop slowly.

This card symbolizes trade and negotiations with other countries or distant cities and may indicate that the querent will need to make lots of trips or establish numerous contacts (via phone or internet) with foreign countries or with places far from their work.

In some cases, The Ship represents someone who works far from their homeland (such as an emigrant).

Unlike The Storks, the emigration represented by The Ship can take a long time.

Card no. 4: The House

The person represented by The House card tends to create a family-like atmosphere in their workspace and cares for their co-workers, looking after their welfare and treating them as family.

In a work-related reading, this card advises the querent to be more approachable, understanding, and friendly to their colleagues and boss. The querent must do everything possible to preserve the good image of the company and their work.

The House card ensures a secure job or a stable professional position. The projects have solid foundations that allow them to be completed and endured.

In my experience, this card also encourages turning a hobby into a profession, which may be inherited from the family. It can also refer to the possibility of working from home.

The House
  + The Broom and The Whip: a maid, cleaning.
  + The Anchor: working near home; stable workplace.

Card no. 5: The Tree

The Tree card indicates that the development of a project will take some time.

Card no. 6: The Clouds

The Clouds card represents a hostile work environment with an overwhelming workload, and inconsistency in tasks.

Card no. 7: The Snake

The Snake card warns of potentially serious issues at work that will demand the querent's full attention. It advises to be cautious of partners, competitors, customers, or colleagues. This card also implies significant complications in business. Be careful when accepting help from a third party or a coworker. The Snake card may suggest that someone at work is causing conflict and turning colleagues against each other. As advice, this card recommends using charm to attract customers or win over coworkers and keeping professional plans secret.

Card no. 8: The Coffin

The Coffin card suggests the professional situation is worrying, and there's a severe crisis, with business coming to a standstill. It may indicate the end of the career due to retirement, leave of absence, or a long period of unemployment. This card points to a significant change in the professional area, such as a new career or job completion. The Coffin also denotes work that is not progressing and construction or renovation that has stopped.

Card no. 9: The Bouquet

The Bouquet represents a well-deserved recognition, promotion, or bonus. In addition, it can indicate a job offer, but in this case, it's important to look at the cards surrounding The Bouquet to be sure whether it's a favorable opportunity.

- The Bouquet + The Moon + The Anchor: recognition of one's own works, a professional celebrity.

Card no. 10: The Scythe

The Scythe card foretells an abrupt interruption or the end of a work contract. It also denotes a job with a deadline or a potential job change.

Card no. 11: The Broom and The Whip

The Broom and The Whips card stands for negotiations, a hostile working environment, including discussions, criticisms, complaints, or stress.

- The Broom and The Whip + The Ring: signing a work contract.

Card no. 12: The Owls

The Owls card indicates, work shifts, short business trips, and a restless and noisy workplace. It also denotes that the querent may have two jobs and business-related phone calls.

Card no. 13: The Child

The Child card represents new professional activity. Sometimes it denotes inexperience in carrying out their professional duties.

Card no. 14: The Fox

This Fox card may denote fierce competition in the professional area or conflict with untrustworthy coworkers. It may also suggest a hostile or deceitful workplace as well as moral harassment or bullying. The Fox card describes a cheater, impostor, trickster, or crafty person. Broken agreements, unfulfilled promises, contracts that aren't honored, and also dishonest business partners are also associated with this card. The querent demonstrates excellent negotiation skills in dealing with customers.

It also represents work autonomy or self-employment work. Sometimes it can suggest that the querent is in the wrong professional field or something is not quite right in their job. It's necessary to pay close attention. I've noticed in my readings that The Fox can indicate either undocumented work or illegal and criminal activities.

Card no. 15: The Bear

The Bear card stands for ambitious goals.

Card no. 16: The Stars

The Stars card indicates professional achievement.

Card no. 17: The Storks
The Stok card suggests a job opportunity for three, six, or nine months. Emigration is a possibility. It may indicate a job promotion, career change, new assignments, or contract extension. The querent might have a desire to explore new things.

Card no. 18: The Dog
The Dog card indicates a reliable and trustworthy colleague who is great to work with as a team. It denotes a good working relationship, as well as a friendly and relaxed atmosphere at work. It also describes an honest and loyal business partner.

Card no. 19: The Tower
The Tower card represents ambitious and long-term projects or a career. It describes someone who prefers to work alone rather than in a team. This person is known for their discipline, responsibility, and dedication to work.

Card no. 20: The Garden
The Garden card shows a harmonious professional evolution characterized by both commercial and artistic success. It indicates valuable connections and new customers. To increase visibility and attract more clients, effective advertising, particularly on social networks, plays a crucial role.

Card no. 21: The Mountain
The Mountain card indicates a significant obstacle that is impeding work progress. It may mean unemployment or overwork leading to exhaustion.

Card no. 22: The Crossroads
The Crossroads card refers to a part-time job or indicates a choice between two jobs, a job alternative, or that the querent is being evaluated for a position. Sometimes, it denotes an offer that requires careful consideration.

Card no. 23: The Mice

The person depicted by The Mice card isn't very committed to their job, may lack motivation (lazy). It may also indicate a decrease in working hours, job insecurity, or possible unemployment. This card is often associated with low-paid or unstable jobs and uncertain and unclear situations. It also represents exploitation, illegal or under-the-table employment.

The Mice

- + The Fox: plagiarism;
- + The Ring: the completion of a contract.
- + The Anchor: job loss, no promotion.

Card no. 24: The Heart

The Heart card represents deep love and passion for work.

Card no. 25: The Ring

The Ring card indicates job security and professional stability, signing an employment contract, a contract extension, a job offer or proposal, or a contractual clause. The Ring can also refer to a successful professional collaboration with others. The querent is working or is part of a team. Organization and discipline are key factors in carrying out a project successfully.

The Ring

- + The Coffin: Termination of a work contract, dissolving a contract, breaking up with a business partner;
- + The Fox: An agreement or contract that isn't honored, agreement or association with criminals, a fictitious partnership;
- + The Garden: Hiring staff.

Card no. 26: The Book

The Book card represents the need for professional requalification, training, or internship. It sometimes appears in a reading to emphasize the importance of improving work performance.

The Book means introducing a new technique in the workplace that requires training for a better understanding, which will lead to more autonomy. This card describes someone highly qualified for their job. It advises keeping confidential information about a work project and professional secrets.

The Book
- + The Rider: Looking for new products or a new job;
- + The Ship: Distance professional training or online course;
- + The Anchor: professional training or professional documents.

Card no. 27: The Letter

The Letter card denotes the possibility of establishing new business connections. You may receive important information about work through email, articles, or advertisement

The Letter
- + The Ring: a contract
- + The Book: a diploma, certificate, attestation.

Card no. 30: The Lilies

The Lilies card suggests a pleasant workplace. The querent demonstrates skills and experience in their work. However, it can also represent a slow pace in business or retirement. The querent may only find a new job in the winter.

Card no. 31: The Sun

The Sun card shows that the querent is reaching the pinnacle of their career. A discovery can bring greater professional visibility, admiration, and prestige, as well as recognition and reward for their efforts. This card also suggests that the querent is highly efficient and takes personal fulfillment and pleasure in their work. The Sun card stands for project progress, career growth, and a leadership position within a group or company. If you're looking for a job, The Sun indicates that a positive response is right around the corner.

Card no. 32: The Moon

The Moon means recognition for a well-done work. The querent is appreciated by their coworkers. This card may predict a promotion, or a night-shift job.

Card no. 33: The Key

The Key card indicates a stable job or the need to come up with new ideas to solve a worrying situation. The querent shows initiative and turns their ideas into real projects, is self-employed, and has the ability to develop their projects autonomously.

The Key

- + Ring: A contract
- + The Anchor: Finding a job

Card no. 34: The Fish

The Fish card represents a self-employed job.

Card no. 36: The Cross

The Cross card indicates burdensome tasks, overtime work, or stress. The querent is under evaluation at work or might face unemployment.

The card meanings:

- The Anchor: A steady job;
- The Fox: A second job;
- The Rider or The Book: Looking for a job;
- The Ring and The Anchor: Finding a steady job;
- The Ring: A contract;
- The Clover or The Bouquet: A temporary job;
- The Book or The Cross: Being on trial at work;
- The Mice: Decrease or little work;

- The Scythe / The Coffin: Interruption, dismissal, or end of a contract;
- The Coffin / The Mountain / The Mice: Unemployment;
- The Coffin / The Mice: Bankruptcy;
- The Snake / The Fox / The Mountain / The Mice: Competitors, professional rivals;
- The Clover / The Bouquet / The Stars: Promotion;
- The Bear / The Tower / The Moon: A high position;
- The Coffin / The Tower / The Lilies: Retirement;
- The Ship / The Storks: Emigration.

The Theme Card Meanings for Professions

Card no. 1: The Rider

The Rider represents all professions that allow autonomy, freedom of action, independence, direct interaction with the clients, as well as communication or spreading of information.

For example: mail carriers, work that involves delivering documents directly, such as the post office, home delivery, representatives for companies (medicine, food, etc.), consultants, drivers, bus and taxi drivers, pilots, transporters, loaders, couriers, salesclerks, street vendors, waiters, waitresses, programmers, technicians, tour guides, professional athletes, members of the military, special correspondents, and emissaries (spokesmen, ambassadors, mediators).

Card no. 2: The Clover

The Cloves stands for punters in various forms of racing (cars, motorcycles, horses), animal fighting, employees in gambling halls (croupier), illusionists, stockbrokers, traders, professional gamblers in betting or casino, lottery ticket sellers, herbalists, botanists, and rare plant breeders.

Card no. 3: The Ship

The Ship card is associated with professions related to the sea, lakes, and rivers, importing, exporting, shipping abroad (international companies), buying and selling (including online platform like eBay and Etsy), and tradespeople. It also relates to professions in the travel and tourism industry, such as sailors, cruise personnel, merchant navy, fishers, and international transportation employees.

Card no. 4: The House

The House card represents a housemaid, architects, real estate agents, family-owned business or small business, craftsmen, construction workers, work-from-home, and domestic assistance.

Card no. 5: The Tree

The Tree card is related to all healthcare professions, including nurses, doctors, pharmacists, etc., as well as ambulance personnel. It stands for relaxation methods such as meditation and yoga. Counselors and advisors. It also denotes professions related to trees and wood, for example, carpenters, foresters, and landscape architects.

Card no. 6: The Clouds

The Clouds card represents meteorologists, laboratory technicians, chemists, pharmacists, factory workers, and tobacconists.

Card no. 7: The Snake

The Snake card stands for pharmaceutical, medical workers, and anesthesiologists. It can also denote dancers, contortionists, prostitutes, fortune tellers, witches, sorceresses, and healers.

- The Snake + The Stars: professionals related to spirituality or esotericism.

Card no. 8: The Coffin

The Coffin card is associated with all professions that deal with death: morticians, gravediggers, homicide detectives, pathologists, and necrologists. It also represents the followers of esotericism, occultism, or spiritism.

This card also represents professions involving human psychology, such as psychologists, psychiatrists, and analysts, or occupations that require absolute confidentiality. I've noted in my readings that this card stands for occupations dealing with terminal diseases and patients in vegetative or pharmacological coma. It also describes organ transplant specialists.

Card no. 9: The Bouquet

Botanists, florists, and gardeners are represented by The Bouquet. It also includes beauty-related professions, such as aesthetics, stylists, hairdressers, fashion designers, models, decorators, and fashion professionals: perfumers and creative artists. It also indicates a hobby that turns into a profession.

Card no. 10: The Scythe

The Scythe represents occupations related to weapons. It also stands for dentists, orthodontists, tattoo artists, seamstresses, tailors, and farmers. It also indicates dangerous tools or a toolmaker.

- The Scythe + The Garden: a farmer.

Card no. 11: The Broom and The Whip

This card is associated with cleaning company workers, athletes, and justice officers.

- The Broom and The Whip + The Snake: A dancer, including the belly dancing, samba, kuduro, merengue, kizomba, etc.

Card no. 12: The Owls

The Owls card represents telephone operators, advertisers, media workers, announcers, columnists, reporters, musicians, chorus girls, receptionists, and tour guides.

Card no. 13: The Child
The Child card is related to educators that work with children or teenagers.

Card no. 14: The Fox
The Fox card represents salesclerks, businessmen, businesswomen, engineers, traders, policemen, and investigators. It's also associated with killers, mobsters, criminals, hunters, and forgers. This card also stands for actors or actresses, politicians, and self-employed.

Card no. 15: The Bear
The Bear card indicates accountants, inspectors, economists, bank clerks, cooks, court officials (lawyers, judges, policemen, etc.), politicians, bosses, and managers.

Card no. 16: The Stars
The Stars card represents scientists, mathematicians, or workers in the audiovisual (television, film, special effects, scenography, etc.) or theater fields. This card also denotes computer programmers, esoteric (numerologists, astrologers, fortune tellers, etc.), spiritualists, and healthcare professionals.

- The Stars + The Crossroads: a palm reader.

Card no. 17: The Storks
The Stork card symbolizes obstetricians and international airport workers, pilots, parachutists, flight attendants, emigrants, and professions requiring a lot of air travel.

Card no. 18: The Dog
The Dog card denotes a security organization (security guards, bodyguards), animal trainers, veterinarians, canine anti-drug unit, animal protection volunteers, and any profession that deals with animals. It also represents counselors, assistants (doctors, nurses), and defense attorneys.

Card no. 19: The Tower

The Tower card indicates professions that require patience, discipline, and deep and detailed analysis: scientists, medical specialists, tower controllers, prison or Vatican guards, and heritage administrators. It also represents professions applied to studying the past: Archeology, History, ancient (dead) languages, and museums. It also stands for self-employed workers or a leadership position. Public servants, business people, tax officials, and someone qualified for their job. It also represents large corporations or government institutions.

The Tower
- \+ The Broom and The Whip: A lawyer
- \+ The Mountain: A prosecutor
- \+ The Lilies + The Broom and The Whip: A judge

Card no. 20: The Garden

The Garden stands for professions that are in contact with many people: public relations, event organizers, salesclerks, receptionists, market vendors, laborers, auctioneers, bank clerks, entertainers, players (soccer, football, etc.), but also gardeners, farmers, and wine growers.

Card no. 21: The Mountain

The Mountain card denotes professions dealing with stones (crystals, gems) and also marble workers, masons, miners, or climbers.

Card no. 22: The Crossroads

The Crossroads card represents palm readers, laborers, ecologists, shoemakers, specialists, and researchers. With The Mice card: street sweepers.

Card no. 23: The Mice

The Mice card signifies teamwork, and also illegal or used goods smugglers, factory or workshop workers, garbage collectors, sweepers, and miners.

Card no. 24: The Heart
The Heart card represents professions related to beauty and creativity: musicians, artists, and painters. It can also denote all humanitarian aid workers, and medical care, such as cardiologists.

Card no. 25: The Ring
The Ring card is associated with professions that involve working in groups or teams, as well as employees under contract and watchmakers. This card can also indicate a person returning to a previous career or resuming an old job.

Card no. 26: The Book
The Book card stands for professions involving books, writing, and documents, such as students, teachers, educators, supervisors, instructors, booksellers, librarians, editors, writers, novelists, journalists, historians, typographers, notaries, and archivists.
This card also includes professions that require professional secrecy or secret actions: investigators, criminalists, secret agents, and occultists. Occupations related to the study of the mind or brain: psychologists, psychotherapists, neurologists, scientists, researchers, and specialists.

The Book
- + The Stars: A scientist
- + The Garden: An editor;
- + The Mice: No knowledge or experience.

Important Note:
This card has two interpretations, and the second card that comes into contact with it has its message. The first message means accumulated knowledge, and the second is that the person lacks professional experience.

Card no. 27: The Letter

The Letter card is associated with professions related to information or written communication: mail carriers, couriers, delivery workers, translators, interpreters, office clerks, and secretaries.

- The Letter + The Garden: an advertiser or journalist.

Card no. 30: The Lilies

The Lilies card represents professionals who work with older people, such as caregivers and social workers. It can also refer to someone who works in a family business.

Card no. 31: The Sun

The Sun card is associated with professions that involve energy, such as electricians, employees in tanning salons, reiki practitioners, hypnotherapists, ophthalmologists, and vulcanologists. It can represent a summer job or day-shift jobs.

Card no. 32: The Moon

The Moon card stands for artists, dream interpreters, and night-shift jobs.

Card no. 33: The Key

The Key card denotes craftsmen, new product promoters, interpreters, security service, detectives, and workers dealing with metal, such as locksmiths and also computer technicians.

Card no. 34: The Fish

The Fish card indicates professions related to finance, such as bankers, financial advisors, stockbrokers, accountants, and cashiers, as well as professionals who deal with numbers, such as mathematicians, physicists, and numerologists. It can also include professions related to the sea or water: sailors, fishermen, coast guards, lifeguards, marine biologists, divers, and swimmers. Importers and exporters of goods, traders, and tax officials.

Card no. 35: The Anchor

The Anchor card stands for dental prosthesis technicians, physiotherapists, and shipbuilders.

Card no. 36: The Cross

The Cross represents theologians, missionaries, priests, nuns, religious volunteers.

Theme Cards for Finances and Money

The theme card for financial matters is **Card no. 34 – The Fish**. As a symbol of fertility, prosperity, abundance, and plenty, The Fish represents money, cash, salary, financial stability, income, and profits from business transactions.

Card no. 15 – The Bear, represents the querent's resources, assets, goods, possessions, inheritance, economy, and savings. The Bear often describes someone who is stingy and a born hoarder, fiercely protecting their wealth. Therefore, The Bear card symbolizes one's own resources.

Card no. 34
The Fish

Card no. 15
The Bear

Theme Cards for Finances

Card no. 1: The Rider

The Rider card indicates incoming financial news, whether positive or negative, will be confirmed by the surrounding cards. For example, favorable cards such as The Dog, The Lilies, and The Fish may indicate a possible loan or financial support. It can also announce a financial transaction, such as sending, transferring, or receiving money (through Wester Union or another similar means), a cash refund, extra money, or a financial reward.

The Rider

- + The Ship: Money coming from far away, transport of valuables;
- + The Ship + The Coffin: News regarding an inheritance;
- + The Coffin: Negative answer on a credit application;
- + The Fox: Inflow of extra money earned dishonestly; a second job;
- + The Bear: Deposit money;
- + The Mountain: Delay in receiving money;
- + The Mice: Debts, extra expenses;
- + The Ring: Regular cash inflow
- + The Letter: Payment order, bank forms for payment of amounts;
- + The Book: Undisclosed information referring to an investment or loan
- + The Fish: Postal order, news about investments, cash inflow.

Card no. 2: The Clover

The Clover card means new opportunities and unexpected possibilities that may lead to a positive turn in financial matters. Most of the time, it indicates a small but welcome extra inflow of money from various sources, such as a bonus, an extra job, a slight increase in salary, a lottery game, or as a gift.

CHAPTER 3: POLARITY AND SIGNIFICATOR CARD

The Clover represents all games of chance, such as lottery or horse racing. If The Fish and The Sun cards are next to The Clover, it suggests that the querent has made significant profits from gambling.

The Clover

+ The Stars: Great wealth
+ The Mice: Loss of small sums of money in gambling;
+ The Sun: Good luck in gambling;
+ The Fish: Cash bonus, the moment is great for gambling: luck will surely be on your side;
+ The Fish + The Sun: Jackpot

Card no. 3: The Ship

The Ship card denotes potential financial gain through international ventures or online platform sales, such as eBay. It can also represent money transfers or income from overseas, cash flow, currency exchange, foreign currency, financial investments, real estate transactions, spending, valuable purchases, stock market involvement, and inheritance.

The Ship

+ The Coffin + The Fish: Inheritance
+ The Bear: Depositing money abroad;
+ The Fish: Profitable business;
+ The Fish + The Rider: A purchase of a vehicle, such as a car, a motorcycle, or a bicycle;
+ The Fish + The Mice: A planned trip may result in financial losses;
+ The Fish + The House: The purchase of a property.

Card no. 4: The House

The House card denotes a stable financial situation. And a strong sense of responsibility towards supporting the family and devoting heart and soul to providing stability and financial comfort at home. It also indicates buying or selling real estate, such as a house, apartment, land, or shop.

- The House + The Fish + The Ship: Selling a property.

Card no. 5: The Tree

The Tree card represents a stable and reliable source of income, as well as steady financial growth, savings, and plenty of money accumulated over many years, or life insurance.

Card no. 6: The Clouds

The Clouds card indicates financial worries and uncertainties; something is unclear. It's a period of financial ups and downs.

Important Note:

If the dark clouds of The Clouds card are covering The Fish card, it means you don't have a clear view of your finances, or the source is obscure. It may also indicate short-term financial setbacks.

Card no. 7: The Snake

The Snake card predicts financial difficulties, involvement in illegal or unethical financial activity, and tendencies toward greed. It may also indicate the ability to deceive others in financial matters.

Card no. 8: The Coffin

When The Coffin card falls next to one of the two theme cards, The Fish or The Bear, it's a warning of bankruptcy, poverty, serious financial problems, loss of money, no money, no profit, financial ruin, and inability to repay a loan or credit. However, if The Coffin card follows a card that represents debt, such as The Ring or The Mice, it announces the end of the debt.

Card no. 9: The Bouquet

The Bouquet card may announce a gift, reward, or prize in the form of money or a valuable gift, as well as generosity and a salary raise. However, it can also suggest bribery.

Card no. 10: The Scythe

The Scythe card stands for a financial cut or dividing assets in situations involving inheritance or separation. It could also indicate receiving money from an ex-partner.

The Scythe

- + The Bear: Closure of a bank account;
- + The Mice: Debt cancellation;
- + The Fish: A sudden loss, interruption of financial support, denial of a loan, dividing money, or the loss of the main means of living.

Card no. 11: The Broom and The Whip

The Broom and The Whip card suggests a dispute over money or a discussion about finance. It can also stand for a fine or penalty.

Card no. 12: The Owls

The Owls card denotes financial stress, talking about money, and financial negotiations.

Card no. 13: The Child

The Child card represents a small amount of money, modest profits, first earnings, child support, new cash inflows, monthly allowances, or financial inexperience and irresponsibility. It may also stand for the playful use of money and spending on children or young people.

The Child

- + The Bear: Start saving
- + The Fish: Tip, inability to manage money, new investments

Card no. 14: The Fox

The Fox card represents the struggle for survival, as well as greed, financial fraud, and dishonesty. This card indicates that someone is enriching themselves at the expense of others, misusing money, making bad financial decisions, using money to pressure others, and bribery. The positive aspect of this card is the ability to solve financial problems.

> **Important Note:**
> When The Fox card shows up, it advises caution in all financial matters.

Card no. 15: The Bear

The Bear card represents economic power, savings, personal finance, income, investments, resources, and wealth accumulation. It can also denote wise money management, financial independence, and creditors and debtors. This card stands for a bank account, good financial management, money accumulation, loan, financing, sponsorship, financial support or assistance, wealth, a broker, banker, or sponsor.

The Bear

+ The House: Home economics, saving money at home;
+ The Coffin: No savings;
+ The Ring: joint account
+ The Fish: Effective money management, financial resources, and deposited money or investments in the areas indicated by the nearby cards. For example, when paired with The House card, it indicates real estate investment in land, buildings, or loans.
+ The Fish + The Coffin: it denotes bankruptcy, financial hardship, or poverty.

Card no. 16: The Stars

The Stars card indicates a positive turn in finances. It stands for a steady income, a consistent flow of money, success, financial plans, or goals for the future, profits, financial expectations, and innovative ideas to increase earnings. Additionally, it predicts the solution to any financial issues.

Card no. 17: The Storks

The Storks card denotes a change in the financial situation. When paired with The Fish card, it points to the repayment, payoff of a debt, or an attitude that improves the financial situation. It also indicates incoming and outgoing cash flow.

Card no. 18: The Dog

The Dog card predicts financial support or help from friends, colleagues, or siblings, as well as loans, financial honesty, and loyalty.

Card no. 19: The Tower

The Tower card represents a safe, financial institution, savings accounts, and taxes, money from institutions, credit institutions, and savings.

The Tower

+ The Fish: A financial institution, such as a bank, dealing with cash, money, and taxes.
+ The Fish + The Clover: casino
+ The Fish + The Bear: tax office, a senior bank clerk.

Card no. 20: The Garden

The Garden card represents public spending or for events, such as concerts, festivals, etc. It can also indicate investing money in a garden or parks, as well as collecting, auction, stock markets, casinos, and gambling halls. This card also signifies customers and a social circle that values money. Along with Ther Rider or The Mice, it denotes used items or antique fairs.

Card no. 21: The Mountain
The Mountain card means blocked funds, delayed payments or salaries, significant financial problems, difficulty repaying loans, risky loans, and no economic guarantee.

Card no. 22: The Crossroads
The Crossroads card denotes financial decisions that require careful consideration of the pros and cons of a potential investment. It may involve choosing between two or more options, money from one or more sources, and handling numerous loans or expenses. When paired with The Fish card, it suggests various sources of income.

Card no. 23: The Mice
The Mice card foretells financial difficulties such as debt, overspending on unnecessary things, theft, loss, scarcity, misery, poverty, and depending on others for financial support. It also suggests reducing prices and buying second-hand items.

The Mice
+ The Fox: a slow deterioration of finances, illicit appropriation;
+ The Bear: Spending the savings, not interested in saving money;
+ The Fish: Receiving less money than expected, consistently losing money, being on guard against thieves, the querent's money is being stolen; mismanagement of one's own money, precarious financial situation, payment.

Important Note:
When The Mice card appears in a financial reading, it recommends you take a closer look at your expenses, consider changing your spending habits, and be more careful with finances.

Card no. 24: The Heart

The Heart card stands for charity, generosity, and donating money. It also indicates a love for money and a tendency to materialism if it's close to unfavorable cards.

Card no. 25: The Ring

The Ring card indicates shared finances, the partner's savings (spouse, boyfriend/girlfriend), credit, ongoing loans, financial agreements, contracts, financial returns, alimony, financial responsibilities, shared payments, quotas, fees, marriage for convenience, money from associations, partnerships (spouse, boyfriend/girlfriend, or partners).

The Ring

- + The House: Rent payment
- + The Fish: Financial agreement, loan

Card no. 26: The Book

The Book card represents accounting, savings accounts, financial records, and hidden money. It can indicate the need to investigate the source of income and deal with the tax office, as well as expenses related to education and training courses.

Card no. 27: The Letter

The Letter stands for shares, a check, a receipt, an account statement, money transfer, receiving or sending money, and payment.

The Letter

- + The Clove: Lottery ticket;
- + The Bear: A bank account, bank account statement, check.
- + The Fish: A bank account, A bank correspondence, or notification of an online purchase or sale.

Card no. 28: The Man and Card no. 29: The Woman

It's important to observe the directional facing law for an accurate interpretation.

- If The Fish card faces the querent's card, it indicates that they're focused on financial issues, determined to achieve independence and future economic stability, and has the ability to make money.
- When The Fish card appears on the querent's back (behind), it means that they're not giving much importance to their financial situation or that current financial events are causing concern.

In any case, check out the surrounding cards for more details.

Card no. 30: The Lilies

The Lilies card suggests financial resources coming from the family or that money holds significant importance for the family. It may also denote that the querent will receive money in the winter or will take some time to arrive. It also means that the querent will receive a loan or financial support. Along with The Fish card, it represents family assets, properties, pensions, inheritance, or even paid sex.

Card no. 31: The Sun

The Sun card predicts success, financial improvement and plenty of money.

Card no. 32: The Moon

The Moon card indicates achieving financial power, receiving a reward or monetary prize, and attaining high social status because of their resources.

Card no. 33: The Key

The Key card represents financial security or investment. The Key combined with The Fish card means searching for a financial solution or opening a bank account. This card also stands for an ATM and security code.

CHAPTER 3: POLARITY AND SIGNIFICATOR CARD

Card no. 34: The Fish

The Fish card is a symbol of financial abundance, salary, food, purchases, and profits.

The Fish

- + The House: Buying a house, investing in real estate, spending on a house;
- + The Tree: Medical expenses;
- + The Scythe: Unexpected money; financial success;
- + The Stars: Salary increase;
- + The Garden: Public money, plenty of customers;
- + The Mountain: Delay in payment or receiving money, blocked account;
- + The Mice: Lack of interest in financial matters, as well as love for money without corresponding interest to work for it, inability to manage finances, and ongoing financial insufficiency;
- + The Mice + The Mountain: Ending of the financial issues
- + The Ring: Steady income; salary
- + The Ring + The House: rent payment or mortgage;
- + The Book: Financial privacy, student and training programs loans;
- + The Sun: Abundance of money;
- + The Anchor: Financial security through a job or a regular income that guarantees a monthly payment such as salary, alimony, and savings.

Card no. 35: The Anchor

It means financial stability (the nearby cards will provide more details about the source of this security), regular income, dependence on money, a permanent income, long-term investment, and savings.

Card no. 36: A Cruz

It predicts burdens, debt, suffering due to financial problems, or church funds.

Namely:

- The House, The Tree, The Tower, and The Anchor cards announce financial stability. However, these same cards can indicate that the finances will remain stagnant without significant changes. Therefore, it's crucial to check out the cards involved in the reading.
- The cards that indicate the cash flow are The Rider (the inflow and outflow of cash), The Clover (extra income), The Ship (the inflow and outflow of cash), The Bouquet (extra money income), and The Storks card (the inflow and outflow). The Fox indicates theft or fraud and The Mice predicts financial loss or expenses.
- The Clouds, The Coffin, The Scythe, The Mountain, The Mice, and The Cross are cards that augur significant financial problems: When these cards show up, they advise you to take steps to improve the situation.
- The cards that indicate low-wage jobs are The Child and The Mice.
- The Ride and The Letter cards represent charges.
- The Coffin, The Crossroads, The Ring, The Mice, and The Cross indicate debts.
- The Bear, The Dog, and The Lilies cards indicate financial help, support, or assistance, which may come as a subsidy, scholarship, or loan. The combination of The Bear and The Lilies card indicates that the querent has received financial advice and help from an institution or family member.
- The cards that represent quantity are: The Broom and The Whip, The Owls (double), The Scythe (half), The Stars and The Fish (much, expansion, multiplication and increase in finances), The Crossroads (various such as several sources of income), The Child and e The Mice (reduction, little);
- The cards that indicate delays in receiving money include The Clouds (for short-term delays) and The Mountain (for long-term delays). In addition, the stop cards, such as

The Tower, The Mountain, and The Anchor, may also denote delay when they're close to The Fish card.
- The Fish or The Bear, along with The Clouds, The Snake, The Fox, The Mice, or The Book indicate money from obscure origin or from an illegal source.
- The Mice card above The Fish card indicates that the querent is spending all their salary, or it may also predict a theft. So be wary of your salary and make sure that your boss or someone else isn't stealing from them.
- The Mice card above The Bear tells us that the querent is spending their savings and fleecing their assets.

THEME CARDS FOR TRAVEL AND VACATION

These five cards represent travel, displacement, and vacation:
- The Rider, The Ship, The Owls, The Storks, The Crossroads

These five cards are divided into two groups:

Group 1

Card no. 1
The Rider

Card no. 12
The Owls

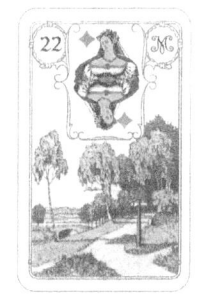

Card no. 22
The Crossroads

The Rider, The Owls, and The Crossroads cards represent short-distance or brief trips, such as sightseeing, excursions, and visits for educational, cultural, personal, or work-related purposes, usually on foot or by bicycle if The Crossroads card is involved.

The Rider stands for a trip by car, motorcycle, or horseback. In some cases, when paired with The Owls, it may suggest air travel, but usually for domestic or regional flights, such as helicopters, small planes, hot air balloons, or paragliding. If The Crossroads card is accompanied by The Ship, it may indicate a longer journey.

Group 2

Card no. 3
The Ship

Card no. 17
The Storks

The Ship and The Storks cards are commonly associated with long-distance or overseas travel.

Interestingly, when The Ship card appeared in the past position, it means that most querents had to leave their homeland to live in another country for work, love, or to escape the war. Similarly, when The Ship card and The Storks card show up in the past, it can indicate immigration.

The Ship stands for traveling by train, bus, or ship; while The Storks card represents air travel. It's worth noting that The Ship card may also refer to mental, spiritual, or astral journeys, as well as the passage from one life to another, including death.

Important Note:

If one of the five cards falls next to the querent's card in a reading about travel, the card will indicate the type of journey, and the cards next to the card that represents the travel will provide more information about it.

Vacation Cards

Four cards can represent vacations. Although I present them separately here, in a reading, they should appear together:

- The Ship card indicates an escape and often points toward a long vacation, international travel for study or business, or a trip to a distant city.
- The Tree card denotes a long vacation filled with relaxation, rest, calmness, peace, and nature. It can also indicate a walk in the fields or woods.
- The Owls card stands for a weekend, a holiday, or a day off. It also refers to tours, walks, visits to places such as museums, or a brief trip.
- The Garden represents a holiday, a day off, or a weekend. It may also refer to entertainment, recreation, hobbies, leisure time, outdoor activities, picnics, concerts, self-care, and escape from stress.

Theme Cards for Health

Although we all know that every theme suggested by the querent deserves a fortune teller's full attention, I believe that health is a particularly important and delicate life area that requires extra consideration.

Cartomancy can predict and confirm a specific disease that is already in progress or is about to arise. As a responsible cartomancy practitioner, I acknowledge this capability, as the deck is a valuable tool that can offer guidance on any matter that troubles us.

In addition, a genuine cartomancy professional brings the knowledge and years of study experience to provide insightful readings. It's proven that Cartomancy can predict and confirm an ongoing sickness or one that is about to manifest.

It would be contradictory for me not to accept this, as I firmly believe that the card deck is a serious tool that we can trust whenever we seek guidance, no matter the issue at hand. A genuine professional card reader has extensive knowledge and expertise gained through years of study and practice.

A professional and responsible fortune teller knows their cards deeply and recognizes that a certain card, when placed next to another specific card, can confirm whether a disease is likely to worsen or improve. It's crucial to accept this truth and not dismiss it, just as we accept and believe in predictions about other life areas.

<u>However, given that health is a sensitive subject and a delicate approach, I recommend fortune tellers who lack medical expertise and solid experience using the cards refrain from making medical diagnoses. Instead, they should advise the querent to see a doctor and only answer questions about the progression of a disease if the querent requests it.</u>

Ultimately, cartomancy can be quite beneficial in maintaining good health.

- The Tree is the significator card for health-related questions and has the function of revealing the querent's overall vitality and well-being.
- The Coffin is the theme card for disease.

Card no. 5
The Tree

Card no. 8
The Coffin

Therefore, pay attention to how close The Tree card is to the querent's card during a reading. If it's near and surrounded by negative cards, the health is affected. However, if it's far from the querent's card, there's no need to worry about health concerns.

The Card Meanings for Health

Card no. 1: The Rider

The Rider generally announces the arrival of something significant related to health. So, it's crucial to check the card next to The Rider as it can provide information about what to expect regarding health matters.

- <u>Organs and body parts</u>: legs, knees (including the meniscus), feet, ankles, tendons, and joints.
- <u>Vehicles</u>: wheelchair, crutches.
- <u>Advice</u>: The Rider encourages movement and sports activities

The Rider

+ <u>The Clover</u>: recovery
+ <u>The Tree</u>: information concerning one's health;
+ <u>The Snake</u>: a worsening health condition;
+ <u>The Bouquet</u>: healing from a disease or the positive outcome from medical treatment;
+ <u>The Letter</u>: the result of a medical examination or a prescription for a new medicine.

Card no. 2: The Clover

The Clover card indicates a quick recovery from fatigue or sickness, or a short-term disease.

- <u>Treatment</u>: alternative medicine, herbs, homeopathic healing, Chinese medicine, and teas.

Card no. 3: The Ship

The Ship can sometimes indicate the need to visit a hospital or travel to a distant (foreign) city for treatment, and medical exams. It can also suggest considering alternative medicine.

- Organs and body parts: organs of detoxification: liver, kidneys, pancreas, gallbladder, bladder, etc.
- Vehicle: ambulance.
- Advice: Take better care of your body and soul.

The Ship

+ The Tree: ambulance;
+ The Snake: gastroenteritis;
+ The Child + The Coffin: natural childbirth;
+ The Mountain: kidney stones
+ The Fish: alcoholism.

Card no. 4: The House

The House card represents the body as a whole, including the physical structure and soul. It also stands for rehabilitation and recovery.

- Organs and body parts: the whole body, the skeleton, and the soul.
- Advice: Get some rest.

The House

+ The Tower: arms, fingers, or the hospital room;
+ The Clouds: the lungs.

> **Important Note:**
> The card touching The House identifies the organ or the body part that needs attention.

Card no. 5: The Tree

The Tree is the theme card for health.

- » <u>Organs and body parts</u>: lungs, airways, skeleton, bones, gums and also DNA, and genes.
- » <u>Disease</u>: a hereditary or long-term disease.
- » <u>Advice</u>: A period of rest and regeneration may be necessary to achieve better health and personal balance.

The Tree
- \+ <u>The House</u>: a clinic, rest;
- \+ <u>The Clouds</u> + <u>The Mice</u>: depression, infection;
- \+ <u>The Coffin</u> + <u>The Cross</u>: serious disease;
- \+ <u>The Tower</u> + <u>The Scythe</u>: urgent admission to the hospital;
- \+ <u>The Mountain</u>: long-term disease

Important Note:

If The Clouds card shows up in a health reading, it indicates that the Querent isn't in their regular state, whether emotionally, psychologically, or physically. In this scenario, it's crucial to check the cards near the dark clouds, as they will provide information regarding the source of the problem. It's also crucial to see a doctor for a check-up. The Clouds card frequently hides a sickness that can lead to serious health problems if not identified in time. If there is a disease, there's a risk of it persisting because of the querent's negligence.

Card no. 6: The Clouds

- » <u>Organs and body parts</u>: lungs, airways, chest.
- » <u>Diseases</u>: malaise, nausea, dizziness, fainting, emotional or mental instability, imbalance. Depression, risk of infection, swelling, bruising, spots, asthma, bronchitis, flu, cold, pneumonia, smoking, intestinal disease, cataracts, myopia, and

diseases caused by the overload (work, relationships, financial problems, etc.). Smoking addiction and lung cancer when combined with The Mice card.

The Clouds
- + The Ship: blisters, nausea;
- + The Bouquet: allergy;
- + The Coffin: fainting, loss of consciousness, depression, psychological problems;
- + The Coffin + The Scythe: suicidal tendencies;
- + The Broom and The Whip: cough;
- + The Mice + The Garden: virus;
- + The Mice + The Fish: bladder inflammation (cystitis);
- + The Book: unknown diseases;
- + The Lilies: pneumonia;
- + The Fish: alcoholism, chemical substance abuse (medications or drugs). The querent is under the influence of medication, drugs, or alcohol. It also denotes dizziness, diarrhea, or metabolic problems.

Card no. 7: The Snake

The Snake card may indicate complications in the mentioned areas referring to diseases, such as roundworms, worms, and other intestinal parasites. It also stands for anesthesia, sleeping pills, as well as the danger of insect or reptile bites.

- » Organs and body parts: veins, intestine, colon, digestive system, umbilical cord, and fetus.
- » Treatment: medication with poison, chemotherapy, antibiotic, or intensive therapy.
- » Advice: Take more care of your health by paying more attention to your intestines and the dorsal spine.

The Snake
- + The Ship or The Fish: urinary tract or diarrhea;
- + The Scythe: poisonous insects or animal bites.

Card no. 8: The Coffin

The Coffin card is the theme card for disease. If The Coffin card is next to The Tree, it indicates the presence of a disease. Pay attention to the surrounding cards for further information about the querent's health. If there are many unfavorable cards, there may be more reason for concern about the querent's health condition.

- » Organs and body parts: anus, rectum, blindness. The Coffin also indicates an organ removal.
- » Disease: The Coffin card indicates serious health problems that require medical intervention. The diseases associated with this card are depression, headache, migraine, and neurological deficiencies. When accompanied by unfavorable cards, The Coffin denotes chronic, severe, or terminal disease, as well as conditions such as coma, paralysis, or disability. Additionally, it can indicate exhaustion, mental and emotional fatigue that requires rest. The Coffin also predicts age-related diseases, such as menopause or premature aging, if it touches The Clover card. However, if favorable cards surround it, The Coffin announces positive changes.
- » Objects: bed, medicine box, coffin.
- » Advice: Get some rest.

The Coffin;

- + The Tree: a hereditary disease
- + The Snake: a long-term disease or health complications;
- + The Scythe: sudden disease or death;
- + The Broom and The Whip: high fever;
- + The Fox: lying about an illness or false symptoms;
- + The Ring: relapse of a disease;
- + The Sun: recovery, reanimation;
- + The Fish: bladder problems;
- + The Anchor: incurable disease.

Card no. 9: The Bouquet

The Bouquet card announces a fast improvement, recovery, or cure from a disease.

- » <u>Organs and body parts</u>: the face and hair.
- » <u>Disease</u>: allergy, herpes, and acne.
- » <u>Treatment</u>: alternative therapies: (oils, creams, ointments, homeopathy, Bach flowers, essences).

Card no. 10: The Scythe

The Scythe card stands for medical emergencies, including fractures and injuries, and also organ amputation or uterine scraping.

- » <u>Organs or body parts</u>: the nails.
- » <u>Disease</u>: fever, wounds, fractures, animal or insect bites, injuries, trauma, excruciating pain, severe misfortune or incidents, tetanus, and inflammation.
- » <u>Treatment</u>: surgery, cesarean section, transplantation, injection, and acupuncture.
- » <u>Advice</u>: It's important to investigate the problem thoroughly or take a biopsy for proper diagnosis.

The Scythe

- \+ <u>The Ship</u> + <u>The Child</u>: cesarean section;
- \+ <u>The Bouquet</u>: esthetic surgery;
- \+ <u>The Mountain</u>: tooth extraction.

Card no. 11: The Broom and The Whips

- » <u>Organs and body parts</u>: throat, tendons, muscles, and hands;
- » <u>Diseases</u>: Colic, cramps, injuries, fever, nerves, speech problems; postoperative pain; chronic diseases.
- » <u>Treatment</u>: physiotherapy.

The Broom and The Whip

- \+ <u>The Sun</u>: high fever.

Card no. 12: The Owls

- » Organs and body parts: the eyes, legs, veins, and nerves.
- » Diseases: eye diseases, sleep disorders, nervous system, and high blood pressure.

Card no. 13: The Child

The Child card indicates the progress of disease treatment or dentition.

- » Diseases: childhood-related disease, an early-stage disease, or deficiency.

The Child

+ The Ship: pregnancy;
+ The Ship + The Scythe: premature birth;
+ The Coffin + The Scythe: abortion;
+ The Owls: twins;
+ The Storks: pregnancy

Card no. 14: The Fox

The Fox card recommends adopting healthy eating habits, such as eating small amounts several times a day. It might also indicate ear, nose, and throat problems.

If the card appears in a health-related reading, it suggests that the querent should pay more attention to the area indicated and seek help from a specialist if necessary. It also implies that the symptoms may not be what they seem. The Fox card can represent a psychosomatic disease or someone faking an illness.

- » Organs and body parts: the nose, ears, throat, and neck.
- » Disease: psychosomatic disease, misdiagnosis.
- » Advice: Ask for a second medical examination.

Card no. 15: The Bear

- » Organs and body parts: hair, fur, the stomach, and belly.
- » Diseases: Obesity, geriatric diseases, and tumor.

Card no. 16: The Stars

The Star card indicates an improvement or recovery from a disease.

- » <u>Organs and body parts</u>: skin, cells, scalp, birthmark, and warts.
- » <u>Diseases</u>: dermatological diseases, diseases at the cellular level, and pimples.
- » <u>Treatment</u>: chemotherapy, radiotherapy, laser, medication, physiotherapy. Attention to medicine overdose.

Card no. 17: The Storks

- » <u>Organs and body parts</u>: legs and womb
- » <u>Diseases</u>: it indicates a reemerging disease or health improvement if you're sick.
- » <u>Advice</u>: You need to adjust your habits and lifestyle, such as smoking, diet, or sedentarism.

The Storks

+ <u>The Mountain</u>: Irreversible changes in the disease.

Card no. 18: The Dog

- » <u>Organs and body parts</u>: vocal cords, mouth, and nose.
- » <u>Diseases</u>: chronic diseases.

Card no. 19: The Tower

- » <u>Organs and body parts</u>: spine, vertebral discs, neck, fingers, legs, and knees.
- » <u>Diseases</u>: the tendency to arthritis, rheumatism, bone disease, circulatory disorders, and diseases requiring isolation, quarantine, or hospitalization.

The Tower

+ <u>The Storks</u>: crutches;
+ <u>The Fish</u> + <u>The Child</u>: fertilization or insemination.

Card no. 20: The Garden

- <u>Diseases</u>: immune system, allergy, or virus.
- <u>Treatment</u>: group therapy or treatment retreat.
- <u>Advice</u>: Get some rest.

Card no. 21: The Mountain

The Mountain card predicts the beginning of a long-term disease.

- <u>Organs and body parts</u>: head, skull, bones, and teeth.
- <u>Diseases</u>: kidney or gallstones, blood clots, breast nodules, cysts, benign tumors, constipation, and also difficult-to-treat infections or possible complications, plastered, and swellings.

The Mountain

+ <u>The Clover</u>: temporary tooth;
+ <u>The Stars</u>: metastasis;
+ <u>The Anchor</u>: toothy.

Card no. 22: The Crossroads

- <u>Organs and body parts</u>: circulatory system, veins, arteries, tendons, and ligaments.
- <u>Diseases</u>: strabismus, high cholesterol.
- <u>Advice</u>: it's necessary to consult a specialist.
- <u>Treatment</u>: clinical examinations.

The Crossroads

+ <u>The Heart</u> + <u>The Mountain</u>: clogged arteries.

Card no. 23: The Mice

- <u>Organs and body parts</u>: digestive organs, stomach, and liver. Physical deformity, or limb loss, the surrounding cards will provide more details:
    - The Storks + The Mice: one missing leg
    - The Letter + The Mice: one missing hand
    - The Tower + The Mice: missing fingers

» <u>Diseases</u>: Infectious and contagious diseases, viruses, nervous system (tic disorder), stomachache and intestinal pain (ulcers), digestive or gastric problems. Food intolerance, vomiting, poisoning, and memory loss (amnesia). Diseases due to poor hygiene, such as tooth decay. Cancer, anxiety, fatigue, stress, depression, anorexia, fecal matter, osteoarthritis, organ failure, and arthrosis.

» <u>Treatment</u>: The Mice card also represents a healing, weight loss, or detoxification center (drugs, alcohol, etc.).

In some of my readings, I've observed a correlation between this card and medication refusal or the presence of parasites and lice.

The Mice

+ <u>The Tree</u>: bone atrophy;
+ <u>The Snake</u>: intestinal bacteria;
+ <u>The Coffin</u>: a slow recovery from a disease, an effective treatment that leads to the definitive cure of a serious disease. (The Mice card has the function of eliminating, reducing, removing, and gnawing the card in front of it)
+ <u>The Garden</u>: infectious disease;
+ <u>The Mountain</u>: osteoporosis, tooth decay;
+ <u>The Sun</u>: loss of vision and energy, apathy;
+ <u>The Fish</u>: bladder inflammation (cystitis).

Important Note:

In a health reading, The Mice card, especially when it touches The Tree card (The Mice + The Tree), indicates that we're dealing with a sick or weakened person (check out the nearby cards to understand the reasons for the problem). The card to the right of The Tree will indicate the diagnosis or specific sickness affecting the querent.

Card no. 24: The Heart

- » <u>Organs and body parts</u>: the heart
- » <u>Diseases</u>: heart problems (cardiopathies), circulatory system, blood, blood pressure, blood vessels. Emotional issues.
- » <u>Advice</u>: it's necessary to take care of the heart and the valves

Card no. 25: The Ring

- » <u>Diseases</u>: the tendency to relapse disease, addiction, chronic pathologies, or circulatory system.
- » <u>Advice</u>: Continuous and regular monitoring of a disease or health is necessary.

Card no. 26: The Book

- » <u>Organs and body parts</u>: head, brain, and navel.
- » <u>Diseases</u>: a health condition that is kept secret or hidden diseases. Mental disorder and visual problems.
- » <u>Advice</u>: It's necessary to perform clinical tests to make a diagnosis.
- » <u>Documents</u>: this card refers to all kinds of health-related documents, such as medical records, laboratory tests,

The Book

+ <u>The Coffin</u>: a disease that is being kept secret or is difficult to diagnose; the querent may be experiencing memory loss or amnesia.

Card no. 27: The Letter

When The Letter card appears in the reading, it brings news about the querent's health condition.

- » <u>Organs and body parts</u>: hands.
- » <u>Diseases</u>: anxiety, restlessness, and headaches.
- » <u>Documents</u>: medical prescriptions, laboratory results.

The Letter
- + <u>The Tree</u>: medical prescriptions, medical leave, make an appointment.
- + <u>The Coffin</u> + <u>The Tree</u>: sickness certificate,
- + <u>The Stars</u>: ultrasound, X-ray.

Card no. 28: The Man

- » <u>Organs and body parts</u>: male organs.
- » <u>Diseases</u>: men's diseases.

Card no. 29: The Woman

- » <u>Organs and body parts</u>: female organs.
- » <u>Diseases</u>: women's diseases.

Card no. 30: The Lilies

- » <u>Organs and body parts</u>: sexual organs.
- » <u>Diseases</u>: diseases related to cold weather, such as colds, flu, etc., urogenital system diseases, hormonal disorders, sexually-transmitted diseases (STDs), and age-related diseases.
- » <u>Treatment</u>: detoxification; slow recovery after a long-term disease.
- » <u>Advice</u>: Get some rest.

Card no. 31: The Sun

The Sun card announces restored energy, good health, and well-being. If you're sick, this card announces a recovery.

- » <u>Organs and body parts</u>: the eyes.
- » <u>Diseases</u>: sunstroke, burns, bruises, and also health problems due to heat, or diseases caused by harmful radiation.
- » <u>Negative aspect</u>: sunstroke, burns, dry skin, dehydration
- » <u>Treatment</u>: a safe and effective treatment for a disease.

The Sun
- + <u>The Coffin</u>: blindness or fainting.

Card no. 32: The Moon

- <u>Organs and body parts</u>: womb, breasts, and female sexual organs.
- <u>Diseases</u>: hormonal and reproductive system disorders and menstruation.

Card no. 33: The Keys

- <u>Organs and body parts</u>: clavicle.
- <u>Treatment</u>: Take mineral salts and vitamins. A new treatment has been found.

Card no. 34: The Fish

- <u>Organs and body parts</u>: kidneys and bladder.
- <u>Diseases</u>: kidney and bladder problems, fluid retention, water intoxication, but also fertilization or sperm problems. The Fish card also represents chemical dependency (alcohol, drugs) when it's next to The Ring or The Anchor cards. It can also indicate constipation and flu.
- <u>Treatment</u>: liquid medication (serum, ampoules, drops, syrup).

Card no. 35: The Anchor

The Anchor card suggests a stable but stagnant condition with no significant change.

- <u>Organs and body parts</u>: pelvis and hip.
- <u>Diseases</u>: occupational or chronic diseases.
- <u>Treatment</u>: There is currently no progress in healing or recovery.

Card no. 36: A Cruz

- <u>Organs and body parts</u>: vertebral discs, spine, marrow, arms, and wrists.
- <u>Diseases</u>: hereditary or chronic illness, misfortune, incident, sickness from past faults (addiction, smoking, drinking), and cancer. It also denotes suffering due to a disease.
- <u>Treatment</u>: hospitalization.

Cards that represent

- Diseases: the cards surrounding The Tree will give information about the querent's health. If The Coffin and The Mice cards fall next to The Tree, it augurs a health problem
- Chronic diseases: The Broom and The Whip, The Ring, and The Cross.
- A disease relapse: The Broom and The Whip and The Ring
- Incurable diseases: The Coffin and The Cross;
- Terminal disease: The Coffin;
- Treatments: The Snake and The Stars;
- Disease complication: The Snake
- Rehabilitation: The Broom and The Whip (physiotherapy);
- Recovery: The Clover, The Bouquet, The Stars, The Garden, and The Sun;
- Analysis: The Crossroads and The Book;
- Laboratory results: The Rider and The Letter;
- Surgery: The Scythe
- Hospitals, clinics and doctor's office: The Tree represents a hospital, a health institute, a medical college. The House indicates a clinic or a doctor's office, but only if they're accompanied by The Tree.

Theme Cards for Physical Death

From the moment we are born, life and death are constant companions. However, there are moments in life; we may not feel or even realize that death is so close until we experience the loss of a loved one or go through a serious disease. During these challenging times, we become aware of a divine force, the Lord of Death, reminding us of the importance of enjoying the remaining moments. Embracing this reality isn't easy, but it's a process that we can learn to live with.

Death isn't a common topic in reading, but there may be occasions where it comes up, like when discussing attending a funeral. However, if you prefer not to "see" death during a reading, it doesn't mean that this topic shouldn't be addressed. I want to remind you that the cards "talk" about any topic we choose to investigate, but not everyone is comfortable hearing about death.

If you decide to explore this subject, you must approach it with great care and sensitivity. Making accurate predictions about someone's death requires advanced expertise and a deep understanding of the cards.

When The Coffin card appears in a reading, it announces an ending or conclusion, but it doesn't necessarily predict physical death on its own. You need to look at the surrounding cards to determine if there might be indications of potential death. Certain cards that, when placed next to The Coffin, could suggest a possible death are:

- The Ship
- The Tree
- The Scythe
- The Tower
- The Roads
- The Lilies
- The Cross

Some combinations that predict physical death:

- The Coffin + The Ship: physical death;
- The Coffin + The Scythe: It announces a premature death due to suicide, murder, or terminal disease;
- The House + The Lilies + The Coffin + The Scythe: It denotes the untimely death of a loved one (premature or traumatic death);

- The Scythe + The Tower + The Coffin: death in a hospital;
- The Cross + The Coffin + The Tree: death after a prolonged disease;
- The Cross + The Crossroads + The Coffin: This combination showed up a few days before my brother passed away from a terminal illness. The Crossroads card serves a similar function to The Ship card, representing the passage from one life to another.

The surrounding cards will describe the reasons and cause of death:
- The Ship: death far from home;
- The Snake: by poisoning or hanging;
- The Coffin + The Tower: by asphyxiation or suffocation;
- The Scythe + The Anchor: occupational accident;
- The Broom and The Whip + The Scythe: by physical violence
- The Tower: old-age death;
- The Lilies: by freezing;
- The Fish + The Anchor: by drowning;
- The Ship or The Fish: in water or bleeding;
- The Rider with cards that announce death predicts an imminent death;
- The House or The Lilies: death of a close relative;
- The Bouquet, The Garden, or The Letter predicts that the querent will attend a funeral.
- The Rider, The Ship + The Storks, or The Roads announce the "passage" from this life to the next (death).

Theme Cards for Magic

In my 38 years as a fortune teller, I've done countless readings and found relatively few querents who were affected by magical powers. Most people who came to me with suspicions of magical influence were actually dealing with everyday life challenges and difficulties. For example:

- They were going through periods of dissatisfaction with life, disappointments, and a lack of courage and attitude to pursue their goals;
- They were influenced by emotional, psychological, and religious factors, as well as by family, friends, and even their community, which impacted their choices and freedom of expression;
- They faced unemployment and financial hardships, leading to anxiety, sleepless nights, and even hunger;
- They were dealing with personal issues, such as divorce, conflicts with the family or partner, and problems with their children related to substance abuse. They may also be suffering the consequences of poor decisions, such as debts, bankruptcy, depression, or even severe disease;
- They became targets of envy, slander, and harmful behavior from others;
- And so on.

These and other situations can cause emotional and mental strain, making people think they might be under the influence of magic. However, it's crucial not to jump to conclusions and blame others without evidence of a magical ritual. Furthermore, accusing an innocent person of committing an evil act can bring powerful and negative energies into our lives, which may slowly lead to ruin and potentially affect our loved ones, such as our spouse or children.

The Petit Lenormand deck has specific cards that can help identify if someone is under the influence of magic, the type of magic, who may have caused it, and what needs to be done to remove it.

The Broom and The Whip card is the primary significator card for spells, but it must always be accompanied by one or more of the following cards:

- The Clouds
- The Snake
- The Coffin
- The Owls
- The Tower
- The Mice
- The Book
- The Cross

THE THEME CARDS FOR MAGIC AND ESOTERISM

Card no. 1: The Rider

The Rider is the messenger from beyond, the divine messenger. When this card appears in a reading, it announces the arrival of something identified by the card next to it.

The Ride
- \+ The Clouds + The Broom and The Whip: magic spell
- \+ The Sun: receiving Reiki.

Card no. 2: The Clover

Herbs and amulets.

Card no. 3: The Ship

The sea, magic water. Magic from distant places or foreigner cultures. Telepathy, astral travel, or astral projection.

The Ship
- \+ The Coffin: a medium or psychic.

Card no. 4: The House

Protection, talismans, magic or traditional family rituals.

The House
- + The Coffin: a tombstone, a grave;
- + The Mice: no protection.

Card no. 5: The Tree

The magic from the trees, the rituals associated with nature, "terreiro," runes, and chakras. When The Tree shows up in a reading, it usually means that the querent has a karmic connection with the past, family, or ancestors.

Card no. 6: The Clouds

Magic, spirits, incense, powder, cigarettes, cigars (cigar reading). The evil eye.

The Clouds
- + The Coffin: it warns of the presence of disturbing spirits;
- + The Coffin + The Stars: black magic, witchery.

Card no. 7: The Snake

Hypnosis, sorcery, and witchcraft. It can also be associated with darker practices such as demon magic, satanism, and devil worship. Ropes, wires, threads, and ribbons are used in magic rituals. It suggests that a spell was cast on the querent as revenge. The hidden adversaries represented by The Snake Card are powerful. This card can represent an ex-partner or a malicious mother-in-law. The Snake combined with The Clouds card may denote that the current ex-partner's partner, or father-in-law is practicing magic or evil against the querent.

The Snake
- + The Fox: A charlatan, a quack;
- + The Ring: Several people are conspiring against the querent. A satanic ritual;
- + The Cross: Satanic mass.

Card no. 8: The Coffin

Necromancy, black magic, a destructive magical effect, or dead people. It can also represent objects like a box or a coffin.

The Coffin
- \+ The Snake: sorcery, witchcraft;
- \+ The Mice: it alerts to the presence of disturbing spirits;
- \+ The Cross: spell performed or buried in the cemetery.

Card no. 9: The Bouquet

Plants, herbs, and aromatic oils.

The Bouquet
- \+ The Stars + The Owls + The Coffin: psychic painting.

Card no. 10: The Scythe

Rituals involving sharp objects like knives, scissors, needles, pins, or blades. Animal or human sacrifices. Karma. As The Scythe has a cutting and eliminating function, it means you'll successfully reverse a negative situation and overcome the enemy.

Card no. 11: The Broom and The Whip

Magic, a sorceress, or a pendulum.

The Broom and The Whip
- \+ The Coffin: black magic;
- \+ The Moon: moon magic;
- \+ The Cross: magic with prayers.

Card no. 12: The Owls

Visions and curses.

The Owls
- \+ The Snake: evil-eye, a healer, or fortune teller;
- \+ The Coffin: invoking the dead people;

- + The Stars: the person has the gift of clairvoyance;
- + The Stars + The Moon: an astrologer;
- + The Book: a fortune teller;
- + The Moon: visions, a medium or psychic;
- + The Cross: prayer.

Card no. 13: The Child

Angels. Magic dolls.

Card no. 14: The Fox

Charlatans and false prophets.

Card no. 15: The Bear

A guardian, shaman, guru, and protector. Power and strength.

- The Bear + The Stars: a spiritual guide.

Card no. 16: The Stars

Clairvoyance, psychics, magic, spirituality, but also geomancy, numerology, and symbols.

Card no. 17: The Storks

Attention! When The Stork card appears next to the whip, it usually announces the return of a spell.

Card no. 18: The Dog

Protection, the guardian angel, and a protector.

The Dog

- + The Tree: runic protection;
- + The Stars: divine protection.

Card no. 19: The Tower

Tao, magic, sorceress, occultism, or a hermit.

- The Tower + The Cross: a church, mosque, or synagogue.

Card no. 20: The Garden
The "terreiro".
- The Garden + The Coffin: magic ritual practiced in a cemetery.

Card no. 21: The Mountain
Crystals and crystal therapy. If a magic spell has been cast on the querent or is in progress, it will be blocked or difficult to reach them. When The Mountain touches the broom side (I'll describe this method later), it acts as a protective barrier.

Card no. 22: The Crossroads
Magical rituals performed at crossroads or on the road. It also reveals the specific type of "magical ritual" necessary to clarify the querent's paths.

Card no. 23: The Mice
Negative influences, witchcraft, and also the presence of disturbing spirits.

Card no. 24: The Heart
Magical rituals involving blood or human organs.

Card no. 25: The Ring
The Ring card refers to rituals, *love binding*[1] or repeating unskilled tasks.

The Ring

+ The Scythe: karmic connections;
+ The Stars: mandalas;
+ The Book: sects, occultism, or esoteric communities;
+ The Cross: magic rituals

---

1. T/N: In Afro-Brazilian religion, love binding refers to rituals and spells to attract or maintain a romantic relationship, strengthen the bond between the partners, or prevent a partner from straying.

Card no. 26: The Book

Secret teaching, the study of occult sciences, the Akashic records, a deck of cards, and astrology charts.

The Book

- + The Coffin: necromancy;
- + The Stars + The Moon: astrology studies;
- + The Crossroads: chirology studies.

Card no. 27: The Letter

Talismans, amulets (Tawiz), photography, and paper.

To protect themselves against their enemy, Islamic warriors used amulets containing excerpts from the Koran written in Arabic on small pieces of paper and placed them inside hand-sewn leather pouches. The writings included phrases such as "Help us against those who reject the faith" and "Save us from this city whose people are oppressors!". They believed that each talisman protected against certain weapons – for example, the "laya" protected from arrows and the "maganin karfe" from knives. An illustration from 1835 depicts a fragment of Arabic text discovered in a Malian amulet (Tawiz), which reads: "Victory comes from Allah!"

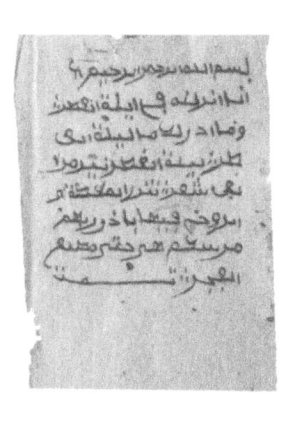

The Letter

- + The Coffin: messages from the dead;
- + The Broom and The Whip + The Stars + The Sun: radionic table;
- + The Owls + The Stars + The Coffin: psychography;
- + The Key + The Coffin: Ouija table.

Card no. 28: The Man and Card no. 29: The Woman

If the querent's card falls on the whip side, examine the other cards closely, as they may indicate that the querent is harming themselves.

Card no. 30: The Lilies

Sexual rituals and also Eastern practices such as yoga.

Card no. 31: The Sun

Magic involving fire and candles and also energy-based practices such as Reiki.

Card no. 32: The Moon

The use of crystal balls and the practice of moon magic.

Card no. 33: The Key

Contacts, connections, interpretation, and revelation. At the entrance of a house.

The Key
- + <u>The Ship</u>: dream interpretation;
- + <u>The Stars</u> + <u>The Ship</u>: tasseography (coffee ground reading);
- + <u>The Stars</u> + <u>The Crossroads</u>: palmistry (hand-reading);
- + <u>The Moon</u>: strong intuition.

Card no. 34: The Fish

Magic involving water, sea, river, and lake.

Card no. 35: The Anchor

Protection.

Card no. 36: The Cross

Rituals using religious objects and icons, such as saint statues, crucifixes, etc. Religious rituals, worship places, temples, and prayers.

When several cards representing animals or birds come up in the reading, it indicates the involvement of animals in the ritual or Totem animals.

The cards that represent the querent's life area that will be or have already been affected by the magic and require a cleansing ritual are:
- The Rider: a vehicle (car, motorcycle, etc.);
- The Clover: luck;
- The Ship: travels;
- The House: the domestic environment;
- The Tree: the health, the body, and life in general;
- The Stars: the spirituality;
- The Dog: pets or friendships;
- The Crossroads: to lose life guidance;
- The Ring: a relationship, marriage, or dating;
- The Book: the studies;
- The Fish: business, or finance;
- The Anchor: the work;
- The Cross: faith.

Note

I created a card spread to identify any magic or negative energy affecting the querent or their environment. It's in Chapter 6: Reading Methods (page 438).

Other Topics

The Meanings of Cards for Places

Card no. 1: The Rider

The Rider card represents any place within the querent's neighborhood (city or nearby country). It refers to a gym, sports training facility, racetrack, stables, and delivery services. It also applies to car and motorcycle dealers. On the road.

The Rider

- + The House: a garage;
- + The Tower: the border, frontier
- + The Garden: golf or soccer field

Card no. 2: The Clover

The Clover card indicates places or buildings for gambling, such as a casino or where lottery tickets are sold. It also includes gardens and areas covered with grass.

Card no. 3: The Ship

The Ship card represents a location geographically distant from the querent's home, such as a foreign city or country. It stands for a train, bus station, port, or tourist destination. This card also refers to areas with water, such as canals, swamps, seas, lakes, rivers, oceans, and continents. In addition, places with plumbing, such as laundries and bathrooms. The Ship may also indicate an embassy or an international company. Bazaars or spice stores that sell various spices and condiments are also depicted by this card.

The Ship

- + The House: a house abroad or a vacation home.
- + The Tower: the border, the custom

Card no. 4: The House

The House card refers to one's own house or apartment. It can also represent where the querent lives or spends most of their time. Along with The Tree card, it denotes a store or a clinic and the querent's neighborhood or city. The House card, accompanied by The Ship and The Stars, stands for a website, such as Facebook, Instagram, eBay, etc.

The House

+ The Clover: a bookmaker;
+ The Ship: an apartment or a house abroad;
+ The Tree: the family's home, birthplace, a furniture store;
+ The Clouds: a tobacco store, a steam room;
+ The Snake: a drugstore;
+ The Broom and The Whip: a laundromat;
+ The Child: a nursery; elemental school;
+ The Bear: the kitchen;
+ The Garden: living room, garden, or yard;
+ The Book + The Garden: elemental or high school;
+ The Letter: post office;
+ The Woman: women's shelter;
+ The Lilies: grandparents' house or retirement home;
+ The Lilies + The Fish: brothel;
+ The Fish + The Garden: restaurant or bar;
+ The Cross: a chapel or small church.

Card no. 5: The Tree

The Tree card represents not only forests, groves, orchards, and plots of land but also the querent's country or hometown. While The House card symbolizes the city or the neighborhood where we live, The Tree card stands for our country, hometown, and origin. Additionally, it refers to agricultural or forestry companies and healthcare facilities. In some cultures, like Candomblé, an African religion, The Tree card also indicates the "terreiro", the sacred place where religious rituals are performed.

The Tree
- + The House: a clinic;
- + The Snake: a drugstore;
- + The Garden: an orchard.

Card no. 6: The Clouds

The Clouds card stands for damp or foggy places, industrial areas, a factory, a tobacco shop, a smoking area, or a steam room. It also means something hidden, behind the curtains. This card is also associated with London.

Card no. 7: The Snake

The Snake card depicts roads, paths, and streets, as well as hospitals, drugstores or healing places. It also indicates stores that sell hoses, pipes, ropes, and wires.

Card no. 8: The Coffin

The Coffin card can indicate cold, dark, enclosed spaces and areas affected by catastrophic events or natural disasters. It refers to tunnels, cemeteries, tombs, mortuaries, caves, or ruins. The Coffin can also represent a flush, landfills, garbage, bathrooms, basements, attics, garages, cupboards, closets, drawers, and shelves. This card also suggests that something is well hidden or buried underground.

The Coffin
- + The Snake: cupboard or medicine box;
- + The Coffin + The Garden: a cemetery.

Card no. 9: The Bouquet

The Bouquet card represents hair salons, beauty clinics, clothing and accessories stores, cosmetics stores, gardens, flower shops, and perfumery. It indicates herb or natural food stores, handicrafts, and art galleries. This card is also associated with The Netherlands.

Card no. 10: The Scythe

The Scythe card is associated with agricultural companies, plowed and cultivated farmlands, and agricultural and mechanics supply stores. It also denotes areas for vehicle dismantling areas, licensed shooting ranges, and auto repair shops. This card may indicate emergency and operating rooms, dentist's offices, and butcher shops.

Card no. 11: The Broom and The Whip

The Broom and The Whip card may stand for places related to physical activities, such as martial arts, boxing, or judo academy, and places like courthouses, police stations, reformatories, or correctional facilities.

The Broom and The Whip

- + The Stars: a music hall;
- + The Stars + The Bouquet: a painting room;
- + The Garden: a dance hall.

Card no. 12: The Owls

The Owls card represents a place you visit regularly or an area associated with birds, chickens, nests, cages, aviary, and chicken coop. It also indicates recording studios, radio stations, telephone and electronics stores, or small airports.

Card no. 13: The Child

The Child card stands for playgrounds, nurseries, and rooms or spaces designed for children or teenagers to play or learn.

Card no. 14: The Fox

The Fox card represents areas for hunting or trapping. This card is associated with China.

Card no. 15: The Bear

The Bear card is related to banks, financial institutions, stock exchanges, and safes. It describes zoos, national parks (with The Garden card), kitchens, dining rooms, and restaurants.

Card no. 16: The Stars

The Stars card depicts cold places or the north. It can represent esoteric stores, planetariums, concert halls, movie theaters, and stores that sell or repairs electronic devices and computers. This card is associated with Israel, a country in Hebrew territory.

The Stars
+ <u>The Garden</u>: theaters, movie theaters, art galleries;
+ <u>The Mountain</u>: gems and crystal store.

Card no. 17: The Storks

The Storks card may refer to stairs, escalators, elevators, roofs, chimneys, atriums, the top floor of a building, and busy places.
If you're looking for something that has been lost, this card indicates that it could be in a high place; the surrounding cards will provide more details.

Card no. 18: The Dog

The Dog card represents pet-related places, such as pet stores, kennels, veterinary clinics, areas reserved for pets, and guardian places.

Card no. 19: The Tower

The Tower card is associated with large cities, capitals, and states. It also denotes multinational corporations, banks, and historical and governmental landmarks, such as monuments, statues, museums, and castles, as well as hospitals, or medical centers, schools, universities, and vocational training institutes are described by this card. This card includes transportation systems like train stations, bus stations, ports, and airports. The Tower card indicates tall structures or high places like cupboards, shelves, elevators, high-rise buildings, and also fences, walls, or on the floor. It can stand for isolation or seclusion, such as in prisons, and also historical statues.

The Tower
- \+ The Tree: a hospital, health care center, health department;
- \+ The Clouds: industrial area, a polluted area in the city;
- \+ The Broom and The Whip: police station, court;
- \+ The Mountain: prison;
- \+ The Garden: public building, shopping center store, hotel;
- \+ The Garden + The Ship: train station or port;
- \+ The Garden + The Owls: domestic airport;
- \+ The Garden + The Storks: international airport;
- \+ The Mountain: the border, frontier, custom;
- \+ The Mountain + The Broom and The Whip: prison;
- \+ The Ring: registry office;
- \+ The Owls: telephone company;
- \+ The Letter: post office;
- \+ The Book + The Garden: library; university;
- \+ The Fish: finance department, taxes;
- \+ The Cross: church, cathedral, sanctuary, convent. The Vatican.

Card no. 20: The Garden

The Garden describes public spaces, including streets, squares, parks, gardens, markets, shopping malls, restaurants, bars, stadiums, movie theaters, theaters, train stations, bus stations, ports, and airports. It may also refer to art galleries, exhibitions, street fairs, concerts, and conference halls. In addition, this card relates to residential complexes, parking lots, dining rooms, living rooms, and any place you visit frequently.

The Garden
- \+ The Tree: a park, a wood,
- \+ The Bouquet: a garden

Card no. 21: The Mountain

The Mountain card indicates high and elevated city areas, like hills, mountains, and rocky terrain far from the coast. It also refers to mountainous countries or cities, like the Alps or volcano regions. This card also represents places with stones or an accumulation of objects, such as piles of clothes or papers, and can denote confinement, like prisons. The Mountain card may also be associated with high places, such as the top shelf.

Card no. 22: The Crossroads

The Crossroads card represents roads, streets, vias, paths, ways, routes, detours, crossroads, a bifurcation, overpasses, and laboratories.

The Crossroads

+ <u>The Snake</u>: road with lots of curves, a detour;
+ <u>The Coffin</u>: dead-end street.

Card no. 23: The Mice

The Mice card stands for impoverished, precarious, or infamous areas where illegal activities, like prostitution or drug smuggling, occur. This card also indicates markets, warehouses, and second-hand stores, as well as storage places, basements, cellars, garages, and underground spaces. It may refer to unpleasant or foul-smelling places like sewers, landfills, recycling centers, or the ground.

Card no. 24: The Heart

The Heart represents your favorite places where you feel comfortable to stay. This card also includes medical facilities that deal with heart-related issues and organ donation.

Card no. 25: The Ring

The Ring card refers to places a spouse or partner frequently visits, such as clubs, associations, or committees, and it also denotes jewelry stores.

Card no. 26: The Book

The Book card represents schools, bookstores, libraries, study areas, and archive or record-keeping spaces. It also stands for offices, publishing houses, reserved or secretive places, and even a confessional.

Card no. 27: The Letter

The Letter card indicates offices, post offices, mailboxes, printing press, and box offices for movie tickets and transportation (buses, trains, etc.). It can also denote reception areas in places like hotels.

Card no. 28: The Man or Card no. 29: The Woman

These cards indicate locations where the querent visits frequently.

Card no. 30: The Lilies

The Lilies card depicts cold, freezing, or snowy regions and northern areas. It may also be associated with Hindu regions or countries.

Card no. 31: The Sun

The Sun card represents warm, southern regions, tropical countries, and deserts. In addition, this card suggests proximity to heat sources, such as a stove, oven, boiler, fireplace, sunny or well-lit areas, saunas, solariums, and electricity-related places. This card is also associated with Japan.

Card no. 32: The Moon

The Moon card indicates illuminated areas and is often associated with Islamic regions, countries, and mosques.

Card no. 33: The Key

The Key card indicates a locked or closed space, such as the entrance door. It can also mean where you keep your keys for the house, car, or TV remote control, and an insurance agency as well.

Card no. 34: The Fish

The Fish card describes flooded or wet areas, oceans, seas, lakes, rivers, pools, bathtubs, whirlpools, sinks, basins, and showers. This card is associated with financial places such as banks or exchange offices. It also includes fishing areas, fish markets, and Japanese restaurants.

The Fish

+ <u>The Garden</u>: a pool, a bar;
+ <u>The Anchor</u>: an island.

Card no. 35: The Anchor

It represents the workplace, coastal zones, port cities, and islands.

Card no. 36: The Cross

The Cross is associated with places of religious worship, such as churches, convents, monasteries, and sanctuaries. It can also indicate a Christian region or a graveyard.

CARDS REPRESENTING BUILDINGS

In the Petit Lenormand deck, card no. 4, The House, and card no. 19, The Tower, identify buildings. In order to deeper understand these cards and the differences between the buildings they represent, it's essential to know the following:

- The House card represents small private or public structures. Keep in mind that, in a reading that requires a significator card, The House will stand for a house, apartment, office, branch of a large company, den, nest, dog or cat house, birdcage, chicken coop, barn, aquarium, etc.

- The Tower card identifies large private or public buildings. In a reading, The Tower depicts the post office building, administrative offices, the telephone company or the electric power company offices, train stations, airports, laboratories, humanitarian (Red Cross, Caritas, UNO) and religious organizations (monasteries, churches, parishes, cathedrals, and monasteries). It also indicates banks, hospitals, courts, police stations, prisons, schools, universities, factories, apartment buildings, monuments, museums, castles, military headquarters, and buildings in general.

Therefore, to accurately identify the building during a reading, you should look closely at the cards that touch The House and The Tower. I will then share some examples from my consultations.

Combinations with The House Card

The House
- + The Ship: a travel agency, a real estate firm (independent), a house by the sea or a houseboat (with The Anchor), also a home abroad, and a foreigner's residence;
- + The Tree: the family home, or a wooden house, like a hut. In a professional reading, this combination indicates a family business. It also means a tree house, a house outside the city, a place in the home country, home acquisition, an outpatient clinic, and a doctor's office;
- + The Tree + The Ship: house for vacations; clinic, outpatient clinics, doctor's offices, nursing homes; plantation;
- + The Tree + The Dog: a veterinary clinic;
- + The Tree + The Lilies: nursing homes;
- + The Clouds + The Dog: a house haunted by spirits;
- + The Snake: drugstores, the competitor's or rival's house;
- + The Bouquet + The Garden: a house with a beautiful garden, cosmetics stores, home accessories or women's products stores, perfumeries, souvenirs stores; flower shops;

- The Coffin: a tomb, a deposit tomb, a cave, a grotto, a wine cellar; a funeral parlor;
- The Broom and The Whip: a gym or a cleaning company;
- The Broom and The Whip + The House: two houses;
- The Child: a small house; a two-room house; a new house or the building of a new house;
- The Child + The Tower: an orphanage;
- The Stars: the dream house, an esoterica house, a house with modern architecture;
- The Storks: a mobile home; moving home;
- The Storks + The House: house renovation;
- The Dog: a friend's house, a neighbor's house, a kennel, the doghouse;
- The Tower: the branch of a large company (the card following The Tower will indicate which company it refers to); the head office; a village; the city council;
- The Garden: a pension house, a hotel; a store
- The Garden + The Fish: a restaurant, a bar, or a pub;
- The Mountain: a house in the mountains, a house made of rock or stone; an alpine hut;
- The Crossroads + The Garden: a motel;
- The Mice: a hovel, an abandoned house;
- The Mice + The House: a ruined or damaged house;
- The Book + The Tower: a private school;
- The Book + The Mice: a second-hand bookstore;
- The Book + The Garden: a second-hand library;
- The Sun: a house for vacation in a tropical country or the South;
- The Fish: a bureau de change (foreign currency) or the sending of money overseas or to more distant places; a real estate agency;
- The Fish + The Child: a toy store;
- The Anchor: the main house;

- + The Church: a church, a chapel;
- + The Rider + The House (keeping in mind that The House card is behind The Rider): a caravan, a campsite.

Combinations with The Tower Card

The Tower

- + The Clover: small buildings, casinos;
- + The House: an apartment in a building, the city hall. If The House card precedes The Fish card, it indicates an apartment in a luxury condominium. If The Garden falls after The House, it represents a shopping center;
- + The House + The Stars (or The Stocks): an apartment on the top floor of a building; a penthouse;
- + The Tree: The Ministry of Health;
- + The Tree + The Coffin: a hospital;
- + The Tree + The Snake: a mental hospital;
- + The Tree + The Storks: a maternity hospital;
- + The Broom and The Whip: police stations;
- + The Stars (or The Moon) + The Garden: movie theaters, theaters;
- + The Garden: shopping centers, malls, public buildings, hotels,
- + The Ring + The Ship: multinational companies;
- + The Book: schools, universities, institutions for vocational training;
- + The Book + The Cross: theology or religion schools;
- + The Book + The Stars: scientific laboratories;
- + The Book + The Garden: libraries;
- + The Fish: bank, financial institution;
- + The Fish + The Bear: financial departments;
- + The Cross: religious institutions, churches, monasteries, convents, etc.

The Objects represented in the Cards

Card no. 1: The Rider
Car, motorcycle, bicycle, or other personal vehicle, such as roller skates and skateboards. Communication items include telephones, cell phones, computers, and other similar items.

Card no. 2: The Clover
Gambling activities (bingo, lottery) and objects that bring luck, good fortune, and protection, such as talismans or amulets.

Card no. 3: The Ship
Foreign currency. Vases, cups, mugs, bathtubs, household appliances, as well as traditional items acquired during travels, replicas of sailboats or boats, nautical and swimming pool equipment and accessories, and water vessels like boats, canoes, kayaks, and surfboards.

Card no. 4: The House
Typical household items, including furniture, trousseaus, and other domestic belongings.

Card no. 5: The Tree
Wooden furniture, sculptures crafted from blackwood or other types of wood, and tools used by carpenters or sculptors.

Card no. 6: The Clouds
Curtains, veils, ceilings, blankets, masks, thermometers, blood pressure measuring devices, accessories for cigarettes and cigars, steamer, fans, and heaters.

Card no. 7: The Snake

Ropes, wires, lines, tubes, pipes, hydraulics, hoses, bamboo, bracelets, and rubber bands. Accessories made of animal skin, such as belts, bracelets, shoes, purses, etc. Items belonging to a rival or lover.

Card no. 8: The Coffin

Containers, boxes, crates, bed trunks, wardrobes, chest of drawers, wallets, and cases. Belongings of the deceased like bags, sports bags, medicine boxes, jewelry boxes, and document boxes. Laundry baskets, trash cans, coffins, and aquariums.

Card no. 9: The Bouquet

Beauty cosmetics and accessories, paints, artist tools, crafts, gardening, ornaments (Christmas or for other festivals), and gifts.

Card no. 10: The Scythe

Metal or cutting and sharp objects, such as knives, forks, needles, pins, syringes, nails, arrows, glasses, and blades. Surgical and dental instruments, scissors, chainsaws, firearms, crossbows, swords, axes, and agricultural and mechanical tools.

Card no. 11: The Broom and The Whip

Pens, pencils, brushes, cleaning tools (brooms, mops, etc.), sticks, bamboo, and pendulum. Gymnastic and sporting items. Objects for sexual or sadomasochism practice.

Card no. 12: The Owls

The devices and gadgets included are hearing aids, microphones, TVs, radios, MP3 players, CDs, floppy disks, and telephones.

Card no. 13: The Child

Toys, games for children, and children's personal belongings.

Card no. 14: The Fox
Masks, disguises, wigs, fake teeth, forgery, fake jewelry, and traps.

Card no. 15: The Bear
Wallets, savings accounts, restaurant-related items, and parents' personal belongings.

Card no. 16: The Stars
Esoteric items, equipment, and electronic devices, including maps, GPS navigators, telescopes, cinematographic equipment, and police badges.

Card no. 17: The Storks
Stairs, ladders, and aircraft accessories.

Card no. 18: The Dog
Best friend's personal belongings. Items associated with pets, such as their house and objects like a brush or collar. Alarms.

Card no. 19: The Tower
Bulletproof vests, tall cupboards, toy cabinets, safe boxes, and items related to government or organizations.

Card no. 20: The Garden
Gardening and farming equipment.

Card no. 21: The Mountain
Meteorites, marble, stones, crystals, and gym weights.

Card no. 22: The Crossroads
Road signs, geographic map, and shoes.

Card no. 23: The Mice
Used and worn items, little value objects. Lost or stolen belongings. Jewelry and trinkets.

Card no. 24: The Heart

Sentimental and significant objects associated with special memories or inherited belongings.

Card no. 25: The Ring

Valuable items and jewelry including rings, bracelets, earrings, and watches. Handcuffs. Round objects and things that belong to a partner, spouse, or group.

Card no. 26: The Book

Books, USB pens, CDs, notebooks, journals, diaries, manuals, sketches, tablets, laptops, passports, photo albums, astrological birth charts, packs, decks of cards, and printers.

Card no. 27: The Letter

Newspapers, magazines, envelopes, mail, packages, papers, documents, cardboards, ID cards, driver's licenses, credit cards, and checkbooks. Signs or advertising materials, business cards, document folders (receipts, bills), tickets (for trains, planes, buses, etc.). Desks, counters, and items found on desks.

Card no. 28: The Man and Card no. 29: The Woman

Personal items belong to the querent or their partner. Clothing and accessories for men or women.

Card no. 30: The Lilies

Refrigerator, freezer. Sexual items.

Card no. 31: The Sun

Light bulbs, batteries, cell phone chargers, matches, lighters, and candles. Heating pad, electrician's equipment, and gold objects.

Card no. 32: The Moon

Silver objects and medals.

Card no. 33: The Key

Small metal items, such as keys, instruments, and tools. Objects that open and close, like padlocks, faucets, switches, remote controls, and cell phones.

Card no. 34: The Fish

Valuable items and coins. Accessories for fishing or aquariums. Hair gel.

Card no. 35: The Anchor

Dental plaques, iron, machinery, engines, and working tools and equipment.

Card no. 36: The Cross

Religious or ritual object.

The Animals in the Petit Lenormand

Card no. 1: The Rider

Transport animals such as horses, donkeys, camels, yaks, reindeers, huskies, elephants (The Rider with The Bear), bulls, and cows.

- The Rider + The Tower: giraffe

Card no. 7: The Snake

Reptiles, scorpions, earthworms, lizards, chameleons, and iguanas.

The Snake

+ The House: snails;
+ The Bouquet: chameleons;
+ The Fish + The Scythe: crocodiles.

Card no. 12: The Owls

Birds, owls, bats, crows, doves, chickens, roosters, parrots, pheasants, and bees.

The Owls
- + <u>The Bouquet</u>: butterflies, hummingbirds;
- + <u>The Storks</u>: swallows;
- + <u>The Letter</u>: carrier-pigeons.

Card no. 14: The Fox

Stray cats and dogs, wolves, foxes, tigers, lions, leopards, wild boars, and other wild predator animals.

Card no. 15: The Bear

Bears, koalas, chamois, pala-palas, deers, buffalos, and elephants.

The Bear
- + <u>The Lilies</u>: polar bears;
- + <u>The Fish</u>: hippopotamus.

Card no. 17: The Storks

Large birds or animals that migrate to warmer places to breed, such as ostriches, peacocks, and swans.

Card no. 18: The Dog

Pets: cats and dogs.

Card no. 23: The Mice

Rodents, mice, groundhogs, squirrels, rabbits, and ants. In my readings, I've noticed that The Mice cards can represent animals that serve as lab guinea pigs.

Card no. 34: The Fish

Microclimate animals, fish, whales, lobsters, crustaceans, cuttlefish, tuna, frogs, seals, dolphins, whales, orcas, and sharks.

The Fish
- + <u>The House</u>: crabs, turtles;
- + <u>The Scythe</u>: sharks, orcas.

Numbers and Quantity in the Cards

The Numbers

- <u>Zero</u>: The Coffin
- <u>One</u>: The Tower
- <u>Two</u>: The Broom and The Whip or The Owls
- <u>Three</u>: The Crossroads
- <u>Four</u>: The Clover or The Cross
- <u>Five</u>: The Rider
- <u>Six</u>: The Snake
- <u>Seven</u>: The Scythe
- <u>Eight</u>: The Stars
- <u>Nine</u>: The Lilies

Quantity

- <u>A lot / plenty of</u>: The Stars
- <u>Little / small amount</u>: The Mice

In Mathematic

- <u>Division</u>: The Scythe
- <u>Addition</u>: The Stars
- <u>Subtraction</u>: The Mice
- <u>Multiplication</u>: The Fish

The Colors on the Cards

- <u>White</u>: The Lilies
- <u>Black</u>: The Coffin
- <u>Gray</u>: The Clouds, The Mountain, and The Mice
- <u>Silver, Gray</u>: The Moon and The Keys
- <u>Gold, Bronze, Copper</u>: The Cross
- <u>Yellow</u>: The Sun
- <u>Blue</u>: The Ship, The Fish and The Man
- <u>Pink</u>: The Woman
- <u>Green</u>: The Clover and The Tree
- <u>Orange, Reddish, Brown</u>: The Fox
- <u>Brown</u>: The Broom and The Whip, The Bear
- <u>Red</u>: The Heart
- <u>Colorful</u>: The Bouquet

Some cards describe the shading of colors: ranging from light to dark, for example:

- The Sun: lighter shades of colors;
- The Coffin: darker shades of color;
- The Stars: bright, luminous, and metallic shades;
- The Mice: bleached colors, discolored colors due time;
- The Bouquet: several shades of color;
- The Child: pastel colors.

For example, The Clover:

+ The Coffin: dark green;
+ The Sun: light green;
+ The Stars: metallic green;
+ The Bouquet: various shades of green.

Food, nutrition, drinks, diet on the cards

- The Rider: beef, horse meat;
- The Clover: vegetarianism;
- The Ship: foreign foods (fruit, vegetables, spices, and condiments);
- The Tree: fruits, olives, chestnuts, nuts, dates, coconut, coffee;
- The Clouds: smoked food;
- The Bouquet: tea;
- The Scythe: flour, grapes;
- The Owls: chicken, duck, and turkey;
- The Fox: boar, hare, and rabbit;
- The Bear: greasy food;
- The Garden: seasonal vegetables and fruit. Vegetarian food;

- The Mice: all discarded food, food has passed its expiration date, and moldy food. Diet food and beverages;
- The Heart: sugar, chocolate, ice cream, sweets, dessert (cakes and puddings);
- The Lilies: canned, pickled, frozen foods, sausages, and cheese;
- The Sun: dry food (meat, fish, fruit);
- The Fish: sea food such as crabs, shellfish, lobster, sardines, tuna, shrimp, seaweed, and alcoholic beverages.

CHAPTER 3: POLARITY AND SIGNIFICATOR CARD

PREDICTING TIME

Fortune tellers often struggle to predict the timing of events accurately in a reading. Querents often ask questions like: "How long will it take me to find a job?" or "When will my son come home?" and so on.

Each fortune teller has their own "secret" way of estimating timing, and I believe that with consistent practice, you'll also develop your own method. Below, I provide some guidelines that can serve as a reference for calculating time in your reading.

To understand the basic rules for determining time in a reading, it's necessary to know the following 5 points.

1. Understanding the card energies

Which are the fast cards?

Dynamic and fast cards represent fast timing. The event can happen on the same day or in the next few days.

- The Rider
- The Owls
- The Clover
- The Storks
- The Clouds
- The Letter
- The Bouquet
- The Key
- The Scythe
- The Fish
- The Broom and The Whip

Which are the slow cards?

Slow cards indicate that the event will take time, but continually developing.

- The Ship
- The Stars
- The Tree
- The Dog
- The Child
- The Book
- The Bear

Which are the stop cards?

The stop cards have no movement. Instead, these cards extend time, delay or prevent the immediate progress of an event.

- The House
- The Coffin
- The Tower
- The Mountain
- The Lilies
- The Anchor
- The Cross

2. Cards that represent the time of day

These cards can define what part of the day the event will happen:
- During the day: The Sun;
- At dawn: The Coffin + The Sun;
- In the afternoon: The Garden;
- At night: The Stars and The Moon.

3. The Seasons of the Year

These cards can determine what time of day the event will take place:
- Spring: The Bouquet;
- Summer: The Sun;
- Autumn / Fall: The Clouds;
- Winter: The Lilies.

The cards that determine the beginning, middle, or end of a season

The Child card indicates the beginning of the season, day, week, month, or year.

The Child
- + <u>The Bouquet</u>: The beginning of the spring
- + <u>The Sun</u>: The beginning of the summer, early morning, at dawn.

The Mice card represents the middle of the season, day, week, month, or year.

The Mice
- \+ The Mountain: The Mice card lessens the delay caused by The Mountain;
- \+ The Lilies: The middle of the winter;
- \+ The Sun: The middle of the summer.

The Coffin represents the end of the season, day, month, or year.

- The Sun + The Coffin: it stands for the end of the year, but also for the end of the summer or the end of the day (sunset, late afternoon);
- The Lilies + The Coffin: the end of the winter.

Important Note:
When The Stork card shows up in a timing spread, it indicates a change of season, day, week, month, or year.

Addition Cards

These cards can increase the number of days, weeks, and years:
- The Broom and The Whip
- The Owls

These two cards double the amount of time of the card next to it. For example:

The Broom and The Whip
- \+ The Tree: it indicates two years since The Broom and The Whip card represents No. 2, and The Tree card denotes one year;
- \+ The Bouquet: two seasons of Spring;
- \+ The Sun: two seasons of Summer.

The same interpretation applies to The Owl card; it always indicates two of something.

TIMING IN THE CARDS

Each card contains a specific timing determined by the energy and the meaning of the symbol it represents. In the following section, I'll present you the time breakdown of the timing in the 36 cards.

Card no. 1: The Rider

» Time: from one to ten days, quickly, soon, a weekend, or a very short-term trip.

» Advice: It's time to act.

> **Important Note:**
> The Rider is a dynamic and fast-paced card. It announces that something is about to happen or is currently on its way. To determine the time accurately, it's essential to check the surrounding cards. For example, if a stop card like The Mountain or The Anchor is nearby, it suggests that the event may occur, but after the initial timing indicated by Ther Rider card.

Card no. 2: The Clover

» Time: A short-term period. Something will occur unexpectedly and surprise the querent. Between two and four days.

Card no. 3: The Ship

» Time: The waiting period can be quite lengthy, ranging from three months to three years. However, if the combination of The Ship + The Clover shows up in a timing spread, it indicates a shorter waiting time. During the vacation.

» Advice: Allow things to unfold naturally. Don't rush! Patient is essential during this time.

Card no. 4: The House

- <u>Time</u>: Something will last for a long time.
- <u>Time of day</u>: During a break or rest period

Card no. 5: The Tree

- <u>Time</u>: For a long time, one year or more.
- <u>Advice</u>: It's a slow-paced card, indicating a slow and gradual development, so be patient.

Card no. 6: The Clouds

- <u>Time</u>: Some setbacks may delay achieving a goal or completing a project. Thus, the timing is still being determined. Fast, quick, and brief.
- <u>Season</u>: Rainy season; autumn (fall).
- <u>Weather and temperature</u>: rainy weather, cloudy skies, and instability.

Card no. 7: The Snake

- <u>Time</u>: Based on my readings, The Snake card predicts a long time due to significant complications caused by third parties. Delays.

Card no. 8: The Coffin

- <u>Time</u>: Never-ending, forever
- <u>Season</u>: At the end of the season.
- <u>Weather and temperature</u>: Cold.
- It'll never happen, so don't persist in a situation that has already ended.

Important Note:
When The Coffin card falls after a card representing a season or time of the day, it announces the end of the day or season.

Card no. 9: The Bouquet

- » Time: A brief period or on the date of a significant celebration.
- » Season: In the spring.

Card no. 10: The Scythe

- » Time: Expiration date. Suddenly, unexpectedly, abruptly. It denotes a fast-developing event.
- » Season: In the autumn (fall)

Card no. 11: The Broom and The Whip

- » Time: Very fast. An event will occur unexpectedly.

Card no. 12: The Owls

- » Time: Brief and fast.
- » Time of day: At twilight or at night.

Card no. 13: The Child

- » Time: In the present, but pointing to the future.

Card no. 14: The Fox

- » Time: Wrong day or time.
- » Advice: Don't do anything right now. Wait and observe. Exercise patience. Play dead and wait until you have a perfect strategy. Pretend you haven't noticed anything and that everything is fine. Be diplomatic. Use the fox's cunning and astuteness to deceive your opponent and attack when they least expect it. It's not the right time.

Card no. 15: The Bear

- » Time: A long-term period, possibly lasting for several weeks or even years (from ten to twenty years).
- » Advice: Calm down.

Card no. 16: The Stars

- » Tempo: In the future.
- » Time of day: At night.
- » Season of the year: In the autumn (fall) or winter.
- » Weather and temperature: cool or cold weather.

Card no. 17: The Storks

- » Time: In three, six, or nine months.
- » Time of day: During the change of the season or in the following period.
- » Advice: It's time to make some changes in your life.

Important Note:
The Storks card always shows a change of season or time of day.

Card no. 18: The Dog

- » Time: It'll last for a long time.
- » Advice: It's necessary to wait and rely on the events.

Card no. 19: The Tower

- » Time: A long-term period.
- » Advice: It's time to take a break and reflect on what has happened. It's recommended to wait for as long as necessary.

Card no. 20: The Garden

- » Time: In three months. During a public gathering, such as a festival, congress, or an outing, like a picnic and excursion.
- » Time of day: At noon, at lunchtime

Card no. 21: The Mountain

» Time: There will be delays, or things won't be done right now. A blockage, a stop. An event might be postponed.
» Advice: Be patient and persistent.

Card no. 22: The Crossroads

» Time: The timing can't be determined as it's still being evaluated.

Card no. 23: The Mice

» Time: It'll be an exhausting and ineffective situation, a waste of time. It'll take a while to achieve the goals.

Important Note:

It's important to note that, in a reading about timing, this card can shorten the time predicted by the card to its right (in front of it).

Card no. 24: The Heart

» Time: A long time.

Card no. 25: The Ring

» Time: On a scheduled or pre-planned event such as a regular commemorative date or prearranged date (mentioned in a contract). Something will happen on a specific, predetermined date.

Card no. 26: The Book

» Time: In the future. Unknown date.

Card no. 27: The Letter

» Time: Soon, from one to fifteen days.

Card no. 28: The Man and Card no. 29: The Woman

» Time: In my readings, I've already noted that when the querent's card comes up in a timing spread, it's crucial to pay attention to the surrounding cards as they will indicate whether the querent is working for or against their purpose.

If there are fast-paced cards nearby, it means that the querent is active and may soon carry out their goals. On the other hand, if there are stop or slow-moving cards nearby, it's likely that they need to be more enthusiastic, put more effort into their endeavor, or may be facing some obstacles along the way.

Card no. 30: Lilies

» Time: During a Christian festival period, such as Christmas, Easter, etc. A long-term period.
» Season: In the winter
» Weather and temperature: Cold, freezing.
- The Clouds + The Lilies: It predicts it will snow.

Card no. 31: The Sun

» Time: Within 24 hours or 365 days
» Time of day: From sunrise to noon. During the day.
» Season: In the summer.
» Weather and temperature: Too hot, scorching, muggy.

Card no. 32: The Moon,

» Time: During the lunar cycle, within 28 days.
» Time of day: In the afternoon or at night.
- Full moon: The Moon + The Sun
- Waning Moon: The Mice + The Sun + The Moon
- New Moon: The Son + The Moon
- Waxing Moon: The Mice + The Moon + The Sun

Card no. 33: The Key

» <u>Time</u>: The querent will set the time.

Card no. 34: The Fish

» <u>Season</u>: During a rainy season.
» <u>Weather and temperature</u>: rainy and wet.

Card no. 35: The Anchor

» <u>Time</u>: a long-term period.

Card no. 36: The Cross

» <u>Time</u>: It can take two or three weeks, but sometimes it can take longer, depending on the event or issues the querent is dealing with and also the surrounding cards.

In my consultations, I use two different procedures to determine timing.

1st procedure

Before drawing the cards, you must set a specific time frame, whether ten days, one, two, or three months, will depend on the querent's question. For example, when I work with the Grand Tableau, I usually set a three-month time frame for a general consultation and a one-month time frame for a specific question. This approach provides a complete understanding of how the situation may unfold within the chosen time frame.

Verified example:

I bought some Russian card decks online last year to add to my collection. It had been a month since my purchase, and I hadn't received my order yet. So, I consulted the cards to determine what was happening and whether I'd receive my package soon.

CHAPTER 3: POLARITY AND SIGNIFICATOR CARD

I asked: "Will I receive my package from Russia within the next ten days?"

- Reading method: The Tree-Card Method
- The cut of the cards: The Rider + The Ship
- Keywords:
    - The Rider: news, movement, delivery, the mail;
    - The Ship: something from abroad, foreign land, long journey, distance.
- My interpretation: the package has been shipped; it's on the way.
- The three cards drawn: The Tower + The Rider + The Mountain
- Keywords:
    - The Tower: authority, government, prison, public, state enterprise or office, government agency, control, customs, border;
    - The Rider: mobility, news, messages to receive or give;
    - The Mountain, stagnation, authority, regulations, restrictions, obstacles, significant delay or problem, patience.
- Card Combinations:
    - The Tower + The Mountain: police, authority, laws, regulations, held under the law of a country, stationary, prison;
    - The Tower + The Rider: communication from the authorities, in the hands of the authority;
    - The Rider + The Mountain: blocked, held back, customs, delay.
- My interpretation: My order will take a while to arrive because it's held up at customs in another country or state. So I won't be receiving it within the next ten days.

I also use to take a look at the last card in the spread to determine if the event will happen on time or be delayed.

In the example above, The Mountain is regarded as a stop card, indicating that there will be a delay.

- Feedback: After 20 days since my consultation, I started making some phone calls (The Rider also represents a search through phone calls and emails, with the help of the Russian seller), and I found out that my order had been held at the Swiss customs in Zurich. I had to prove that the object in the order was for personal use and not for selling, and I also had to pay a fee. Anyway, a big headache.

2nd procedure

The second procedure involves asking a direct question and drawing a single card from the deck. This is the easiest way to determine the timing of an event.

For example:

Suppose the querent asks: "Will I receive my medical results this week?"

- Card: The Bear
- Answer: NO. It will be a long time before I receive my medical result. This is a slow-paced card.

Another example:

- Question: When will Paula get in touch with Chiara?
- Card: The Rider
- Answer: Quite soon. In fact, Ther Rider card represents a situation or event that is already in progress and about to occur in the querent's life.

Another example:

- Question: When will Claudia find a steady job?
- Card: The Lilies
- Answer: It will take some time. The Lilies card represents winter, most likely next winter.

2

CHAPTER 4:
THE LOPES MAZZA CODES

The Petit Lenormand isn't merely based on meanings, symbols, and reading methods; it goes far beyond that, like any other divinatory instrument – Tarot, Sibilla, Kipper, Belline, Geomancy, Astrology, Numerology, etc.).

To use it properly, you need to clearly and unequivocally understand its basic rules. Each card has a specific role in the reading, and some cards have a decisive role depending on their position in relation to other cards. Therefore, when working with the Grand Tableau, it's crucial to consider the direction the figures are facing and the position of certain cards, whether to the left or right, above or below the card being analyzed.

At first, it may seem a bit cold, calculated, mathematical, and systematic to you. However, over time, these techniques will provide you with valuable support and motivation to better understand the topics covered in the readings. It may take some time before you feel completely comfortable and truly grasp the Petit Lenormand, so don't rush through this step, no matter how challenging it may seem. I assure you it'll be worth it. Applying these techniques correctly will make your readings more detailed and insightful.

My codes combine techniques from Philippe Lenormand's instruction sheet, the German school's directional technique, and other methods I've learned through my consultations and studies. I developed this habit of closely observing the cards back in 1970 when I learned to read the traditional cards and realized how important the movement of the court cards was for accurate interpretations. I've applied it to other decks like the La Vera Sibilla Italiana, Tarot, Petit Lenormand, and Kipper.

In 2010, I began organizing my techniques to make them easy for my students to understand. I think I've done a good job when I see them using my codes in their own consultations, lectures, courses, and books they write. They're my pride and joy

The name Lopes Mazza Codes comes from my Swiss, Italian, and Brazilian students, who have lovingly named the techniques I've taught them over the years.

The codes provided here are not complete, but they're the essential starting point for studying. There are five codes:

- Philippe Lenormand's Law or The Method of Distance (MOD);
- The Directional Facing Law;
- The Law of Position;
- The Law of Predominance;
- The Law of Movement.

PHILIPPE LENORMAND'S LAW
Or The Method of Distance (MOD)

The method used here is based on the traditional Petit Lenormand technique, known as Philippe-Lenormand Method in Switzerland, and the Near/Far Method or Method of Distance by traditionalists in the United States and England.

It respects the three principles established in the instruction sheet written by Mlle Lenormand's supposed heir in 1846 when the Petit Lenormand deck was first introduced.

The three rules are:

1. The function of the querent's card
2. The Near/Far Law or The Method of Distance
3. The four cards reading code

CHAPTER 4: THE LOPES MAZZA CODES

Rule 1

An excerpt from the instruction sheet says:

"The Person consulting the cards is represented by No. 29, if it be a lady; or by No. 28, if a gentleman."

The card no. 28, The Man and the Card no. 29, The Woman have the sole function of physically representing the querent in the reading.

Rule 2

The following excerpt states:

"We must concentrate on cards No. 28 and No. 29 – The Gentleman and The Lady The whole pack refers to either of these cards, depending, if the person whose fortune is being told is either a Lady (No. 29) or Gentleman (No. 28). The signification of the Personal card depends largely on the position it assumes in dealing the cards in the rows, and the meaning and force of all the other cards are modified by their distance from or contiguity to the Personal card".

We understand that the first step in a reading is to focus on the two cards that represent the querent (The Man and The Woman), as the entire reading develops through these cards. The remaining 34 cards in the deck gain importance depending on how close or far they are from the querent's card (Grand Tableau).

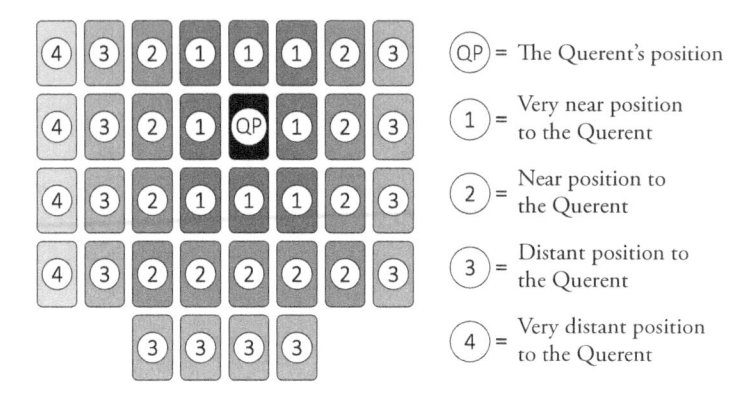

(QP) = The Querent's position
(1) = Very near position to the Querent
(2) = Near position to the Querent
(3) = Distant position to the Querent
(4) = Very distant position to the Querent

The closer a card is to the querent or a significator card, the more intense its impact. On the other hand, the further a card is from the querent or from a significator card, the less intense its effect on the querent's life.

Therefore, during a reading, our attention should first be directed to the cards close to the querent's card, in positions 1 and 2, which are the strongest positions; consequently, they have a much more significant impact.

The influence of Position 3 on the querent's life is weak, so it has little impact. However, the querent will be greatly impacted if this card has a very negative value, such as The Coffin card. In position 4 (depending on where the querent's card falls, the distances can go beyond the four positions shown here), the querent doesn't feel the impact of the cards. As a result, we understand that the value of a card increases when it's close to the querent's card and decreases when it's far away.

Let's take The Coffin card as an example. Of course, we won't go deeper into the meanings, reading techniques, and context as we would in a reading; instead, we will focus solely on The Coffin card, according to Philippe Lenormand's meaning.

"No. 8. – A Coffin, very near to the Person, means, without any doubt, dangerous diseases, death, or a total loss of fortune. More distant from the Person, the card is less dangerous."

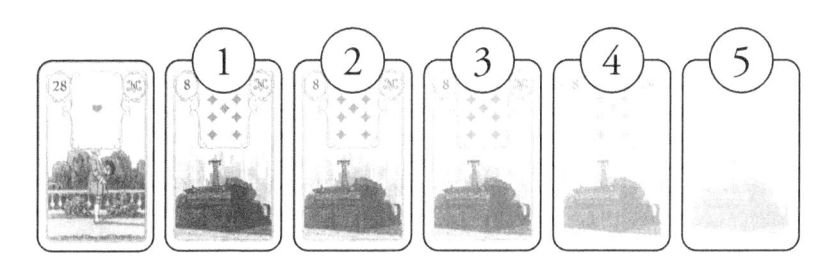

As the card gets closer to the querent's card in positions 1 and 2, its color intensifies, while in position 3, the card's color lessens.

Rule 3

Pay attention to the following four cards.

Card no. 4: The House

"No. 4 – The House is a certain sign of success and prosperity in all undertakings; and though the present position of the Person may be disagreeable, yet the future will be bright and happy. If this card lies in the centre of the cards, under the Person, this is a hint to beware of those who surround him or her."

Card no. 6: The Clouds

"No. 6 – Clouds, if their clear side is turned towards the Person, are a lucky sign; with the dark side turned to the Person, something disagreeable will soon happen."

Card no. 25: The Ring

"No. 25 – The Ring, if on the right of the Person, prognosticates a rich and happy marriage; when on the left, and distant, a falling out with the object of your affection, and the breaking off of a marriage."

Card no. 30: The Lilies

"No. 30 – The Lilies indicate a happy life; surrounded by clouds, a family grief. If this card is placed above the Person, they indicate the same as being virtuous; if below the Person, the moral principles are doubted."

The Philippe Lenormand method is a very interesting technique, and it will be further examined in Chapter 7 of this book, where we will study the Grand Tableau reading method.

THE DIRECTIONAL FACING LAW

The reading is based on the direction the figures are facing.

THE QUERENT'S CARD
Card no. 28: The Man and Card no. 29: The Woman

The querent's cards play a major role in a reading. This is the first lesson we learn from Philippe Lenormand's instruction sheet:
"We must concentrate on cards No. 28. & No. 29 – The Gentleman and The Lady. The whole pack refers to either of these cards, depending, if the person whose fortune is being told is either a Lady (No. 29) or Gentleman (No. 28). The signification of the Personal card depends largely on the position it assumes in dealing the cards in the rows, and the meaning and force of all the other cards are modified by their distance from or contiguity to the Personal card".

The Philippe Lenormand Method, also known as the Traditional Method, doesn't take into account the directional facing law. So how did traditionalists distinguish between the past and the future?

The cards to the left of the querent's card represent the past, and the cards to the right represent the future, as seen in the illustration.

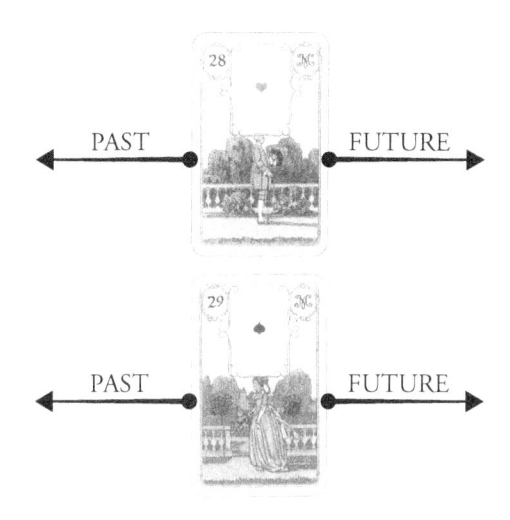

PAST ← → FUTURE

PAST ← → FUTURE

As we've just seen, the direction the figure is facing doesn't matter, but all the cards to the right of the querent's card represent the future, and those to the left, always starting from the querent's card, represent the past.

On the other hand, the German Method follows a different approach. In this method, it's important to pay attention to the direction the figure faces, known as the "facing law". This valuable technique helps determine the location of past, present, and future events concerning the investigated subject. Therefore, this is a very important technique to keep in mind if you intend to "work" with the Grand or Petit Tableau Lenormand Method.

The Directional Facing Law is a technique that has its origins in past centuries. One of the earliest examples of its use can be found in the "Tarocchino Bolognese" deck, created around 1420. This Tarot consists of 22 major arcana, 40 minor arcana (with the 2, 3, 4, and 5 of each suit removed), and 1 - The Joker. A reading with the deck uses 50 cards arranged in 10 horizontal lines of 5 cards each (known today as The Master's Method, The Board, or Grand Tableau).

The reading begins from the position of the querent's card (the King of Clubs for the man and the Queen of Clubs for the woman), observing the direction that the figure is facing. The cards in front of the querent's card represent the future, while the cards behind it represent the past.

In my research over the years, I haven't found any written records about the origin and author of this technique. Still, I believe that, as happened to me, all the secrets of cartomancy were passed down orally through generations. In the past, many people were illiterate, which is why there are fewer written records about this topic.

How to interpret the querent's card

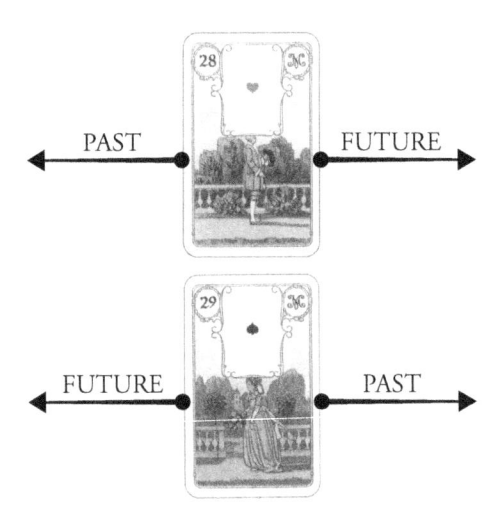

◄── PAST ● [card 28] ● FUTURE ──►

◄── FUTURE ● [card 29] ● PAST ──►

In addition to representing the future, the cards in front of the querent's card (according to the facing law) also provide insight about the following:

- The direction the querent is currently heading;
- The events that the querent is giving attention to or interested in;
- What the querent still needs to learn, know, or discover;

- People the querent may not know or be aware of or who may play a role in future events if a court card or another card representing a person shows up.

The cards facing the opposite direction, back-to-back, represent the person's past. This position also provides information about:
- Where the querent came from;
- What the querent has left behind or moved away from;
- The querent's experiences and knowledge;
- The people the querent is familiar with or who were involved in past events, if a court card or another card representing a person shows us.

The two querent's cards may fall next to each other. Is this relevant to the reading? Absolutely! Especially when a relationship reading, such as friendship, love, marriage, or partnership

When the querent's card figures face each other

When the two querent's cards figure face each other, it indicates:
- Communication and shared interests and goals,
- They're connected;
- They're supportive;
- There is a sense of closeness between them.

The cards surrounding the querent's cards or the cards that fall between them will reveal:
- What connects them;
- What they have in common;
- The issues they're currently dealing with.

Let's take an example of a reading about a professional issue between my client Miguel and his boss Vera. The cards shown here are from the Grand Tableau reading. Notice that there are three cards between Miguel's and Vera's cards: The Key, The Storks, and The Anchor. These cards will provide insight into the subject being investigated at that moment.

The interpretation of the cards is as follows:

Miguel's boss values and relies on him (The Woman + The Anchor) due to his professional competence (The Key + The Anchor). Consequently, Miguel will be offered a more responsible position at work (The Man + The Key + The Storks + The Anchor).

WHEN THE TWO QUERENT'S CARD FIGURES ARE BACK-TO-BACK

Those who aren't familiar with the described technique may jump to premature conclusions such as:
- The couple has already broken up;
- The couple will break up in the future.

Unless other cards confirm the couple's separation or divorce, these two cards should be interpreted in the following way:
- The couple is likely going through a crisis at the moment;
- Some serious issues or problems are keeping them apart;

- They have different interests, aspirations, and goals, resulting in distance and a lack of shared projects;
- There's a significant incompatibility between them;
- They're avoiding each other;
- There's no cooperation between them;
- They might be distracted or uninterested in each other's lives.

In this case, it's crucial to pay close attention to the cards surrounding and between the querents' card to understand the reason for their distancing or misunderstanding.

For example, in the combination below, the reason may be:
- The Woman + The Tree + The Mice + The Man: a disease;
- The Woman + The Ship + The Anchor + The Man: a business trip;
- The Woman + The Heart + The Snake + The Man: a potential betrayal.

Important Note:

The technique mentioned above must be applied even if the querent's cards appear horizontally, vertically, or diagonally in the Grand Tableau.

THE LAW OF POSITION

This Law of Position consists of eight laws that respect the placement of certain cards in a reading.

1. THE BEFORE AND AFTER LAW

This law emphasizes the importance of paying attention to certain cards when they fall before or after another card.

These cards include:
- The Rider, The Ship, The Tree, The Coffin, The Scythe, The Mountain, The Mice, The Book, The Letter, The Key, The Anchor, and The Cross.

2. THE LAW OF INFLUENCE

The Law of Influence is based on observing the cards according to their position, whether above or below, in relation to other cards.

This technique can be used with all 36 cards, but some cards require more attention:
- The Rider, The Tree, The Clouds, The Scythe, The Fox, The Storks, The Mountain, The Rats, The Book, The Man, The Woman, The Lilies, The Anchor, and The Cross.

This technique can be applied to all 36 cards, but some require more attention. It is used exclusively in larger spreads such as the Grand Tableau, Grandma's Method, and others, where many cards are involved.

CHAPTER 4: THE LOPES MAZZA CODES

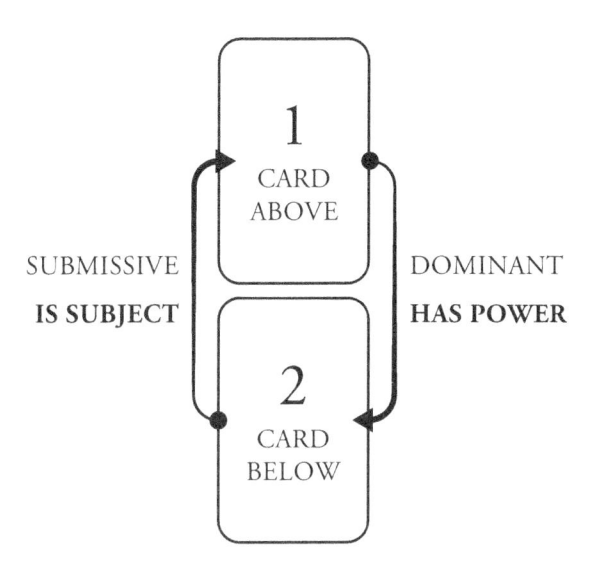

```
         ┌─────────┐
         │    1    │
         │  CARD   │
         │  ABOVE  │
SUBMISSIVE│         │ DOMINANT
         │         │
IS SUBJECT│        │ HAS POWER
         │    2    │
         │  CARD   │
         │  BELOW  │
         └─────────┘
```

Position 1:

The card above controls the card below. It's also said it has weight, strength, power, and control over the card below.

If the querent's card is in this position, it means they're in control of the situation, the life area, or the person represented by the card below.

Position 2:

The card below is controlled by the card above it. Therefore, the card in this position has no control over the situation, life area, or person represented by the card above. But beware! Some cards can act with all their energy in this position, such as the stop cards, indicating that the querent or the life area represented by the card above is stagnant, not evolving, or that the querent isn't taking action.

Important Note:

The technique mentioned above must be applied even if the querent's cards appear horizontally, vertically, or diagonally in the Grand Tableau.

3. The Law of Orientation

This law respects the direction that certain symbols (animals and objects) are facing.

These cards are:

- The Snake, The Scythe, The Fox, and The Dog.

4. The Law of Relevance

The Law of Relevance is based on the power of certain cards to neutralize or cancel the effect of the other cards, particularly the stop or negative cards. I affectionately call them the "eliminator cards".

These cards are:

- The Coffin, The Scythe, and The Mice.

When **The Coffin card** comes after another card, it puts an end to the card that precedes it. Examples:

- The Ship + The Coffin: canceled trip or the end of a trip;
- The Snake + The Coffin: end of a betrayal or extramarital relationship;
- The Broom and The Whip + The Coffin: end of discussions and conflicts;
- The Stars + The Coffin: no expectations;
- The Storks + The Coffin: no change or the end of a change;
- The Mountain + The Coffin: no delays, end of obstacles;
- The Anchor + The Coffin: end of a professional task;
- The Cross + The Coffin: end of a mission or an important position.

When **The Scythe card** falls before another card, it removes, cuts, breaks, or separates the card in front of it, whether it's for better or worse.

Examples:

- The Scythe + The Snake: eliminating a rival;
- The Scythe + The Coffin: no ending;
- The Scythe + The Bear: a breakup or separation with one of the parents;
- The Scythe + The Mountain: removing an obstacle or problem represented by The Mountain;
- The Scythe + The Mice: cutting unnecessary expenses;
- The Scythe + The Book: revealing a secret;
- The Scythe + The Letter: breaking or interrupting communication.

The Mice card reduces, lessens, weakens, and takes away the card's strength in front of it. Unlike the quick cut of Scythe, The Mice card indicates a slow and gradual loss. Examples:

- The Mice + The Coffin: relief, a slow ending, pain or sadness that slowly goes away;
- The Mice + The Broom and The Whip: a slow decrease in tension;
- The Mice + The Mountain: slowly and gradually overcoming an obstacle;
- The Mice + The Cross: relief, lessening of burden.

5. The Law of Repetition

Certain cards positioned after other cards indicate the repetition of situations represented by the preceding card(s).

These cards include The Broom and The Whip and The Ring.

The Broom and The Whip card represents tools used to beat (whip) and shake (broom) in a frantic and repetitive movement.

The Ring card stands for a continuous and circular motion, creating a repetitive connection until the querent breaks free from this dependency.

Here are some examples:
- The Coffin + The Ring: chronic disease;
- The Broom and The Whip + The Ring: discussing the same subject;
- The Owls + The Broom and The Whip: always talking or repeating the same things;
- The Fox + The Ring: repeating the same old mistakes; continuous acts of criminality;
- The Anchor + The Ring: always repeating the same tasks at work or renewing a contract.

6. The Bridge Law

Some cards serve as a link or bridge between two other cards, and when they appear in a reading, it's necessary to pay close attention to the cards that fall before and after them.

These cards are:
- The Rider, The Ship, The Storks, The Crossroads, and The Key.

Let's see an example with the following cards: The Anchor + The Crossroads + The Stars.

According to my interpretation, my querent is thinking about taking some time off to decide whether he should quit his current job (The Anchor + The Crossroads) and pursue a career related to spirituality (The Anchor + The Stars).

If The Crossroads card appears in a reading, it indicates several available options. To better understand the situation, checking the card that falls before it is essential, as it denotes the factors that led to the decision or choice. Additionally, the card that follows it will reveal what the querent wants to achieve or the outcome of their decision or choice.

Important Note:

It's important to observe that the bridge cards represent the passage from one place to another, so that, in rare cases, these cards announce one's death or the change from one state to another.

7. The Law of the Double

The Clouds and The Broom and The Whip cards feature two main symbols on the same card

The Clouds card displays both light and dark clouds. Light clouds mean enlightenment and relief, even if it appears next to a negative card. Dark clouds bring annoyance and problems, and their negativity increases when it's next to a negative card. This law was introduced by Philippe Lenormand in 1846.

The Broom and The Whip card features two symbols, a broom, which removes, cleans up, and purifies dirty places or negative energies, and a whip, which, on the contrary, aims to punish and defend against attacks. In India, hanging a broom and a whip behind the door is common to ward off negative energies or unwanted visitors.

When someone or something negative is present, or even if you feel something bad is about to happen at home, strike a whip on the floor and then sweep the house from the inside out to remove any disturbance.

This ritual inspired my Method of Magic technique, in which the cards touching the whip show the active energy in the querent's life or home, while the cards touching the broom will guide you on how to eliminate current negativity if confirmed by the group of cards on the side of the whip.

8. The Law of Addition

This law is based on adding an extra card to the end of a line, which will provide further details and deeper interpretation. Therefore, if there are no cards in front of the querent's card (The Facing Law) or in the direction of objects and animals (The Law of Orientation), or the last card is neutral, another card needs to be added to complete the reading.

This law is used in smaller card spreads, such as the three-card, five-card, or seven-card lines, as well as the Celtic Cross. However, it's not applied in larger spreads like the Grand Tableau, which uses all 36 cards in the reading. For example, in a romantic reading using the "Three-Card Method," you draw three cards to represent the intentions and state of the relationship, and the cards drawn for my querent's husband were:

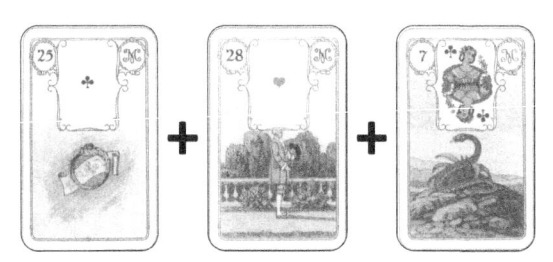

- <u>The Ring</u> + <u>The Man</u> + <u>The Snake</u>: It indicates the presence of a woman (Queen of Acorns), who is linked to this man (The Snake + The Ring).

My querent's husband seems to be focused on another woman (The Man + The Snake), causing him to neglect his responsibilities in the marriage (The Ring). To understand the situation better, we need to focus on The Snake. As you may know, the direction in which The Snake moves reveals its interests, and what lies behind it gives us clues about The Snake's true intentions or goals.

After drawing a card from the deck, The Heart card appeared next to The Snake, confirming that my querent's husband is having an affair (The Ring + The Snake + The Heart).

The other woman is in love (The Snake + The Heart) and wants a stable and committed relationship (The Snake + The Ring). Therefore, we can conclude that my querent's husband has no feelings for her and is involved and attracted to another woman.

Reading Code in some cards
The Law of Position

Card no. 1: The Rider

Reading code:
- The Law of Position: Orientation, Influence, Bridge, and Addition

> **Important Note:**
> When two cards with techniques appear together, the technique on the first card that should be considered first in the reading.

When reading The Rider card, it's essential to pay attention to the direction in which the horse is facing, as well as the position of the horse's muzzle and tail. It's also necessary to consider the direction the horse is galloping. So, when The Rider card shows up, you need to check the four positions listed below (see the illustration).

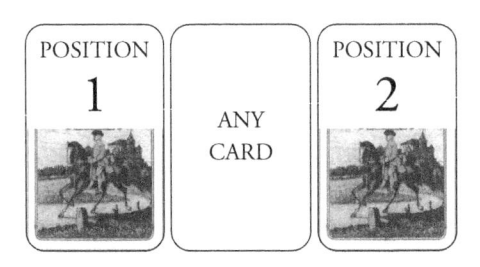

POSITION 1	ANY CARD	POSITION 2

Position 1: The Rider card before another card (tail)
Where it comes from

The cards in this position indicate The Rider's origin, the purpose of his journey, what he's about to bring, what he carries with him, and what is on the way (events, news, messages, people, etc.). This information needs to be delivered or communicated to someone.

For example:
- The Rider + The Clover: It brings new opportunities and energy;
- The Rider + The Clouds: We assume that The Rider's "baggage" is not the best. The Rider will undoubtedly bring something unpleasant and bothersome;
- The Rider + The Coffin: Something is coming to an end, or the querent will react differently due to the issue being investigate. This combination announces that the circumstances will change drastically. A definitive answer is on the way. The message will cause immense pain. It can also reveal a severe disease or someone's death if accompanied by cards that confirm this prognosis. It also indicates the arrival of a package (as The Coffin card can stand for a box);
- The Rider + The Stars: It indicates the arrival of new ideas or inspirations and brings clarity to previously unclear subjects. It heralds the awakening of spirituality or spiritual growth;
- The Rider + The Storks: it announces someone's return or significant changes taking place;
- The Rider + The Dog: A friend or new friend's arrival. It might also identify the imminent arrival of a friend or brother who wears a uniform. Sometimes it may bring messages or news from friends;
- The Rider + The Anchor: a job offer or achieving the desired stability.

In this position, The Rider can always indicate an exit, a departure, or a distancing from the situation or life area represented by the card positioned in the tail. For example:
- The Rider + The Ring: It may denote someone who doesn't want to go into a relationship or make a commitment. Therefore, they tend to run away from any situation that could restrict or "imprison" them. As The Ring card represents dependencies and enslavement, it may imply that the querent is moving away from dependence.

Position 2: The Rider card after another card where The Rider is going to

The card in front of the horse's muzzle indicates the destination or where The Rider is heading. The card in this position represents the "recipient" or the place where something needs to be delivered or the goal to be achieved.

For example:

- The House + The Rider: returning home;
- The Clouds + The Rider: unpleasant consequences (observe the card that falls before The Rider to understand the origins of the problem);
- The Coffin + The Rider: the message won't reach its destination;
- The Lilies + The Rider: reconciliation, the return of someone or something that brings peace.

Let's take as an example the three cards shown here, The Book + The Rider + The Anchor. This exercise aims to understand The Rider card technique when it's close to other cards.

First, let's look at the card positioned behind The Rider: The Anchor, which is the significator card for work and employment (obviously, The Anchor has other meanings, but for simplicity's sake, I've decided to use only these meanings). The card in front of The Rider is The Book, which stands for studies, learning, and the unknown.

My interpretation would be:
The querent will soon receive (The Rider) a new professional task (The Anchor), which will require further training or course (The Book).

Other examples I've pulled from my consulting journal:

- The Anchor + The Rider + The Moon: a professional (The Anchor) promotion (The Moon);
- The Mountain + The Rider + The Child: a new project (The Child) that will face significant challenges (The Mountain) to be completed;
- The Tree + The Rider + The Sun: health (The Tree) recovery (The Sun).

Position 3: The Rider card above another card

The card positioned below The Rider, especially if it represents the querent (The Man or The Woman cards), refers to their projects and plans. It also indicates that the querent is waiting for news from someone, and the card next to or below it will show the specific life area it relates to.

Position 4: The Rider below another card

The card positioned above The Rider represents what the querent is currently being dealt with and what they'll achieve. It also announces that the querent has received prior information and is aware of something that allows them to act on the matter at hand.

Card no. 3: The Ship

Reading code:

- The Law of Position: Before and After

| POSITION 1 | ANY CARD | POSITION 2 |

Position 1: The Ship card before another card

Means the remembering of an event, the arrival (for a visit or an event), progress, achievement, conquest, and exploration. So, the cards lying after The Ship show the destination (where you're heading or what you'll find out).

For example:

- The Coffin: something is coming to an end; it may be the end of a journey, a project, or a task; it also announces a trip to attend a funeral;
- The Broom and The Whip: a trip or action leading to discussion;
- The Child: a new beginning; desire to get pregnant; pregnancy;
- The Mountain: a task that won't be easy to accomplish; postponed plans.

Position 2: The Ship card after another card

Indicates transition, change, departure, leaving, moving away, letting go, distancing, absence, and abandonment. The Ship moves onward, leaving behind the subject brought up by the preceding card. Therefore, the card(s) preceding The Ship inform which life area is changing. For example:

- The House: leaving the comfort zone or home;
- The Coffin: distancing oneself from suffering, pain, sadness, past habits, or people. It also indicates a profound and long-awaited

transformation by the querent, such as gender transition. In a reading about illness, this combination indicates that the disease has entered a new stage or phase and may progress. If a positive card, such as The Bouquet, The Lilies, or The Sun, falls after The Ship, it suggests recovery. However, when paired with The Cross, it may augur physical death;

- <u>The Broom and The Whip</u>: it indicates running away or distancing oneself from problems, stress, or someone who causes conflicts. In a specific case, my Italian client has a daughter who worked as a journalist during the Gulf War in 1991. When she hadn't received any communication from her daughter for a while, she sought my guidance to locate her. The cut of the deck was The Broom and The Whip + The Ship, indicating that her daughter was leaving the conflict zone at that very moment. Later the same day, her daughter contacted her to inform her that she had indeed left Baghdad for security reasons and was in Saudi Arabia;

- <u>The Child</u>: it announces the end of pregnancy, the birth of a child. But also the departure of a young person or a child who has left home to live alone or to study in a distant place;

- <u>The Mountain</u>: it predicts that a period of great difficulty has been left behind or that solutions have been found solutions to get out of difficult situations;

- <u>The Heart</u>: distancing oneself from love or an emotional situation. Making rational rather than emotional decisions to solve a problem;

- <u>The Ring</u>: The partner has broken up the relationship or is moving away.

Important Note:
When The Ship is the last card at the end of a line, it foresees events or situations (indicated by the cards placed before The Ship) that will "carry" for a time.

Card no. 5: The Tree

Reading code:
- The Law of Position: Before and After, Influence

| POSITION 1 | ANY CARD | POSITION 2 |

Position 1: The Tree before another card

- Nature of the disease;
- Care, treatments, and operations;
- Overcoming or not the disease;
- Health facilities (medical center, hospital, and clinic).

For example:

- The Tree + The Fox: an incorrect diagnosis; or pretending to have a disease if The Coffin card is also nearby;
- The Tree + The Tower: hospital admission.

Position 2: The Tree card after another card

- Health personnel (doctors, nurses, etc.);
- The querent's health and living conditions;
- Consultations;
- Clinical exams.

For example:

- The Clouds + The Tree: feelings of discomfort or illness;
- The Dog + The Tree: healthcare staff;
- The Letter + The Tree: medical exam results, medical prescription, and making an appointment;
- The Book + The Tree: medical exams.

Position 3: The Tree card above another card

Reveals what is firmly rooted in the querent's life. For example, The Tree above:

- The Coffin: a chronic or severe disease;
- The Child: a person who resists growing up;
- The Dog: a lifelong friendship or enduring loyalty;
- The Tower: a hospital or a long period of isolation;
- The Heart: balanced and strong feelings;
- The Ring: a solid and committed relationship or union; a long-term contract;
- The Book: can represent two different things:
    o Secrets not revealed or a family that has long-held secrets;
    o Knowledge passed down through generations, or the person has expertise in the subject of the reading; heritage.
- The Fish: savings or family finances;
- The Cross: family karma.

Position 4: The Tree card below another card

Indicates what grows and expands. In the case of disease, the card above The Tree, like The Stars, may show the progression or spread of the disease. For example:

- The Ship + The Tree: a medical trip for rest or a vacation;
- The Letter card above The Tree means various health certificates or prescriptions;
- The Mice above The Tree: weakness;
- The Man or The Woman above The Tree indicates that a person needs to take better care of themselves and their health;
- The Fish above The Tree predicts financial growth; healthcare expenses if The Coffin is nearby.

Card no. 6: The Clouds

Reading code:
- Philippe Lenormand's,
- The Law of Position: Double and Influence

"No. 6. – Clouds, if their clear side is turned towards the Person, are a lucky sign; with the dark side turned to the Person, something disagreeable will soon happen."

Philippe Lenormand, 1846

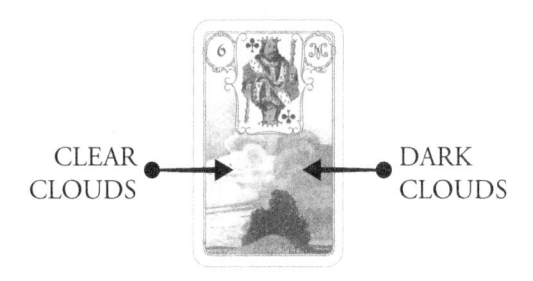

CLEAR CLOUDS → ← DARK CLOUDS

According to Philippe Lenormand, how we interpret The Clouds card depends on its position in relation to other cards. This card has both clear and dark clouds, and we consider these elements when reading it.

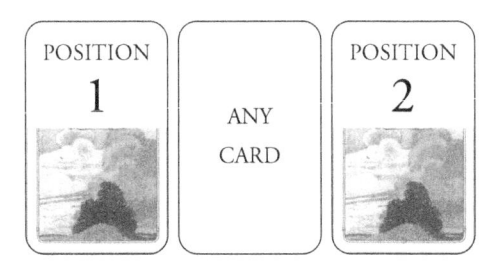

POSITION 1 — ANY CARD — POSITION 2

Position 1: Dark clouds

The card touching the dark clouds receives its negative influence, regardless of whether it's a negative or positive card. The dark clouds also cast a shadow over the card in this position, hiding something or keeping it secret. For example, The Clouds + The Fox denotes something wrong, fraudulent, or deceptive.

The Clouds card covers up and hides the truth behind these lies. Another example is the pairing of The Clouds + The Ring. The Ring stands for any unions, partnerships, or relationships. These cards together indicate betrayal, deceit, but also a hidden agreement or secret alliance. Since one of the meanings of The Lilies card is sexuality, the combination of The Clouds + The Lilies suggests that the querent is hiding their true sexual orientation.

If dark clouds are touching a significator card, it reveals where the querent's concerns and problems lie. If the querent's card is in this position, it may indicate uncertainties, secrets, or unclear aspects of their life.

Position 2: Clear clouds

These clouds bring calmness and peace during difficult times and clarify ambiguous situations. If we examine the clear clouds closely, we'll notice traces of the dark clouds. It's a sign to protect yourself from a potential "storm", indicating that the problems are still present and need to be solved once and for all. Keep in mind that clouds are constantly moving, coming and going depending on the weather and the moment. The clear clouds soften the impact of negative cards. The problem is still there, but the querent is aware of it and handles it safely.

Position 3: The Clouds card above another card

It's a red flag and a threat to the card below it. It's a dangerous position that requires attention. When The Clouds card lands above the querent's card, it indicates that the querent is emotionally disturbed, psychologically stressed, worried, and nervous. Since the problems remain unresolved, it's necessary to look for other alternative approaches. However, the querent is unable to focus due to a distorted or unclear perception of the situation. They feel scared, distressed, and anxious. It's a difficult moment of psychological pressure, and sometimes it may indicate a potential bipolarity. If The Clouds card is above a significator card, it implies that the corresponding area of the querent's life will be significantly impacted. It's recommended to stay calm and delve deeper into the issue as something isn't clear or right.

Position 4: The Clouds below another card

The Clouds card positioned below the querent's or significator card foretells a chaotic, disorganized, and uncertain life. It refers to an unhealthy lifestyle by excessive use of medications, cigarettes, alcohol, drugs, or overeating. Additionally, it predicts instability or misfortune. This instability can often lead to conflicts.

Important Note:

When reading for a teenager or a troubled person, it's crucial to check the cards surrounding The Clouds, such as The Scythe and The Coffin, which may suggest depressive thoughts or suicidal tendencies. It indicates that the person isn't in their usual state.

Card no. 7: The Snake

Reading code:
- The Law of Position: Orientation

The card The Snake faces

Reveals which aspect of life area it will impact or attack. It serves as a warning to the querent to be cautious and attentive in that particular area.

Some examples:
- The Garden + The Snake: betrayal on social network;

THE HEAD'S DIRECTION

THE TAIL

- The Heart + The Snake: emotional manipulation;
- The Ring + The Snake: betrayal in a relationship.

The card that faces The Snake's tail

Reveals what is hidden.

Some examples:
- The Snake + The Fox: deceit;
- The Snake + The Stars: esoteric ability or knowledge;
- The Snake + The Heart: a lover;
- The Snake + The Book: information that can be used when necessary; esoteric knowledge; a fortune teller.

Card no. 8: The Coffin

Reading code:
- The Law of Position: Before and After, Influence, and Relevance

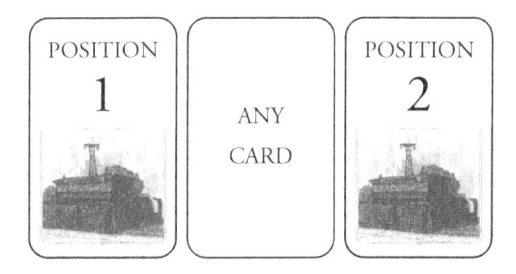

| POSITION 1 | ANY CARD | POSITION 2 |

Position 1: The Coffin before another card
- A fresh start;
- A resurrection;
- Remaking the future.

If The Coffin is the first card in a spread, it implies that a past situation still deeply affects the person, plunging them into a mental and emotional gloom. This is particularly true if the following card is also negative or if there are cards that indicate the situation remains unchanged, such as The Tower, The Mountain, and The Anchor.

For example, The Coffin

- + The Clover: a trauma that will soon be overcome;
- + The Child: new ventures;
- + The Tower: It's two cold and stop cards that indicate loneliness and isolation. This combination may describe a totally lonely person. It also denotes a severe disease requiring hospitalization or possible isolation due to an infectious or immunological disorder. In some cases, these cards can even announce the possibility of death if the: The Cross, The Tree, and The Lilies, among others, are nearby;
- + The Ring: the recurrence of chronic disease;
- + The Woman: a traumatic experience;
- + The Fish: inheritance;
- + The Cross: deep pain, suffering, or attachment to the past.

Position 2: The Coffin after another card

It means the end and the conclusion of something. But it also represents the release from a burden or the letting go of the past or old vices, or the discovery of something new.

For example:

- The Snake + The Coffin: overcoming the enemies or rivals;
- The Scythe + The Coffin: past secrets or revelations that shock those close to the querent;
- The Broom and The Whip + The Coffin: The end of conflicts or aggression, no competition. The end of a trial and punishment;
- The Tower + The Coffin: The Tower stands for solitude, pause, separation, and physical seclusion from the outside world, which can often represent a prison for the person. If The Coffin is in this position, the time of isolation and solitude, a release from confinement;

- The Ring + The Coffin: breaking a cycle; ending a love relationship to begin a new one if The Child falls after The Coffin;
- The Man + The Coffin: a traumatic experience;
- The Fish + The Coffin: a significant financial loss or bankruptcy;
- The Anchor + The Coffin: hopelessness or unemployment.

Position 3: The Coffin above another card

Intensify its power upon the card below it. The Coffin has impacts on another card.

The Coffin above:

- The Tree: physical fatigue or disease;
- The Bouquet: a funeral or mourning;
- The Ring: if the reading is about health, it predicts a chronic disease; instead, if the reading is about a relationship (whatever that may be), it indicates a definitive separation;
- The Fish: significant financial damage that leads to poverty.

Position 4: The Coffin below another card

Any card above The Coffin acts upon it

The Coffin below:

- The Rider: news may not reach its destination; meeting someone from the past;
- The Ship: if The Tree is positioned before The Coffin, it augurs death and if The Cross or The Tower falls after it. It also denotes a dying wish or contact with the dead;
- The Tree: it predicts serious disease;
- The Mountain (or any stop card): something remains hidden, a prolonged period of sadness or being bedridden;
- The Mice: Energy loss;

- The Letter: diagnosis of a disease, death certificate; news of a death;
- The Book: inheritance documents, keeping a disease a secret, or a breakup;
- The Man: a radical change in the querent's life;
- The Cross and next to The House and The Lilies: a family grave.

Card no. 10: The Scythe

Reading code:
- The Law of Position: Orientation, Influence

THE HANDLE ← → THE BLADE

The Scythe card's meaning depends on its position in relation to other cards, particularly the querent's card.

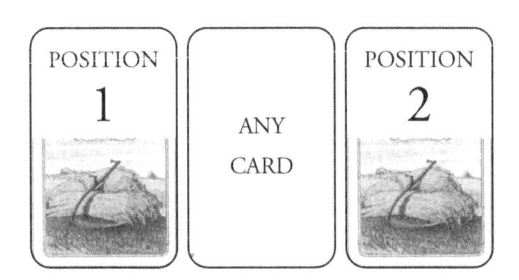

POSITION 1 | ANY CARD | POSITION 2

Position 1: The card the blade is facing

Will receive a cut, an abrupt end, for better or worse. The blade also points to the area or situation that requires the querent's close attention because it's in danger or is threatened by something.

For example, The Scythe

- The Rider: a canceled date or interview, risk of an accident involving a car, motorcycle, bicycle, skates, or scooter, and sports-related accident; leg, tendons, or ligaments injuries; broken contact or connection;
- The Mountain: overcoming obstacles and restrictions;
- The Book: interruption of studies or revealing secrets;
- The Letter: a break in communication;
- The Anchor: job completion or dismissal.

Position 2: The handle of the scythe

Pay close attention to the card to the left of The Scythe as it accurately indicates the speed of an event. For example, If The Anchor card is in this position, the time will be longer but still shorter than what The Anchor card alone predicts, which is one year. The Scythe adds a sense of urgency and hastens the events represented by the previous card, often leading to their conclusion within 72 hours. Keep in mind that The Scythe in this position also denotes an unexpected event represented by the preceding card. Therefore, with positive cards, The Scythe intensifies its positivity, while with negative cards, it can strengthen its negativity.

For example:

- The Coffin + The Scythe: It announces a tragic and sudden ending, an unforeseen and serious disease, a sudden death (heart attack or fatal accident), or a danger like an incident or traumatic event (such as an earthquake or loss of a loved one).

    I have a personal experience to share. When my dog Dolly fell sick, I initially thought it was a passing discomfort. However, the cards I drew, The Coffin + The Scythe + The Dog, clearly predicted her sudden death, which sadly happened the day after the reading;

- The Storks + The Scythe: an unexpected and sudden change or disruption;

- The Mountain + The Scythe: an unplanned obstacle that will delay the completion of a project;
- The Letter + The Scythe: a telegram, an immediate response, or an unexpected message.

Position 3: The Scythe above another card

Announces danger, a threat, or the cutting out of something (represented by the card below). This is a highly dangerous position when reading for adolescents or adults facing difficulties. When The Scythe is above a card representing a person, it may indicate negative thoughts about committing suicide or self-destructive or violent impulses. In other cases, The Scythe in this position suggests thoughts of division, separation, or the need for a significant life change. The person has reached a breaking point, and their life requires a cleansing by removing what no longer makes sense.

For example, The Scythe above:

- The Ring: the querent or their partner wants to end the relationship;
- The Book + The Ring: the inability to keep a secret or hide a relationship.

Position 4: The Scythe below the querent's card

Indicates an ongoing elimination process. I've already observed in my readings that The Scythe in this position suggested that the querent was very selective and undergoing a period of personal growth. On the surface, they appeared egotistical, cold, and harsh in their words and actions, but their focus was on improving their life or accomplishing a relevant project. For example, The Scythe below The Ring card indicates that it's time to let go of anything unnecessary in the relationship, with cards confirming that the separation can be effective

Card no. 14: The Fox

Reading code:

- The Law of Position: Before and After, Influence, and Addition

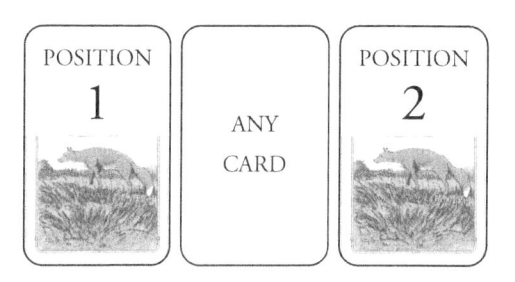

Position 1: The Fox card before another card

When The Fox card shows up in a reading, it's crucial to check the direction its muzzle is pointing. That direction can provide clues about what is wrong, false, deceptive, disguised, hidden, or at risk of sabotage and deceit. When working with the Grand Tableau, pay close attention to Fox's position relative to the querent's or significator card. In other words, observe if The Fox is in front of, behind, above, or below the significator card.

For example, the combination The Fox + The Man indicates that the querent or the man in question:

- Is intelligent, cunning, and analytical;
- Analyzes his steps carefully;
- Is quiet, silent, and patient;
- Doesn't reveal his true intentions;
- Is discreet and reserved;
- Maintains a sense of caution and suspicion;
- Hides something;
- Works on projects confidentially;
- Can be of great help and is skilled in strategy.

Other examples, The Fox

+ <u>The Crossroads</u>: living a double life;

- + The Ring: keeping lying, having an extramarital affair, hiding being married, or being connected to the querent's enemy;
- + The Book: concealing relevant knowledge or secrets.

Position 2: The Fox card after another card

Indicates deception, falsehood, or things not being what they seem. It shows which life area will be affected by lies, sabotage, manipulation, or being spied on. It also suggests that the querent may be heading in the wrong direction.

For example, The Man + The Fox, indicates that the querent or the man in question:

- Uses his charm to get what he wants;
- Has hidden motivations and didn't approach with real intentions;
- Is deceptive, dishonest, and a liar;
- Tends to exaggerate and twist the truth when describing situations;
- Is dealing with someone who is scheming or deceitful;
- Talks a lot but doesn't keep his word or promises;
- Is untrustworthy and ambiguous in his actions.

Other examples:

- The Ship + The Fox: someone lying about a trip;
- The Snake + The Fox: a psychopath;
- The Scythe + The Fox: exposing a charlatan or a liar. Detecting a scam in time;
- The Heart + The Fox: hidden or disguised feelings;
- The Ring + The Fox: Beware, something is wrong with contracts and agreements;
- The Letter + The Fox: the document contains false information or is a forgery;
- The Book + The Fox: someone pretending to have knowledge they don't have; plagiarism; well-disguised falsehoods;

- The Lilies + The Fox: having a wrong attitude towards family matters;
- The Keys + The Fox: lies and deceit; finding solutions through well-planned strategies;
- The Fish + The Fox: misuse of money, financial loss; possible deception, or fraud.

Position 3: The Fox card above another card

Indicates something sneaky, wrong, or false. In my readings, I've found that when The Fox is above the querent's card, it suggests that the person is:

- Is suspicious and on high alert, keeping a watchful eye;
- Might be digging deeper into a particular subject, weighing the advantages and disadvantages, and using all the fox's traits: cleverness, cunning, and strategic thinking.

Therefore, we can conclude that:

- The expectations are mistaken or based on illusions;
- The querent is making incorrect assumptions about someone or a situation;
- If The Snake touches The Fox card, it suggests that evil plans are being developed;
- The person is focused on preparing a strategy to solve a problem. Since this card represents falsehood, illusion, deceit, and harmful intentions, it's necessary to warn the querent to carefully review their actions and projects, as things may not go as planned;
- Sometimes, when The Fox is above the querent's card, it indicates they're being deceived or manipulated.

Other examples of The Fox card above another card:

- The Ship: cunning in business dealings;

- The Tree: living a deceptive or wrong lifestyle; false identity;
- The Coffin next to The Tree card: an imaginary disease or pretending to be sick; incorrect diagnosis, seek another doctor;
- The Bouquet: false happiness;
- The Storks: a deceptive change or the need to pretend that a change is taking place;
- The Crossroads: the querent is surrounded by lies and deceit.

Position 4: The Fox card below another card

When I learned to work with the directional facing technique, I was taught that when The Fox appears below the querent's card, it means that the person is honest, not easily deceived, and has a clear view of reality. But in practice, I realized that The Fox card in this position didn't mean honesty but the following:

- The querent lives in a fictious situation based on lies;
- The querent is a victim of fraud or deceit.

Or:

- The querent is acting dishonestly, playing unfairly, or involved in a scam. The victim of the scam will be identified by the card in front of The Fox;
- The querent lies to survive;
- The person is acting like a real Fox.

Examples of combinations:

- The Ship, next to The Coffin and The Fish, above The Fox card: falsehoods regarding an inheritance;
- The Broom and The Whip The Fox: arguments or conflicts caused by lies;
- The Owls above The Fox: slander or the spreading of lies;
- The Mountain above The Fox: A secret that will be difficult to uncover.

The Fox and the Law of Addition

If the drawn cards were The Bouquet + The Fox, it suggests an invitation that may have hidden motives; adding another card after The Fox is necessary to understand the true intentions.

If The Garden card shows up, it indicates that the person aims to join the querent's social circle. I wanted more information, so I drew a second card, The Anchor, that I placed next to The Garden card. Therefore, I interpreted it as the person is using flattery, courtesy, and invitations to take advantage of the querent's professional expertise.

Card no 17: The Storks

Reading code:
- The Law of Position: Before and After, Bridge, Influence, and Addition

Position 1: The card before The Storks

Describes:
- The motivation for change;
- Changing the position;
- Where the change comes from;
- Where the change is taking place (in which life area);
- What should be changed;
- What the querent wants to change their situation;
- Where it comes from.

For example:
- <u>The Clover</u> + <u>The Storks</u>: small changes;
- <u>The Tree</u> + <u>The Storks</u>: Your health will undergo some changes, and the next card will reveal if it's for better or worse. For instance, if you draw The Sun or The Bouquet after The Storks, it means a recovery or improvement in health. But, if the next card is The Snake, it means serious complications that will worsen your health. If you draw The Stars, it may indicate the spread of the disease, requiring chemical treatment to overcome it;
- <u>The Clouds</u> + <u>The Storks</u>: feeling anxious about a change; fear of changing something;
- <u>The Dog</u> + <u>The Storks</u>: A friend will experience significant changes; friendship, loyalty, or honesty will change;
- <u>The Tower</u> + <u>The Storks</u>: leaving seclusion or isolation;
- <u>The Ring</u> + <u>The Storks</u>: changes in relationship or partnership, a union that will bring about life changes; alterations in a contract;
- <u>The Anchor</u> + <u>The Storks</u>: changes in work or professional tasks.

Therefore, The Storks card indicates a change or shift in the situation represented by the card to its left or before it. When it appears as the final card in a spread, it indicates that the issue at hand will take a different turn or that a change is necessary. To understand the outcome of this change, add another card to the right of The Storks (Addition Law). For instance:

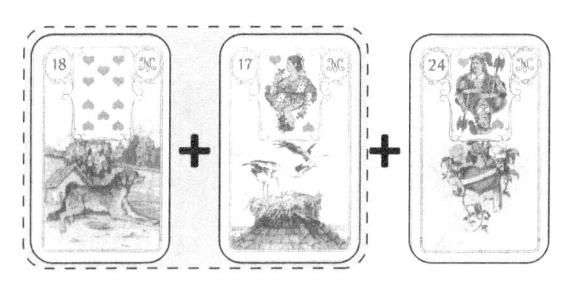

- The Dog + The Storks + The Heart: a friendship (The Dog) turns (The Storks) into love (The Heart).

Another example:

- The Anchor + The Storks: changes in the stable and well-structured lifestyle.

Position 2: The Storks card after another card

Describes:

- The consequences of motivation;
- Where will this change take you;
- The chosen direction;
- What it brings back.

For instance:

- The Storks + The Coffin: the conclusion of a change in the situation indicated by the previous card; a change that will lead to nothing;
- The Storks + The Child: changes that promote personal growth;
- The Storks + The Dog: a change that brings new confidence into life; the arrival of a friendly and trustworthy person; reconciliation, the return of an old friendship; or adoption of a pet;
- The Storks + The Book: confidential or secret changes.

To better understand the Bridge Law technique, I'll use an example with three cards: The Man + The Storks + Bouquet.

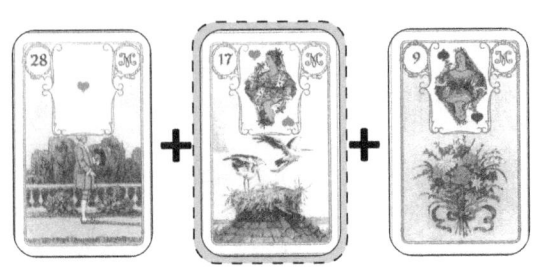

My interpretation:
A man plans to make a change (The Man + The Storks) in his appearance or behavior (The Bouquet). We know that the bouquet represents not only esthetics and beauty but also good manners, kindness, and proper etiquette.

The following two techniques, position 3 and 4, are used in larger spreads where more cards are involved, such as The Granny Method, The Grand Tableau, or The Petit Tableau.

Position 3: The Storks card above another card

When The Storks card is above another card, it influences and impacts the card below it. It indicates what will be changed or modified.

For example, The Storks above the:

- The House: breaking from daily routines, moving away, or distancing from home or the city. The card in front of The Storks card points to the desired destination or goal. If paired with The Ship card, it denotes a journey overseas or possible new cultural experiences for studying or working;
- The Broom and The Whip: continuous changes or moving away from conflict;
- The Mountain: getting out of a difficult situation;

- <u>The Man</u> or <u>The Woman</u>: the person is evaluating their life or reconsidering a decision. The cards next to The Storks will reveal what it is about. For instance: The Book + The Anchor: the querent is examining the possibility of furthering their professional education to enhance their career;
- <u>The Anchor</u>: It refers to someone using alcohol to escape from reality. If the combination of The Clouds + The Fish falls in front of The Storks, it indicates the use of chemical substances (medicines or drugs). The Clouds + Stars and The Storks above The Anchor card can also predict a change from a stable position to another.

Position 4: The Storks below another card

Describes:

- What makes or forces the querent to make the change.

In my Grand Tableau journal, I found an interesting reading for a lady that showcases my technique. Let me share it with you:

The Anchor + The Storks + The Scythe, with The Cross above The Storks and The Lilies below The Storks, announce changes in the querent's routine (The Anchor + The Storks) will occur suddenly and unexpectedly (The Storks + The Scythe), bringing heavy burdens (The Cross + The Storks) and sufferings for the family (The Cross + The Storks + The Lilies).

To understand the cause of these changes and hardships within the family, it's necessary to look at the card that falls before The Cross, which is The Coffin. Therefore, The Coffin above The Anchor card indicates that the job loss is the cause of the family will face difficulties.

Card no. 18: The Dog

Reading code:
- The Law of Position: Orientation

The card the dog's muzzle

Points to shows what the querent can trust, whether it's a situation, life area, or a person. It indicates what the dog is devoted and loyal to. In my readings, I've noticed that when The Dog card appears before cards like The Snake, The Fox, or The Mice, it reveals the betrayals, falsehoods, and lies represented by those cards.

Some examples:

The Dog
- + The Tree: a trustworthy cure; a loyal friend;
- + The Stars: trust your intuition;
- + The Lilies: devotion to family.

The card on The Dog's "tail"

Shows what is being protected.

Some examples:
- The Child + The Dog: protecting their children;
- The Book + The Dog: safeguarding their knowledge or a secret;
- The Lilies + The Dog: preserving their peace and serenity.

Card no. 21: The Mountain

Reading code:
- The Law of Position: Before and After, Influence

| POSITION 1 | ANY CARD | POSITION 2 |

Position 1: The Mountain card before another card

The card to the right of The Mountain indicates overcoming a difficult situation. However, if a negative card, such as The Scythe, shows up in this position, it announces dangers or unexpected obstacles that will block the positive development of the situation. But if The Coffin card appears in this position, it means that those obstacles will be removed (The Law of Relevance).

If The Anchor card, a stop card, is to the right of The Mountain, it denotes a long-lasting obstacle. It's also possible to predict a stagnation regarding the matter represented by the card to the left of The Mountain. For example:

The Mountain
+ The Clover: minor problems; short-term blockage;
+ The Snake: a complex and complicated problem;
+ The Ring: long-term obstacles;
+ The Key: overcoming hardship due to the querent's initiative.

Position 2: The Mountain card after another card

Indicates:
- Delays and significant obstacles;
- A project that won't progress or continue;

- Inability to move forward;
- Failure to solve the issue represented by the previous card;
- The situation will remain unsolved;
- Progress will come to a standstill;
- What will remain stagnated.

The Mountain card difficult the progress of the card to its left. In fact, this card serves as a barrier, an obstacle, a blockage that hinders the development of the situation represented by the previous card.

However, The Mice and The Scythe cards (The Law of Relevance) are the only cards that aren't affected by The Mountain. For instance, The Mice card slowly and persistently reduces difficulties, while The Scythe swiftly cuts through the obstacles, clearing the path ahead. For example:

- The Coffin + The Mountain: bedridden, a disease that doesn't progress;
- The Bouquet + The Mountain: postponing a visit;
- The Child + The Mountain: a new start is obstructed;
- The Crossroads + The Mountain: difficulty in making decisions at the moment;
- The Ring + The Mountain: delays in implementing a contract;
- Book + The Mountain: feeling blocked in study; undiscovered knowledge, illiteracy;
- The Letter + The Mountain: messages that won't arrive, delayed news.

Position 3: The Mountain card above another card

Presses, imposes a burden, a weight. For example, The Mountain above:

- The House: a burden affecting the family; difficulties in accessing a home, an app, or an account on online platforms such as Facebook, Instagram, etc.;

- The Man or The Woman: this person resists changes and may tend to isolation and loneliness, or maybe he or she is dealing with a concerning issue;
- The Keys: unavoidable problems.

Position 4: The Mountain card under another card

Blocks the card above it. For example:

- The Bear above The Mountain: a blocked relationship with the parents;
- The Stars above The Mountain: a lack of objectivity; a hindrance to spiritual growth;
- The Tower above The Mountain: seclusion, prison; a lonely person;
- The Man or The Woman above The Mountain: stagnation and a lack of progress in the person's life, where nothing significant seems to be happening;
- The Fish above The Mountain: limited income;
- The Anchor above The Mountain: the person prefers a stable life; stubbornness.

Card no. 22: The Crossroads

Reading code:

- The Law of Position: Before and After, Bridge, Addition

| POSITION 1 | [Card 22: The Crossroads] | POSITION 2 |

Position 1: The card before Crossroads card describes

- The motivation behind the choice;
- The reasons for leaving;
- A decision to be made;
- What is under evaluation;
- The last word has not yet been spoken;
- Nothing has been decided yet.

When The Crossroads card shows up as the final card in a spread, it indicates that a solution for the situation hasn't been found yet. It means that currently, a way out has yet to be found. For example, suppose the querent is seeking guidance regarding a specific job contract, and the cards drawn are The Ring + The Crossroads:

[Card 25: The Ring] [Card 22: The Crossroads]

Then the interpretation would be as follows:

The proposal is still under evaluation, along with other candidates. As the last card in a reading, The Crossroads card signifies an UNCERTAIN outcome where neither a positive nor a negative answer can be determined. In this case, it's recommended to draw another card and add it (The Law of Addition) to the right of The Crossroads card to gain more exact information about the subject to be analyzed.

Other examples:

- The Ship + The Crossroads: a business trip choice; considering whether or not to go on a business trip;
- The Tree, or any "stop" card + The Crossroads: making a decision will take a long time. In the health context, it suggests an undiagnosed disease that will require several medical tests to identify;
- The Coffin + The Crossroads: Seeking treatment for an illness; deciding to end something;
- The Child + The Crossroads: choosing a new path in life;
- The Stars + The Crossroads: having to make many decisions;
- The Garden + The Crossroads: making decisions that involve several people.

Position 2: The card after The Crossroads card

Describes the "path" or the consequences of the decisions or choices. For example, if The Coffin card falls in this position, it indicates a dead end. If the reading refers to a change, it suggests that it won't happen or will be canceled.

For example, The Crossroads + The Ring:

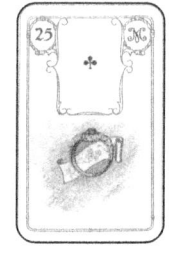

The answer would be that the querent will be chosen among several candidates after a careful evaluation. The contract will be successfully signed. So the answer is YES.

Other examples, The Crossroads

- + <u>The Child</u>: a decision that will lead to a new situation;
- + <u>The Garden</u>: decisions that will become public;
- + <u>The Mice</u>: no immediate need to make a decision;
- + <u>The Book</u>: decisions that are still unknown.

The Bridge Law with The Crossroads card

For example:

<u>My interpretation</u>:

The combination of The Anchor + The Crossroads + The Tree cards indicates that the querent has to choose between two jobs (The Anchor + Crossroads) and will choose the job that will offer them stability for a long time (The Crossroads + The Tree).

Card no. 23: The Mice

Reading code:

- The Law of Position: Before and After, Influence

```
POSITION      ANY        POSITION
   1          CARD           2
```

Position 1: The Mice card before another card

Indicates:

- What can be lost;
- What is gradually losing or decreasing in value;
- What is in risk of disappearing from our lives.

The Mice card weakens the cards in front of it, like in the combination of The Mice + The Fish. In this position, The Mice slowly and steadily "gnaw" and "deplete" whatever is in front of them. In a reading about finances, for example, this combination may suggest that the person is spending or wasting their resources recklessly, as well as financial debt.

Other examples:

- The Mice + The Ring: a relationship that gradually weakens; a union or commitment that gradually dissolves;
- The Mice + The Book: gradual or partial disclosure of a secret;
- The Mice + The Letter: slow loss of communication, theft or loss of information or documents;
- The Mice + The Anchor: decrease in; a part-time job.

Position 2: The Mice card after another card

Indicates:

- Something that has already been lost;

- Loss of interest;
- Loss of value;
- Something has been taken away;
- Something that has been used;
- Something that has been damaged or destroyed;
- A situation with no solution or remedy;
- Something that must be ignored;
- Something that has been rejected.

For example, The Fish + The Mice

In this example, The Mice card is the final card in the spread. The Mice in this position means that the positive qualities associated with The Fish card, such as abundance, well-being, and wealth, among other meanings, are being negatively affected or devalued by The Mice card. In a financial reading, this combination may indicate an economic decline or that the querent doesn't value material possessions.

Other examples:
- The Bouquet + The Mice: an impolite or deceitful person;
- The heart + The mice: lack of love; no interest or feelings;
- The Ring + The Mice: a single or divorced person, not desiring a committed relationship;
- The Letter + The Mice: a lost mail or message, spam, ignored information or mail;
- The Lilies + The Mice: no harmony or peace; sexual impotence; a long time without sex;
- The Fish + The Mice: disinterest in money, loss of financial support;
- The Anchor + The Mice: unemployment; or a lack of interest in work.

Position 3: The Mice card above another card

Contaminates and spreads its negativity, causing substantial damage and losses to the card below it. For example, The Mice above:

- The Ship: loss of inheritance, involvement in illicit trade, or dealing with second-hand goods;
- The House: damage to the house or the presence of vermin;
- The Ring: a breach of contract;
- The Man or The Woman: destructive distress, worried, anxiety; low self-esteem, a ghost visitation; someone who is unclean or emits an unpleasant odor;
- The Lilies: loss of values, morals, and dignity;
- The Fish: excessive spending; financial worries, debts; receiving less money than expected, and theft;
- The Cross: duties or responsibilities that diminish.

Position 4: The Mice card below another card

Indicates what has lost interest, for example, The Mice card below:

- The Tree: a disabled person; no health or energy;
- The Clouds: minor or insignificant concerns;
- The Letter: unimportant communication or mails;
- The Man or The Woman: an impure or weak person.

Card no. 26: The Book

Reading Code:
- The Law of Position: Before and After, Influence

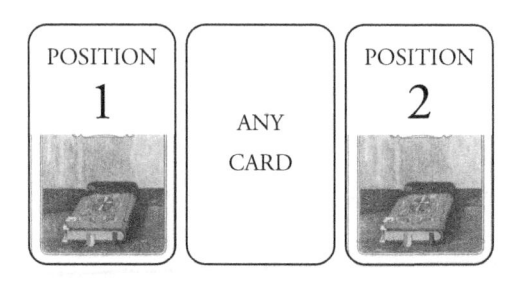

| POSITION 1 | ANY CARD | POSITION 2 |

Position 1: The Book card before another card

Denotes the discovery or knowledge of something important that may help resolve the issue being investigated. For example:

The Book

- + The Clover: obtaining information or secrets by chance;
- + The Owls: revealing secrets or confidential issues; disclosing several pieces of information; confessing, exchanging knowledge;
- + The Fox: pretending to have knowledge or expertise in a subject;
- + The Stars: esoteric studies, spiritual teaching;
- + The Ring + The House: documents or deeds relating to a house or a shop.

> **Important Note:**
> The secret or the answer to a question remains hidden only with the following cards: The Tree, The Coffin, The Tower, The Mountain, and The Anchor.

Position 2: The Book card after another card

Indicates confidential information or something that must be kept confidential or hidden. It may also suggest that the querent lacks knowledge or that something is unclear at this point. The unknown!

Important Note:
The cards The Scythe, The Mice, and The Keys are the only cards that can open The Book when they fall before it.

For example:
- The Rider + The Book: a secretive meeting;
- The Clouds + The Book: an unknown threat;
- The Snake + The Book: hidden enemies;
- The Owls + The Book: confidential information; private conversations; two secrets, confidences; shared secrets; a conversation where not everything is said;
- The Child + The Book: an illegitimate child;
- The Bear + The Book: an unknown father;
- The Storks + The Book: something that changes in a total silence;
- The Dog + The Book: a secret kept by friends; concealment of the truth;
- The Crossroads + The Book: unknown or unfamiliar paths, uncertainty about the way forward;
- The Heart + The Book: a lover; a secret admirer; someone concealing their emotions;
- The Man + The Book: an unknown or reserved man.

Position 3: The Book card above another card
- Something concealed;
- What the querent doesn't want to reveal;
- What's necessary to learn;
- What the querent needs to know;

- What is hidden or unknown and needs to be explored or investigated;
- A mystery.

For example: The Book above:
- The Ship: a journey to an unknown destination;
- The Ring: an extramarital relationship or a secret agreement;
- The Lilies: the concealment of one's sexual orientation;
- The Fish: payment or involvement with dirty money;
- The Anchor: a job or task that requires secrecy.

Position 4: The book card below another card

Reveals what is already known.

For example, The Book card below:
- The Ship: a trip related to studying or training;
- The House: revealing a family secret;
- The Tree: solid education;
- The Clouds: mental confusion, lack of attention;
- The Coffin: end of the school year, completion of a training or course.

Card no. 27: The Letter

Reading code:
- Position Law: Before and After, Bridge, Addition

| POSITION 1 | ANY CARD | POSITION 2 |

Position 1: The Letter card before another card

Indicates:
- Who the recipient of the message is;
- The effect that the content of The Letter will cause.

For example, The Letter

+ The Bouquet: happy news, a potential promotion or recognition for a job well done;
+ The Book: messages or confidential mail or an anonymous message.

Position 2: The Letter card after another card

Indicates:
- Who the sender is;
- The content.

For example:
- The Ship + The Letter: news from a distant place or related to business, a postcard;
- The Coffin + The Letter: an announcement of someone's death or sad news;
- The Stars + The Letter: news that through the internet;
- The Mice + The Letter: a bill or invoice through mail.

The Bridge Law

My interpretation:

The announcement (The Letter) of a job offer (The Bouquet + The Anchor) will bring happiness (The Bouquet + The Sun) to the querent.

Card no. 33: The Key

Reading code:

- The Law of Position: Before and After, Addition

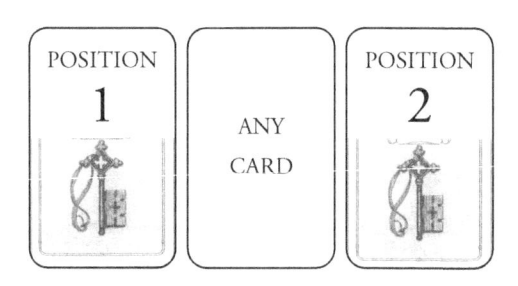

Position 1: The Key card before another card

- Opens;
- Points to a solution;
- Advises to act with your own will.

For example, The Key

+ <u>The Tree</u>: health recovery or improvement;

+ The Coffin: completion of a project or work; or reopening old wounds;
+ The Anchor + The Moon: achieving career success.

Position 2: The Key card after another card
- Closes;
- Protects and supports.

For example:
- The House + The Key: supported by the family;
- The Ring + The Key: a security union or relationship;
- The Fish + The Key: financial security.

Card no. 35: The Anchor

Reading code:
- The Law of Position: Before and After

Position 1: The Anchor card before another card
Indicates:
- The querent's profession;
- What is the most suitable profession;
- Where to find work.

For example: The Anchor + The Bouquet:
- A job related to a hobby;
- A florist or gardener;
- A stylist.

Position 2: The Anchor card after another card
Indicates:
- Information about the querent's professional status;
- The querent's professional conditions.

For example: The Bouquet + The Anchor:
- An offer or professional invitation;
- Congratulations on a job well done;
- A satisfying job;
- A joyful professional environment.

Card no. 36: The Cross

Reading code:
- Position Law: Before and After, Influence

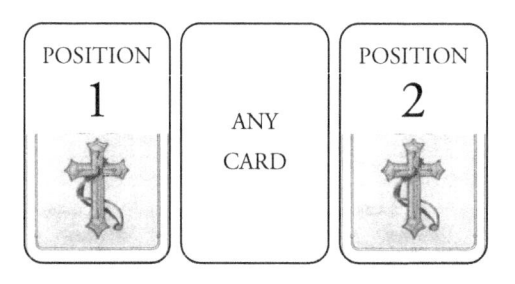

POSITION 1	ANY CARD	POSITION 2

Position 1: The Cross card before another card
Indicates it's necessary to pay attention to the card that comes after The Cross, as it can modify or strengthen the energy of The Cross. For example, The Tree, The Tower, The Mountain, and

The Anchor cards (the "stop" cards) can intensify the negative aspects of The Cross. Some examples

The Cross

+ <u>Clover</u>: a small sacrifice; short-term hardship; relief;
+ <u>The Coffin</u>: serious disease; end of a depressing phase; grief; an irreversible or painful situation; depression; death, mourning;
+ <u>The Mountain</u>: resignation or failure pain; a time of great obstacles; stuck in a painful past experience; a karmic blockage; limitations imposed by religious beliefs.

Position 2: The Cross card after another card

The cards before The Cross suffer its impact, except for The Scythe and The Mice, which can cut away, eliminate, and diminish the negativity of The Cross card (The Law of Relevance).

Some examples:

- <u>The Mice</u> + <u>The Cross</u>: religious crisis, loss of faith; concerns or burdens that decreases;
- <u>The Heart</u> + <u>The Cross</u>: love that requires sacrifice; fanaticism; restlessness; heartache; dissatisfaction in love life; self-sacrifice;
- <u>The Ring</u> + <u>The Cross</u>: an unhappy relationship; a promise or oath made on behalf or connected with God.

Position 3: The Cross card above another card

Suggests a challenging situation or a heavy burden that is hard to bear. It may represent overwhelming, fateful, or inherited events. For example, The Cross above the card:

- <u>The House</u>: significant family responsibilities or obligations;
- <u>The Tree or The Coffin</u>: hereditary disease;

- <u>The Ring</u>: karmic relationships; an unfavorable contract; contractual obligations; relationship tests and tribulations;
- <u>The Book</u>: heavy mental burden;
- <u>Man, a burden</u>: something deadly; a heavy burden; torment;
- <u>The Anchor</u>: great responsibility at work.

Position 4: The Cross card below another card

The Cross, due to its potentiality, is influenced by the card above it. For example, The Cross below:

- <u>The Ring</u>: religious union;
- <u>The Man</u>: overcoming a test.

Cláudia was concerned because her son Sérgio had been sad lately, and she asked me for a card reading to figure out what was bothering him. This example is part of my reading for Sérgio using the Grand Tableau in 2009. I got the first insight when I noticed that the card representing Sérgio (The Man) had no cards below it.

This indicated that Sérgio felt discouraged, oppressed, frustrated, and didn't know what to do. When the querent's card falls in this position in a Grand Tableau reading, it means a lack of guidance or support for the querent. The cards above Sergio's card represent his thoughts.

The central cards, The Book, The Cross, and The Lilies, indicate the focus of his thoughts. When analyzing these three cards, I immediately paid attention to The Cross card, which stands for suffering, anguish, and mental strain in relation to the card below it, The Book, which implies that Sérgio was feeling pressured about his studies (The Cross + The Book) and that this pressure came from his family (The Lilies).

Analyzing the cards flanking the theme cards, I concluded that Sérgio was making sacrifices by suppressing his desires, interests, and passions (The Heart + The Cross), which had led him to a state of sadness and depression (The Cross + The Coffin), to the point that made him contemplate putting an end to this suffering (The Heart + The Coffin).

CHAPTER 4: THE LOPES MAZZA CODES

Sergio's family (The Lilies) is traditional (The Tree + The Lilies) and held a respected position in the medical field (The Tree + The Lilies + The Moon), particularly in surgery (indicated by the mirrored cards The Tree + The Moon + The Scythe), and expected Sérgio to keep the family tradition.

The three cards (The Scythe + The Book + The Stars) revealed Sergio's desire to break away from his studies (The Heart above The Scythe cutting The Book card) and follow his vocation (The Book + The Stars), something connected to death (The Cross + The Coffin) or scientific investigation (The Book + The Stars).

Today Sérgio works in the scientific investigation department of the Italian police (RIS).

THE LAW OF PREDOMINANCE

The Law of Predominance is based on observing the groups of cards that predominate in the reading. The deck is divided into energies (positive and negative), categories (movement, slow, and stop cards), and suits. Each group of cards generates a specific energy that helps us during the reading. This technique allows you to gather first impressions about the question being investigated before focusing on the individual meanings of the cards and the combinations that will provide more information.

Take note of the following points:

- It's important to consider the number and position of the groups in the reading. Are they in the past, present, or future? Which group is dominant in the past and present? For example, if the group of stop cards predominates in the past and the group of movement cards dominates in the present, we can infer that the querent went through moments of inactivity or inability to act in the past (the cards in the past position will provide more information about what caused them to stop) and is now actively pursuing their goals in the present;

- Pay attention to the position of the predominant groups of cards. If they're close to the querent's card or a significator card, this indicates the dominant energy in that specific life area or the querent's emotional and behavioral state. For example, if the reading shows a predominance of movement cards next to the querent's card, this announces that the querent is going through significant changes.

    The context of the reading and the surrounding cards help to figure out what these changes may be. For example, if the question is about business, the presence of the movement card group suggests that the querent should prepare for a significant change in this area. Additionally, if there are cards of Acorn suits, it indicates that these changes will cause considerable financial difficulties;

- Analyzing the absence or predominance of certain groups is also essential when starting the reading. For example, if there are more movement cards in the future position, this announces that the querent will experience significant changes, such as changes in the financial area if the question refers to business. On the other hand, the absence of movement cards in the future means that there will be no development or progress in this area. In this case, consider which group is prevailing in the future position to provide guidance about the consequences of the querent's current actions.

The Meaning of the Group of Cards in a Reading

Predominance of the positive card group:

The presence of several positive cards in a reading, announces that all difficulties will be overcome with success, bringing satisfaction, joy, happiness, well-being, good health, vitality, and strength.

Predominance of the neutral card group:

This group of cards appears quite often in readings when an issue or situation isn't yet stable, is changing. They may also suggest that changes are necessary to move forward.

Predominance of the negative card group:

The presence of many negative cards in a reading generally indicates unpleasant, problematic or negative situations. A high number of negative cards can significantly impact any positive card. For example, if one or more negative cards fall after one or more movement cards, it could indicate that a change or action taken may have disastrous consequences, or that a change is coming to an end.

Predominance of the movement card group:

When several movement cards show up in a reading, it means that the person is entering a period of change and that there may be shifts in projects and plans.

Predominance of the slow card group:

The presence of many slow cards in a reading announces that something will take longer than expected.

Predominance of the of stop card group:

the presence of several stop cards in a reading means that there is no action, progress or development in an issue. It's likely that the querent is holding onto something, such as an addiction, past memories, etc., and is unable to move forward.

> **Important Note:**
> The delays represented by the slow cards are temporary, while the stop cards indicate longer delays.

Predominance of the cards from The Hearts suit group:

The presence of several cards from The Hearts suit cards in a reading denotes that the dominant themes are related to emotions, relationships, friendship, domestic life, and everything that brings happiness to the querent.

Predominance of the cards from the Leaves suit group:

The presence of several cards from the Leaves suit group in a reading indicates an active social life, with a high level of communication and interaction, both in personal and professional spheres. The querent is eager to take advantage of all opportunities that come their way.

Predominance of the cards from the Bells suit group:

The presence of several cards from the Bells suit in a reading indicates that the focus is on material matters, such as financial gains and losses. The querent is focused on the material aspects of life.

Predominance of the cards from the Acorns suit group:

The presence of several cards from the Acorns suit in a reading predicts pain, suffering, sacrifices, and numerous challenges. The querent is undergoing difficult times and will require courage, determination, and strength to overcome them.

THE LAW OF MOVEMENT

Movement cards:

Keywords:
- Change, alteration, movement, activity, action, impulse, dynamism, energy, mobility, shift, progress.

Generally, when cards representing movement show up frequently in a reading, it usually suggests a process of change, mutation, transformation, or action. These cards indicate that the situation isn't yet stable. Their purpose is to announce a process of change, development, progress, evolution, expansion, growth, and renewal of a subject, for better or worse, depending on the surrounding cards

The cards are:
- The Rider, The Clover, The Ship, The Clouds, The Snake, The Coffin, The Scythe, The Broom and The Whip, The Owls, The Child, The Fox, The Storks, The Crossroads, The Mice, The Ring, The Letter, The Key, and The Fish.

As you can see, The Coffin card has been included in the list of movement cards because it symbolizes the conclusion of something already "dead" and no longer makes sense to "feed", making room and impulse for new beginnings in life. These new events will completely change the person's life.

Important Note:
The Clouds, The Snake, The Coffin, The Scythe, The Fox, and The Mice cards announce changes that are out of our control, whether by a natural disaster – The Coffin – such as an earthquake, flood, accidents, misfortunes, death, and so on, or by the action taken by others – The Clouds, The Snake, The Scythe, The Fox, and The Mice. These changes can be unwanted or caused by external or sometimes unseen forces.

Stop cards:

Keywords:
- Stop, nothing happens, unchanging, waiting, delay, boundaries, obstacles, blockage, prison, isolation, limits, restriction, monotony, demotivation, stagnation, dissatisfaction, frustration, fear, addictions, habits, disability, disease, resistance, persistence, stuck, paralyzed, suffering, frustration, pessimism, stubbornness, selfishness, pride, and disinterest.

And also:
- Balance, stability, perseverance, security, protection, calm, and patience.

When stop cards appear in a reading, they usually indicate that the querent is stuck in something, such as a habit, addiction, dependency, attachment, or relationship. This means they can't move forward or progress in life. These cards predict a period where nothing happens; there's no evolution or progress.

The problems aren't being solved, and the querent may resist change or have no goals in life. The reasons for the blockage can be indicated by surrounding cards.

The cards are:

- The House, The Coffin, The Tower, The Mountain, The Lilies, and The Anchor.

Important Note:

The difference between the slow and stop cards is their impact on progress. Slow cards denote a delay, meaning that the evolution or progress is taking place but at a slower pace than expected. On the other hand, stop cards indicate a lack of movement or progress, suggesting that the situation remains unchanged. Slow cards imply a temporary setback, while stop cards denote a complete stoppage.

Slow cards:

Keywords:

- Delay, slow, late, tardy.

In general, when slow cards appear in a reading, they indicate that a particular issue is progressing slowly and may take longer to achieve the desired outcome.

The cards are:

- The Ship, The Tree, The Child, The Bear, The Stars, The Storks, The Dog, and The Book.

2

CHAPTER 5:
COMBINATION TECHNIQUE

As mentioned in the topic about the meaning of the 36 cards, a Petit Lenormand reading with two or more cards is the most effective. Trying to perform a reading with just one card doesn't allow you to grasp the true message of a subject. Only by combining the cards will you find out what is behind the question, and it's possible to tell a story. In my courses, I encourage my students to practice reading daily, as it's the only way to learn interpretive language. I don't believe in memorizing the card combinations for two reasons:

- It's impossible to memorize all the possible card combinations in a reading because the interpretation of two cards can vary significantly depending on the context and the question being asked;

- By using "cheat" combinations from books or the internet, you miss out on connecting with the true essence of the cards and establishing your own interpretive language. In addition, when using such "cheats," the readings become cold and meaningless. Therefore, consider the proposed combinations from books and websites as suggestions rather than absolute combinations.

The ability to read the cards fluently will depend on your understanding of the 36 cards and their techniques. Without this knowledge, it's common to experience moments of uncertainty or feeling stuck, commonly referred to as a "lack of vision" or "I can't see anything". Becoming proficient in card reading takes time and dedication. It involves thoroughly studying all the aspects of the deck and regularly practicing to refine your skills.

HOW TO PERFORM A CARD COMBINATION

The secret of successfully performing a card combination depends on several elements. If you've read all the arguments in this book, you'll know it's essential to consider some points before you start card reading.

1. Knowing the 36 cards very well means:
   - To familiarize with the traditional German card reading;
   - To understand the meaning of all 36 cards;
   - To recognize each card's role in interpreting different life areas, such as emotions, relationships, work, finances, health, etc.

2. Understanding the card polarity (positive, neutral, and negative) and energy (movement, slow, and stopped cards). The group of movement cards initiates change and motion to a situation, the group of slow cards brings eventual resolutions, and the group of stop cards causes stagnation and blocks the progress of an issue.

3. Learning the card reading codes.

4. Knowing the significator cards.

CHAPTER 5: COMBINATION TECHNIQUE

STEPS FOR COMBINING CARDS

The result of a combination depends on three points: the context, the question, and the interpretation.

The context defines the theme of the reading

Having a clear understanding of the subject is crucial for interpreting the cards. The initial conversation with the querent is vital to the reading to determine the motivation and purpose of the consultation. Once you grasp the context, you can confidently define:

- The purpose of the reading;
- The objectivity and clarity of the question;
- The choice of the appropriate method;
- An objective and clear reading.

The question allows you to get a clear and objective answer

When we're mentally confused and dissatisfied with our lives, our thoughts, and actions become unclear. Everything seems confusing and uncertain, right? Similarly, if we ask vague and unclear questions, the cards will respond, but we'll be unable to understand the message clearly and objectively, leaving us confused. So, to ensure accurate answers, it's of the utmost importance to learn to formulate clear and specific questions for the cards. Remember, the way you pose the question has a significant influence on the answer. Stay focused on the question. Bear that in mind.

When posing a question, keep in mind the following:

- Always use affirmative statements

  For example, "Will Gloria pass the math exam?" instead of "Won't Gloria pass the math exam?".

- Avoid double questions

  Double questions allow two possible answers or cover two different themes.

  For example: "Is Clara going on vacation or not? If so, when?", "Should I go out with John or Tom?", "Will Paul call me today or not?", "Will Simone solve her financial situation and find a job soon?" and so on. These questions make obtaining clear and objective answers from the cards difficult and will only complicate things. Here are some suggested examples of how to ask questions:

  o What are the true intentions of (person's name) for (querent's name)?
  o What should (querent's name) do to solve the problem with (person's name)?
  o How will the (querent's name) financial situation develop in the coming months?
  o How can (querent's name) and (person's name) overcome marriage difficulties?
  o Will (person's name) grant the loan requested by (querent's name)?
  o How will the business develop in the next three months?
  o In what field is (querent's name) most likely to find a job?
  o Will (querent's name) sell their property at a price they have set?
  o What prevents (querent's name) from achieving their goals?
  o Will (querent's name) find their lost keys?
  o How can (querent's name) help their child (child's name) to overcome the situation they're experiencing?
  o And so on.

- Don't ask about unrealistic facts

    We shouldn't ask the cards abstract questions. For example, it makes no sense to ask the cards if we will become Olympic champion swimmers without even knowing how to swim or intending to learn someday, don't you think so? The cards work based on current situations in our lives and the future, deeply rooted in our past and present. Always practice with real situations for a better understanding of the subject and to identify where you need to deepen your studies.

- Self-reading

    My grandmother always told me, "… You need to feel, see and live things within yourself before sharing them with others", "… Maturity comes only with practice with our life situations". I always take this and other wise advice with me and apply it personally and professionally. Is it possible to read the cards to yourself? Yes, of course! And I'm not the only one who says so.

    During the learning phase, it's common for the fortune teller to use personal situations as an object of study. After all, is it possible to learn something without having personally experienced it? Even if you know everything about swimming technique, that doesn't make you a good swimmer if you don't put that knowledge into practice, right? The same is true for the cards.

    The more you work with them, practicing the theories you've learned in the courses and through research, the more you'll understand their language and feel confident in your ability to read them. Therefore, self-readings are a valuable and beneficial form of learning, especially for those who want to become a professional fortune teller.

    In my classes, I observe that those who study the cards using personal issues for their card readings tend to perform better than those who don't.

    Does self-reading bring bad luck or cause a blockage? There are conflicting opinions on this subject, some based on superstition or "rules" imposed by fortune tellers who believe that the cards won't answer if you read for yourself or that it's even possible to lose the gift of fortune-telling.

I think it's time to demystify these old beliefs that no longer make sense today. As I have mentioned before, we aren't born fortune tellers; it requires a journey of hard work and theoretical and practical studies. The fortune teller has no paranormal abilities other than their intuition that grows over time.

There is no basis for the claim that self-reading leads to a block for the reading. The cards will always respond when they're questioned. The blockage actually lies with the fortune teller, not with the cards. Reasons for this blockage can include fatigue, sickness, and personal worries, among others. These factors can prevent the fortune teller from achieving the necessary focus to perform an accurate reading.

- It's not recommended to ask the cards the same questions

Asking the cards the same question can negatively affect mental health and growth in card study. This behavior can result in dependency and insecurity. The dependency argument should be taken seriously, and it's important to be careful when reading cards for yourself and others. A fortune teller, whether a beginner or a professional, must keep self-control and avoid encouraging obsession in those who constantly look for convenient answers. The cards will always answer the first question. This answer is understandable, and it's necessary to wait a few days before asking again about the same topic.

In this sense, it's also crucial to remember that the role of a fortune teller, or anyone who uses divination tools for personal growth or therapeutic purposes, is to contribute to the well-being of those who seek their assistance and to encourage them to use their free will, if necessary.

Based on my extensive experience, the fortune tellers should educate their clients by setting boundaries and ensuring neither party (fortune teller and querent) exceeds them. This is what is called professional ethics.

- Timing Prediction

    It's common for the querent to follow up their answers with "When". This type of inquiry requests a date. When this happens, include a specific time frame in the question.
    For example: "Will Albert find a job within a month?" "Will Sarah go on vacation in August 2023?" "Will Veronica receive the medical results within ten days?"

    Establish a time frame if you use a specific reading method, like the Grand Tableau. For general readings, I typically set the Grand Tableau for three to six months. I set the time according to the querent's needs using fewer cards or specific methods, such as the three- or five-card line. This topic has already been covered, and I suggest further study in case of any doubt.

Interpreting the cards

As a general rule, when interpreting the cards, it's necessary to take into account the following:

1. **Keep in mind that the interpretation of cards isn't done individually.** The meaning of single card may change depending on the context and the relationship to other cards in the reading.

    The interpretation is based on reading the groups of cards. Think of the 36 cards as pieces of a puzzle that come together to form the whole picture. I use to say that each card has its own unique personality and posture that changes depending on the context, the question, and the surrounding cards.

    For instance, consider The Heart card to understand a mother's reaction to her child after receiving negative news about his behavior at school. Usually, The Heart card overflows with love, intense feelings, passion, joy, kindness, and charity, isn't it? However, if the next card is the Broom and The Whip, the message takes on a completely different meaning, don't you agree?

Let's see how.

My interpretation:
The mother is dissatisfied and hurt and may take a strict and authoritarian attitude toward her child. Punishment is a possibility.

But the scenario may be different if instead of The Broom and The Whip card, we have The Lilies No. 30.

My interpretation:
The mother is likely to handle the situation calmly and maturely, helping her child take responsibility for his actions. Maturity and responsibility.

As you can see in these examples, the meaning of each card is influenced by the card next to it. Therefore, keep in mind that the message can change depending on the cards that are next to another card, so it's necessary to consider the polarity and techniques (codes) when interpreting the cards.

2. **The cards are interpreted based on the theme of the reading,**
   Which includes the context and the question. For example, if the combination of the cards The Bouquet and The Fish shows up in a romantic context and the question is "What's Paul's true intention toward Anne?", the answer would indicate that Paul's interest and investment in a relationship with Anne rather than financial gain or salary. Similarly, If The Heart and The Anchor card appear in the same context, and the question is "Are Arthur's feelings sincere?", we won't talk about his complete devotion or absolute dedication to the job, but that he has sincere and deep feelings for the querent. Keep focused on the main topic, and don't get distracted by other issues that have nothing to do with the theme.

3. **When the cards don't respond.**
   It's important to understand that the cards always respond. This is a proven fact. There is no such thing as an error, blockage, or lack of response from the cards during a reading. So why do some fortune tellers believe this? According to my experience, when it happens, it's due to the fortune tellers themselves, not the cards. Below I list the reasons why I believe it's a blockage on the part of the fortune tellers.

   3.1. The main reason is the lack of knowledge about the card's symbolic language. During a reading, the fortune teller faces symbolic images they need to know how to interpret based on their prior knowledge. Each deck of cards has its unique identity, a history that includes information about its creator. To work effectively with a deck, you must first gather information about it and know its origins and the symbolic meaning of each card according to its creator. We can't interpret a card based on our cultural superstitions or even worst, our personal ideas. If, during a reading, a fortune teller claims to "see nothing", in fact, they really don't have enough knowledge of the deck's symbolic language. For a better understanding, consider the following example: When we travel to a foreign country, we only know a few words of the local language, such as "hello," "good morning," "thank you," and "please," don't we?" We can't talk fluently with someone in a foreign country if we know only a few words of the local language. And someone talks to us, we don't understand the language, our brain seems to shut down, and we feel like we can't hear anything. When we don't recognize something, our memory creates a vacuum, as if we're in the dark. Likewise, if we don't master the cards' language, we will simply see darkness and won't be able to see anything.

3.2. Panic and insecurity may also cause blockage. Again, this is related to what was previously mentioned: insufficient knowledge, lack of preparation and practice.

3.3. The mental, emotional (problems, anxiety, worries, nervousness), and physical (fever, pain, illness, medication) conditions can greatly affect clarity and concentration, which are essential for a successful consultation. So don't try to blame external factors like evil spirits, spells, or other reasons for blockages in your readings. The solution is to study your cards seriously.

4. **Can the cards be wrong?**
No, absolutely! Those who believe the cards can be deceived aren't working properly with their deck. What we see during a reading is accurate and truthful. Only the fortune teller's lack of solid knowledge can lead them to assume that the cards' message is incorrect. Lack of deep knowledge, due to poor preparation can lead to insecurity and make it difficult to interpret the cards' messages clearly. Only through dedicated and hard study and practice it's possible to gain a deep understanding of the cards.

5. **The stalking cards**
A stalking card is a card that keeps coming up over and over when cutting the deck or falls out of the deck while you are shuffling. Even though this doesn't always happen, it's worth

paying attention because the card sends you an important message. If this occurs during a reading, the message is intended for the querent. However, if you're reading for yourself, the message is directed at you.

How to interpret the stalking cards? You interpret them based on their keywords. If they show up with other cards, the stalking cards are the main theme and the others give further details.

6. **Some behaviors can also cause frustration and failure in a reading,** particularly when choosing a method and applying its rules correctly. It's always recommended, especially for beginners, to opt for smaller and positional methods.

But what exactly is a positional method? Think of the structure of a method as a theater set. Each object (furniture, doors, windows, etc.) has a specific position. Now imagine that the cards represent the actors, who take their respective positions on the stage set as they enter the scene. The interpretation of the cards is guided by definitions closely related to each positional house. A positional method includes all these reading methods and contains several areas called houses. Each house is assigned keywords that play a specific role during the reading.

For instance, in the Energy of the Day Method, the 1st house represents the energy of the day, while the 2nd house shows how to manage the energy brought by the card in the 1st house.

Another example is the Three-Card Method, where the 1st house indicates the past, the 2nd house represents the querent's present or current situation, and 3rd house the future or the development of the situation in the following few days.

When a card lands in a house, its interpretation is based on the energy represented by the keyword associated with that house. For example, if The Heart card is in a house representing obstacles, it means that the querent is unable to express their feelings or that they have a weight in their heart preventing them from acting naturally. On the other hand, if The Heart card is placed in a house representing the present, we can say that the querent is emotionally involved with current events and is doing their best to make things conform to their wishes.

But is it important to work with a positional method? Absolutely. It's especially important if you're starting your studies or want to go deeper into a particular topic. As mentioned, a good positional method contains houses full of analytical possibilities to give you as much information as possible about a subject.

7. **Bear in mind that cards in the position A + B don't have the same interpretation if they're in the opposite position B + A.**

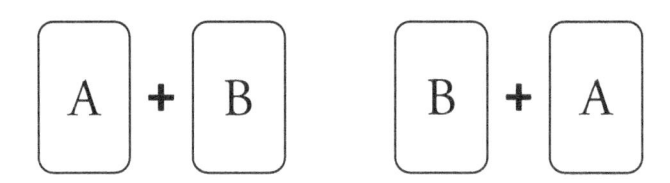

For example:

Position A + B: The Ship + The Coffin
- The end of a journey or trip;
- The trip is canceled;
- The final journey;
- No movement;
- A health-related trip or mourning;
- An inheritance.

Position B + A: The Coffin + The Ship
- Traveling abroad to seek medical treatment;
- Nausea, motion sickness;
- After the end of a standstill phase and the gradual start of progress or movement;
- Passage to another life (possible death);
- Leave behind past experiences or painful situations.

Another example:

Position A + B: The Scythe + The Ship
- o A trip might be interrupted;
- o Overseas travel accident or far from home;
- o The trip is canceled unexpectedly.

Position B + A: The Ship + The Scythe
- o A sudden trip;
- o An emergency trip;
- o A quick trip.

8. **If you're starting your studies, it's normal to struggle with interpreting the cards,** but don't worry, stay calm and follow these steps 1) Give each card three or more keywords related to the reading's theme. Since each card has many possible meanings, focus on the associations most relevant to the subject you're exploring. 2) Interpret the cards according to the reading's context. 3) Write down all your readings. This way, you can see if the prediction came true and create a personal record of card combinations.

9. During a reading, it's crucial to look at both the first and last cards. The first card shows us the current situation, while the last card points to the outcome or development of the question under analysis.

10. A card reading is based 50% on technical and intellectual knowledge acquired through study and much practice and 50% on intuition. We all have this precious gift of intuition.

TWO-CARD COMBINATION

Start studying combinations with only two cards. You can use the "Two-Card Method" or draw two cards randomly from the deck and place them in front of you from left to right:

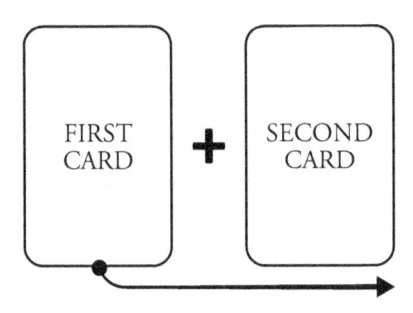

- The first card drawn represents the focus of the reading (my grandmother called it the domain card). This card's function is to establish the main theme, which is of greater importance in the issue being analyzed.

- The second card drawn offers further insight into the theme indicated by the first card. It can also change the value of the preceding card.

For example

Suppose the theme of the reading is to understand the cause of a 14-year-old- young man's antisocial behavior towards his family at home (true reading). The cards drawn are The Broom and The Whip + The Lilies.

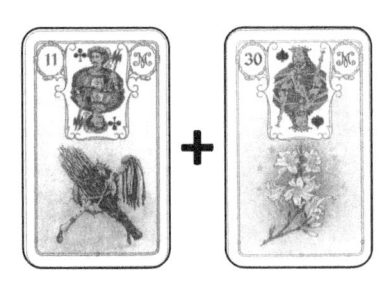

The Broom and The Whip card
- Keywords: disagreements, conflicts, aggression, abuses, oppression, submission, domination, criticism.

As the first card, the Broom and The Whip card indicates tension and conflict. Therefore, the major concern is related to the person's experience of aggression and the punishment they're enduring.

The second card, The Lilies, provides information and details about The Broom and The Whip card.

The Lilies
- Keyword: peace, harmony, calmness, honor, family, tradition, sex, morality, support.

Interpreting the two cards:
The Broom and The Whip card shows that the young man was facing a conflict that took away his inner peace (The Lilies). When I saw these two cards, my intuition told me that the boy was struggling with his sexuality (The Broom and The Whip + The Lilies) and was afraid to tell his family about what was afflicting him. The boy's mother had a friendly conversation with him about sex and gained his trust. He admitted that he was homosexual and that he suffered greatly for upsetting his parents. After talking to his family, the problem was solved, as both his mother and father embraced and supported their son.

Example of another reading:
Querent's name: Giancarlo
- **Step 1 – Reading Context:** Work
- **Step 2 – Question:** How will Giancarlo develop professionally within a month?
- **Step 3 – Drawn cards:** The Ship + The Fish

- **Step 4 – Keyword of each card:**
    - The Ship: trade, buying and selling, interchange, movement, progress, a foreign country, distant places;
    - The Fish: abundance, money, business, trade, wealth, fertility, growth.

- **Step 5 – Interpreting the cards:**
In this reading, I see the querent's ability to "swim" the troubled waters of challenges in his work to reach his goals. He needs to express himself, grow, explore new opportunities, and move away from what limits him. The querent has already implemented his project, promoting his work through different channels such as the internet. He may even be negotiating with foreign products or traveling frequently on business. Therefore, the cards promise professional growth, well-managed business, new customers, and financial gain.

CHAPTER 5: COMBINATION TECHNIQUE

COMBINING MORE THAN TWO CARDS

You apply the same procedure used in the Two-card Method. Combine the cards in pairs, starting by combining the first with the second, then the second with the third, the third with the fourth, and finally, the fourth with the fifth, as shown in the image below.

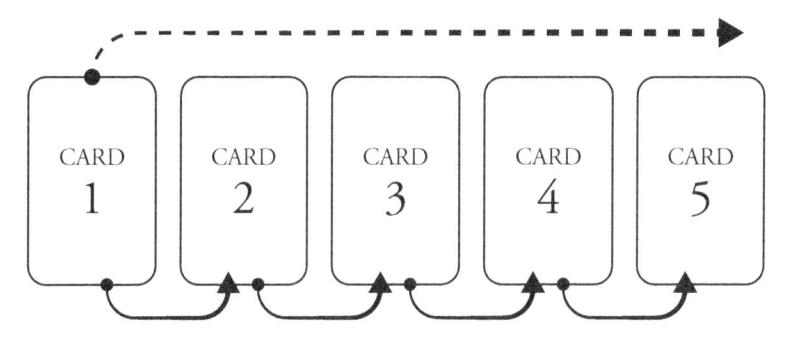

| CARD 1 | CARD 2 | CARD 3 | CARD 4 | CARD 5 |

Demonstrative example:

Querent's name: Giancarlo

- **Step 1 – Reading Context:** professional
- **Step 2 – Question:** How will Giancarlo develop professionally within a month?
- **Step 3 – Cards drawn:** The Ship + The Fishes + The Crossroads + The Ring + The Anchor
- **Step 4 – Keyword for each card:**
    o The Ship: trade, buying and selling, travel, foreign, new horizons;

- o The Fish: business, commerce, prosperity, money, finance;
- o The Crossroads: choice, decision, research, different paths, other possibilities, several paths;
- o The Ring: union, contract, signature, something regular and solid;
- o The Anchor: employment, work, determination, stability, bond, commitment

- **Step 5 – Combining the cards:**
  - o The Ship + The Fish: a business trip, desire to increase earnings;
  - o The Fish + The Crossroads: selling goods, expanding one's own business;
  - o The Crossroads + The Ring: choice regarding a contract or a professional union;
  - o The Ring + The Anchor: work contract, a steady job, a secure professional association.

- **Step 6 – Possibilities of card interpretation:** Based on these card combinations, the querent may be
  - o Seeking new business partners;
  - o Considering different business offers;
  - o Researching ways to stabilize his business;
  - o Deciding between two contracts that could bring financial stability to their business;
  - o Planning to market his products to multiple companies;
  - o Traveling abroad in search of work due to the crisis in his country.

As you saw in the previous example, there are numerous possibilities for interpreting the cards in a reading. The key is to trust the cards in front of you and yourself and keep calm while analyzing each card and its combinations.

It's time to start your practical journey with the cards. I wish you a pleasant trip and great success. And may your knowledge and understanding about the cards help those in need.

CHAPTER 5: COMBINATION TECHNIQUE

THE HIDDEN CARD

The hidden card is meant to clarify, offer advice, or provide a final answer to the question. It's important to determine the hidden card's role in the consultation. In my readings, I've established that the hidden card will serve as guidance to take action or deal with the situation being analyzed. For example, if the hidden card is:

- The Tree card means that the situation is developing and that it's necessary to wait patiently for the events' development, keep working on the projects, and stick to the previously established plan.

- The Clouds card indicates that the situation is still being evaluated, so it's not the right moment to make decisions or take action. I advise waiting a little longer and letting things settle down before making any moves. It's important to avoid rushing or acting impulsively.

- The Mountain card denotes that the problem will only be solved with great effort.

- The Mice card denotes that new troubles will arise, and you may not get what you desire as time passes. Therefore, the analyzed situation will lead to nothing; it's a waste of time.

- The Book card tells us the importance of delving deeper into the question to gather all the necessary information and thoroughly explore the topic for a more comprehensive analysis. It can indicate that the querent is not sufficiently prepared to perform a specific task.

Is it necessary to find the hidden card in every reading method? The answer is no. However, so it's crucial to respect the principles and procedures of the chosen method.

How to obtain the hidden card?

Method 1:
Add up all the numbers corresponding to the card pip numbers. For example, if the cards in the reading are The Rider (1), The Scythe (10) + The Ship (3), the pip number of the hidden card is obtained by adding: 1 + 1 + 0 + 3 = 5. The hidden card is then The Tree (5).

Method 2:
Another way to add up all the pip numbers. Using the cards from the previous example: The Rider (1) + The Scythe (10) + The Ship (3), the hidden card pip is the sum: 1 + 10 + 3 = 14. In this case, the hidden card will be The Fox (14). To better analyze the problem, you can look for another hidden card that depends directly on the card obtained using the previous methods.

Determining the Second Hidden Card

It's very easy to obtain the second hidden card. Read the pip number obtained by the previous methods from right to left. Since the deck contains only 36 cards, if the number exceeds 36, subtract it from 36. Thus, the result will be the second hidden card of the reading.

For a better understanding, let's take the result of the example where the hidden card was The Fox (14). When we read the pip number from right to left, we get 41, which exceeds 36, so we subtract 36 from 41 and get 5 (41 - 36 = 5). This gives us the second hidden card in the reading: The Tree (5).

The hidden cards The Fox (14) + The Tree (5) aim to reveal what is still concealed regarding the subject at hand but which is about to happen in the querent's life. This valuable information can help them prepare for the impact of the event or look for solutions to overcome any challenges.

2

CHAPTER 6:
READING METHODS (DRAWINGS)

In this chapter, we apply what we've learned in the previous five chapters. Choosing the proper drawing method can be challenging, especially for those just starting to work with the deck. At this stage, it's common for beginners to feel eager to demonstrate their skills and choose complex methods, such as the Grand Tableau. However, this isn't the best way.

It's crucial to understand that when we start new things, we have to give ourselves time to assimilate them. The same goes for studying decks. Starting with simple methods that allow you to focus on a few cards will help you to understand the messages more clearly.

Once you feel ready to read with a large number of cards, you can move on to more complex methods like the Grandma Method, which is explained in this chapter, and the Grand Tableau, which will be covered in Chapter 7.

Before presenting the reading methods, I'd like to take a moment to answer some questions, especially from those who are just starting their journey in the world of cartomancy.

THE PLACE OF CONSULTATION

Traditionally, the consultation took place in a specific and private room, such as the living room or bedroom, away from prying eyes. In countries like Africa, Portugal, and Brazil, fortune tellers have their own dedicated space in their homes decorated with objects, plants, and saints that are part of their religious beliefs. However, times have changed, and the consultation space has evolved to include tables in bars, restaurants, discos, fairs, call centers, TV, radio, and other places.

Nowadays, fortune tellers are adapting to the modern world and are willing to travel long distances to serve their clients. Although there are different opinions about the new methods of fortune-telling consultations, I disagree with those who judge these professionals negatively.

Fortune tellers can still be serious professionals even working in an unconventional place, whether in front of a camera, at a fair table, over the phone, or through a webcam. They can create a calm and appropriate environment for conducting their reading with seriousness. No two people are alike. Each person has the ability to absorb and release energy, it varies from person to person. Thus, fortune tellers must always uphold and values fortune-telling by being transparent, honest, and respectful to themselves and others.

Whether consulting in front of a camera, at the microphone, over the phone (call center), or performing a show, the fortune teller should always remember their role.

How should the consultation place be?

The place for the reading should have the following characteristics:

- Free from distractions (TV, radio, computer, phone) to keep the focus;

- Decoration that reflects the fortune teller's personality;

- A welcoming and comfortable atmosphere.

The environment affects the fortune teller's work. Therefore, it's essential to pay special attention to the workspace. In Arab countries and India, the card reading or coffee ground readings are performed by women in the kitchen, a place where men aren't allowed to enter. In Mozambique and Angola, it's customary to consult while sitting on mats on the floor.

In Arab countries, India, and Africa, divination practices like card reading are still considered taboo and are usually done secretly, out of men's eyes in the house. As you can see, the consultation place depends on the cultural norms and the personal lifestyle. The important thing is to respect and value your work.

The Reading Table

I suggest following your religious beliefs or personal motivations. The fortune teller's table is traditionally covered with a white cotton tablecloth, and utensils are placed on it to help absorb negative energies:

- Incense (to your liking);
- White candle;
- A saucer with sea salt;
- Glass of water (mineral still water);
- Crystals or coins.

In addition, the box in which the cards are kept should also contain paper and a pen to write down the querent's information and the drawings.

The Duration of the Consultation

How long should a consultation last? That varies depending on the fortune teller. Each professional has their rituals and the choice of card-drawing methods. Therefore, it's a good sense, to communicate the estimated duration of the session in advance.

When a client contacts me for an appointment, I always ask if they want a comprehensive reading about all aspects of their life or focus on a specific issue. Some querents prefer not to talk about certain issues during the consultation, and this request should be respected.

Based on this initial contact, the client's expectations for the reading are established, which will determine the drawing method choice and the consultation duration. For instance, I schedule an hour and a half to two hours for an extensive Grand Tableau reading. Alternatively, if the reading is focused on a single topic, the session may last around 45 to 50 minutes.

THE TIME INTERVAL BETWEEN CONSULTATIONS

Setting a date for each reading based on the subject established with the client is the best approach. This allows the fortune teller to plan future appointments and track the development of the situation.

The querent may reach out for a re-evaluation either on the same day or a few days later. What to do in this situation? I usually keep a record of my appointments in a journal. Consulting these notes helps me clear up any questions the client may have without needing to schedule a new appointment. But we can schedule another consultation if the querent wishes to discuss a different topic. For example, as I primarily work with the Grand Tableau Lenormand method, it sometimes happens that the querent contacts me days later to go more in-depth on a specific topic, such as finance, work, friendship, and so on. In such a case, scheduling another appointment for a particular topic isn't a problem.

It's essential to "educate" the querent to be patient and allow the situation to unfold, understanding that cartomancy isn't a solution to their problems but rather a tool to aid self-awareness and personal growth. As fortune tellers, our responsibility is to convey the messages from the cards without imposing our own opinions or influencing the querent's free will.

CHAPTER 6: THE METHOD OF READING (DRAWINGS)

TO PAY OR NOT TO PAY FOR THE CONSULTATION?

"The fortune teller has a gift, so he or she shouldn't receive any compensation for their consultations."

This statement is commonly heard when someone asks for a consultation with a fortune teller. However, it's important to clarify that no one is born to be a fortune teller.

Becoming a fortune teller extensive and time-consuming study, covering both theory and practice. Serious fortune tellers invest significant time and resources in professional courses, books, and research to develop their skills, which can be pretty costly. Their reputation and professionalism are often built upon recommendations from satisfied clients.

When seeking the guidance of an experienced and professional fortune teller, clients can benefit from the extensive knowledge gained through years of dedicated study. Given these considerations, I believe that fortune tellers deserve to be fairly compensated for the valuable services they provide.

COVERED CARDS: YES, OR NO?

What does it mean when a card is "covered" or "hidden"? Covered or hidden cards refer to the cards laid face down on the table without revealing their image, so they remain unidentified until the reading begins.

This isn't a mandatory practice, and you're free to place the cards face down or not, depending on the chosen reading method. For example, for the methods like Grand Tableau, three-card or five-card spread, the cards are arranged face up, with their images exposed.

On the other hand, with methods like the Celtic Cross or the 12 astrological houses (mandala), among other methods, it's possible to keep the cards covered in their positions until they are read within their respective "hosted" houses."

Shuffling the Cards

Shuffling the cards is an essential part of the consultation ritual. It's at this point that the magic of reading begins. But why is shuffling important? It allows the cards to mix and rearrange, resulting in a new arrangement for the next reading. By this process, we ensure that the cards are reorganized and avoid drawing the same cards again. However, if that still happens, it's considered a "divine will."

It's important to shuffle the cards well and stop when you feel it's the right time. My grandmother used to ask the querent to say "stop" to indicate the conclusion of shuffling and I take this inheritance with me to my consultations.

Different shuffling techniques, such as overhand, Hindu, and cascade, can be used based on personal preference. What really matters is to find a technique that works for you and to handle the cards carefully, avoiding bumping or pressing too hard, which could damage the edges. If you have trouble shuffling, apply a small amount of baby powder to make the cards slide more smoothly.

Should the querent shuffle the cards?

Should the querent perform the card-shuffling ritual? Whether the querent should participate in the card-shuffling ritual depends on the fortune teller and their personal beliefs. In my practice, I don't allow the clients shuffling, cutting, and choosing the cards themselves. I believe they may not be emotionally stable during the reading, and there is a risk of potential damage to the deck due to their lack of practice in shuffling.

What should you do when the cards fall out of the deck?

It's common for the cards to accidentally fall out of the deck while shuffling or moving them from one place to another. What should we do in such situations? What behavior should be adopted? Should we take the cards falling cards ignore them or take them as a message? First, it's necessary to evaluate your relationship with the deck.

If the fortune teller has a strong connection, as I do, it's natural to pay attention to them since they may convey important messages that we should listen to.

What should you know about the cards that fall out of the deck?

Here are some guidelines that will help you to deal with falling cards:

1. Consider only the cards that fall with their image facing up.
2. These cards always offer valuable messages such as alerts, advice, warnings, or important information. They can provide clarification, reveal insights, or provide further details about something significant.
3. If you're conducting a reading, this falling card's message is intended for the querent and relates to the topic being explored.
4. If you're moving the deck from one place to another, or studying the cards without intending to consult them, then the message from the falling cards is meant for you.

Based on my extensive experience, I strongly emphasize that falling cards should be taken seriously during a reading.

THE READING METHOD (DRAWINGS)

THE ENERGY OF THE DAY METHOD

I have an old deck of cards on a small table in the living room, and I habitually draw out two cards every morning to know the energy of my day.

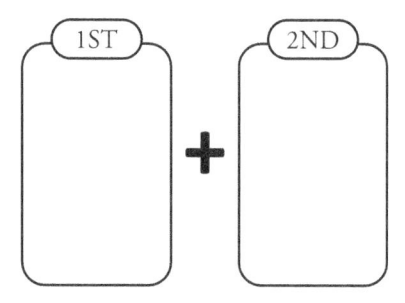

```
  1ST        2ND
 ┌───┐      ┌───┐
 │   │      │   │
 │   │  +   │   │
 │   │      │   │
 └───┘      └───┘
```

- **The First Card:** This card represents the day's energy. It'll reveal significant events and happenings that will take place on that day. This energy can be caused by the querent, other people, or situations that the querent has no control.
- **The Second Card:** This card represents how to deal with the day's energy, offering guidance and suggesting how to handle it effectively

An example with this method:

One morning in 2017, my friends, whom we'll call Danielle for privacy, requested me to draw some cards for the day because she had a disturbing dream.

Querent's name: Danielle

Drawn cards: The Clouds + The Anchor

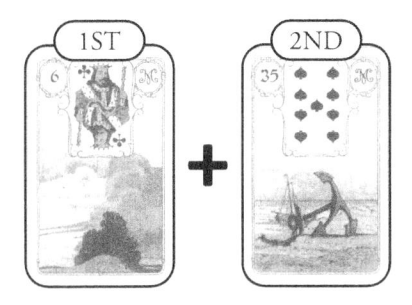

1st Position: The Clouds

- Keywords: misunderstanding, dimness, doubts, uncertainty, confusion, chaos, and eagerness

When The Clouds card comes up in a reading, it usually means that something unpleasant has suddenly arisen, causing panic and anxiety. It may be necessary to draw another card to delve more into what caused the situation. This additional card is known as a complementary card, and you can draw as many cards as you need to understand better what The Clouds card is trying to say. The complementary card will be placed on top of The Clouds card.

Complementary card drawn: The Owls

- Keywords: verbal communication, conversations, disagreements, encounters, gossip, stress, confusion, and small group of people.

Feeling unsatisfied, I decided **to draw a second card** that complements the situation: The Snake.

- Keywords: deceit, betrayal, lies, or a complicated situation

When I saw the combination of The Clouds + The Owls + The Snake, I understood that Danielle would be involved in a heated argument with a woman that day. The Owls and The Snake suggest that this woman could be a fortune teller or a sorceress.

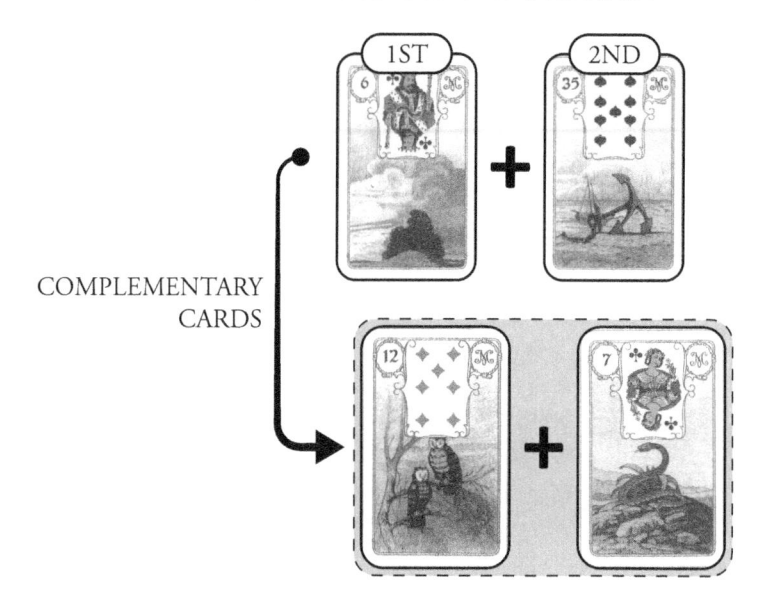

COMPLEMENTARY CARDS

Out of curiosity, I drew another card to figure out where this event would take place, and I got The Garden card.

- Keyword: a public place, or social networking groups.

Now we have in the 1st position the cards, The Clouds + The Owls + The Snake + The Garden

My interpretation:

The energy of that day energy would be terrible for my friend as she would be involved in a chaotic situation (The Clouds) caused by a woman (Queen of Club) due to disagreements, judgments, and fierce criticism (The Owls + The Snake) in a social network (The Garden). Most likely in a small closed group (The Owls + The Clouds). The combination of The Owls + The Snake + The Garden indicated that this woman would be responsible for spreading lies and slander on social media, resulting in many people making hurtful comments against Danielle.

2nd Position: The Anchor

- Keywords: stability, firmness, stopped, not moving.

My interpretation

So, based on The Anchor card's guidance, I advised Danielle not to take any action. Instead, I recommended that she focus on her personal and professional tasks and avoid communicating with the woman who caused the conflict or anyone else who sought her out to discuss the situation. As we know, situations brought on by The Clouds card pass quickly..

Update:

My friend was part of a small study group focused on cartomancy, where they shared knowledge and experiences. On that particular day, she found out that someone within the group was using her material without her permission and offering courses based on it. This sparked a heated argument and offensive remarks. Additionally, this person spread slanderous rumors about my friend in other cartomancy groups.

For ten days, hurtful comments were exchanged, but my friend handled them calmly and avoided getting into confrontations, eventually letting the situation calm down. Danielle decided to stay away from this person and the social media groups where she was subjected to insults. Sometimes it's better to prioritize peace over being proven right.

THE THREE-CARD METHOD

The Three-card method has several possibilities of use. It can be used for reading any topic you want to investigate:
- Love;
- Relationship;
- Work;
- Finances;
- Health;
- Timing questions;
- Asking about the current state of a situation;
- Yes / no questions;
- Daily advice;
- and so on.

As I previously stated, this method can be applied to any aspect of life. Unlike the Three-Card Timing method (1st house for the past, 2nd house for the present, and 3rd house for the future), there is no positional house in the Three-Card Method, and the fortune teller relies on keywords for guidance. This method is particularly suitable for someone starting to venture into the study of card reading, as it facilitates learning the combination technique and increases one's confidence as a fortune teller.

However, this method isn't appropriate for a general consultation. Instead, it's important to focus on doing the readings based on clear and specific questions, always answering within the context of the topic.

THE PHYSICAL STRUCTURE OF THE METHOD

This method consists of three houses where the cards drawn from the fan are placed in the order they were drawn.

CHAPTER 6: THE METHOD OF READING (DRAWINGS)

The Reading Technique

1. The first step is to focus on the central card, which is the second card.

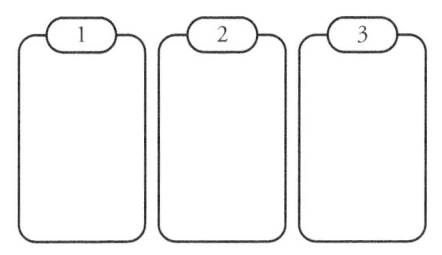

2. The second step is to focus on the second house. The "guest" card in this house is very important, as it will reveal crucial information for the reading.

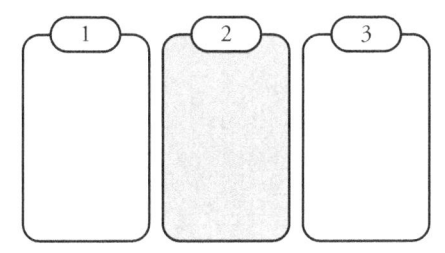

3. The third step is first to connect houses 1+3

4. Then the houses 1+2:

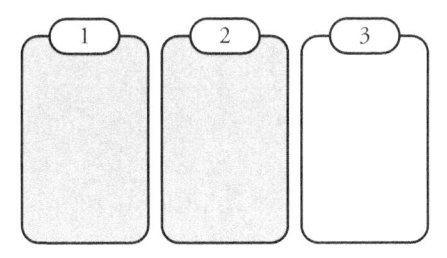

5. And finally, the houses 2+3:

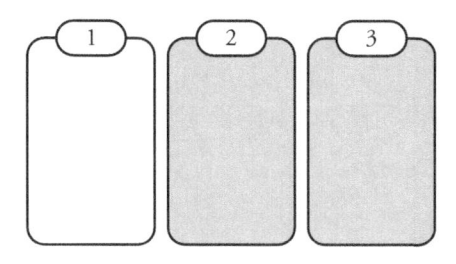

The combinations are read in pairs, not together. It's more effective to read each pair separately and save the summary for the end of the entire reading. It's recommended to practice this technique with a specific example to make it clearer.

Important Note:

In this method, it's not necessary to calculate the sum of the three houses to get an additional card for guidance. You can always do a new reading if you need advice or suggestions on an important topic.

Example 1

(The examples presented here were taken from my journal)

Consultation date: February 4, 2009

Querent's name: Gabriella, 32 years old.

Reading theme: Financial

Question: Will Gabriella's economic situation improve in the next three months?

Deck cut: The Anchor + The Mountain

These two cards reveal a long-standing stagnant situation. In fact, Gabriella confirmed that her work as a seamstress had faced setbacks for the past five months, leading to financial difficulties. The Anchor is the significator card for work, and The Mountain in front of it represents an insurmountable obstacle that has hindered progress in Gabriella's professional life.

These two cards belong to my "stop" card category, meaning they don't allow any advancement or news. They are static and remain fixed in the same position, causing long project delays and preventing any improvement in Gabriella's professional and financial situation.

The three cards drawn:

- The Storks + The Fish + The Anchor

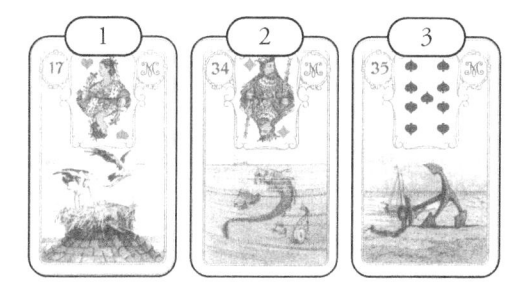

Keywords from the three cards:

I tried to identify the keywords from each of the three cards based on the reading question, to determine the most helpful ones

- The Storks: changes, action, modifications, movements, transmission, and alterations.
- The Fish: finances, money, material values, business, and businessman.
- The Anchor: work, hope, continuous, static, and stability.

Analysis of the three cards:

The central card, The Fish, stands for finances and money. It's amazing how it shows that money is the reading's main theme.

Now we'll see the three-house combinations:

- The Storks + The Anchor (house 1 + house 3): Gabriella is going to experience significant changes in her work. She'll probably try to change the way she works;

- The Storks + The Fish (house 1 + house 2): It indicates a return or improvement of financial status. This combination also indicates fertility;
- The Fish + The Anchor (house 2 + houses 3): The Fish card indicates increase, growth, and multiplication. With The Anchor card, I think of increasing work or income and providing financial stability.

My interpretation:

I really enjoyed these three cards, and I'm sure you did too. I told Gabriella that she would undergo significant changes in her work, ensuring her a stable income and financial stability.

Then Gabriella asked me how these changes would come about since she had no idea where to start. So, based on Gabriella's question, I reshuffled the cards, fanned them out on the table, and drew the following three cards:

Keywords from the three cards:

I tried to identify the keywords from each of the three cards based on the reading question, to determine the most helpful ones.

- The Fish: finance, money, investment, business, material values, procreation;
- The Ship: travel, moving, foreign, international, import-export, miscellaneous;
- The Garden: public, crowd, advertising, customers, social network, parade, being noticed.

Analysis of the three cards:

The central card is The Ship, which represents new adventures and contacts with new things and situations that may be intellectually and culturally enriching. It also stands for trade, negotiations, networking, and connection with distant people and places.

The Ship card in the central position is an invitation to Gabriella to expand her professional horizons, explore different market possibilities, promote her products, and take advantage of the vast opportunities offered by the internet.

Now let's see the house combinations:

- The Fish + The Garden (1st house + 3rd house): The word "customer" immediately came to mind when I saw this combination. But I also thought of possibly offering Gabriella's products online.

- The Fish + The Ship (1st house + 2nd house 2): This combination had already come up a few times and indicated business or the sale of products on the international market.

- The Ship + The Garden (2nd house + 3rd house): This combination indicates connections with foreign countries and people and "surfing" on the internet for business purposes. It also reveals that there will be a contract with people from other countries.

My interpretation:

I suggested to Gabriella to abandon her old ideas of work and adapt to the modern world, where everything revolves around the Internet. I encourage her to browse blogs and websites to research the most popular products in the clothing and sewing industry, given her expertise as a professional seamstress.

By offering her products online, Gabriella could reach, for sure, broader international customers.

Update:

Gabriella wasted no time to set to work. She reached out to a friend who was well-versed in the Internet and social media to help her research and promote her work. She started showcasing her handmade bags online, even sharing a couple with me since she knew I'm crazy about bags. Her products caught the attention of an Israeli stylist who offered her a position on his team of seamstresses.

Gabriella visited me in March 2013 while passing through Switzerland, and I was thrilled to see her thriving and happy. Today she works for a wide range of satisfied customers worldwide. I must admit that I feel immense joy knowing that my "little French cards" helped Gabriella to find her true calling and achieve professional goals, success, inner peace, and serenity. May her journey of prosperity and fulfillment continue for many years to come.

Example 2

Consultation date: December 13, 2012
Theme: Day's horoscope.
Question: How will my day be today?
Deck cut: The Scythe + The Woman

At that time, I was going through a difficult period of my health struggles. So, you can imagine how I felt when I saw these two cards! Nonetheless, I made an effort to set these feelings aside and wrote down in my journal, in red capital letters, "I'M EXPECTING A GREAT SHOCK".

CHAPTER 6: THE METHOD OF READING (DRAWINGS)

Then I fanned out the cards and drew three: The Rider + The Snake + The Letter, placing them in front of me:

Keywords from the three cards:

I tried to identify the keywords from each of the three cards based on the reading question, to determine the most helpful ones.

- The Rider: arrival, novelty, thought, fast transmission of information, delivery, interview, and direct contract.
- The Snake: a rival, an enemy, poison, conspiracy, serious complication, detour, betrayal, and infidelity.
- The Letter: written communication (MSN, email, chat, letter, SMS), signal, and warnings.

Analysis of the three cards:

The Snake as the central card worried me a bit since it's a potentially unfavorable card whose effects can cause long-term annoyance or even be fatal.

Let's see the house combinations:

- The Rider + The Letter (house 1 + house 3): I'll get a message from someone who wants to tell me something personal.
- The Rider + The Snake (house 1 + house 2): This gentle Rider brings me news of a betrayal, a conspiracy against me. It's worrying!
- The Snake + The Letter (house 2 + house 3): I interpreted these two cards as a warning, an alert. The Rider brings an important and disturbing message about the occult and the esoteric world, possibly a fortune teller.

My interpretation:

What caught my attention about these three cards was the presence of The Rider as the first card. I sometimes follow my instincts and look at the direction the figure is facing and the movement of objects and tools on the cards. In this case, we can see The Rider galloping swiftly toward its destination and goal, carrying The Snake and The Letter.

This led me to think that something unpleasant might happen behind my back, and a messenger (since The Rider symbolizes a messenger) would soon deliver urgent news through a fast communication method like a telegram, email, or chat. The message will bring shocking and painful information (The Scythe + The Woman). That's what I wrote in my journal on that day.

Update:

Later that day, I received a private message on my Facebook profile from a dear friend from South Africa, whose considerable contributions to the research and study of the Petit Lenormand and her expertise as a fortune teller I really admire and appreciate.

She notified me in her message that my second book, "L'Oracol di Mademoiselle Lenormand", had been plagiarized. This revelation took me entirely by surprise, especially given that

I had been dealing with the challenges of battling breast cancer and had just undergone chemotherapy earlier that day. You can imagine how deeply this news affected me at that time. However, the message conveyed by the cards were so clear.

CHAPTER 6: THE METHOD OF READING (DRAWINGS)

THE THREE-CARD METHOD (EXTENDED)

Author: Odete Lopes Mazza

Proposal 1 — for a relationship

You can use this method to assess the state and development of any relationship, such as love, friendship, partnerships, rivals, and family.

Draw nine cards from the deck and arrange them on the table in the order indicated in the figure below.

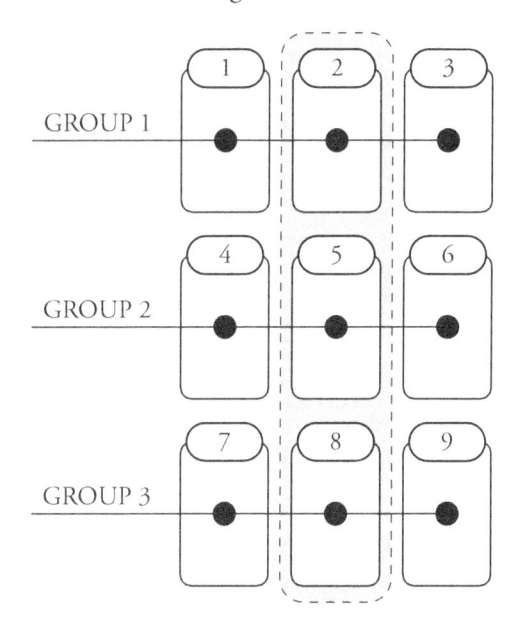

```
             ┌───┐ ┌───┐ ┌───┐
             │ 1 │ │ 2 │ │ 3 │
GROUP 1 ─────┤ ● ├─┤ ● ├─┤ ● │
             └───┘ └───┘ └───┘

             ┌───┐ ┌───┐ ┌───┐
             │ 4 │ │ 5 │ │ 6 │
GROUP 2 ─────┤ ● ├─┤ ● ├─┤ ● │
             └───┘ └───┘ └───┘

             ┌───┐ ┌───┐ ┌───┐
             │ 7 │ │ 8 │ │ 9 │
GROUP 3 ─────┤ ● ├─┤ ● ├─┤ ● │
             └───┘ └───┘ └───┘
```

Card Definitions

- **Cards from Group 1:** These cards show the querent's situation, how they deal with the relationship, as well as attitudes and goals concerning the partner.

- **Cards from Group 2:** These cards represent the other person's perspective and involvement in the relationship (be it a romantic partner, friend, family member, or rival). They reveal the person's thoughts, feelings, attitudes, and goals towards the querent. If it's a romantic reading and there's no other person in the querent's life, they'll describe the current state of the querent's love life.

- **Cards from Group 3:** These cards give insight into the couple's current situation. If the querent doesn't have a partner, these cards will provide information about the future of their love life or a potential relationship.

- **Cards from Group 4:** The future evolution is obtained in two ways:
    o By adding up the value of the cards from the three groups and reducing them to a card between numbers 1 and 36 or;
    o By interpreting the central (vertical) cards, which are depicted in gray in the illustration

Let's take, for example, a reading I conducted in 2014 for a woman named Margherita in French-speaking Switzerland. Margherita had met Jean-Pierre on a dating app, and they were in the early stages of getting to know each other. At first, their relationship seemed to be going well, and they even made plans to travel to France together. But then something happened that made Margherita seek me for a consultation to understand his behavior and to see how their relationship would evolve over the next three months.

- **Group 1**: It represents Margherita. I drew the following cards: The Clouds + The Broom and The Whip + The Stars
  During the consultation, Margherita was feeling confused, agitated, and upset (The Clouds + The Broom and The Whip) due to her partner's lack of clarity (The Clouds + The Stars). She began to doubt Jean-Pierre's feelings for her (The Clouds above The Heart card).

CHAPTER 6: THE METHOD OF READING (DRAWINGS)

GROUP 1

GROUP 2

GROUP 3

- **Group 2:** It represents Jean-Pierre. I drew the cards: The Heart + The Fox + The Crossroads.

    Margherita's doubts are justified, as the combination of The Heart + The Fox cards indicates that Jean-Pierre's feelings and intentions are ambiguous and deceitful. Furthermore, the cards suggest that he may be secretly (The Fox + The Crossroads) seeking romantic adventures (The Heart + The Crossroads), possibly through online platforms (The Stars above The Crossroads card).

- **Group 3:** It denotes the couple's current situation. I drew the following cards: The Owls + The Letter + The Mountain.

    To avoid explaining and clarifying his already complicated situation, Jean-Pierre blocked contact and communication with Margherita (The Letter + The Mountain) so she couldn't control him on WhatsApp (The Owls + The Letter).

- **Group 4 (vertical central cards):** These cards indicate the couple's possible romantic evolution: I drew: The Broom and The Whip + The Fox + The Letter

Margherita's constant pressure to uncover the truth (The Broom and The Whip + The Fox) led her to spy on her partner's contacts in an attempt to find out something (The Fox + The Letter + The Owls). Despite her efforts, however, Margherita won't receive any clarification from Jean-Pierre.

Proposal 2 – for professional or financial issues

House Definitions

- **Group 1:** It provides information about the querent's work or finances, depending on the topic of the question. They reveal the querent's attitudes towards the question and offer insights into their financial or professional situation.
- **Group 2:** These cards describe the querent's current professional or financial condition.
- **Group 3:** These cards reveal the professional future or financial developments.

Here's an example of a financial reading

In January 2017, Carlos Miguel requested a consultation to see how his finances would evolve over the next three months. The cards drawn were:

CHAPTER 6: THE METHOD OF READING (DRAWINGS)

GROUP 1 — cards 1, 2, 3

GROUP 2 — cards 4, 5, 6

GROUP 3 — cards 7, 8, 9

- **Group 1:** The Mice + The Bear + The Coffin
  The combination of The Mice + The Bear cards indicates a substantial financial loss due to a long-standing and painful situation (The Coffin) that has depleted his bank account. Unfortunately, this withdrawal of funds was unavoidable.

- **Group 2:** The Crossroad + The House + The Anchor
  In fact, the querent had to withdraw his entire savings from the bank to resolve an important family matter.

- **Group 3:** The Cross + The Clover + The Tree
  Thanks to Carlos Miguel's ability to overcome difficult times (The Cross + The Clover), he'll will be able to recover his savings (The Clover + The Tree).

Important Note:

When working with the Grand Tableau techniques or the Lopes Mazza's codes, it's common to certain interesting aspects in the "game". For example, the corner and central cards can provide additional information to the reading, pointing to the root cause of the problem and explaining why the querent had to use his savings. In this particular case, the cards reveal that the reason behind it was the disease (The Coffin + The Tree + The Cross + The Mice) of a family member (The House).

Here's an example for professional reading

Xavier seeks guidance on his job situation over the next three months.

- **Group 1:** The Stars + The Fox + The Rider
  The combination of The Stars + The Fox cards suggests that Xavier is concerned about the success of his promising project (The Stars) because he's dealing with an unhealthy work environment that's full of traps and deceit (The Fox + The Rider).

- **Group 2:** The Snake + The Mountain + The Bear
  Actually, Xavier is surrounded by deceitful and crafty people who plot against him and cause problems (The Snake + The Mountain). Therefore, he must make a great effort (The Bear) and sacrifices to overcome them.

- **Group 3:** The Tower + The Ring + The Child
  The Tower card stands for serious and long-term work, and when combined with The Ring card, it also indicates an agreement or a new business contract (The Ring + The Child), which will give the querent energy and motivation. The corner cards The Tower + The Stars + The Rider + The Child indicate a company that values creativity, imagination, and innovative ideas. Consequently, Xavier has all the necessary skills to succeed in his career at the company where he works.

CHAPTER 6: THE METHOD OF READING (DRAWINGS)

GROUP 1

GROUP 2

GROUP 3

SHOULD I TRUST METHOD
Author: Odete Lopes Mazza

"Trust is a fragile thing. Once earned, it affords us tremendous freedom. But once trust is lost, it can be impossible to recover. Of course, the truth is, we never know who we can trust. Those we're closest to can betray us, and total strangers can come to our rescue. In the end, most people decide to trust only themselves. It really is the simplest way to keep from getting burned."

Mary Alice Young (BrendaStrong)
Desperate Housewives

THE CARD LAYOUT

The cards are placed on the table according to the position suggested in the following illustration.

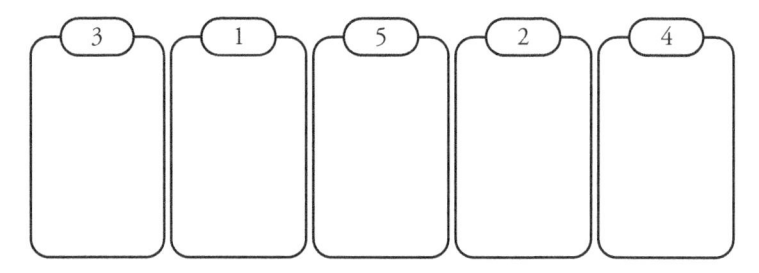

```
 ┌───┐ ┌───┐ ┌───┐ ┌───┐ ┌───┐
 │ 3 │ │ 1 │ │ 5 │ │ 2 │ │ 4 │
 │   │ │   │ │   │ │   │ │   │
 │   │ │   │ │   │ │   │ │   │
 └───┘ └───┘ └───┘ └───┘ └───┘
```

HOUSE DEFINITIONS

- **House 1:** It reflects how the other person presents themselves to the querent, including verbal behavior and attitude towards them.

- **House 2:** It reveals what the person is keeping hidden from the querent, something that is not yet known. There are two possible reasons for this behavior.
    - The person may have built a barrier or doesn't have good intentions towards the querent.
    - The person may be fueling doubts about the querent based on the same concerns that led to the inquiry.

CHAPTER 6: THE METHOD OF READING (DRAWINGS)

- **House 3:** House 3: Represents what the person intends from the querent. The guest card in this house reveals the person's real intentions and goals towards the querent.
- **House 4:** This card provides information about the development and quality of the relationship. It can answer questions like:
  - What can I expect?
  - Should I break up the relationship or continue it the with this person?
- **House 5:** It answers the querent's question – Can I trust him or her? This house gives the definitive answer on whether this person is trustworthy.

Here's **an example** of a reading I did for a woman I'll call Gloria some time ago.

Querent's name: Gloria

Question: Should Gloria trust her new friend Alberto?

Drawn cards:

- **House 1:** This is how Alberto presents himself to Gloria: The Bouquet card.

  Keywords: happiness, courtesy, kindness, appreciation, and interest.

  My interpretation: Alberto shows interest in Gloria's friendship. He's friendly, polite, generous, and very thoughtful.

- **House 2:** This card represents what Alberto is hiding from Gloria: The Fox card.

  Keywords: lies, deceit, trap, theft, premeditation, spying, taking advantage, seduction, and manipulation.

My interpretation: The Fox isn't a good card for assessing someone's true character or attitude towards the querent. In Alberto's case, he's hiding something, most likely his real intentions or goals in his friendship with Gloria.

Important Note:

House 2 is connected to house 3, and house 3 holds more information about The Fox card.

- **House 3:** It reveals Alberto's true intentions: The Mice card.
  Keywords: betrayal, theft, loss, taking possession of someone's belongings.

Important Note:

It's important to notice whether the cards in houses 2 and 3 belong to the same category and whether they have similar meanings and energies. In this spread, The Fox and The Mice in these two houses are negative cards and denote betrayal, theft, loss, and taking something away. It's a warning signal advising Gloria to be careful in her relationship with this man. So I suggest drawing a complementary card to figure out his aims or to get more details about the theft or the trap he is setting up for Gloria.

Complementary card: The Book card

CHAPTER 6: THE METHOD OF READING (DRAWINGS)

<u>Keywords</u>: a secret, intellectual knowledge, important information, instruction, important documents.

<u>My interpretation</u>: Therefore, The Fox + The Mice + The Book cards announce concealed information or documents. This was particularly concerning to me since Gloria is a writer. In this combination, it's pretty clear that Alberto's amiability and kindness towards Gloria were to find out details about her new book.

- **House 4:** It shows the evolution of Gloria and Alberto's friendship: The Coffin card.

  <u>Keywords</u>: ending, conclusion, resignation, disappearance, and goodbye.

  <u>My interpretation</u>: Their relationship has no future.

Important Note:

The houses 4 and 5 are interpreted together.

- **House 5:** Should Glory trust Alberto? The Ship card.

  <u>Keywords</u>: action, slow motion, distancing, and going away.

  <u>My interpretation</u>: Gloria shouldn't trust Alberto. The Ship card indicates they'll distance themselves until the relationship comes to an end (The Ship + The Coffin).

Update:

On the day of Gloria's reading, I heard unpleasant things about Alberto from some acquaintances. I found out that he had previously plagiarized another writer, confirming the suspicions raised by the cards. As a result, Gloria began distancing herself from Alberto and stopped responding to his messages and calls. This happened three years ago, and they haven't had any contact since then.

METHOD TO IDENTIFY MAGIC
Author: Odete Lopes Mazza

This reading method is used to detect magic, witchcraft, or any negative energy that is disturbing the querent or their environment.

How to proceed:

1. Take The Broom and The Whip card from the deck and place it in the center of the table.

2. Shuffle and cut your deck as usual.

3. The cards obtained by cutting the deck are significant since they provide the first information and reveal the energies in the querent's life

4. Lay the cards out in front of you in a fan shape, choose eight cards, and distribute them according to the positions indicated in the chart.

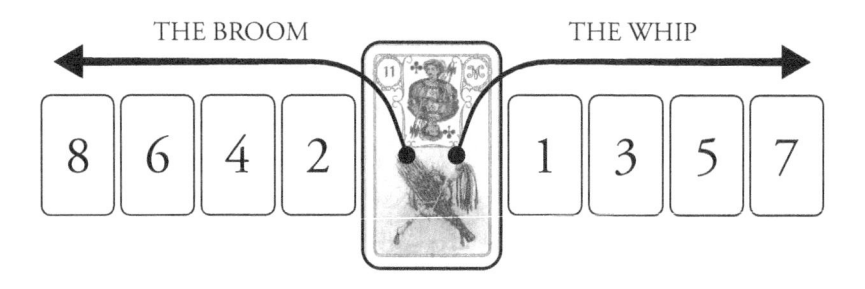

```
        THE BROOM                    THE WHIP
    ←                                         →
   [8] [6] [4] [2]  [WHIP]  [1] [3] [5] [7]
```

- The four cards in contact with **the whip** identify spells or negative influences affecting or disturbing the querent. The cards in this position can reveal the origin (who sent it), the type of magic used, and its location (whether it's indoors, buried, etc.).

- The four cards on **the broom** side will offer guidance and advice on how to clear the energies present in the whip group.

Two important points to consider when court cards appear in a reading:

1. Determine if the court cards belong to The Whip group or The Broom group (according to the magic method below).
2. Identify which suit the court cards belong to.

Therefore, if you find one or more court cards from the Acorn suit placed in the whip group, it means that there are malicious people who have harmful intentions or intend to ruin the querent's life. Dealing with these individuals requires preparing for a battle to protect in order to neutralize the enemy.

The Hearts or Leaves suits represent those close to the querent, like family and friends, who may also be affected by the spell. However, the Acorn court figures in the broom group are a good sign as they represent professionals such as healers, sorcerers, and psychs who can help the querent. The Hearts and Leaves suits also indicate therapists and gurus.

Bear in mind that:

- The Kings: experienced male professionals;
- The Queens: experienced female professionals;
- The Jacks: less experienced professionals.

» The Rider, The Ship, The Owls, The Storks, and The Letter cards announce the arrival of some **negativity or magic**.

» The House, The Tree, The Bear, The Stars, The Dog, The Mountain, The Keys, and The Anchor cards represent **protection**.

For your better understanding, I've included a reading I did for a woman who believed she was under the influence of a spell. The cards were as follows:

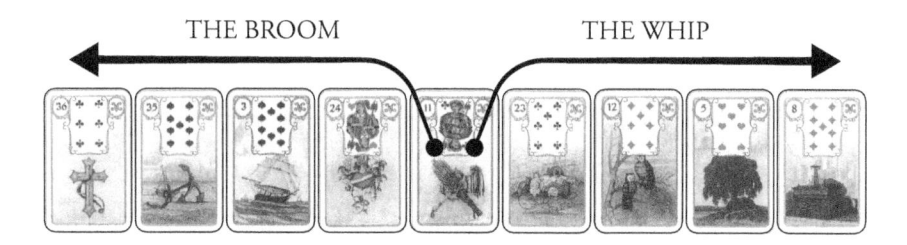

THE BROOM   THE WHIP

- The four cards in The Whip (magic) group were: The Mice + The Owls + The Tree + The Coffin
- The four cards in The Broom (cleaning) group were: The Heart + The Ship + The Anchor + The Cross

The reading begins with the four cards on the whip side, showing the energies in the querent's life:
- The Mice + The Owls + The Tree + The Coffin.

The first step is to check if any cards indicate the presence of magic or negative energies. As you can see, we got three cards: The Mice, The Owls, and The Coffin. This cluster of cards clearly confirms that the querent is affected by magic, especially the combination (mirroring) of The Mice + The Coffin, which means black magic.

Next, we check for theme cards, such as The Tree card, which suggests that the spell was intended to harm the querent's health (The Tree + The Coffin). Another indication is the mirroring of The Mice and The Coffin cards. In addition, the combination of The Mice and The Owls cards indicates the involvement of several people, most likely from an African country (The Tree + The Coffin). Finally, The Owls + The Tree + The Coffin cards describe the presence of two powerful sorcerers.

Once the magic has been identified, we must focus on the cluster of cards that fell on the broom side, which will give us clues on how to "clean" what was predicted in the cluster on the whip side:

- The Heart + The Ship + The Anchor + The Cross.

The Jack of Hearts suggests the presence and interference of a young "magician" or fortune teller apprentice. Despite the lack of expertise, he intervenes in the search (The Ship) for a solution. Moreover, the presence of this young apprentice tells us that the querent hopes (The Ship + The Anchor) that he'll be able to help her overcome this difficult moment (mirroring The Heart + The Cross). This young man's intervention (The Heart + The Ship + The Anchor) will calm the situation with prayers (The Cross) and faith (The Heart + The Cross). As a result, at this time, there will be no solution that can permanently remove the querent's spell.

Getting a similar conclusion, I suggest adding up the card numbers to get guidance that can help solve the problem considering the cluster of cards placed on the whip side. In this case, the total would be:

- 24 + 3 + 35 + 36 = 98 – 36 = 62 – 36 = **26** = The Book card advises the querent should look for someone with relevant experience and knowledge to help them deal with the situation.

THE GRANDMOTHER'S METHOD

I've been using this reading method since I began studying the cards. It was a method that my grandmother worked with, in addition to the Master's Method, now known as the Grand Tableau. This method requires expertise and practice with the cards, so it should be chosen only by those who have already acquired a solid theoretical and practical knowledge of the cards.

This reading method allows you to give precise and clear answers to questions in different life areas, such as love, career, finances, health, and more.

- **Step 1**: To "work" with this method, it's important to define the life area you want to investigate: love, career, finance, friendship, health, and so on.
- **Step 2**: Once you determined the reading context, select the significator card (as explained in previous chapters). For instance, choose The Anchor card if the context is work-related matters. If the context is about a romantic relationship, choose two cards: The Heart and The Ring.
- **Step 3**: After drawing the significator card from the deck, shuffle the remaining 35 cards and draw 19 to go along with the theme card, making a total of 20 cards. If you're doing a love reading, as explained in step 2, you'll need to draw two theme cards: The Heart and The Ring. It means that you'll draw 18 cards to go with the two theme cards, resulting in 20 cards.
- **Step 4**: The remaining deck is set aside.
- **Step 5**: Shuffle the 20 cards and place them on the table following the order illustrated in the figure below. If you prefer a different layout, you can arrange the cards in rows from 1 to 20 side by side, going from top to bottom and left to right, respecting the number of 4 cards in each row.

CHAPTER 6: THE METHOD OF READING (DRAWINGS)

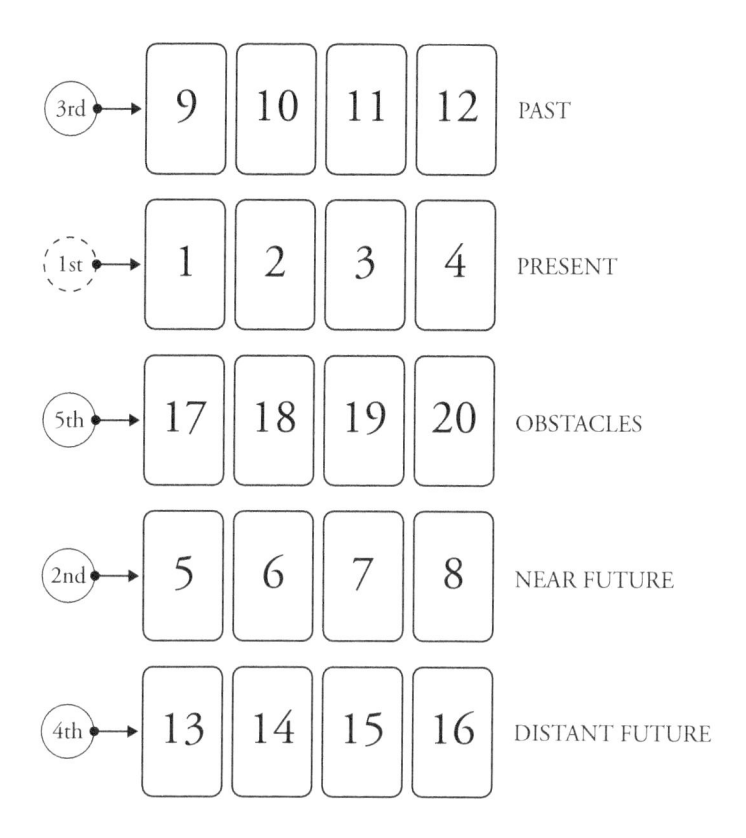

```
(3rd) → [ 9 ][ 10 ][ 11 ][ 12 ]   PAST

(1st) → [ 1 ][ 2 ][ 3 ][ 4 ]   PRESENT

(5th) → [ 17 ][ 18 ][ 19 ][ 20 ]   OBSTACLES

(2nd) → [ 5 ][ 6 ][ 7 ][ 8 ]   NEAR FUTURE

(4th) → [ 13 ][ 14 ][ 15 ][ 16 ]   DISTANT FUTURE
```

- **Step 6**: The four groups of cards set the pace for the reading and provide a chronological timeline of events: Past, Present, Near Future, and Far Future:
    - THE PAST – The cards in this group provide crucial information because they reveal the events impacting the current situation. They show the past events or outstanding factors connected with the present and obstacle groups of cards.

    The following two groups are analyzed together.
    - THE PRESENT: These cards describe the current situation of the problem.
    - THE OBSTACLES: These cards describe the main obstacles and provide additional information about the circumstances that the present group has revealed.

The following two groups of cards will provide insight into the development of the question.

- o NEAR FUTURE: The cards in this group reveal upcoming events.
- o FAR FUTURE: These cards will depict the development of the situation until the reading time frame.

In 2017, I did a reading for a client whom I'll call Monique to preserve her anonymity. Monique is a well-known artist in Switzerland and wanted to know how her friendship with Sebastian would evolve over the next three months. I chose The Dog as the significator card for friendship, and these were the other cards drawn for the reading:

- **The Past:** The Man + The Bear + The Scythe + The Heart
  These four cards indicated that Monique's friendship with Sebastian had suddenly ended recently (The Scythe above The Dog card). The Man card, representing Sebastian, showed me that he could be a vengeful and cold person (The Man + The Bear + The Scythe) who might use his power and abilities to harm those he considered his adversaries. Moreover, the pairing of The Scythe + The Heart indicated Sebastian's unrequited feelings and coldness towards Monique.

- **The Present:** The Mountain + The Mice + The Dog + The Broom and The Whip
  Considering the events revealed in the "past" group of cards, the "present" group shows that Monique feels frustrated and powerless (The Mountain) due to Sebastian's cold and indifferent behavior (The Man above The Mountain + The Mice), which led to arguments and mutual accusations between them (The Dog + The Broom and The Whip). The three Jacks (Bells, Hearts, and Acorns) next to each other, along with the combination of The Dog + The Broom and The Whip cards, may suggest that Sebastian's sexual orientation is homosexual, which could be the reason for their disagreement.

CHAPTER 6: THE METHOD OF READING (DRAWINGS)

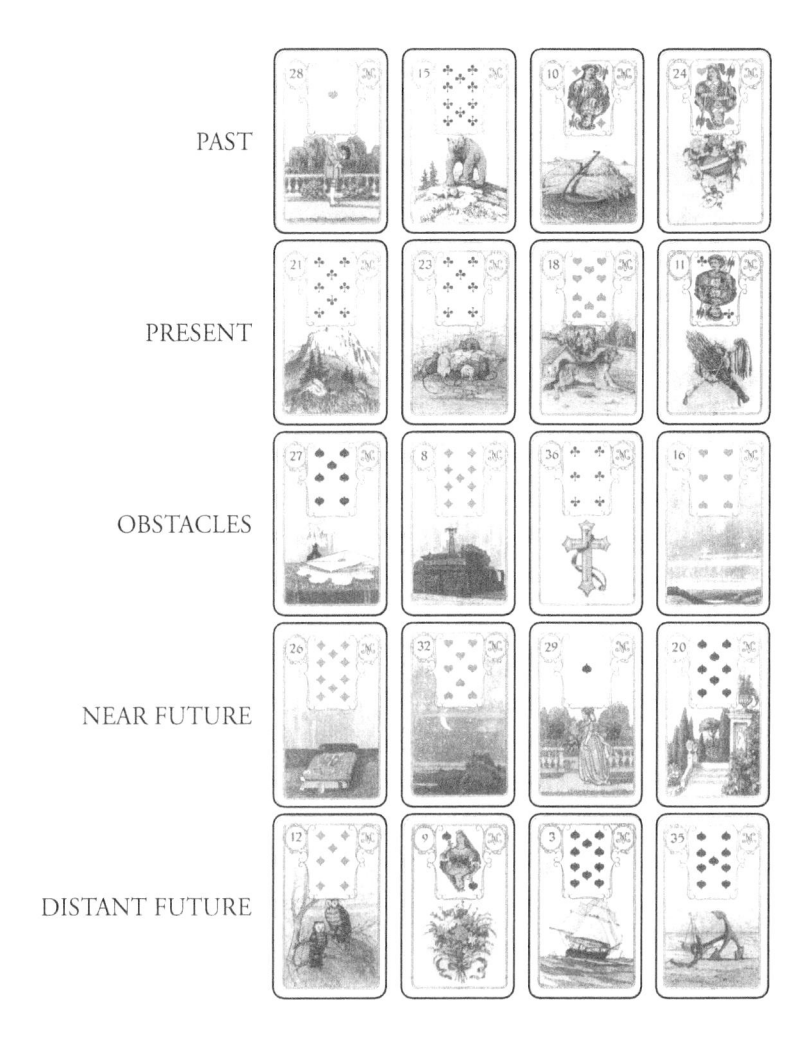

PAST	28	15	10	24
PRESENT	21	23	18	11
OBSTACLES	27	8	36	16
NEAR FUTURE	26	32	29	20
DISTANT FUTURE	12	9	3	35

Important Note:

For those familiar with Grand Tableau reading techniques, it is possible to apply them in this method to obtain more detailed information about the case, such as the bridge technique, which shows the cards that connect the two querents' cards and represent the central theme. In this example, the connecting cards are The Scythe + The Book, indicating Monique's revelation of a secret since the card The Book is close to The Woman card. Additionally, The Owls + The Moon cards above The Bouquet card denote romantic invitations from Monique to Sebastian.

- **The Obstacles:** The Letter + The Coffin + The Cross + The Stars

  The cards in the "Obstacles" group indicate that a lack of communication (The Card + The Coffin) is causing deep pain (The Coffin + The Cross) and also making it impossible to recover from an already complicated relationship (The Coffin + The Cross + The Stars), despite several desperate attempts at clarification (The Broom and The Whip above The Stars card).

- **The Near Future:** The Book + The Moon + The Woman + The Garden

  In the near future, due to the lack of communication and unresolved issues with Sebastian, Monique focused on her opera scores (The Book) and her performance on stage, where she experiences a sense of fulfillment and appreciation from her fans (The Moon + The Woman + The Garden).

- **The Far Future:** The Owls + The Bouquet + The Ship + The Anchor

  Over time, Monique had the opportunity to meet Sebastian at international music stages (The Ship + The Garden above The Anchor card). They engaged in a polite conversation (The Owls + The Bouquet), but their relationship remained limited to a social level in order to maintain a professional image.

2

CHAPTER 7:
THE GRAND TABLEAU

The Grand Tableau is a structure formed by 4 rows of 8 cards and an additional row of 4 cards in the center, resulting in 36 areas called houses. It was named after Mademoiselle Le Normand and means The Great Table in English.

This system is also known by other names:

- 8 x 4 + 4, 9 x 4 or 6 x 6, depending on the chosen structure
- Royal Table
- The Board
- The Board of Life

The origins of the Grand Tableau method are lost in the mists of time. It's known for centuries that fortune tellers used to read the cards with methods that involved the whole deck.

Some documents and books published long before the Petit Lenormand deck, such as the prototype of the Lenormand deck and the Game of Hope (1778/9), which used a 6 x 6 structure, confirm this thesis.

The connection between the method and the Petit Lenormand deck was made in Philippe Lenormand's instruction sheet in 1846 when the deck was first published.

What's the function of the Grand Tableau in someone's life?

In simple terms, the primary function of the Grand Tableau is to provide a complete view of the querent's life. It's a powerful tool that helps the querent and others better understand themselves by shedding to light what is going on in their minds and hearts, and by providing clarity about current events and uncovering factors that may have contributed to the problems that they're experiencing. This awareness enables the querent to identify their current situation, strengths, and weaknesses, so they may face life's challenges at the most appropriate moment and focus on what truly matters for their productivity.

Studying the Grand Tableau

In the beginning, diving right into the card readings can be tempting. However, reading the Grand Tableau can be challenging, even for those with experience with the deck. Although it's a fascinating reading method for Lenormand lovers, interpreting it is technically complex if you have no idea how it works. Since this reading method involves all 36 cards and techniques, it isn't easy to master. You need to be patient and have plenty of practice to become gradually familiar with it.

The way of working with the Grand Tableau can differ from fortune teller to fortune teller. The approaches may be derived from different Lenormand styles (traditional, German, French, etc.), traditions, or personal experiences. All methods are equally valid, and there's no right or wrong way; it's simply a matter of personal preference. In this book, I'll present my approach to working with the Grand Tableau. Over the years, I've experimented with and been inspired by various approaches and techniques that I've learned from my family or colleagues I've met throughout my professional career. I've improved and incorporated some techniques into my practice until they were complete for me. As you gain experience, you, too, will find your way of working with the Grand Tableau.

Chapter 7 is structured as follows:

1. **The Grand Tableau layout** – What are the main layouts used in the Grand Tableau? Where do these layouts come from?

2. **The Bases of the Grand Tableau** – In this section, you'll learn the three main bases of readings used in the Grand Tableau and how to work with them:
   o The Philippe Lenormand Method (also known as The Method of Distance or The Traditional Method);
   o The Timeline Method;
   o The Method of Houses.

   In the Grand Tableau reading, as you'll see in the step-by-step section in point 4, I've incorporated elements from each technique of the three main bases. In my experience, this combination is very enriching, even though each technique can be used independently. However, the choice of each procedure to use is individual.

3. **Auxiliary techniques** – Many ancient techniques, including mirroring, have been generously passed down by fortune tellers and shared their expertise and discoveries. Although they

all hold value, some may be complex to apply in a reading. In this section, I introduce techniques that are more accessible to beginners without compromising their significance. I recommend you explore each of them and find out which one suits you the most.

The first three points focus on theory. Once you understand the concepts in each point, moving on to point four will be easy.

4. **Steps for interpreting the Grand Tableau** – As you can see, the Grand Tableau reading involves several techniques. Especially for beginners, it's essential to know where to start and what to "look" at in order to give accurate answers to the querent's dilemmas. Therefore, this section is a practical guide to help you interpret the Grand Tableau accurately.

> **Important Note:**
> Reading a Grand Tableau requires a basic knowledge of the Petit Lenormand deck (covered in chapters 1 to 6). Believe me, starting with a strong foundation can make all the difference in learning. It's worth emphasizing that cartomancy requires a solid understanding to achieve successful readings and help the querent become aware of their own life. The key to going from an amateur to a professional fortune teller is fully committing yourself to learn everything you can about your deck.

CHAPTER 7: THE GRAND TABLEAU

THE GRAND TABLEAU LAYOUT

There are many layouts of Grand Tableau in the world. The three layouts I present here are the traditional ones and the most widely used on fortune-tellers' tables.

The first Grand Tableau was introduced in 1778/79 with The Game of Hope deck, and the following sentence can be found in the instruction leaflet:

"The 36 illuminated sheets are laid out in a square, that is, in 6 rows of 6 sheets each according to the numbers on top of the cards, that is 1, 2, 3 and so on, up to 36."

Das Spiel der Hofnung (The Game of Hope)
Johann Kaspar Hechtel (1778/79)

In Europe, this first layout is known as Grand Tableau Hechtel (named after the author of The Game of Hope deck) or as 6 x 6 Grand Tableau due to the layout of the 36 cards (6 cards in 6 rows and columns). However, this structure is rarely used in readings because it takes up too much space on the table.

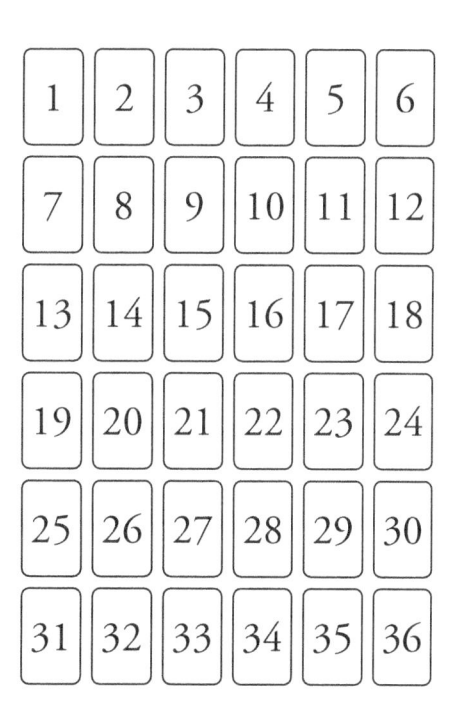

1	2	3	4	5	6
7	8	9	10	11	12
13	14	15	16	17	18
19	20	21	22	23	24
25	26	27	28	29	30
31	32	33	34	35	36

The second layout has accompanied the Petit Lenormand deck since its first appearance on the market in 1846. Philippe Lenormand's instruction sheet states:

"After shuffling the cards and cutting them with your left hand. Distribute them into five rows of eight cards each; the cards in each row are laid from left to right; the remaining four cards are then laid in, under the middle of the last rows, as shown in the diagram."

This Grand Tableau is called Philippe Lenormand or 8x4+4 Grand Tableau. It's a very popular layout on the fortune teller's table, which I use in my readings.

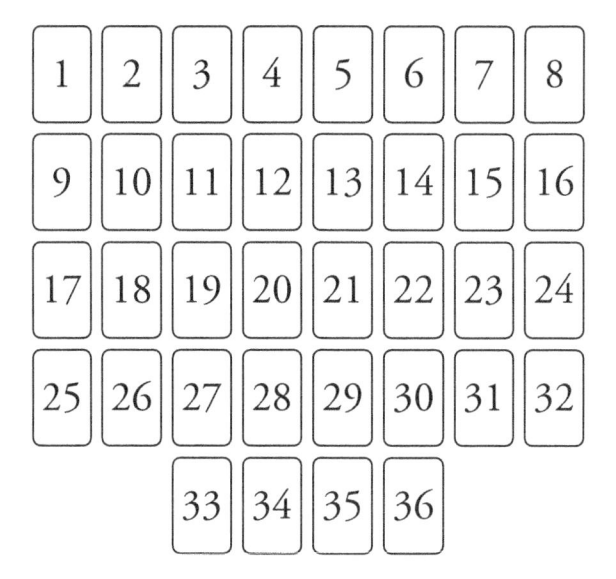

```
 1  2  3  4  5  6  7  8
 9 10 11 12 13 14 15 16
17 18 19 20 21 22 23 24
25 26 27 28 29 30 31 32
      33 34 35 36
```

The third Grand Tableau layout is known by different names, including The Master's Method, Mademoiselle Lenormand's Tableau, and the 9x4 Grand Tableau. These names come from the arrangement of the cards on the table, which consists of four rows with nine cards in each row.

According to the book "L'Oracle Parfait or Le passe temps des Dame, L'Art detirer les cartes avec explication," published in 1875, Mademoiselle Lenormand used a Grand Tableau divided into 36 houses for her readings, as shown in the image.

Each house represents a life area, for example, house 1 for projects, house 2 for satisfaction, house 3 for positive outcomes, etc. I'll provide more details about this layout in the section on The Grand Tableau Houses.

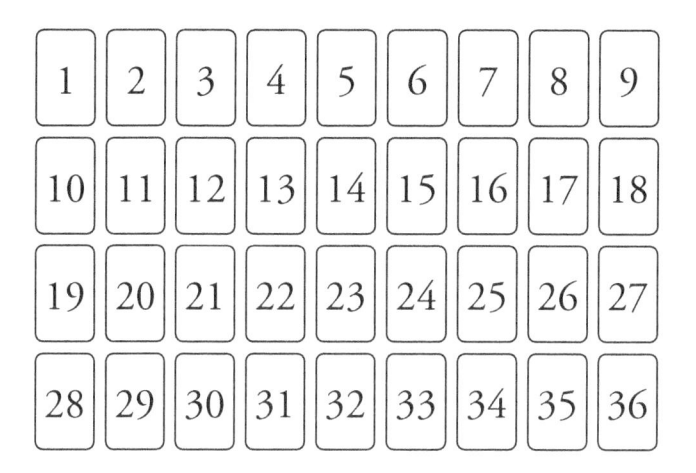

1	2	3	4	5	6	7	8	9
10	11	12	13	14	15	16	17	18
19	20	21	22	23	24	25	26	27
28	29	30	31	32	33	34	35	36

THE FOUNDATIONS OF THE GRAND TABLEAU

THE PHILIPPE LENORMAND METHOD

This method is also referred to the 8x4+4 Grand Tableau, The Method of Distance, or The Traditional Method.

The Grand Tableau has accompanied the Petit Lenormand deck since its first recorded appearance in 1846. The deck's instruction sheet was written by Philippe Lenormand, who introduced the Near/Far technique, commonly known as the Traditional Method. Here in Switzerland, it's known as the Philippe Lenormand Method as a tribute to the author of the instruction sheet.

From 1971 to 1990, I exclusively used the Philippe Lenormand Method since it was the only method to work with the "francesinhas" (little French cards), as my grandmother fondly called the Petit Lenormand deck. I have vivid memories of my grandmother teaching me how to interpret the Petit Lenormand. It was so enjoyable to look for the querent's card and identify the unfavorable cards (The Clouds, The Snake, The Coffin, The Scythe, The Broom and The Whip, The Owls, The Fox, The Mountain, The Mice, and The Cross), observe the surrounding cards and calculate the distance between certain cards, especially those representing the querent. The same approach applied to The Man card, representing the husband, boyfriend, or suitor, The Ring for the relationship, The Child for the children, and The House for the family or other people living in the house. At that time, only women sought my grandmother's consultation for information on these topics. Unlike today, we didn't have an extensive list of theme cards or available reading techniques back then.

The Philippe Lenormand Method has evolved over the years to adapt to the changing times, incorporating techniques from the German tradition and the reading techniques from the playing card deck. In fact, some card meanings and techniques used in the Grand Tableau correspond with the German Lenormand tradition and the playing card deck. For example, The Snake also represents eyeglasses or contact lenses; The Storks can indicate long legs, air travel, and immigration, while The Tower can stand for authority, bureaucracy, and legal matters. There was a period when the use of the Grand Tableau Houses and the Grand Tableau Timeline, along with their techniques, such as the four corner houses, the heart of the table, and the four fate line cards, faced opposition from traditionalists. However, these techniques were widely used in Germany, Austria, and Switzerland. Today, these techniques have gained acceptance by the "traditionalists" due to their grandeur and practicality.

I believe that since the 1980s, most fortune tellers have moved away from the Philippe Lenormand Method due to the lack of techniques and other rich details that the modern Philippe Method offers today. However, thanks to Andy Boroveshengra, fortune teller, master, and author of the book "Lenormand Thirty-Six Cards", the Philippe Lenormand Method has rekindled and made a leap in quality. If you look closely, you can find some similarities with techniques of the German method, but not only with it.

When I read the Grand Tableau, I combine techniques from both the Traditional and German schools, where I made my first steps as a card reader, following the teachings I received from my grandmother and using the Philippe Method. In addition, I base myself on Erna Droesbeke's studies, which give me a quick overview of my client's life and enable me to start the reading more confidently.

How does the technique work?

The explanation of the Philippe Lenormand Method is based on the Philippe Lenormand instruction sheet written by Philippe Lenormand in 1846 and on my extensive experience with the Grand Tableau over the years.

- **Step 1:** Arrange the 36 cards on the table in four rows from left to right, with each row consisting of eight cards. Then add a fifth row of four cards, from the third to the sixth column, as shown in the chart below.

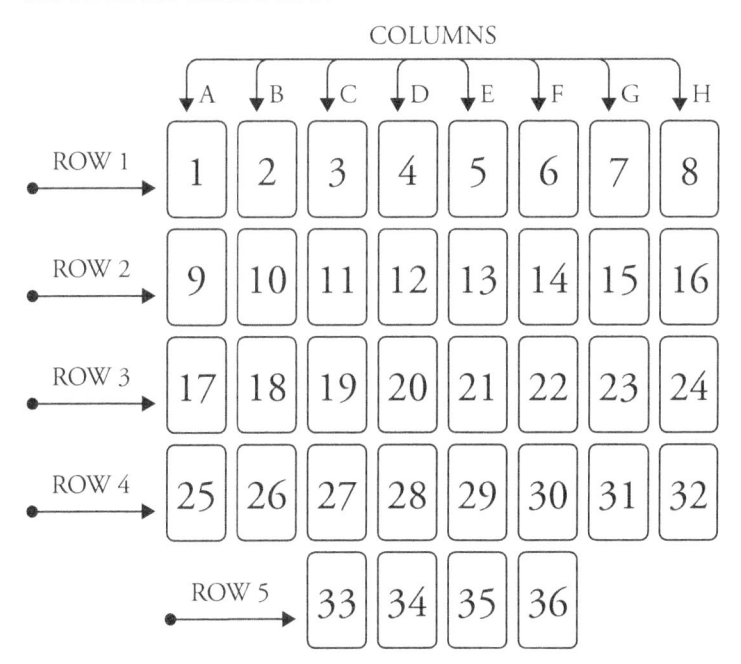

COLUMNS

	A	B	C	D	E	F	G	H
ROW 1	1	2	3	4	5	6	7	8
ROW 2	9	10	11	12	13	14	15	16
ROW 3	17	18	19	20	21	22	23	24
ROW 4	25	26	27	28	29	30	31	32
ROW 5			33	34	35	36		

- **Step 2:** The provided excerpts from the original document offer insights into how the cards are interpreted within the system:

"If the person querying is a woman, one starts from sheet 29, spinning a jocular tale from the cards nearby around the figures on display. If it is for a man, the tale is started from sheet 28 and again makes use of the cards surrounding this one."

Das Spiel der Hoffnung (The Game of Hope)
Johann Kaspar Hechtel (1778/79)

"The greatest attention must be paid to these cards – Nos.28 and 29. Their position signifies the future happiness or misfortune of the person; all the other cards take their meaning from these, and in such a way, that their position, as it near or more distant from these, rule the destiny."

Philippe Lenormand 1846

This method assumes that a complete reading begins from the card representing the querent and that the cards have different energies depending on their position in relation to the questioner's card, whether near or far.

But how to calculate what is near and what is far in the Grand Tableau?

To better to grasp the concept of the near and far system Let's imagine what happens when we throw a stone into a lake. You've probably either tossed a stone into a lake or witnessed someone doing so, right? When you throw a stone into a lake, waves form on the surface at the spot where the stone falls.

The strongest waves originate from the point where the stone hits the water (like points 1 and 2 in the illustration here). As the waves move away from the impact point, they gradually lose intensity until they eventually disappear (points 3, 4, and 5). Now, let's imagine these waves turning into energy fields in our lives, considering that the point where the stone falls represents our

S. (Stone) = Querent's card

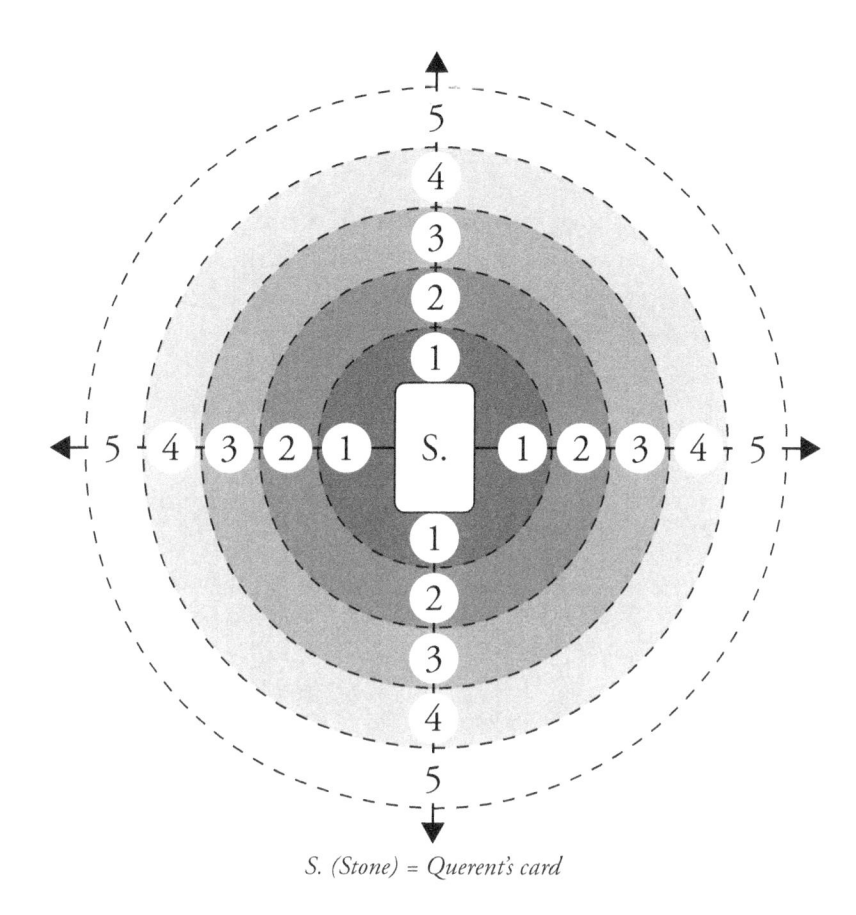

or the querent's position. Which energies will have the strongest impact in our lives? It'll be those nearest (point 1) or near us (position 2). And which energies will have minimal or no effect on us? It will be the ones distant (position 3) and further away from us (positions from point 4). These four zones of the energy field clearly determine what we'll feel, experience, and envision.

The same principle applies to The Grand Tableau. The querent's card position determines what is near and far. But, as you'll notice, when you do a reading using the Grand Tableau system, the querent's card may not always land in the center of The Grand Tableau. Thus, before providing examples of possible querent's card positions, it's essential to know how to apply the "wave theory" in the Grand Tableau.

If you understood the above explanation, you should be aware that nearness and farness are defined by where the stone falls. You'll also understand that there are four different energy frequencies, right?

The Grand Tableau follows the same principle, the position where the querent's card lands determine what is near and far. Let's take, for example, the Grand Tableau layout presented here, with The Man as the querent's card.

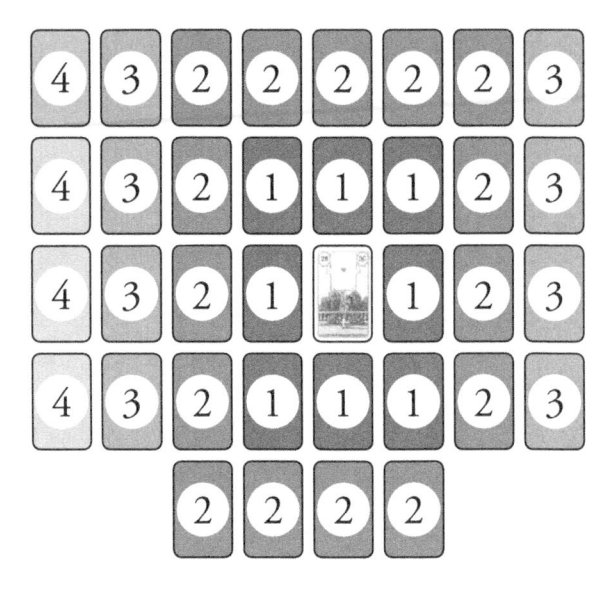

4	3	2	2	2	2	2	3
4	3	2	1	1	1	2	3
4	3	2	1	★	1	2	3
4	3	2	1	1	1	2	3
		2	2	2	2		

The varying shades of gray define the degree of intensity of a card's position in the Grand Tableau. Darker shades of gray represent the cards closer to the significator card, and as you move further away from the significator card, the shade becomes lighter and loses intensity.

Therefore, starting from The Man card, it's defined that:

- **Position 1:** It's determined by the cards touching the querent's or the significator card (theme card) These are the cards that are positioned very near to the querent or significator. In this group of cards, it's possible to identify:
    - Important events and circumstances that are intensely felt by the querent;

- o What is experienced and touched by the querent;
- o What the querent knows or pays the most attention to.

- **Position 2:** It's considered near all cards touching the cards that are very near the querent's card (in position 1). The group of cards in this position is also extremely important and influences the querent's current state.

When observing positions 1 and 2, it's crucial to consider the following points:

» Take into account the worst cards in the deck:
- o The Clouds (King of Acorn)
- o The Snake (Queen of Acorn)
- o The Coffin (9 of Bells)
- o The Scythe (Jack of Bells)
- o The Broom and The Whip (Jack of Acorn)
- o The Owls (7 of Bells)
- o The Fox (9 of Acorn)
- o The Mountain (8 of Acorn)
- o The Mice (7 of Acorn)
- o The Cross (6 of Acorn)

This same procedure must also be applied to the predominance of any other suit, especially the Acorn suit that, as you are aware, is unfavorable and indicates problems and suffering. The closer these cards are to the querent's card or the theme card, the stronger the negative impact they have on the person's life, especially if there are many of them in position 1.

» You should also consider whether the following groups of cards appear in these positions, especially in position 1: movement cards, slow cards, or stop cards. For example, if a large amount of stop cards are present in the group, this denotes resistance to change for different reasons, which the surrounding cards will explain.

Take a closer look at the theme cards, which indicate what life areas are important to the querent. For instance, if The Anchor card is near the querent's card, it implies that the querent is focused on professional matters. The cards nearby The Anchor will give further details. Now suppose The Heart card, the theme card for emotions, desires, enthusiasm, and priorities, falls next to a group of stop cards. In that case, it may announce a lack of enthusiasm, action, or even an emotional inability to deal with situations or circumstances represented by the other surrounding cards. This scenario may indicate that the querent is resisting change or an inevitable conclusion.

What has been understood so far is that positions 1 (very near) and 2 (near) are more sensed and within the querent's grasp.

- **Position 3:** The cards touching the near cards (position 2) are considered far. This group of cards will indicate the following:
  o What is moving away from the querent;
  o What is losing interest, importance, or priority for the querent.

- **Position 4:** The group of cards in this position is considered to be very distant and indicates:
  o What the querent has moved away from;
  o What is no longer of interest or priority to the querent;
  o What the querent is ignoring;
  o What the querent doesn't see.

Bear in mind that certain negative cards, such as The Clouds, The Snake, The Coffin, and The Cross, have a more significant impact in the Grand Tableau. For example, suppose The Coffin card is in position 4, which is very far from the querent's card (see the example below).

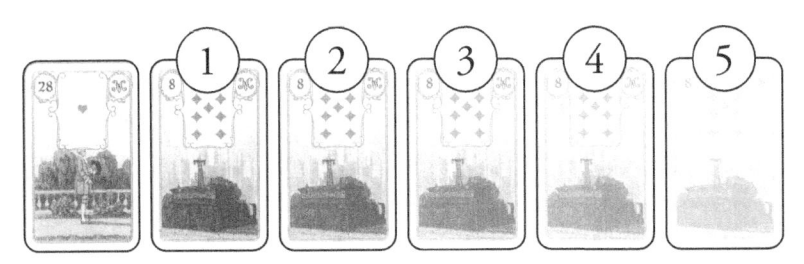

In that case, its harmful energy will still affect the querent, although with less intensity than if The Coffin card fell in positions 3 and 2, which are very near and near The Coffin card. Obviously, it would be alarming if The Coffin were in positions 3, 2, or 1 because the closer the card is to the significator card (person or theme), the more it acts with all its natural energy.

The same applies to some positive cards like The Stars, The Sun, and The Moon. These cards radiate all their positive energy even when positioned in zone 4, but their energy weakens as they move away from the significator card (positions 5 onwards).

How to read the cards surrounding the significator card?

The analysis of the cards, whether in the very near, near, far, and very far positions, must be done in a clockwise direction, starting from position 12 (as indicated in the diagram), covering all the cards and conclude the analysis to position 12.

As previously mentioned, the card representing the querent may land in different positions in the Grand Tableau. Consequently, it can be located 4, 5, 6, or 7 positions away from the significator card, as illustrated in the following examples.

THE COMPLETE BOOK OF THE PETIT LENORMAND

4 POSITIONS

4	3	2	2	2	2	2	3
4	3	2	1	1	1	2	3
4	3	2	1	★	1	2	3
4	3	2	1	1	1	2	3
			2	2	2	2	

5 POSITIONS

4	4	4	4	4	4	4	5
3	3	3	3	3	3	4	5
2	2	2	2	2	3	4	5
2	1	1	1	2	3	4	5
			★	1	2	3	

6 POSITIONS

2	2	2	2	3	4	5	6
1	1	1	2	3	4	5	6
1	★	1	2	3	4	5	6
1	1	1	2	3	4	5	6
			2	2	3	4	

7 POSITIONS

★	1	2	3	4	5	6	7
1	1	2	3	4	5	6	7
2	2	2	3	4	5	6	7
3	3	3	3	4	5	6	7
				4	4	4	5

Philippe Lenormand Method includes techniques beyond what has been described so far. However, as I use the three basic techniques, as I explained in the introduction to the Grand Tableau, it's sufficient to learn the near/far approach, which is one of the primary keys to correctly interpreting Lenormand cards. The significance of this approach will become clear when you combine the three techniques.

THE TIMELINE METHOD
Also known as The Line of Life or The Fate Cross

The timeline is used to establish the chronological order in the Grand Tableau of PAST, PRESENT, and FUTURE events related to the querent's life. It develops horizontally, vertically, and diagonally, starting from the querent's card, respecting the directional facing law.

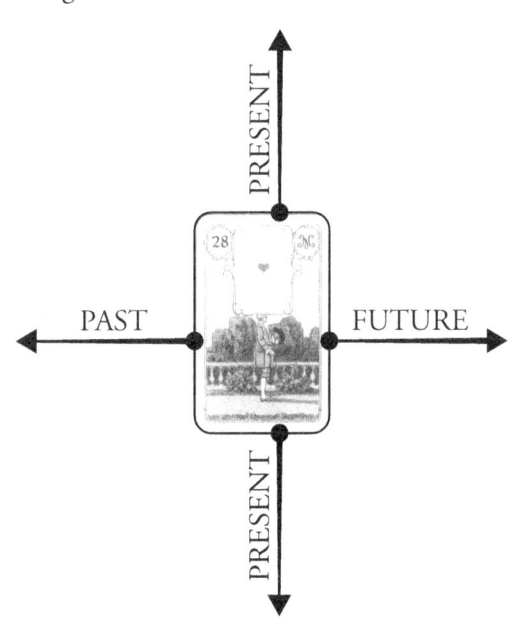

Therefore:

1. All the cards positioned in the direction that the figure faces (the horizontal line, starting from the querent's card) refers the FUTURE events. These cards provide information about events or the development of an issue or situation. Thus, when reading the future line, you must take into account all the events mentioned in the present, as well as the cards surrounding the querent's card, because they'll influence the events in the future.

2. All the cards positioned behind the figure (the horizontal line, starting from the querent's card) are related to the querent's PAST. These cards provide information about past events and their origin. This information will help you understand the querent's current situation in the PRESENT.

3. All the cards positioned vertically in the column of the querent's card represent the PRESENT and provide information about the current situation. These cards indicate the issues that the querent is experiencing and may have a connection to the past. Therefore, when reading the present cards, it's necessary to analyze the cards that land in the past.

Reading the Timeline

The Grand Tableau is divided into three vertical and two horizontal parts.

The vertical division

Results from the position of the questioner's card, which divides the Grand Tableau into three vertical parts:

1. The cards <u>behind the querent's card</u> form the first group and represent the PAST;

2. The cards that <u>go through the querent's card</u> form the second group and represent the PRESENT.

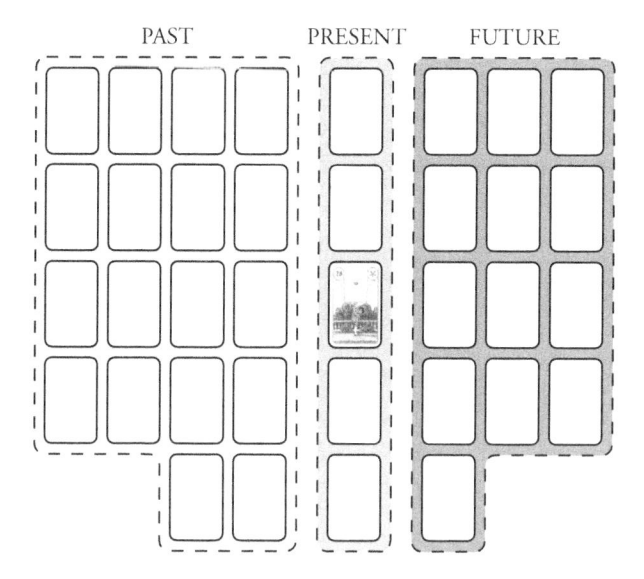

3. The cards <u>in front of the querent's card</u> form the third group and represent the FUTURE.

The horizontal division

Is obtained by dividing the Grand Tableau into two horizontal parts from the querent's card, as shown in the graphic below:

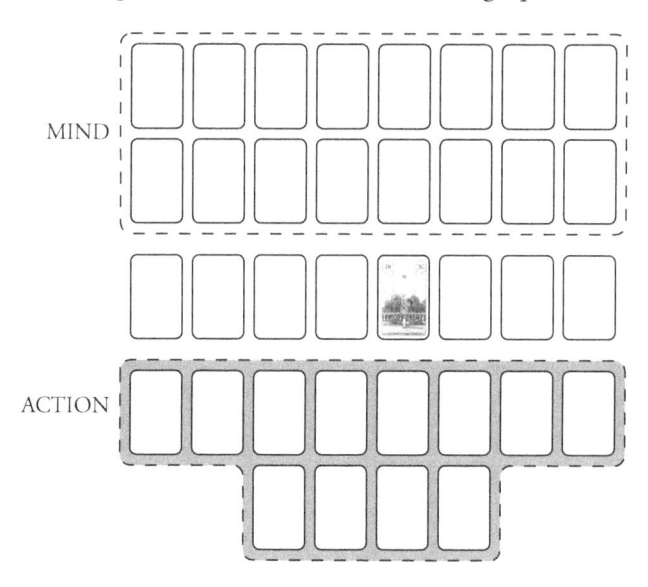

This division defines:

- Above (Mind) - The group of cards above the querent represents their rational aspect. These cards reveal what is going on in the querent's mind, such as hope, fear, anxieties, worries, what weighs on the conscience, memories, plans, projects, ideas, goals, and intentions. They represent the querent's psychological and mental temperamental process.

- Below (Action) – The group of cards below the querent's card is known as the "action cards". These cards reveal the person's experiences and actions and what they are actively contributing or doing to achieve their goals. They also show the effects of past events.

The Diagonals

The diagonals are obtained by forming an X-line that goes through the querent's card, as in the provided illustration. As studied above, The Grand Tableau is divided as follows:

- Vertical: Past, Present, and Future
- Horizontal: Mind and Action

Therefore, the diagonals are in the past and future positions, and when we divide the Grand Tableau into two horizontal parts, we get:

- The diagonals above the querent's card will represent their mental issues;
- The diagonals below the querent's card represent their experiences, behavior, accomplishments, and attitudes.

Before explaining the meanings of the diagonals, let me first share how I assigned the meanings to the four diagonal positions. Back in 1990, during my studies with Erna Droesbeke, I learned that the diagonals on the left represent the causes of events, while the diagonals on the right reflect the consequences or effects of the events announced on the diagonals of causes.

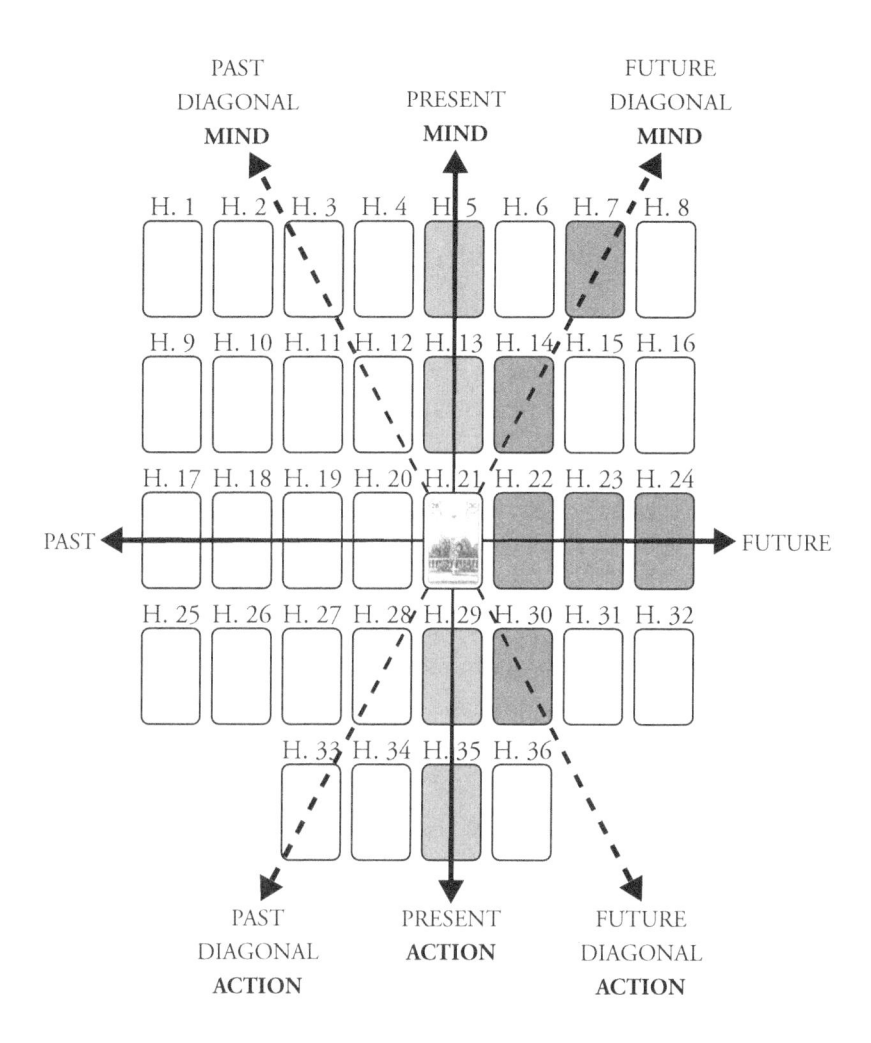

CHAPTER 7: THE GRAND TABLEAU

```
        PAST                              FUTURE
      DIAGONAL        PRESENT            DIAGONAL
        MIND           MIND                MIND
```

[Grand Tableau diagram: 4 rows of 8 houses (H.1–H.8, H.9–H.16, H.17–H.24, H.25–H.32) with additional row H.33–H.36 below, showing PAST ← → FUTURE axis horizontally and MIND ↑ / ACTION ↓ axis vertically, with diagonal arrows to PAST DIAGONAL ACTION and FUTURE DIAGONAL ACTION]

```
        PAST                              FUTURE
      DIAGONAL        PRESENT            DIAGONAL
       ACTION         ACTION              ACTION
```

However, I found Erna's assignments of cause and consequence to the diagonals insufficient to comprehend my querent's situation, and I felt compelled to analyze my readings, paying close attention to the past and present diagonal positions (I always wrote down my readings), as well as the conversations I had with my clients during the readings and throughout the time.

After thorough analysis, precisely by the end of 1991, I finally developed my own meanings for the diagonals.

I've defined that the diagonals above that represent the mind are interpreted as follows:

- **The Past Diagonal – MIND:** It represents significant events that have shaped the querent's memory, such as celebrations, accomplishments, or even traumas. However, in certain situations, especially if the cards in this position reinforce it, it may indicate psychological disorders or obsessions that originated in the past. A careful analysis of the cards representing the querent's thoughts can reveal if this psychological condition still affects them.

- **The Future Diagonal – MIND:** It represents the querent's future thoughts, including their projects, goals, and intentions concerning their current experience.

The diagonals below the querent's card represent action that are read as follows:

- **The Past Diagonal – ACTION:** It shows what the querent has rejected or is rejecting, has given up or is giving up, has avoided or is avoiding, hasn't accepted or is not accepting. These cards indicate what the querent is trying to move away from or free themselves from, such as work, relationship, disease, debts, people, and so on.

- **The Future Diagonal – ACTION:** It represents the immediate progression the situation will take in the next few days

Important Note:

I recommend that my students pay special attention to the diagonal group of cards in the mental area and past action, as well as the cards in the present line, those near the querent's card, and the future line, especially when reading for clients who are facing difficulties or have self-destructive tendencies, such as self-harm or suicidal thoughts. The mind diagonals can reveal the person's intentions, whereas the diagonals of past action may indicate whether the person no longer wants to live. The cards in the present and future positions will reveal whether the person will act on these intentions.

Reading the Past, Present, Future Lines and Diagonals

Two points must be highlighted for effective line reading:

1. Following the correct reading direction.
2. The line reading technique.

Point 1: The correct direction when reading the cards:

As learned in the study of Philippe Lenormand Law and the Philippe Lenormand Method, all cards touching the querent's card hold a more significant influence on the querent's life, while the cards further away have a lesser impact. Applying this concept to The Grand Tableau, the reading always starts with the querent's card, as shown by the arrows in the past, present, future, and diagonal positions, indicating the reading direction. Once you understand this concept, you know that:

- **The PAST line:** The cards near or very near the querent's card (depending on the number of cards) represent the recent past, whereas the far or very far cards represent the distant past. If only a few cards are in this position, it indicates that the recent events have significantly impacted the present moment.

- **The PRESENT line:** To this line, it's necessary you divide your explanation into two parts:
  - The MENTAL line: The cards that are very near or near the querent's card provide information about the querent's current priority thoughts, while the cards that are far or very far are not as significant as those that are very near or near. However, they are still present in the querent's mind, albeit with less intensity.
  - The ACTION line: The cards that are very near or near the querent's card represent a priority situation at the present moment. Those cards that are far or very far refer to issues or events that are still present but have less importance or relevance to the querent.

- **The FUTURE line:** The cards that are very near or near the querent's card announce upcoming events that will likely occur shortly. On the other hand, far or very far cards stand for the distant future.
- **The DIAGONALS**: To explain the diagonal lines, it's also necessary to divide them into two parts:
  - **The MENTAL lines**
    - The Past Line: The cards that are very near or near the querent's card indicate recent events that have been imprinted on their memory. On the other hand, the far or very far cards represent memories from a distant past that may relate to childhood.
    - The Future Line: The cards that are very near or near the querent's card reveal the person's primary thoughts, while the very far or far cards are less prominent but still arouse the person's interest.
  - **The ACTION lines**
    - The Past Line: The cards very that are near or near the querent's card indicate what the querent is currently moving away from or rejecting in their life, whereas the far or very far cards show what has already been removed or rejected.
    - The Future Line: The cards that are very near or near the querent's card denote the person's next steps. When you're reading this line, It's also essential to check out the cards that are very near or near the future line, as they're interconnected.

Point 2: The technique of reading the cards in the lines

Knowing how to "read" the cards in the lines is also important. Let's use the Present Line as an example to read the cards in the lines correctly.

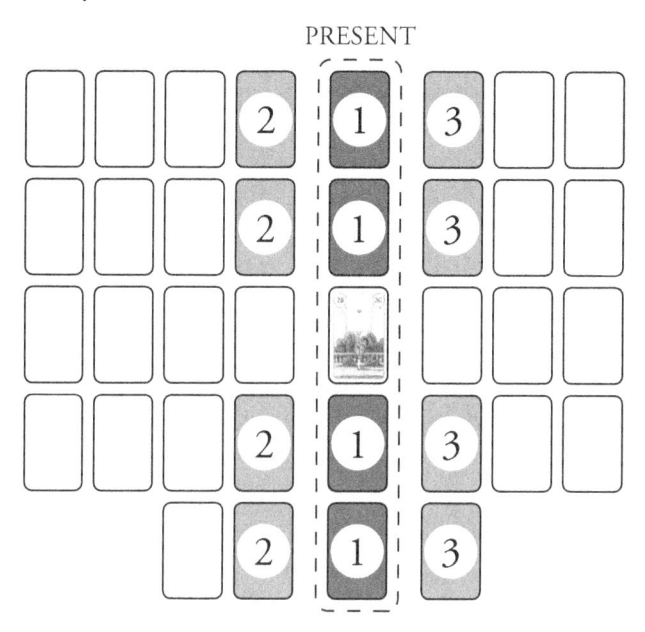

As you've learned, what's above the questioner's card reveals their thoughts, while the card below shows what will happen. However, it's essential to keep the following points in mind when reading it:

- The central cards with the number 1, which I refer to as the focus cards, represent the central theme or the subject of thought;
- The cards near the focus card (1), marked with numbers 2 and 3, which I'll call auxiliary cards, will provide additional information about the topic addressed by the card at position 1.

Let's use this example to understand how to interpret the group of cards in the mental zone, as shown in the figure. In the very near area, we have three cards: The Clouds card in the 1st position, The Owls card in the 2nd position, and The Ring card in the 3rd position.

How should we interpret these three cards? The Clouds card directly above the querent's head is the focus card, indicating that the person is experiencing a severe mental strain (The Clouds + The Owls) and constant agitation (The Owls + The Ring) caused by a compromise or an agreement (The Ring).

Then, examining the cards in the near zone, we can see that The Keys card in the 1st position is the focus card. The Mice in the 2nd position and The Fish in the 3rd position are the auxiliary cards. In the mental position, The Keys card always represents the search for solutions, while The Mice + The Fish combination suggests debts or financial losses.

Examining the group of cards in both the very near (The Clouds + The Owls + The Ring) and near positions (The Keys + The Mice + The Fish), we can infer that the person is currently going through a very anxious and stressful period, and is desperately looking for a solution to pay off a debt.

It's worth noting that these cards can be interpreted in different ways, but for the purpose of explaining the technique, I've provided an academic reading.

The same procedure for reading the present line must be applied to the diagonal lines. However, I've never found examining the cards above and below the past and future lines necessary. Only when there is only one card in the past or future positions, I combine the card above with the card below.

The Chronological Time of Events in the Lines

To estimate the time frame for an event or situation discussed in the lines, you need to consider the following factors:

1. It's important to set a specific time frame for the reading, which can range from 10 days to three months or even more, depending on the question posed by the querent.

2. It's essential to check out which cards are in the last position in the Past, Present, Future, or Diagonal lines, which will help you to determine if the events will occur within the set time frame or if they will be delayed. If the last card in the future line is a stop card, resolving the issues indicated by the preceding cards will take longer than expected, and there will be no significant progress. It will take longer to happen than the time frame for the reading. For example, If the question is whether an order from abroad will arrive within ten days, and the last card in the future line is a stop card or one that represents delays, it may indicate that the order will arrive much later than expected.

The Four Corners in the Grand Tableau

The four corner cards in the Grand Tableau, which correspond to the cards in the 1st, 8th, 25th, and 32nd positions, show the querent's primary concerns.

Even if the querent presents a different issue as the major focus of the reading, these cards indicate the overall theme and the querent's primary concerns and wish. The four cards in the 5th row aren't considered in this technique.

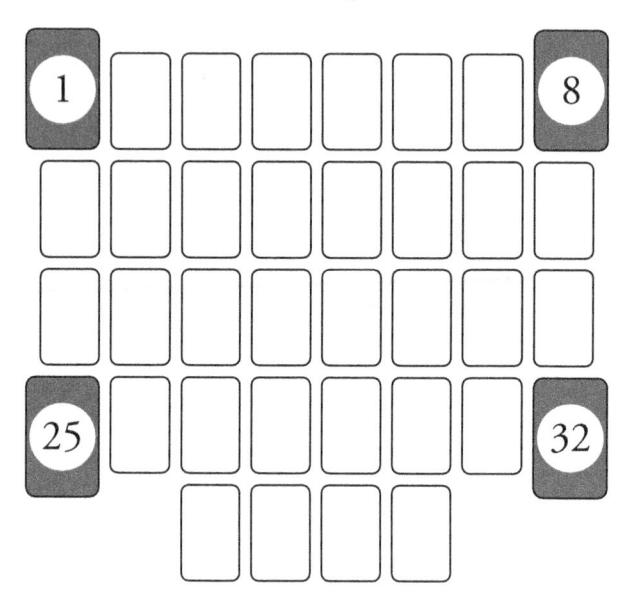

According to German tradition, the card that falls in the 1st house represents the central theme, and the cards in the 8th, 25th, and 32nd houses describe the topic expressed by the 1st house. However, based on my readings, I've noticed that the corner cards don't always emphasize a single issue, especially if the querent is undergoing a difficult period. Therefore, during a reading, it's possible that one, two, or all four corners of the Grand Tableau highlight themes or issues concerning the querent. Then, depending on the purpose of the reading, whether it's general or specific, the reading of the corners may be as follows.

- If you follow the German tradition, keep in mind that the card in the 1st position represents the major theme, while the cards in the 8th, 25th, and 32nd positions provide details about the topic presented by the card in the 1st position. The corners are read in a diagonal combination between the 1st and 32nd positions and the 8th and 25th.

- Instead, if the corner cards present more than one subject, they're read individually, and the surrounding cards will provide further details on the subject represented by the theme card, as follows:
    - The card in the 1st position must be read with the cards in the 2nd, 9th and 10th houses;
    - The card in the 8th position must be read with the cards in the 7th, 15th and 16th houses;
    - The card in the 25th position must be read with the cards in the 17th, 18th and 26th houses;
    - The card in the 32nd position must be read with the cards in the 23rd, 24th and 31st houses.

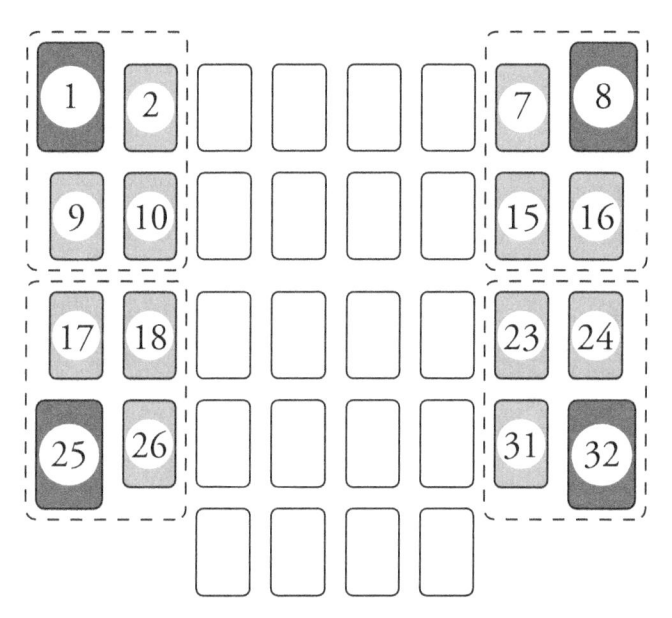

Important Note:

The information obtained from the four corner cards plays a significant role in the reading, as they reveal what really matters to the querent. Depending on the highlighted topics, the reading proceeds analyzing the mental area, the present, and the houses, representing the life areas or themes that have appeared in the reading.

The Heart of The Grand Tableau

The cards in the 12th, 13th, 20th, and 21st positions are The Heart of the Grand Tableau.

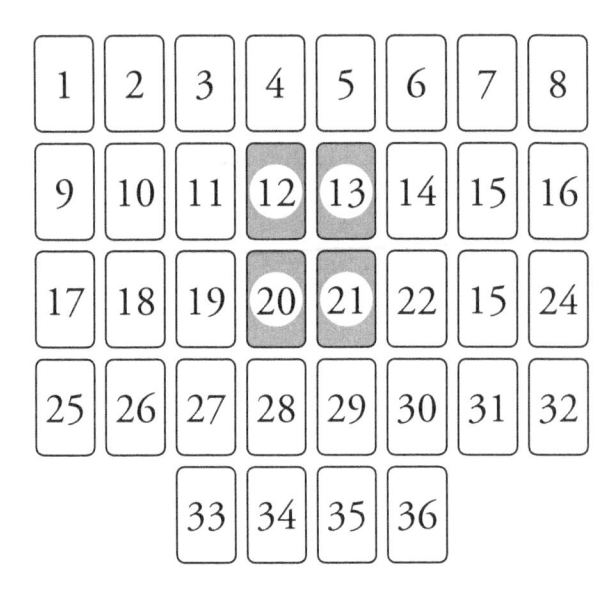

```
 1   2   3   4   5   6   7   8
 9  10  11  12  13  14  15  16
17  18  19  20  21  22  15  24
25  26  27  28  29  30  31  32
            33  34  35  36
```

I've emphasized these four cards so the querent can focus on their attitude and behavior during the reading.

- These four cards are read diagonally, 12 + 21 and 13 + 20.

Important Note:

Pay attention to whether the card representing the querent or another person (represented by a court card or other card) is present in this group of cards, as this will indicate what the querent needs to focus on, their attitudes, behavior, or the other person mentioned. Additionally, look at the theme cards to identify the life area or situation that requires attention and should be the main focus during the reading.

CHAPTER 7: THE GRAND TABLEAU

The Fate Line

The four houses in the last line: 33rd, 34th, 35th, and 36th houses, are called the fate line.

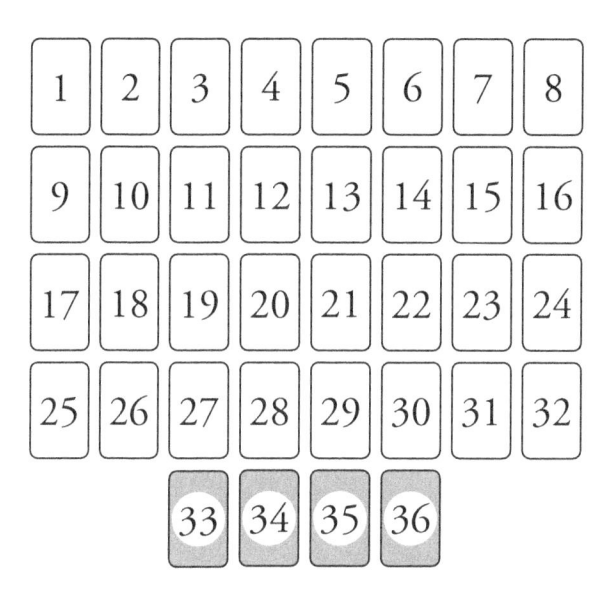

1	2	3	4	5	6	7	8
9	10	11	12	13	14	15	16
17	18	19	20	21	22	23	24
25	26	27	28	29	30	31	32
		33	34	35	36		

These four houses that comprise this line reveal events that will inevitably happen, and there's no way to avoid them. It represents the final outcome or the development of the question being explored. The events announced in this line will be the consequences the querent will experience, regardless of their will.

The Fate Line and the Future Line are connected in a certain sense. The Future Line shows how the situation will develop, while the Fate Line shows the outcome of this development. These events will affect the querent during the time frame set in the beginning of the reading.

For example, if the time frame in the Grand Tableau is six months, this line will show the events that will happen within this period. The cards must be read in pairs, from left to right (from the 33rd to the 36th house), connecting one card to the other, 33 to 34, 34 to 35, and 35 to 36, as shown in the next figure.

```
●- - - - - - - - - - - - - - - ->
[33] [34] [35] [36]
●↩↪●↩↪●↩↪→
```

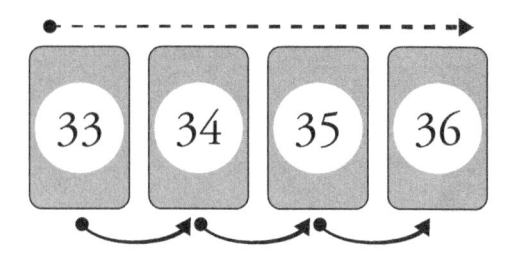

Important Note:

If the card representing the querent lands in the Fate Line, it strongly indicates that they'll play a significant role in the events depicted in this line. The same applies for any other card representing a person. It's also essential to consider the theme cards in this group of cards, as they indicate the life areas where the events will occur or have the most significant impact.

THE METHOD OF HOUSES

Back then, fortune tellers commonly used comprehensive methods, such as the Grand Tableau, in which each house corresponded to a specific life area or event.

Mademoiselle Le Normand's deck and reading method is mentioned in the book "L'Oracle Parfait ou Le Passe-Temps Des Dames Art De Tirer Les Cartes" written by Etteila in 1875, as well as in police interrogation records and her books.

According to Etteilla, Mlle Le Normand used an ordinary 36-card playing deck with nine cards in each of the four suits: King, Queen, Jack, Ten, Nine, Eight, Seven, Two, and Ace. She used a layout of nine cards in four rows that make a total of 36 houses, known as 9x4 Grand Tableau Lenormand, representing different aspects of life, emotional states, or events. This layout, known as the Grand Tableau Lenormand Houses, was a reference

L'Oracle Parfait ou Le Passe-Temps Des Dames Art De Tirer Les Cartes

for readings and is still widely used in Switzerland, Germany, Austria, and France. Is this how Mlle Le Normand used to read the cards? It's uncertain whether Mlle. Le Normand used this layout in her readings since she didn't provide much information about it.

The 36 cards of Mademoiselle Le Normand's Grande Tableau

It's known that this method was initially designed exclusively for an ordinary playing card deck. The keywords associated with each House may seem vague, however the book provides few details regarding their meaning.

1	2	3	4	5	6	7	8	9
Projet.	Satisfaction.	Réussite.	Espérance.	Hasard.	Désir.	Injustice.	Ingratitude.	Association.
10	11	12	13	14	15	16	17	18
Perte.	Peine.	État.	Joie.	Amour.	Prospérité.	Mariage.	Affliction.	Jouissance.
19	20	21	22	23	24	25	26	27
Héritage.	Trahison.	Rival.	Présent.	Amant.	Élévation.	Bienfait.	Entreprise.	Changement.
28	29	30	31	32	33	34	35	36
Fin.	Récompense.	Disgrâce.	Bonheur.	Fortune.	Indifférence.	Faveur.	Ambition.	Indisposition.

Besides, the book "L'Oracle Parfait ou Le passe-temps des Dames, L'Art detirer les cartes avec explication" plagiarized another French book entitled "Étrennes Nouvelles de L'Horoscope de l'Homme e de la Femme," published in 1788, which contained Henricus Cornelius Agrippa's knowledge.

Henricus Cornelius Agripa (1486 – 1535)

If you're curious, you can access the book "L'Oracle Parfait ou Le passe-temps des Dames" for free on the website: *gallica.bnf.fr*

In 1970, I took my first steps in traditional cartomancy using the standard 36-playing card deck, consisting of nine cards of each suit: Ace, King, Queen, Jack, Ten, Nine, Eight, Seven, and Two (French method).

My grandmother taught me the Grand Tableau layout, known as the 6x6 method, which is the same one used in The Game of Hope deck. Later, in 1974, my grandmother gifted me a small book from Portugal entitled "Your Destiny in the Cards: How to Unravel the Mysteries of the Future with 36 Cards". This method includes the Master's Method that explains the 36 Houses and the cards' meanings in each of the 36 positions. It was the first time I had ever seen a cartomancy book, which I still keep as a precious treasure, and I have since shared it with my students who have had the privilege of handling it.

The book "Le Grand Livre de la Cartomancy", written by Gerhard von Lentner and published in 1984, is another highly regarded reference book on cartomancy. I bought this book in Paris, France and I can attest that it contains a vast amount of information, having 920 pages filled with details on methods, techniques, the meanings of the cards and houses individually, and finally, the meaning of the cards in the houses. Although the book presents the Grand Tableau with 32 Houses, the techniques can be adapted to the Master's Method of the 36 Houses.

THE GRAND TABLEAU LENORMAND HOUSES

The houses are what make reading the Grand Tableau truly fascinating, as each house represents a different aspect of life, such as relationships, work, finances, health, and travel. Additionally, they depict people such as fathers, mothers, children, family, husbands, wives, lovers, rivals, friends, and partners. Furthermore, the houses also indicate different places like home, away from home, streets, roads, and cities. They also represent pleasant or unpleasant situations that a person may experience, for example, births, joys, successes, sadness, losses, and diseases. The houses reveal the challenges or experiences the querent is facing or will face in these areas.

The Grand Tableau is divided into 36 sectors, also known as houses, each house corresponding to the cards of the Petit Lenormand deck in numerical order.

- House no. 1 corresponds to card no. 1, The Rider
- House no. 2 corresponds to card no. 2, The Clover
- House no. 3 corresponds to card no. 3, The Ship
- House no. 4 corresponds to card no. 4, The House
- House no. 5, corresponds to card no. 5, The Tree
- And so on.

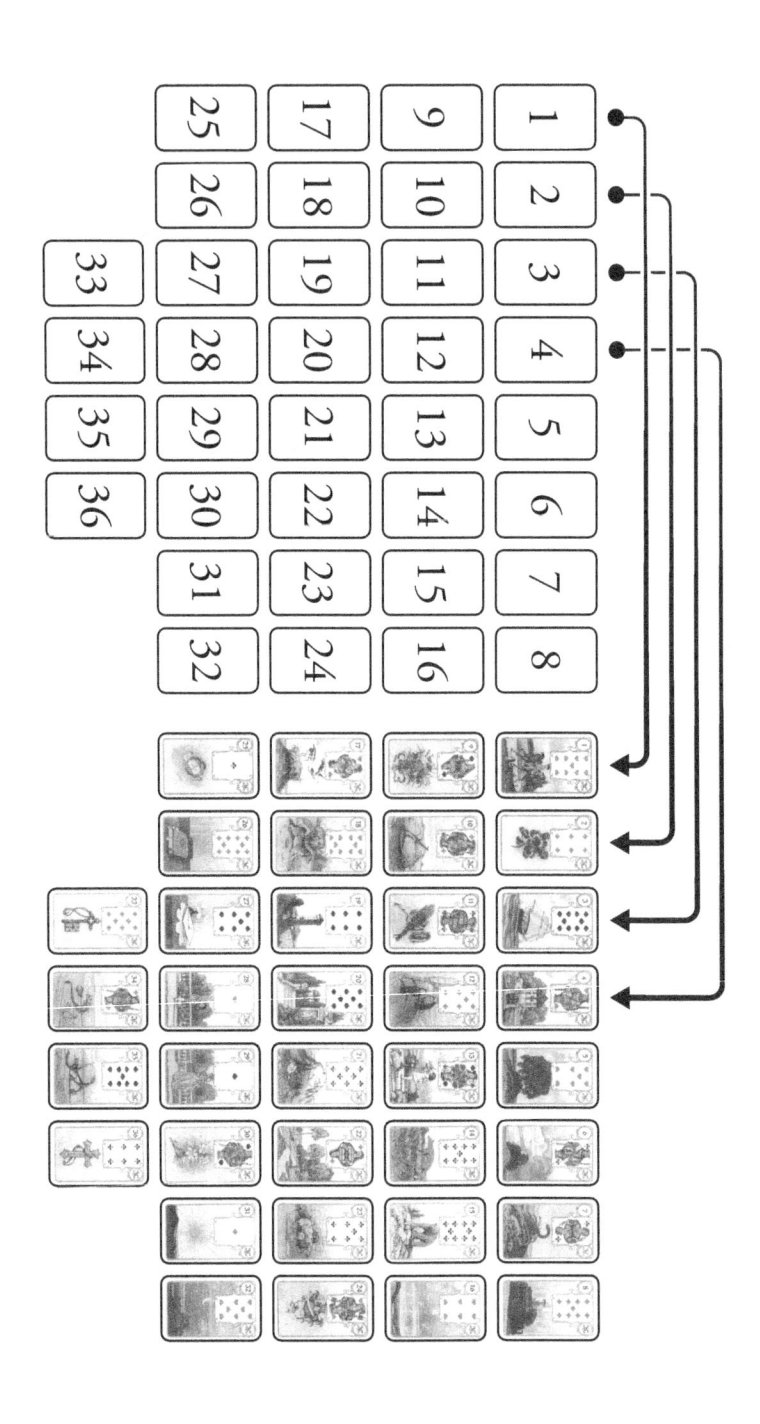

THE COMPLETE BOOK OF THE PETIT LENORMAND

484

Understanding that each of the 36 houses is represented by one of the cards in the deck (technically called the natural house) is essential to understanding what each house represents in a reading. For example, the house no. 32 represents honor, fame, distinction, and social status in the public eye. This means that this house reflects the level of prestige and social status that someone has acquired through their behavior, attitude, and commitment to accomplishing a specific goal.

Important Note:

The house meanings presented here are based on the German Lenormand tradition. If you use the Brazilian system or the Gypsy Deck, some houses in the Grand Tableau will need to be adapted according to the system you usually use. For example, in the Brazilian system:

- The 2nd house means short-term difficulties, trials, and obstacles;
- The 6th house means fears, torments, confusion, and indecisions;
- and so on.

The Language of Houses

Now that you understand the importance of the houses in the Grand Tableau, it's time to deepen your knowledge of the 36 houses.

It's worth mentioning that although each house corresponds to all the 36 card meanings of the Petit Lenormand deck, it's recommended to assign them only a few meanings initially. As you advance in your practical studies and master the meanings and techniques, you can gradually add more meanings to the houses.

House no. 1

- » **Ruled by:** Card no. 1, The Rider
- » **Phrase:** "I bring news."
- » **Purpose:** Revealing important incoming news, whether it's favorable or unfavorable, depends on the card on it.
- » **Keywords:** News, the arrival of something.

Example of some cards in The House no. 1:

- The Ship: arrival of something or someone coming from a distant place;
- The Clouds: vague information; confusing situations;
- The Snake: interference by a third person in the querent's affairs; harassment;
- The Coffin: sad news; a funeral;
- The Bouquet: a small promotion; visits; an apology;
- The Owls: the proximity of someone who will reveal something; receive a phone call;
- The Bear: receiving news or information from an influential person, such as a lawyer, a boss, or a parent;
- The Dog: the arrival of support or help; regaining confidence in yourself or someone else;
- The Mountain: immobility or stagnation;
- The Mice: possibility of recovering something stolen or lost;
- The Heart: a new passion or love; the arrival of a loved one or a new romantic interest;
- The Letter: communication through mail, e-mail, fax (if The Ship card is nearby, it indicates that the communication is coming from far away or abroad); the arrival of a visit or a new contact;
- The Lilies: the arrival of a period of peace and calm; reconciliation;
- The Key: the arrival of an answer or solution to a problem;

- The Fish: the arrival of money; banking transactions (investment);
- The Anchor: new job; new professional opportunities; the arrival of something or someone that brings hope or stability.

House no. 2

» **Ruled by:** Card no. 2, The Clover
» **Phrase:** "I bring a little luck and new opportunities!"
» **Purpose:** Revealing the opportunities will work in your favor, even if for a short time, and advise you to enjoy it.
» **Keywords:** A stroke of luck, new opportunities, small pleasures and satisfactions, all forms of gambling (horse racing, sports betting, lottery, and speculation).

Examples of some cards in The House no. 2:
- The House: temporary accommodation;
- The Stars: good luck in games of hance; an opportunity to clarify a situation;
- The Mice: missed opportunities;
- The Ring: a second chance in a relationship;
- The Fish: a stroke of luck; an opportunity to earn extra money or receive a tip;
- The Lilies: reconciliation.

House no. 3

» **Ruled by:** Card no. 3, The Ship
» **Phrase:** "I bring adventures in faraway places and knowledge of new cultures!"
» **Purpose:** Revealing events that will happen beyond the querent's reach.
» **Keywords:** Trade, business, enterprise, import and export, long-distance travel, vacation, foreign lands, absence, longings, desires, yearning, nostalgia.

Examples of some cards in The House no. 3:

- The Rider: frequent travel; separation, or abandonment;
- The House: business transactions; buying or selling property; homesickness;
- The Clouds: delayed trip;
- The Coffin: canceled trip; funeral; inheritance;
- The Stars: spiritual journey; browsing the Internet;
- The Storks: air travel; changes in the querent's life; travel for business;
- The Tower: a foreign country; border; traveling alone; a foreign company;
- The Book: educational trip or exploration; traveling to an unknown or secret place; confidential business;
- The Letter: long-distance correspondence; connecting with different cultures or ethnicities;
- The Sun: a lucky trip;
- The Fish: a business trip; profitable trade; international money transfer; inheritance; alcoholism;
- The Cross: pilgrimage or travel for religious reasons.

House no. 4

- » **Ruled by:** Card no. 4, The House
- » **Phrase:** "I bring comfort and show the querent's home environment!"
- » **Purpose:** Revealing all that happens at home or in the querent's surrounding environment, including relationships with close family and friends. It also identifies where and with whom the querent feels most comfortable.
- » **Keywords:** The querent's home and properties, daily routine, domestic situation, neighbors, personal and private affairs, emotional well-being, comfort, habits, and tradition, the querent's inner world and personal foundation.

Examples of some cards in the house no. 4:

- The Ship: distancing from domestic affairs; moving away from or leaving home (to understand the reasons for this distancing or departure, check out the surrounding cards and the card in The House no. 3; stepping out of the comfort zone; selling a property;
- The Tree: keeping calm; resting; recovering after a disease or prolonged period of stress; taking a retreat; self-discovery;
- The Dog: a friend's home; a pet;
- The Tower: isolation;
- The Ring: the couple's House, a shared residence;
- The Lilies: living with family; a family home; a harmonious and welcoming home;
- The Sun: energy therapy or Reiki.

House no. 5

» **Ruled by:** Card no. 5, The Tree
» **Phrase:** "I bring well-being."
» **Purpose:** Providing insight about the querent's current health condition, showing the karmic experience.
» **Keywords:** Health (vitality, disease, and recovery potential), medical care, medicine, ancestry, origins), the origin of an event, ramification.

Examples of some cards in The House no. 5:

- Clover: herbal or natural treatment;
- The Clouds: indisposition or malaise;
- The Coffin: disease;
- Bouquet: alternative or non-traditional treatments;
- The Stars: spiritual growth;
- Rats: loss of vitality; sick body; weak immune system;
- The Ring: long-term relationship; continuous treatment;

- The Sun: vitality; good health;
- The Anchor: good health or stability; convalescence.

House no. 6

» **Ruled by:** Card no. 6, The Clouds
» **Phrase:** "I bring misunderstandings, confusions, and ambiguous events."
» **Purpose:** Revealing situations that are causing confusion, anxiety, and uncertainty.
» **Keywords:** Problems, annoyances, worries, short-term setbacks, instability, uncertainty, volatility, misunderstanding, misconceptions, threats, fears.

Examples of some cards in The House no. 6:
- The Ship: It indicates moving away or distancing from the ex; trouble in a trip or business;
- The Clouds: suggests the presence of negativity and multiple minor problems rather than a big issue;
- The Snake: an ex-partner or a rival may join forces to harm you;
- The Coffin: indicates a past that still causes suffering;
- The Bouquet: denotes kindness that is not fully understood;
- The Broom and The Whip: abusive behavior;
- The Stars: misunderstanding cleared up; illusions about a project;
- The Ring: frequent setbacks;
- The Letter: a brief delay in a written communication; feelings of apprehension or anxiety about news; excitement about a message;
- The Fish: financial problems, minor annoyances, or temporary financial difficulties;
- The Anchor: a delay in completing a professional task.

House no. 7

- » **Ruled by:** Card no. 7, The Snake
- » **Phrase:** "I bring betrayals and complications."
- » **Purpose:** Revealing hidden enemies.
- » **Keywords:** Potential enemies, rivals, or adversaries, sins, betrayal, complication, deception, detour, envy, jealousy.

Examples of some cards in The House no. 7:
- The Tree: medication;
- The clouds: a hidden enemy or rival, witchcraft or sorcery;
- The Stars: chemotherapy or other chemical treatments for disease;
- The Heart: emotional or romantic problems, pure malice or cruelty;
- The Ring: a female lover, severe complications in a relationship, disappointment with a partner;
- The Book: technical problems, a hidden rival, the possibility of magic or sorcery.

House no. 8

- » **Ruled by:** Card no. 8, The Coffin
- » **Phrase:** "I bring the end of everything."
- » **Purpose:** Revealing what will come to an end and what is no longer valuable or essential in the person's life.
- » **Keywords:** end, death, grief, sadness, pain, severe disease, bankruptcy, a significant loss.

Example of some cards in The House no. 8:
- The Rider: cancellation of a planned visit or trip;
- The Ship: end of a journey or a relocation process;
- The Tree: health problems in general; conclusion of a therapeutic treatment;
- The Clouds: contamination;

- The Snake: victory over a dangerous enemy;
- The Bouquet: the cancellation of a ceremony;
- The Owls: becoming sick due to worries;
- The Tower: a severe disease that requires isolation; end of isolation; stay in a hospital; end of one's life; demolition of a building;
- The Garden: cancelation of a public event; emotional disease;
- The Mountain: resignation, facing great difficulties in projects; extended stay in bed;
- The Mice: epidemic or the outbreak of a disease;
- The Ring: dissolution of a partnership, employment contract, or relationship; chronic disease;
- The Book: unknown disease;
- The Moon: lack of recognition or awards;
- The Anchor: completion of a professional activity or obligation; bankruptcy; or unemployment;
- The Cross: death; intense pain or great suffering.

House no. 9

» **Ruled by:** Card no. 9, The Bouquet
» **Phrase:** "I bring joy and beauty."
» **Purpose:** Revealing joy and surprises
» **Keywords:** Surprise, invitations, gifts, happiness, joy, satisfaction, offer, awards, visit, and hobbies.

Example of some cards in The House no. 9:
- The Clover: a surprise;
- The Clouds: an uncertain invitation;
- The Stars: artistic talent;
- The Garden: an invitation to a party or performance;
- The Heart: falling in love; an affair; a genuine invitation;

- The Ring: an invitation to a wedding, marriage proposal, or offer of cooperation;
- The Moon: great recognition; promotion;
- The Fish: a gift of great value or a monetary gift.

House no. 10

» **Ruled by:** Card no. 10, The Scythe
» **Phrase:** "I bring the elimination of unnecessary things."
» **Purpose:** Revealing the dangers and risks that threaten the querent's life and also separating the "wheat from the chaff."
» **Keywords:** danger, risky, fierceness, warning, threat, shock, accident, cutting away, separation

Examples of some cards in The House no. 10:
- The Ship: an accident; cutting short a trip;
- The Tree: breaking the bones;
- The Clouds: being attacked by an ex-partner;
- The Snake: taking out a rival; being attacked by an ex-partner;
- The Coffin: suicidal thoughts; an accident or violent death;
- The Owls: cutting off a call or the telephone line;
- The Fox: invitation with ulterior motives;
- The Bear: splitting the assets;
- The Dog: severing ties with a friend, colleague, acquaintance, or neighbor;
- The Garden: isolation from social events; need to get rid of helpers;
- The Mountain: overcoming obstacles that hinder the realization of something;
- The Ring: the termination of a contract;
- The Letter: lack of communication or contact, receiving a letter
- From the querent: assertive attitude;
- The Lilies: sexual harassment or rape;
- The Fish: a decrease or loss of income.

House no. 11

- » **Ruled by:** Card no. 11, The Broom and The Whip
- » **Phrase:** "I bring conflict and discord."
- » **Purpose:** Revealing where or with whom conflicts arise and how disagreements are resolved.
- » **Keywords:** disputes, disagreements, controversies, punishment, accusation, abuse, aggression, addictive, magic, spell.

Examples of some cards in The House no. 11:
- The House: domestic conflicts; emotional or soul pain;
- The Tree: physical pain;
- The Snake: negative criticism; legal complications;
- The Owl: verbal attack;
- The Child: futile discussions; disagreements caused by irresponsibility;
- The Bear: conflict with a superior or a parent;
- The Dog: discussions due to loyalty; security alert;
- The Tower: legal action;
- The Garden: public attack;
- The Lilies: pressure to make a decision;
- The Heart: disagreements with a loved one;
- The Ring: a conflictual relationship;
- The Book: criticism for intellectual reasons;
- The Lilies: a lawyer; tensions in the family;
- The Cross: condemnation.

House no. 12

- » **Ruled by:** Card no. 12, The Owls
- » **Phrase:** ""I bring a little agitation, restlessness, and chatter."
- » **Purpose:** Revealing how you express yourself and communicate with others.
- » **Keywords:** verbal communication, rumors, agitation, anxiety, restlessness.

Examples of some cards in The House no. 12:
- The Bouquet: a formal conversation;
- The Child: a conversation about a child or a new beginning;
- The Stars: video call; a cell phone;
- The Crossroads: anxiety about what path to take or decision to make;
- The Ring: regular phone contact, discussing an agreement or a contract;
- The Book: certain things left unsaid; a confession; a private conversation;
- The Keys: a cell phone;
- The Cross: a prayer; talking about something that causes grief and suffering.

House no. 13

» **Ruled by:** Card no. 13, The Child
» **Phrase:** "I bring something new."
» **Purpose:** Revealing what is new in the person's life and how they deal with their children or young people.
» **Keywords:** children, adolescents, a new beginning, fresh start, first steps, initial phase.

Examples of some cards in The House no. 13:
- The Ship: new directions or beginnings abroad;
- The Clouds: a confused or bipolar young man; the beginning of a period of chaos and confusion;
- The Owls: twins; two children or young people;
- The Stars: a new vision; new ideas;
- The Heart: a new love;
- The Book: a new edition of a book; a new book;
- The Pisces: small investments, small gains, a small amount of money;
- The Anchor: a new job or work opportunity.

House no. 14

- » **Ruled by:** Card no. 14, The Fox
- » **Phrase:** "I bring deceit and mistakes."
- » **Purpose:** Revealing what's wrong and unreliable
- » **Keywords:** a warning, falsehood, mistake, deceit, a trap, lie, illusory situation, intrigue, illegality.

Examples of some cards in The House no. 14:

- The Ship: the wrong time to depart or take a trip; lies or deceit related to a trip;
- The Tree: an incorrect medical diagnosis; leading a double life;
- The Snake: a significant lie;
- The Coffin: faking an illness; misdiagnosing a disease;
- The Bouquet: favoritism; false flattery; rude behavior;
- The Garden: lies involving many people; ability to take advantage of others;
- The Ring: constantly lying or deceiving; wrong behavior in a relationship or partnership;
- The Querent's Card: manipulation of a situation to take advantage;
- The Fish: inappropriate relationship with money; counterfeit money.

House no. 15

- » **Ruled by:** Card no. 15, The Bear
- » **Phrase:** "I bring protection, courage, and strength to face life's challenges."
- » **Purpose:** Revealing possessions, personal and financial resources
- » **Keywords:** strength, power, courage, the parents, superior, assets, savings.

Examples of some cards in The House no. 15:

- The House: properties and real estate;

- **The Broom and The Whip**: conflictual relationship with one's parents;
- **The Fish**: the savings, financial security; the ability to manage money or assets well;
- **The Lilies**: grandparents, a specialist, a judge, a lawyer.

House no. 16

» **Ruled by:** Card no. 16, The Stars
» **Phrase:** "I bring inspiration to achieve goals."
» **Purpose:** Revealing expectations and future projects.
» **Keywords:** expectations, inspirations, plans, goals, achievements, successes, talent, spirituality (spiritual belief), mysticism, esotericism, technology.

Examples of some cards in The House no. 16:
- **The Tree**: healing; recovery;
- **The Clouds**: unclear goals; side effects of medication;
- **The Garden**: social network;
- **The Crossroads**: unfinished projects;
- **The Heart**: a desire for true love;
- **The Sun**: a huge victory; achievement of one's goals;
- **The Moon**: unexpected success; great recognition;

House no. 17

» **Ruled by:** Card no. 17, The Storks
» **Phrase:** "I bring changes."
» **Purpose:** Revealing what is or should be changed or altered in one's life.
» **Keywords:** changes, modifications, alterations, transformations, transitions, transference, pregnancy, birth.

Examples of some cards in House no. 17:
- **The House**: a change of house or domestic environment;

- <u>The Tree</u>: changes in lifestyle or a change that will take a long time to complete;
- <u>The Child</u>: pregnancy;
- <u>The Dog</u>: a reliable change, a change of attitude towards a friendship;
- <u>The Mountain</u>: complex and challenging changes;
- <u>The Ring</u>: renewal, amendments, or changes to a contract, a need to change something in a relationship;
- <u>The Fish</u>: financial changes.

House no. 18

- » **Ruled by:** Card No 18, The Dog
- » **Phrase:** "I bring loyal and reliable friends or situations."
- » **Purpose:** Revealing the person's attitudes towards friendship and the kinds of friends they attract; what is pure; who is trustworthy and honest
- » **Keywords:** loyalty, trustworthiness, honesty, friendship, pet, support

Examples of some cards in The House no. 18:
- <u>The Tree</u>: a friend from childhood or a longtime friend;
- <u>The Snake</u>: a harmful friendship; a friend who betrays the querent's trust; a "friend" who plots against the querent;
- <u>The Scythe</u>: an arrogant or aggressive friend, colleague, acquaintance, or neighbor;
- <u>The Fox</u>: dangerous friendships;
- <u>The Bear</u>: influential friends;
- <u>The Stork</u>: changes in the circle of friends;
- <u>The Tower</u>: friendship with limitations;
- <u>The Mice</u>: a profiteering or opportunist friend;
- <u>The Fish</u>: financial support from a friend or acquaintance;
- <u>The Anchor</u>: a co-worker; loyalty and commitment to work.

House no. 19

- » **Ruled by:** Card no. 19, The Tower
- » **Phrase:** "I bring restrictions and order."
- » **Purpose:** Revealing how the person deals with authority
- » **Keywords:** a large building, government institutions, authorities, laws, bureaucracy, isolation, loneliness.

Examples of some cards in The House no. 19:
- The Ship: a multinational corporation;
- The House: an introverted person;
- The Tree: a hospital; a long period of solitude;
- The Bear: a hospitalized or incarcerated parent; a judge;
- The Garden: public institutions or organizations;
- The Mountain: imprisonment; restrictions; border; customs;
- The Heart: charity;
- The Ring: separation; loneliness within a relationship, official registration;
- The Lilies: a retreat; reflective moments, isolation from the family;
- The Moon: a mosque;
- The Cross: a church.

House no. 20

- » **Ruled by:** Card no. 20, The Garden
- » **Phrase:** "I bring new beliefs and fun outside the comfort zone."
- » **Purpose:** Revealing the person's attitude towards others and social life in general.
- » **Keywords:** social life, external affairs, public event, society, audience, community, entertainment, fun, recreation.

Examples of some cards in The House no. 20:
- The Clover: an unexpected encounter;

- The Tree: recovery, vacation;
- The Snake: a bad company;
- The Coffin: a funeral, a trash can;
- The Bouquet: a pleasant company, a birthday party; a joyful event;
- The Scythe: a dangerous social event (with The Broom and The Whip card, it may indicate aggression in a public demonstration);
- The Ring: social networking app for relationships; a group belonging to a society, such as school or religious organization; regular encounters or meetings;
- The Book: literary publications; limited public access (forum, community, etc.);
- The Moon: admiration and public respect; becoming famous or well-known;
- The Key: a forum or event open to all;
- The Fish: many fans and followers; customers; auction;
- The Anchor: a stable customer base.

House no. 21

» **Ruled by:** Card no. 21, The Mountain
» **Phrase:** "I bring huge challenges and obstacles."
» **Purpose:** Revealing the obstacles that prevent people from accomplishing their goals.
» **Keywords:** obstacles, blockade, delays, difficulties, resistance.

Examples of some cards in The House no. 21:
- The Clouds: obstacles of unknown origins; an unseen adversary;
- The Coffin: difficulty in finishing something;
- The Child: difficulty in starting something new; challenge in having a child;
- The Tower: imprisonment;

- <u>The Crossroads</u>: challenges in choosing a direction among several possibilities or making a decision;
- <u>The Heart</u>: feeling indifferent;
- <u>The Ring</u>: relationship is prevented or blocked (check out the card close to The Mountain); obstacles in signing a contract or entering into a union;
- <u>The Book</u>: a psychological or mental block; struggling to learn, training, research; trouble in mastering a subject;
- <u>The Fish</u>: debts;
- <u>The Anchor</u>: difficulty in accomplishing a task.

House no. 22

» **Ruled by:** Card no. 22, The Crossroads
» **Phrase:** "I bring choices."
» **Purpose:** Revealing uncertainties and decision-making process.
» **Keywords:** decision, choice, options, alternative to be evaluated.

Examples of some cards in The House no. 22:
- <u>The House</u>: house choices;
- <u>The Tree</u>: a second medical opinion;
- <u>The Clouds</u>: uncertainty and difficulty in making a decision;
- <u>The Mountain</u>: a blocked decision;
- <u>The Heart</u>: several love interests or relationships;
- <u>The Ring</u>: infidelity; adultery; separation; several commitments;
- <u>The Querent's card</u>: the querent is evaluating their life or facing an important decision (it may be a separation);
- <u>The Fish</u>: multiple sources of income.

House no. 23

- » **Ruled by:** Card no. 23, The Mice
- » **Phrase:** "I bring stress and losses."
- » **Purpose:** Revealing what you are losing or lessening in your life.
- » **Keywords:** loss, theft, stress, worries, fear, anxiety, depriving, damage, disinterest.

Examples of some cards in The House no. 23:

- The Rider: a damaged car, motorcycle, or bicycle;
- The House: theft of personal information;
- The Tree: physical exhaustion or fatigue;
- The Clouds: infection, contamination, virus;
- The Broom and The Whip: avoiding discussions; reducing hostility;
- The Fox: corruption; decreased resources;
- The Bear: weight loss;
- The Stars: stress during the execution of a project;
- The Dog: a small circle of friends;
- The Garden: virus;
- The Heart: loss of affection;
- The Ring: theft, deception; a slow breakup in a relationship; failing to fulfill promises;
- The Book: memory loss; dementia, Alzheimer's disease;
- The Fish: financial losses, theft, decreased profits, salary cut; precariousness; financial insecurity and instability; greed, materialism;
- The Anchor: professional setbacks; job loss, small professional tasks; lack of job stability and security; exploitation.

House no. 24

- » **Ruled by:** Card no. 24, The Heart
- » **Phrase:** "I bring love and accomplish what's in your heart."

- » **Purpose:** Revealing what is in your heart, your feelings, what you love, appreciate, and admire.
- » **Keywords:** love, romance, affection, passion, attraction, affinity, desire, pleasure, taste.

Examples of some cards in The House no. 24:

- The House: appreciation of domestic life; a desire to own a home;
- The Tree: endless love; stable feelings;
- The Snake: poisoned heart; sadistic desire for revenge;
- The Coffin: emotional exhaustion and feeling drained;
- The Bouquet: flirting; falling in love;
- The Broom and The Whip: anger and a desire to hurt;
- The Stars: esoteric or spiritual interests;
- The Ring: a desire for a committed relationship; a couple in love;
- The Book: interest in occult studies, astrology, or cartomancy; a secret or forbidden passion;
- The Lilies: strong attachment to family; calm and peace;
- The Anchor: love and devotion to one's job or career; a great love; stable feelings.

House no. 25

- » **Ruled by:** Card no. 25, The Ring
- » **Phrase:** "I bring the guarantee that everything will be fulfilled in accordance with the law."
- » **Purpose:** Revealing information about a relationship or contract.
- » **Keywords:** any relationship, an official union, a merger, a contract, a partnership, commitment, an agreement, cooperation, obligations, and duties.

Examples of some cards in House no. 25:
- The Ship: a foreign partner; commercial partnerships; foreign or remote collaborations; long-distance relationships;
- The House: the acquisition of property;
- The Tree: a routine check-up for health;
- The Clouds: uncertainties in the relationship or union;
- The Snake: adultery;
- The Bouquet: an official commitment made or engagement;
- The Scythe: a divorce or separation, if the querent is in a relationship, the termination or cancellation of a contract or agreement;
- The Owls: a verbal agreement; a stressful union;
- The Stars: spiritual connections;
- The Tower: a long-distance relationship; agreement on the timing of a proceeding; a contract or agreement with some restrictions;
- The Garden: social commitments;
- The Mountain: going in circles, no way out; a problematic or stalled contract or agreement; no deal is currently possible;
- The Mice: a worn-out relationship;
- The Book: secret agreements or partnership; the partner (spouse or business partner) is hiding something;
- The Letter: a written contract or agreement;
- The Lilies: a romantic relationship with an older person;
- The Sun: financial success through a business partnership or collaboration;
- The Fish: a relationship based on financial interests; a regular payment, such as leasing, rent, or salary); financial agreement; financial commitment (the person is financially dependent on another person);
- The Anchor: an employment contract, a contract renewal, a long-term and solid relationship.

House no. 26

- » **Ruled by:** Card no. 26, The Book
- » **Phrase:** "I bring knowledge, but I can also hide the truth."
- » **Purpose:** Revealing issues related to learning and the unknown.
- » **Keywords:** unknown, secret, mystery, occultism, education, school, teaching, learning, studies (such as course, training, or seminar), research, investigation, memory, concealment, and secrecy.

Examples of some cards in The House no. 26:
- The Ship: urine analysis; studying abroad or taking online courses; planning a trip; travel documents such as passport, visa, etc.;
- The House: studying from home; documents related to a house;
- The Tree: medical examinations;
- The Snake: secret enemies, spell, or witchcraft.
- The Coffin: a will; hiding the actual state of health.
- The Child: learning positive things.
- The Fox: intelligence used for fraudulent purposes.
- The Stars: the study of the Occult Sciences.
- The Tower: higher education, considering a separation, a legal process;
- The Mountain: a long-held secret;
- The Heart: a secret and platonic love, a secret admirer, interest in occult studies and mystery;
- The Ring: clandestine, extramarital relationship; review of a book or document; a new book edition;
- The Letter: secret affairs;
- The Lilies: family secrets; secrets in one's sex life;
- The Sun: the revelation of a secret; success in education;
- The Fish: financial-related secrets;
- The Anchor: work-related secret; mastering new skills;
- The Cross: religious studies; painful secrets.

House no. 27

- » **Ruled by:** Card no. 27, The Letter
- » **Phrase:** "I bring news."
- » **Purpose:** Revealing issues related to learning and the unknown.
- » **Keywords:** unknown, secret, mystery, occultism, education, school, teaching, learning, studies (such as course, training, or seminar), research, investigation, memory, concealment, and secrecy.

Examples of some cards in The House no. 27:

- The Rider: registered mail;
- The Ship: travel-related information, news from abroad, international mail, online contact;
- The Tree: medical report or prescription;
- The Clouds: contact or news from the ex-male partner; disturbing email or message; unclear information;
- The Snake: contact or news from the ex-female partner;
- The Bouquet: an invitation;
- The Scythe: a legal document for divorce or contract termination if The Ring card is next to it;
- The Broom and The Whip: a fine; communication from a police officer or lawyer if The Bear card is in the 1st house;
- The Owls: an online chat via WhatsApp, Duo, Messenger, Skype, etc.; a phone call;
- The Stars: an x-ray; online contact; or chat;
- The Storks: news about a change;
- The Tower: news or notifications from authorities;
- The Garden: a chat room; comments on social media platforms like Facebook;
- The Heart: mail or messages from an important person; a love message;
- The Ring: messages from a partner or spouse;

- The Book: anonymous letters or email; test results (especially if The Tree card is near, indicating medical tests); unknown symptoms; or confidential information;
- The Fish: a checkbook; a credit card; bank statement; an invoice; and also fertility;
- The Anchor: professional resume.

Houses no. 28 and no. 29

» **Ruled by:** Card no. 28, The Man
» **Ruled by:** Card no. 29, The Woman
» **Phrase:** "I bring energies for the querent."
» **Purpose:** Revealing what is influencing the partner's life.

House no. 30

» **Ruled by:** Card no. 30, The Lilies
» **Phrase:** "I bring peace and serenity."
» **Purpose:** Revealing one's sexual orientation and situation, how the querent deals with their family, as well as their sense of peace and harmony.
» **Keywords:** family, harmony, peace, sexual life

Examples of some cards in The House no. 30:
- The Child: nephews and nieces, grandchildren, heirs;
- The Scythe: violent sex;
- The Bear: assistance from an influential person;
- The Dog: support and help from a friend, self-confidence, and self-esteem;
- The Tower: living separately from the family;
- The Ring: reconciliation; peace achieved through an agreement;
- The Anchor: retirement; professional experience.

House no. 31

- » **Ruled by:** Card no. 31, The Sun
- » **Phrase:** "I bring great success."
- » **Purpose:** Revealing what will make you happy.
- » **Keywords:** great fortune, success, happiness, optimism, vitality.

Examples of some cards in The House no. 31:
- The Clouds: bipolarity; depression;
- The Ring: success through cooperation or partnership;
- The Moon: great recognition and prestige;
- The Cross: success through sacrifices and suffering.

House no. 32

- » **Ruled by:** Card no. 32, The Moon
- » **Phrase:** "I bring honor and recognition."
- » **Purpose:** It reveals how respected and honored you are, but also the reflection of your actions.
- » **Keywords:** status, fame, honor, recognition, reputation, prestige, merit.

Examples of some cards in The House no. 32:
- The Stars: a well-deserved award; praise and recognition; guaranteed success in the esoteric or technical field;
- The Sun: successful or personal career, good reputation.

House no. 33

- » **Ruled by:** Card no. 33, The Key
- » **Phrase:** "I bring solutions."
- » **Purpose:** Revealing a certainty or a solution.
- » **Keywords:** certainty, solutions, resolution, answer, access.

Examples of some cards in The House no. 33:
- The Fox: A problem solved using cunning, strategy, or deceit;
- The Ring: Feeling secure in a relationship;

- The Querent's card: Taking control of one's life; the solution depends on the querent;
- The Fish: financial accessibility; a loan agreement;
- The Anchor: job security; a solution is guaranteed.

House no. 34

» **Ruled by:** Card no. 34, The Fish
» **Phrase:** "I bring prosperity and abundance."
» **Purpose:** Revealing the financial conditions and the relationship one has with money.
» **Keywords:** abundance, finance, money, income, business, investment.

Examples of some cards in The House no. 34:
- The Clover: extra money;
- The Ship: money inherited or from afar; financial support from afar; money transfer; international market;
- The House: real estate investment;
- The Clouds: financial concerns; drunkenness;
- The Dog: friend's help and financial support;
- The Mountain: money that will take a long time to arrive; locked finances;
- The Mice: illegal money;
- The Ring: a joint account;
- The Book: hiding income; hidden money;
- The Sun: fulfillment of one's hopes or aspirations;
- The Anchor: financial security, a stable income, a long-term investment; a businessperson.

House no. 35

» **Ruled by:** Card no. 35, The Anchor
» **Phrase:** "I am hope, but I also bring stability and security."

- » **Purpose:** Revealing the professional situation.
- » **Keywords:** work, job, occupation, hope, stability, routine.

Examples of some cards in The House no. 35:
- The Rider: a new job; new professional opportunities;
- The House: a solid connection to home;
- The Tree: stability in life;
- The Clouds: professional uncertainty;
- The Snake: workplace harassment or inappropriate behavior;
- The Broom and The Whip: disputes at work;
- The Stars: new professional prospects;
- The Mountain: unemployment;
- The Crossroads: professional proposals that must be carefully considered;
- The Mice: an underpaid or undervalued job; lacking stability or guarantee;
- The Book: secrecy at work;
- The Letter: professional correspondence;
- The Fish: a well-paid job;
- The Cross: overwork or heavy professional responsibilities.

House no. 36

- » **Ruled by:** Card no. 36, The Cross
- » **Phrase:** "I bring suffering and tests."
- » **Purpose:** Revealing what is troubling you, what is painful and what must be endured.
- » **Keywords:** karma, sacrifice, suffering, affliction, torment, pain, burden, examination, mission, religion.

Examples of some cards in The House no. 36:
- The Clouds: misfortune;
- The Snake: a shocking event or situation;
- The Coffin: great anguish, deep pain, guilt;

- The Broom and The Whip: ordeal; martyrdom;
- The Heart: regret, guilt, heartbreak;
- The Querent's card: the person can do remarkable deeds, including self-sacrifice;
- The Anchor: professional overload.

The Special Houses

When reading the houses using the Grand Tableau, it's not recommended to read all 36 houses, as the reading would be contradictory, confusing, and too long. The purpose of the special houses is to focus the reading on specific houses and provide a more targeted analysis.

The special houses are:
- The theme houses;
- The additional houses;
- The verification houses.

The Theme Houses

Certain houses in the Grand Tableau are associated with specific life areas or topics, such as love, emotions, relationships, finances, work, health, etc. For instance, if you want to know about someone's married life, you would focus on house no. 25, which is the house for official relationships and official unions. To understand their financial situation, turn to house no. 34, which represents all financial issues, including income and salary.

The theme houses can be interpreted in two ways:
1. In a general reading, they provide an overall view of the querent's life;
2. In a specific reading, the house theme is chosen based on the specific topic brought up by the querent.

Important Note:
The interpretation of theme houses may vary depending the tradition you follow (traditional, German, French, Brazilian, etc.). In the Brazilian tradition (or gypsy deck), the house no. 2 represents temporary obstacles and challenges; the house no. 4 represents family; the house no. 11 stands for sex; the house no. 15 indicates envy and jealousy; the house no. 22 means open paths, the house no. 32 represents intuition, mediumship, and illusion, and the house no. 36 stands for destiny, victory, and success. Therefore, you need to adapt the meaning of the houses according to the tradition you follow as long as you feel comfortable during the reading.

The Additional Houses

In a reading, the theme house and additional houses work together. The additional houses correspond to the topic addressed by the querent or emphasized by the card in the theme house. They allow you to answer the querent's several questions and clarify any doubts that may come up during the reading.

For example, if the querent seeks a professional reading and says they're currently selling handmade products and want to know if they'll find a permanent job soon. In this case, the theme card would be number 14, representing self-employment, and the additional card would be card number 35, indicating a permanent job. The card that lands in this house will provide insights into whether the querent will finally find a permanent job. Let's suppose that The Ring card falls in the additional house, it may announce that an employment contract is on the horizon, suggesting a permanent job. Instead, if The Mice card lands in this house, it indicates unemployment or temporary and low-paying jobs.

The Verification Houses

All 36 houses are considered verification houses. They allow a better understanding of the issue being investigated and provide information that can help the querent to prepare for events, gain awareness of some facts, and focus on their goals.

In the example above, to offer objective guidance, you need to consider house no. 1, which indicates professional news, and house no. 33, which will give clues about where to seek a permanent job.

As you can see, by combining the three techniques of the special houses, it's possible to delve deeper into a particular topic or life area, providing valuable information for the querent to solve their problems.

TABLE OF VERIFICATION HOUSES

Houses	Answer The Following Questions
No. 1	What's on the way? What's coming up? What's the news? How should you approach the problem? What's in motion? Who's involved or intervening? Is it the right time to take action?
No. 2	What new opportunities should be seized?
No. 3	What does the querent need to distance themselves from? What should be left behind? What's moving away? What changes have already taken place? What do you miss the most?
No. 4	How's the querent's inner and personal world? How's the environment where the querent lives in? What are the querent's habits? What makes the querent feel most comfortable?

Houses	Answer The Following Questions
No. 5	What's the person's true nature or the issue being investigated? What requires healing? What emotional or psychological baggage does the querent carry from their past? (Karma)
No. 6	What's currently worrying the querent? What's the querent struggling to handle? What's unclear? What makes the querent upset, uneasy, or anxious?
No. 7	Who are the querent's hidden enemies? What factors or circumstances will complicate things for the querent?
No. 8	What does the querent need to get rid of? What needs to come to an end? What's causing the querent to feel unhappy and unfulfilled?
No. 9	What brings the querent joy? What deserves to be celebrated? In what situation is delicacy required?
No. 10	What needs to be removed? What decisions should be made? What are the dangers and risks for the querent?
No. 11	What needs to be defended or confronted? What needs to be fought or struggled for? Who or what situation is causing the conflicts for the querent?
No. 12	What causes stress or excitement for the querent? What information must or will be conveyed to the querent?
No. 13	What's in the initial phase? What is growing up and needs to be healed?

Houses	Answer The Following Questions
No. 14	What's wrong? What or who should not be trusted? Where is the deception coming from? What's being hiding?
No. 15	What are the querent's financial resources? How strong is the querent?
No. 16	What are the querent's expectations? What goal does the querent want to achieve? What are the querent's spiritual values?
No.17	What's changing? What needs to be changed, modified, or altered?
No. 18	What can the querent trust? What's true? What should be protected? What help or support does the querent receive and from whom?
No. 19	What should the querent reflect on? What prevents the querent's interaction with others or limits their freedom?
No. 20	How is the querent's interaction with others? Does the querent have good social skill and get along we well with others?
No. 21	What's current being blocked or prevented? What should be blocked or prevented? Who's responsible for the blocking or prevention?
No. 22	What factors should be considered before making a decision? What are the current alternatives or options? What's the path to follow?

Houses	Answer The Following Questions
No. 23	What or who is the source of the querent's anxiety and stress? What's currently losing strength? What's the querent wasting time with? What is being taken away from the querent?
No. 24	What does the querent's feel in their heart? How's the querent doing emotionally? What's the querent's deepest desire?
No. 25	What has the querent committed to? What are their responsibilities and obligations?
No. 26	What's in the querent's mind? What remains unknown? What's hidden? What requires further investigation? What's the querent's educational and cultural background or level?
No. 27	Is it necessary to get in touch with someone? Who are the querent's most important contacts? What announcement should be communicated?
No. 30	What brings calm and peace in the querent's life? What's necessary to do to achieve a sense of calm and peace? Is there someone with whom the querent needs to reconcile or make peace? What are the querent's moral values?
No. 31	How is the querent's vitality? What makes the querent happy? In which life areas has the querent experienced the most success?

CHAPTER 7: THE GRAND TABLEAU

Houses	Answer The Following Questions
No. 32	How do other people perceive the querent? What's the reputation or image the querent has among others? How's the querent recognized or known by others? What actions are necessary for the querent to gain recognition or notoriety?
No. 33	What's in the querent's hands? What actions or steps need to be taken to achieve the desired outcome? What outcome will be expected?
No. 34	What values are most important to the querent?
No. 35	What can't be changed? What are the querent's hopes? What makes the querent feel secure or safe?
No. 36	How does the querent deal with their own faith? What must be sacrificed? What's causing the querent to suffer? What mission must be fulfilled?

The questions presented in the table above aren't set in stone. Instead, they're meant to show the types of questions that can be asked for each house when applying the verification house technique. As you become more familiar with the meanings of the houses, you may develop numerous other questions that will help you in your reading.

Natural Houses

When a card falls in its own house, it's called a natural house. So, for instance, if:

- The Clover is in the house no. 2
- The Snake is in the house no. 7
- The Sun is in the house, 31
- The Cross is in the house 36
- and so forth.

But why are natural houses important in a reading? In my experience, I've observed the following points:

- When a card lands in its own house, it points to areas or events that will be relevant in the reading period. For example, if The Snake falls in the house no. 7, it's a warning of danger. On the other hand, if The Sun is in the house no. 31, it announces a period of great vitality, self-confidence, and enthusiasm that will help the querent overcome any adversities in life, despite any challenging situations presented in the reading.
- The card's energy has greater intensity when it falls in its own house. For example, if The Snake is in the house no. 7, it suggests that the person is caught in an endless nightmare where every event or situation is damaging and complicated. If the card representing the querent is near or very near, they might be in touch with their darker side and they'll be driven by their wicked instincts (seductive, sinful, sinister, and cruel) to accomplish their goals, with harmful outcomes and long-term irreparable consequences. In addition, this position may indicate the existence of malicious rivals and opponents who can inflict severe harm to the querent and cause their downfall. In this case, it's crucial to check out the surrounding cards for further information about the nature of this threat and what specific the querent's life area will be affected.
- I've noticed that the only cards that sometimes behave differently when falling in their own houses are: The Coffin,

The Scythe, and The Mice.
- o The Coffin in the house no. 8: it announces a period of intense despair caused by a worsening situation or a huge and profound loss, such as mourning, bankruptcy, or failure. It's also possible that the querent is still dealing with the negative effects of a significant tragedy or loss from the past. On the other hand, The Coffin card in the house 8 may also predict a relief to put an end to something, which the surrounding cards will identify. For example, if The Tree card is nearby, it might signal the end of a severe disease or a past event.
- o The Scythe in the house no. 10: it might indicate a severe and immediate danger, such as an accident or an attack, or the sudden and unexpected end of something, such as a relationship or a job. However, it can also represent the removal of danger or threat.
- o The Mice in the house no. 23: it can be a warning sign of a difficult period with worries, stress and significant losses, such as financial or professional ruin or damage to reputation. But, this card in this position can also indicate the reduction of these problems or losses.

Important Note:

In the reading of the natural houses, also consider the cards that are very near or near and the surrounding cards.

How to Read The Houses?

One of the difficulties I've noticed in the courses I teach is that the students often struggle to interpret the cards in the various houses of the Great Tableau. As we've already seen, houses correspond to different life areas (love, work, finances, health, etc.) and situations, conditions, and concerns that many people experience, such as happiness, opportunities, hope, conflicts, obstacles, and so on.

It's crucial to understand and accurately interpret the cards' role when placed in the houses. Assuming that the cards express 36 different energies and events., when placed in the houses, they indicate what is happening or how people are dealing with certain life areas represented by the houses. To better understand this concept, keep in mind that:

- The cards indicate events;
- The houses represent the life areas where the events announced by the cards will take place. Thus, when a card "visits" a particular house, it reveals the energy and events that the querent is experiencing in that specific life area:

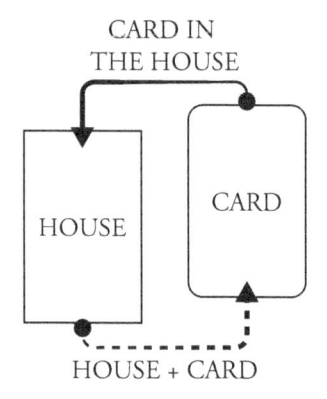

```
         CARD IN
         THE HOUSE

    ┌──────┐  ┌──────┐
    │      │  │      │
    │      │  │ CARD │
    │ HOUSE│  │      │
    │      │  │      │
    └──────┘  └──────┘
         HOUSE + CARD
```

The second fundamental concept is understanding how to read the cards accurately when placed in the houses. It's important to know that the cards don't modify the house they occupy. Instead, they serve as "GPS" that locates the life areas. Therefore, the cards reveal the situations and energies in these areas.

To read them correctly, you should first observe the house in question and then the present card's energy: house + card.

For instance, The Ring card falls in the 10th house, representing danger, risk, rupture, separation, or interruption, while The Ring card means bond, relationship, promise, association, and repetitive cycle, among other meanings.

CHAPTER 7: THE GRAND TABLEAU

CARD IN
THE HOUSE

HOUSE
10

Some possible readings:

- Unexpected changes (house no. 10) in a relationship or contract (The Ring card);
- The person has decided to end (house no. 10) a relationship (The Ring card);
- Interruption or cancellation (house no. 10) of an agreement or contract (The Ring card).

Now let's change the positions: What would the reading be if The Scythe card lands in the house no. 25?

- An agreement (house no. 25) for the division of assets or separation has finally been signed (The Scythe card);
- A relationship (house no. 25) is in danger (The Scythe card).

Important Note:
When reading a house, it's important to take into account not only the card hosted in the house, but also to pay attention the house represented by the card hosted.

To better understand the concept, let's consider this example:
Suppose the querent wants information about their finances. The house no. 34 represents this life area, right? The card found in this house is The Mice, which indicates financial problems, uncertainty, excessive expenses, losses, and financial difficulties, among other things. So, we can conclude that the querent is going

through a financially challenging time. To better comprehend this technique, follow my explanation by looking at the Grand Tableau below point by point.

First, we locate The Fish card, the theme card for finance in the Grand Tableau, which is in the house no. 35, which symbolizes work, employment, and hope. The Fish card in the house no. 35 indicates salary or profit from a business or steady job. Now we move on to the house no. 34, where we find The Mice card, which stands for loss, reduction of something, or expenses. The Anchor card in the house no. 23 suggests a decrease in work opportunities.

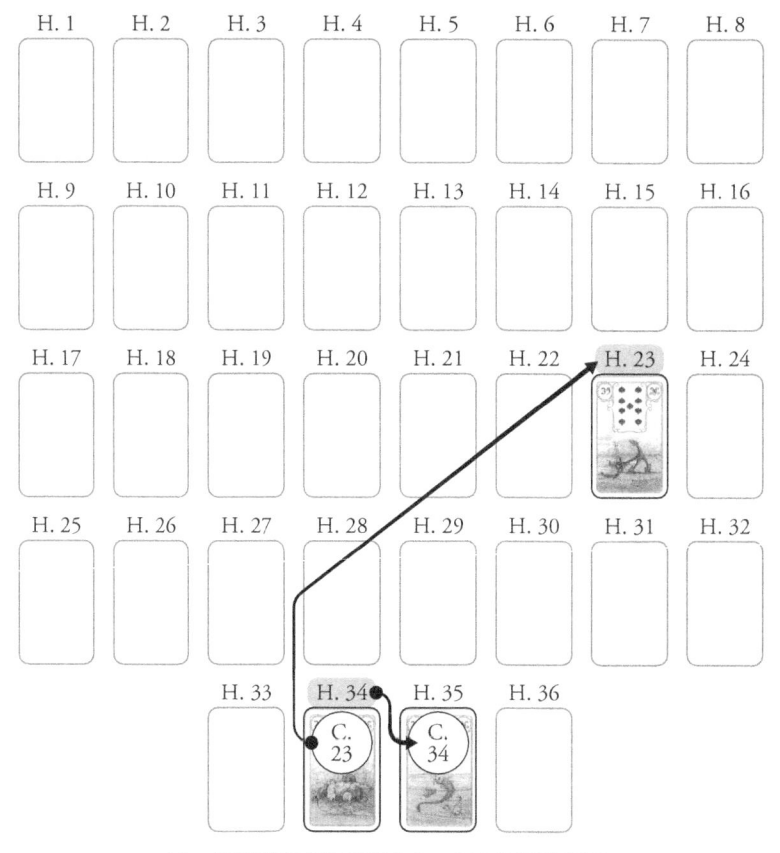

H. = HOUSE NUMBER | C. = CARD NUMBER

My interpretation would be as follows:

The querent is making from their work less profit than expected.

As you can see, this reading technique is known as the chain technique (some refer to it by a different name, which I will explain in detail when discussing the auxiliary techniques of the Grand Tableau). By using this technique, you will discover valuable information that answers questions about the processes and reasons leading to the situation described by the card in the theme house

The Querent's Card in The Houses

As previously mentioned, the querent's card is the most important card in the Petit Lenormand deck since the reading is developed from it. Furthermore, the position of this card in the Great Tableau determines its condition and tendency towards the issue (depending on the reading's context). Now, what's necessary to understand is how to read the querent's card when it falls in a house in the Grand Tableau.

The house where the querent's card falls shows:
- What the querent is currently busy with or focusing on.
- What's most important to the querent;
- How the querent responds to events or situations.

For example:
If the querent's card lands in the house no. 8 or no. 17, it means that the querent is reevaluating their behavior or has become aware of something that requires change. Especially when the card falls in the house no. 8, it points to major changes or the querent recognizes it's time to end unnecessary situations and embark on new journeys. However, this change of direction can lead to significant losses.

While reading, it's essential to consider the following points:
1. Observe where in the Grand Tableau the querent's card is: at the top, in the middle, below, at the ends, or in the center?

2. Analyze the cards surrounding the querent's card.

3. Observe the card in the querent's house, as it shows the issues or energies that the person is experiencing, which has led to their current situation. For instance, if the reading is about professional questions and the querent's card is in the house no. 26, and The Child card is in the querent's house, this may suggest that new projects (Child in the house no. 28) are prompting the querent to acquire the necessary skills (through courses) to perform their job competently.

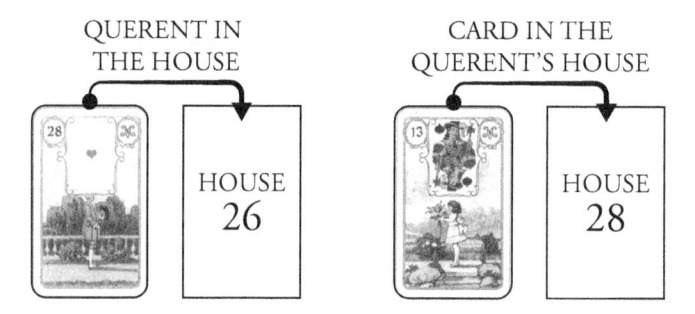

QUERENT IN THE HOUSE	CARD IN THE QUERENT'S HOUSE
HOUSE 26	HOUSE 28

4. Use the chaining technique If you need more information;

5. If the querent's card is in an unfavorable or negative house, such as the no. 6, no. 7, no. 8, no. 10, no. 11, no. 12, no. 14, no. 21, no, 23, and no. 36, it indicates that the person is going through a difficult and delicate period.

CHAPTER 7: THE GRAND TABLEAU

THE AUXILIARY TECHNIQUES

These techniques play an essential role in reading the Grand Tableau. I call them auxiliary techniques because they're tools that you can use to clarify any unclear points that may arise during the reading.

The auxiliary techniques are as follows:
- The position of the querent's card in the Grand Tableau
- The importance of the first and last card
- The bridge technique
- Identifying a person in the Grand Tableau
- The chaining technique
- The knighting technique
- The queen move technique
- The mirroring technique
- The counting round (the counting to 7)

THE POSITION OF THE QUERENT'S CARD IN THE GRAND TABLEAU

When beginning a Grand Tableau reading, the first thing to do is to locate the position of the querent's card. As you will notice in your readings, the querent's card won't always fall in the center of the Grand Tableau. Sometimes it will lie at the top, at the ends, in the center, or at the bottom.

The position of the querent's card in the Grand Tableau will tell you a lot about them because each position represents a different state of mind, posture, and attitude towards their situations. Therefore, this information will help you understand the querent's psychological and emotional state and allow you to guide them to deal with the challenges in a smoother and more productive way.

First of all, it's important to know how the positions in the Grand Tableau are divided. The Grand Tableau is divided into eight vertical columns and five horizontal rows.

The eight columns of the Grand Tableau are identified by the letters of the alphabet (as shown in the graphic), and the last four cards of the fifth row are also identified with four letters of the alphabet. However, the four positions marked as 4.1 in the fourth row don't have a corresponding letter because they have a different function in the reading.

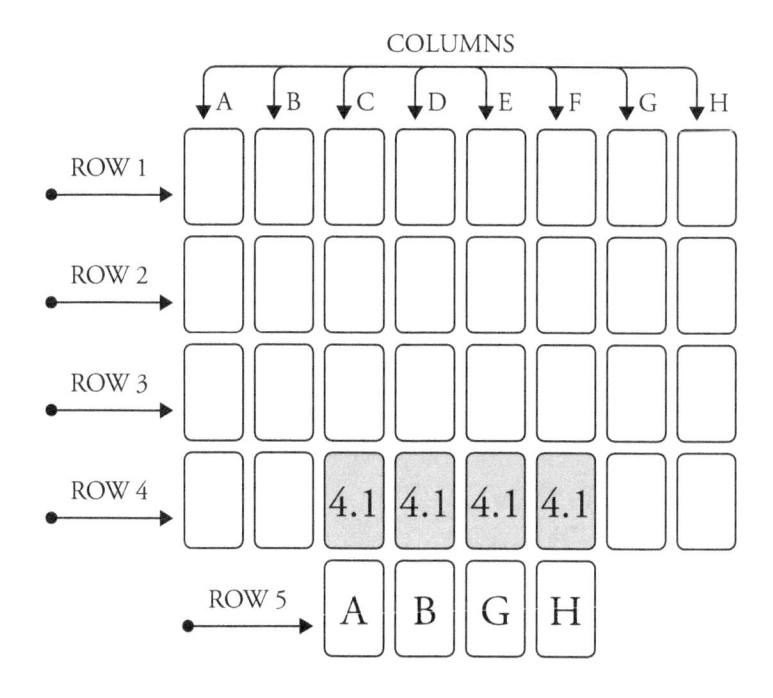

The Eight Columns

To ensure a correct reading, it's necessary to respect "the directional facing law." As previously explained, this law states that the direction in which a figure is facing represents the future or the focus at the current priority, while the direction in which the figure's back is facing represents the past. Let's use The Man card as an example to understand this technique better.

Positions A and H

These positions represent the ends.

Position A:

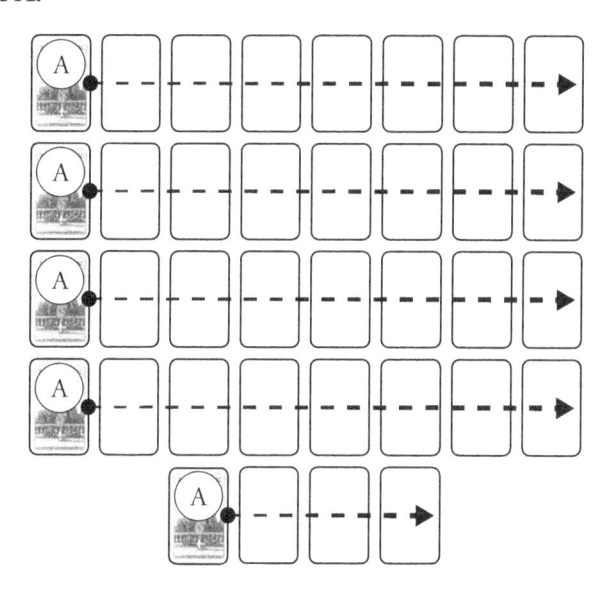

When the querent's card is at an end, and there is no card behind it, it means that:
- The querent is experiencing a period of renewal.
- The querent is at the beginning of a new phase of life.
- The querent is focusing on the future. The past is not relevant at the moment.

- A new path is revealed to resolve an issue or give a new direction.
- The querent has completed a significant phase in their life and is now ready for new challenges.

Position H:

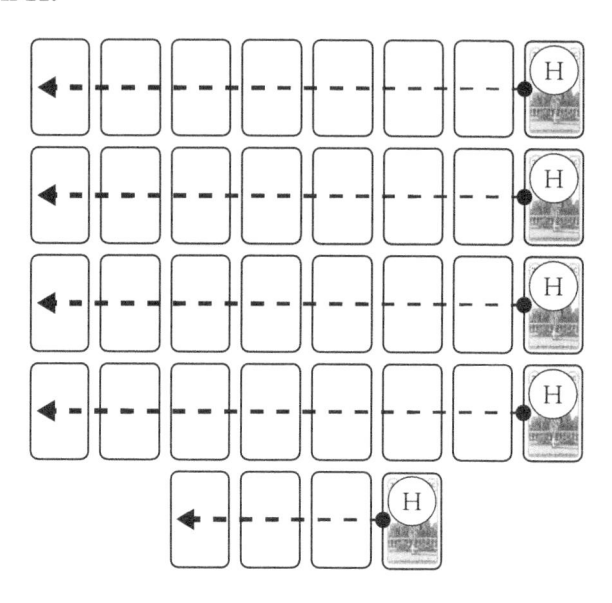

When the querent's card is in the corner and facing the void, as depicted in the illustration., it means that:

- The past is controlling the querent's present life;
- The past is painful or has not yet been fully overcome;
- The querent feels stuck in a difficult situation;
- The querent is afraid to let go of something significant from the past;
- The querent is not free to make decisions or take action;
- The querent needs to resolve a past situation in order to move forward.

Therefore, when the querent's card is in this position, it indicates that they are stuck in old situations or patterns that still strongly influence their current life.

To better understand the situation, I recommend paying attention to the cards surrounding the querent's card, along with the cards in the past line, to identify the events that are still influencing the querent so strongly and causing them to feel stuck or unable to progress. This analysis can also help you determine if the situation is temporary or will last for a long time.

Positions B and C – F and G – D and E:

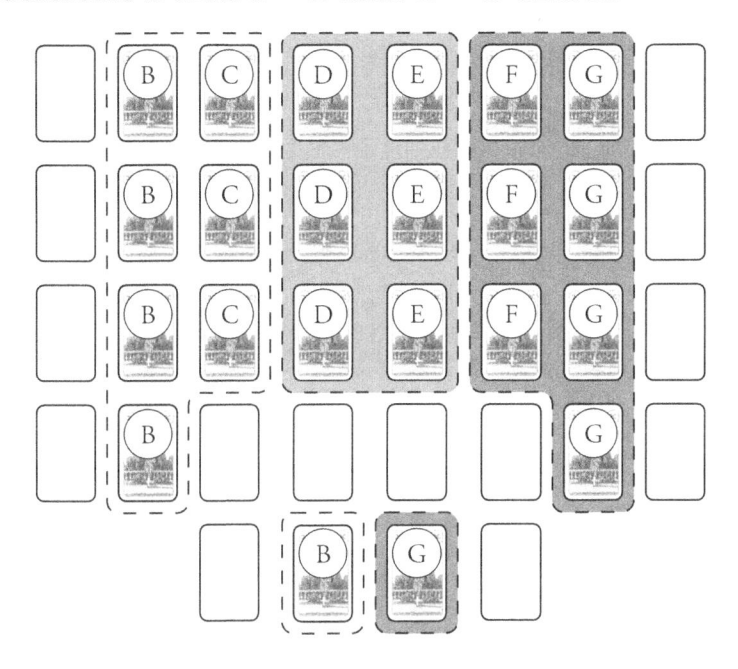

Positions B and C:

When the querent's card falls near the ends of the Grand Tableau with only one or two cards behind it and many in front of it, it means that although they have advanced into the future, there are still unresolved past situations.

Positions F and G

When the querent's card lands near the end of the Tableau with one or two cards in front of it and many behind it, it indicates that:

- The person is moving forward through hard work;

- The querent is making progress but faces challenges;
- A new path is emerging, which may bring difficulties.

Positions D and E:
When the querent's card falls in either column D or E, it denotes a balanced position and the querent has a clear vision of both the past and the future.

The 5 Lines

When reading the lines, the "Law of Influence" is applied, meaning that the card above has an influence and dominate the card below it.

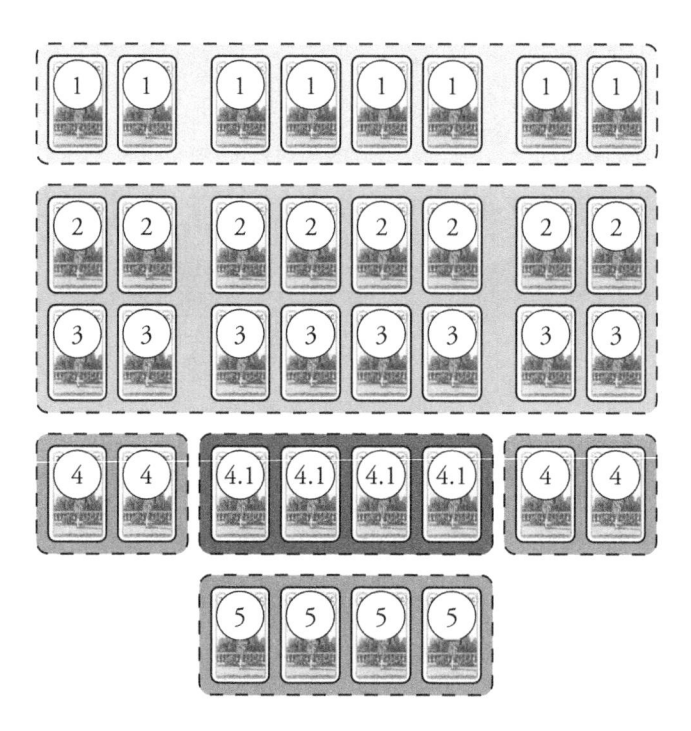

The Line 1:

When the querent's card falls in the line 1, it means that the querent:

- Is confident;
- Is in control of the situation;
- Is an active person with the strength to overcome any obstacles.

The Lines 2 and 3:

When the querent's card falls in the lines 2 or 3, it suggests that the querent is able to think and act in a controlled way.

The Lines 4 and 5:

When the querent's card lands in the lines 4 and 5, the querent is being submitted or controlled by the events or situations represented by the cards above it. When the querent's card is in this position, it may also indicate that the querent is:

- Feeling overwhelmed;
- Thinking a lot without taking action;
- Feeling tired and exhausted;
- Being dominated or controlled by the problems;
- Feeling directionless or lacking purpose;
- Is being heavily dominated by external events or by other people;
- Is being strongly influenced by the opinion of others;
- Is being influenced by events that are deeply rooted in their mind;

The Houses 4.1:

Over the years, I've observed that when the querent's card is in one of the four positions of the 4.1 zone, this indicates that the person is going through a moment of voluntary or forced loneliness and is trapped by addictions or bad habits, such drugs, alcohol, smoking, overeating, sex, or fears that paralyze them.

I've also noticed that any difficult and imprisoning situation in which the querent finds themselves, willingly or not, leads them closer to self-knowledge, both positively and negatively. Over time, I've called this position the "calvary zone".

In a reading, it's essential to join the line and column and interpret them according to the position of the querent's card.

So, for example, if the reading is for a man, he'll be represented by The Man card. If it falls in the 4-H position (as depicted by the illustration below), I'd say that the querent is facing a difficult phase, feeling overwhelmed, depressed, and mentally exhausted and are unable to free himself from a past situation.

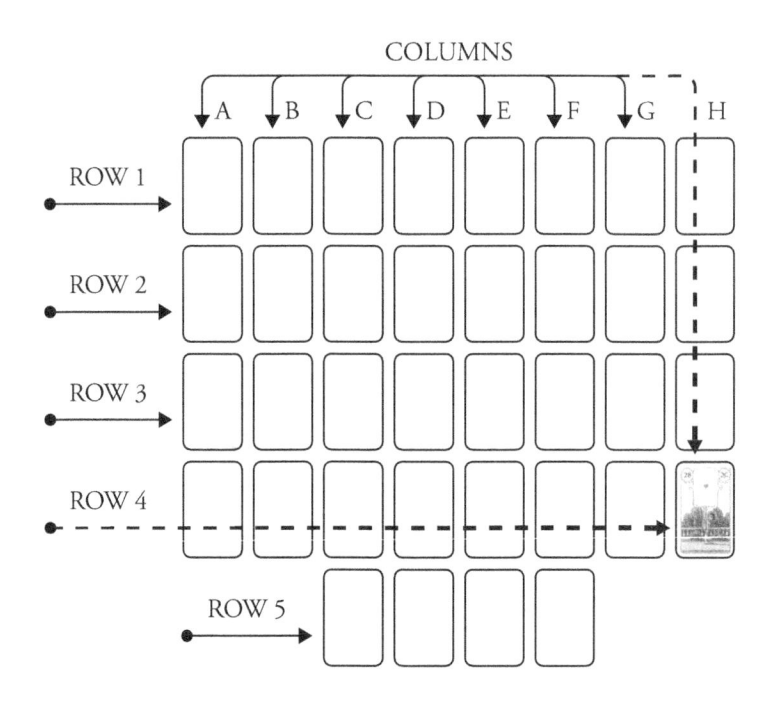

However, to provide an accurate reading of the querent's card and its position in the Grand Tableau, it's necessary to consider the reading's context, as well as the cards that fall in the past, above it (to understand their thoughts and influences), and, finally, the cards surrounding the querent's card in order to understand the actual situation.

CHAPTER 7: THE GRAND TABLEAU

THE IMPORTANCE OF THE FIRST AND LAST CARD

"Little Odette, my daughter, one of the secrets of a card reading is to pay attention to the first and last card drawn" my grandmother used to say. According to her, these cards will summarize the entire reading. With this technique, I have a preview of the beginning and outcome of the reading, which serves as a guide and a template.

This practice of looking at the first and last card has stayed with me since I was a little girl, and I still use it in all my readings, whether with the Grad Tableau or another spread.

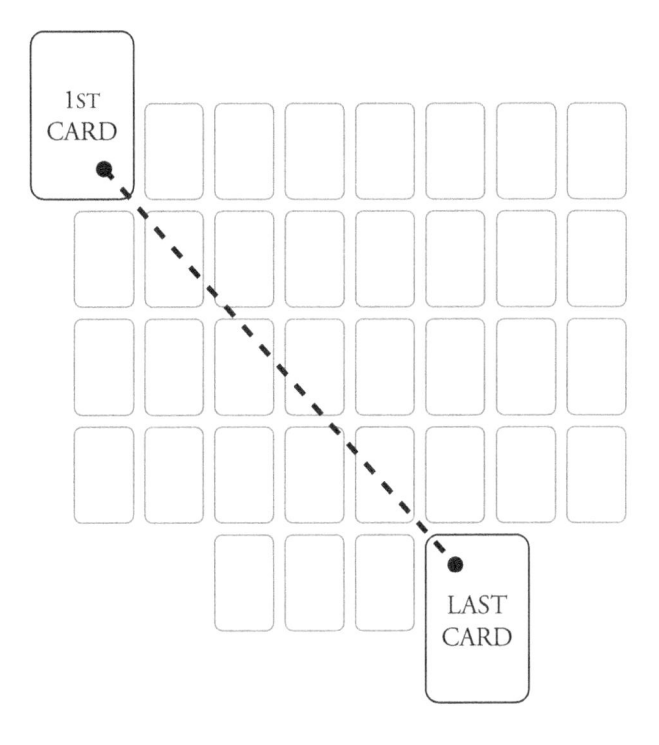

This initial reading phase gathers information about the card under examination. Then we combine the first and the last card to obtain supporting information for the reading. However, the result obtained in this phase shouldn't be communicated to the querent, as the reading is still in its early stages. In addition, many other factors must be taken into account for a successful reading.

As mentioned in the introduction to the Grand Tableau, various techniques help the fortune teller better understand an issue that seems complex or confusing and requires in-depth analysis.

Important Note:
Firstly, these two cards should be read separately, while also considering the cards around them.

THE BRIDGE TECHNIQUE

The Bridge Technique refers to the cards that connect the querent's card to another card representing another person or a theme card that stands for the purpose of the reading.

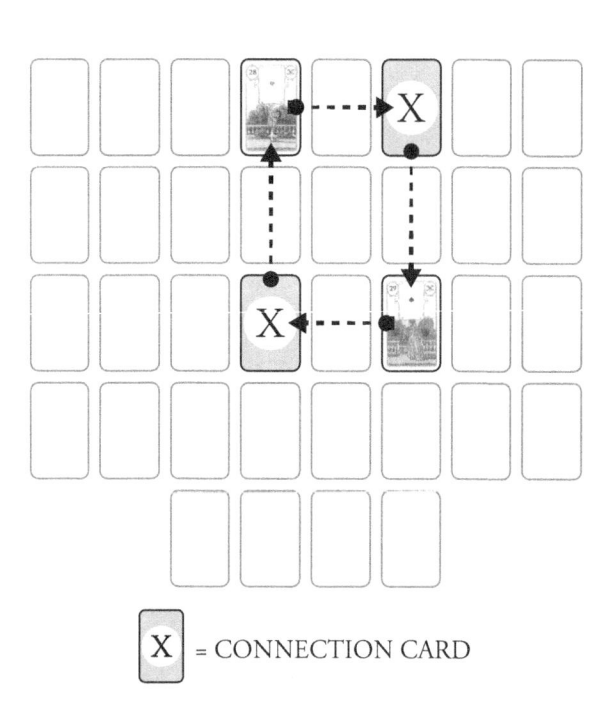

X = CONNECTION CARD

CHAPTER 7: THE GRAND TABLEAU

These two linking cards (depending on the position of the two cards, there may be only one linking card) represent the theme being discussed between two people, and the cards inside the bridge tell a story about these linking cards' themes.

It's also important to check if there are any theme cards between these cards because, along with the linking cards, they can point to other topics discussed between the two people or in a life area if the reading focuses on a specific theme.

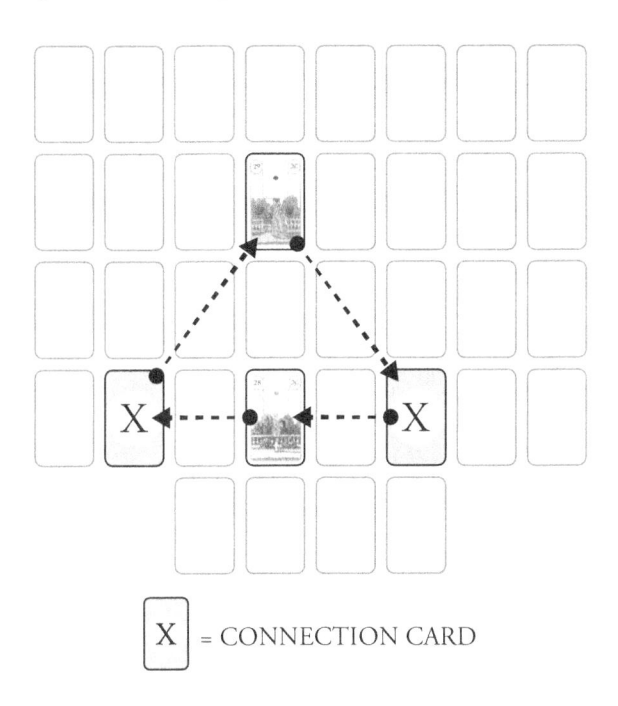

X = CONNECTION CARD

Identifying a Person in The Grand Tableau

Using the Grand Tableau or other reading methods, it's possible to find out the person's physical characteristics and their role in the querent's life, either examining either the card that represents the querent or a court figure. To obtain this information, you need to check the surrounding cards.

A method I use when I'm not working with the Grand Tableau is the 3x3 box. First, I pull the querent's card from the deck - The Man, if the reading is for a man, or The Woman, if it's for a woman - and place it in the center of the table. Then, I shuffle the cards and draw eight more cards, which I arrange on the table following the numerical order as shown in the graphic.

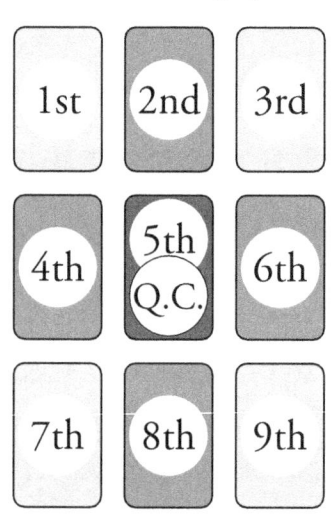

```
| 1st | 2nd | 3rd |
| 4th | 5th Q.C. | 6th |
| 7th | 8th | 9th |
```

Q.C. = QUERENT'S CARD

The reading rules are as follows:
1. The cards in 2nd, 6th, 8th, and 4th positions will give clues about the person's physical characteristics. The reading begins with the querent's card, moves on to the card above it (in the querent's head), and proceeds clockwise to 2nd, 6th, 8th, and 4th positions.

CHAPTER 7: THE GRAND TABLEAU

2. The cards in 3rd, 9th, 7th, and 1st positions will provide information about the relationship, situation, or area in which that person acts in the querent's life. These cards are also read clockwise, starting from 3rd 9th, 7th, and 1st positions.

If you are working with the Grand Tableau Lenormand, you can apply the same system by locating the card representing the person you want information about and considering all the cards surrounding the querent's card.

As an example, I'll share a reading I did in February 2013. In this particular reading, I didn't attribute an identity to The Man card.

The reading starts from the card in the 2nd position, above the querent's head, and then move clockwise, considering only the cards in the cross position (6th, 8th, and 4th). It's worth note the number of cards in the position where the querent's card is located may vary, as shown in the example. Even with few cards, always read them clockwise. In this particular Grand Tableau, the cards in the 2nd, 6th, 8th, and 4th positions are as follows:

- The Lilies: a fair-skinned person with gray hair;

- The Tower: a tall person;
- The Mice: a bald person or with very little hair;
- The Ship: a foreigner

These cards suggest a mature and tall man who is either bald or has little hair. The Lilies + The Tower indicate he is elegant, polite, and conservative.

Moving on to the cards in the corner positions, we'll start from the 3rd position and always proceed clockwise to the 9th, 7th, and 1st positions.

- The Bear card indicates a person who holds authority and occupies a significant position in life. It's curious to note that if we look carefully at the Grand Tableau (which serves as an example), the card next to The Bear is The Anchor, the theme card for work, which implies that my relationship with this man is purely professional;
- The Book card is associated with books and manuscripts;
- The Moon represents status, fame, recognition, admiration, and prestige;
- The Bouquet: stands for surprises, satisfaction, and kindness.

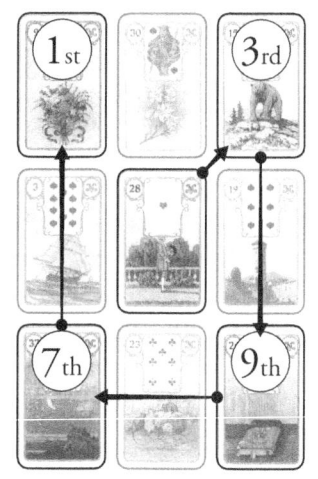

The cards describe a mature man (The Lilies), distinguished and influential (The Lilies + The Bear + The Tower), very straightforward, honest (The Lilies + The Bear), and cultured (The Tower + The Book). He owns a publishing house (The Bear + The Tower + The Book), and his position in the publishing world is highly respected and admired (The Bear + The Book + The Moon + Bouquet). He has a strong character and is determined to pursue his goals (The Mice), especially in challenging times (The Tower + The Book + The Mice).

These three cards reminded me of the financial crisis that the publishing house faced on November 14, 2012, caused by the flooding of the book warehouse, affecting several parts of Rome and destroying all the materials in the warehouse. It was a tough time, but the publisher's courage, determination, and expertise (The Lilies + The Bear + The Tower + The Book) helped to save the company, which continues today in its splendor, publishing esoteric books.

After analyzing all the card information, I concluded that the man portrayed was Giovanni Canonico, my Italian publisher and the owner of the Mediterranee publishing house in Rome. As you can see from the photo, Mr. Canonico is tall, elegant, and bald. But, of course, since I'm Suiss, he was a foreigner to me.

A few days after this reading, Mr. Canonico called to inform me he was bringing all the writers together to propose public meetings and new manuscripts to help the publishing house overcome its current crisis.

Giovanni Canónico

The Chaining Technique

The term "chaining" is used to describe a card-reading technique that connects the houses and cards. This technique is most often used in a general reading, as it provides more clarity to a specific life area. The cards obtained through the chaining technique indicate the current situation and offer a glimpse into the near future, usually within 7 to 10 days.

I'd like to emphasize the relevance of the chaining technique in a Grand Tableau reading. You'll be using it frequently in your readings, so getting as much experience as possible with this working tool is essential.

There are two kinds of chaining technique:

1. The traditional technique, which provides you with a larger number of cards but requires more familiarity so that you don't get lost while reading;
2. The simplified technique, which focuses on a few houses and cards.

How should you put this technique into practice? Before starting, I recommend the following:

- Being very clear about the reading's theme;
- Identifying the theme house that best represents the question. For example, questions related to:
    o A journey – house no. 3;
    o Health – house no. 5;
    o Magic, misunderstandings, and abuse – house no. 11;
    o Spirituality – house no. 16;
    o Legal, juridical, or judicial issues – house no. 19;
    o Social life, manifestations, events, lectures, or meetings – house no. 20;
    o A relationship (marriage, engagement, or dating), partnership, or contracts – house no. 25;

- o The family or sex – house no. 30;
- o Business or money – house no. 34;
- o Work – house no. 35;
- o Religion, belief, and faith – house no. 36.

To help you understand how the chaining technique works, I'll give you a step-by-step reading example sample of the traditional and the simplified versions. While both Grand Tableaus are accurate, these examples aim to demonstrate the technique's procedure.

THE TRADITIONAL CHAINING TECHNIQUE

During a reading, my client asked me to analyze two essential issues for him: his health and his professional situation. For the sake of example, I will only focus on the professional. As you know, the house no. 35 is the theme house for work, and we start our reading from this house. In the traditional chaining technique, the reading ends when we find the theme card, which in this case, is The Anchor.

Step 1

In the first step, it's necessary to consider the card in the theme house, which in this case is The Mice.

Important Note:

When you first start learning and practicing card readings, it's common to face difficulties interpreting the cards, especially the Grand Tableau. That's why it's important to learn the keywords associated with the houses and the cards. Additionally, it's critical to trust your intuition and emotions during the reading and pay attention to what they are saying to you. It's essential to observe and feel what that particular card in that specific card. Let's take The Mice card as example.

H. = HOUSE NUMBER | C. = CARD NUMBER

Generally, The Mice card brings a negative energy to the reading, indicating deterioration and loss and a state of stress and nervousness caused by worries.

What can we conclude based on the information obtained?
In my view, it shows that my querent's professional situation was unsatisfactory at the time of the reading. The Mice card always brings a sense of loss, diminishment, and dissatisfaction regardless of the house it falls in. In this case, this card denotes a possible frustration of not being able to fully exercise his knowledge and expertise, as well as the possibility of a decrease in work opportunities

As I previously stated, this reading aims to demonstrate the technique. Therefore, I won't provide a complete reading. First, however, I'd like to share some essential guidelines that you should keep in mind and apply when using this technique:

1. Always observe the cards surrounding the card you are reading since they provide important information that can help you understand the issue.
2. Check the distance between the querent's card and the theme card. As you learned in the Philippe Lenormand Method, all cards that are very near and near to the querent's card have more significant influence, while the distant cards have little weight or less impact on the querent.
3. Observe in which house the querent's card falls in. The querent's card position determines what the querent is focused on, their attitudes, and behavior at the reading time.

Back to our reading.

So far, we've learned that the querent was going through tremendous stress and anxiety due to his worries. As you can see, the reading has been vague, which may have left the querent feeling unsatisfied and without answers that could help him understand the situation and solve his problem. Always bear in mind that our role as fortune tellers is to help the client by opening up their worldview with all the information they can acquire from the readings. And it is through this search for knowledge that the chaining technique can be extremely useful.

Step 2

The next step is to locate the house that represents the card that falls in the theme house (The Mice), house no. 23, that represents losses and faults, the house no. 23, The Mice, directly to the natural house that falls in the theme house. The house no. 23 indicates losses and damages.

So, this card will indicate about:
- What is decreasing?
- What is being cancelled?
- What is no longer strong?
- What is being damaged?

The Garden card is in the house no. 23, representing the public, people, customers, and employees.

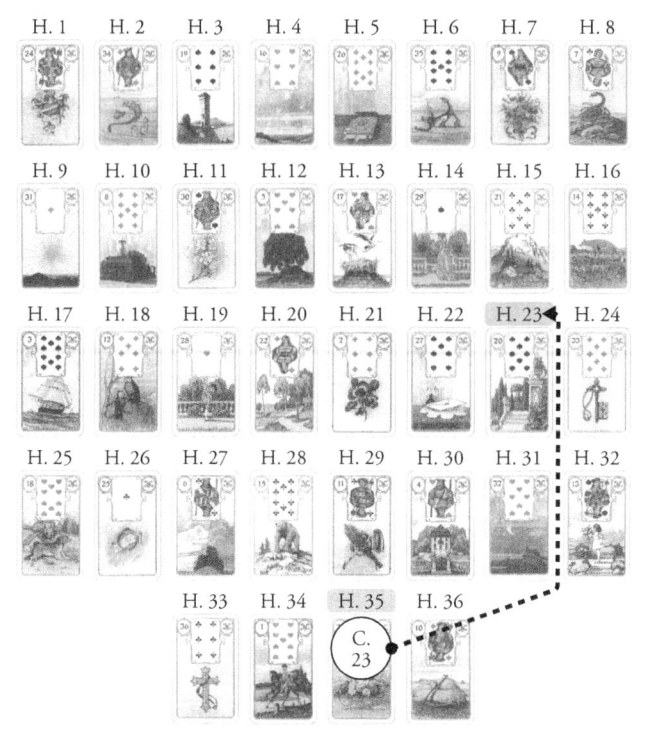

H. 1	H. 2	H. 3	H. 4	H. 5	H. 6	H. 7	H. 8
H. 9	H. 10	H. 11	H. 12	H. 13	H. 14	H. 15	H. 16
H. 17	H. 18	H. 19	H. 20	H. 21	H. 22	H. 23	H. 24
H. 25	H. 26	H. 27	H. 28	H. 29	H. 30	H. 31	H. 32
			H. 33	H. 34	H. 35 (C. 23)	H. 36	

H. = HOUSE NUMBER | C. = CARD NUMBER

Important Note:

From now on, it's essential to connect the interpretation of the cards with the subject raised by the first card placed in the theme house, which in our case is The Mice card, because it's from this point that the story will develop.

Taking into account what was mentioned in step 1, and with The Garden card in the house no. 23, at that moment, I understood the reasons behind my querent's frustration. He was worried about the decrease in customers leading to a lack of work, causing dissatisfaction.

CHAPTER 7: THE GRAND TABLEAU

Step 3

Repeat the previous process by finding the natural house of the card in the house no. 23, The Garden, and then go to the house no. 20.

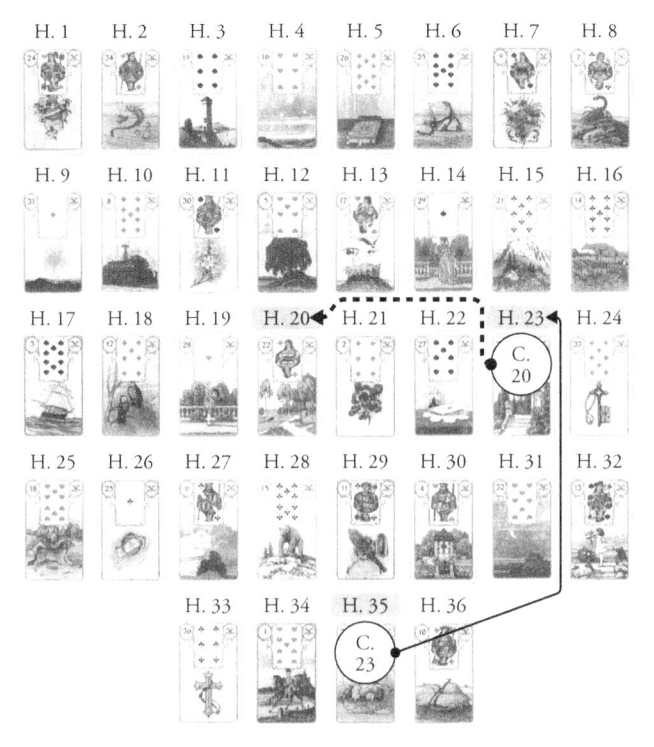

H. = HOUSE NUMBER | C. = CARD NUMBER

This house represents what is happening around the querent and provides insight into his social life, society, and the community where he lives. In this specific context, it will reveal information about his professional environment.

The Crossroads card is in the house no. 20, which means:
- The need to make an important decision;
- A choice;
- Alternatives to be considered.

My interpretation:
A group of people were making an important decision concerning the employees.

Step 4

We'll continue the same procedure as before by locating the natural house of the card in the house no. 20, The Crossroads, which is the house of choices, evaluations, and decisions to be made.

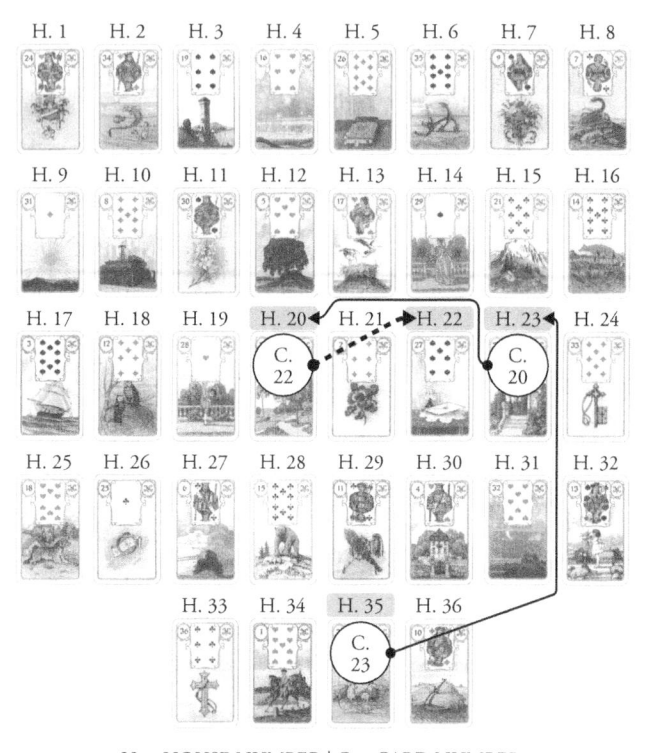

H. = HOUSE NUMBER | C. = CARD NUMBER

In the house no. 22, we find The Letter card, which stands for news and written communications.

My interpretation:
It indicates that there is a significant amount of information regarding a decision that needs to be made

CHAPTER 7: THE GRAND TABLEAU

Step 5

Repeat the previous step by identifying the natural house of the card in the house no. 22, The Letter, which will lead us to the house no. 27.

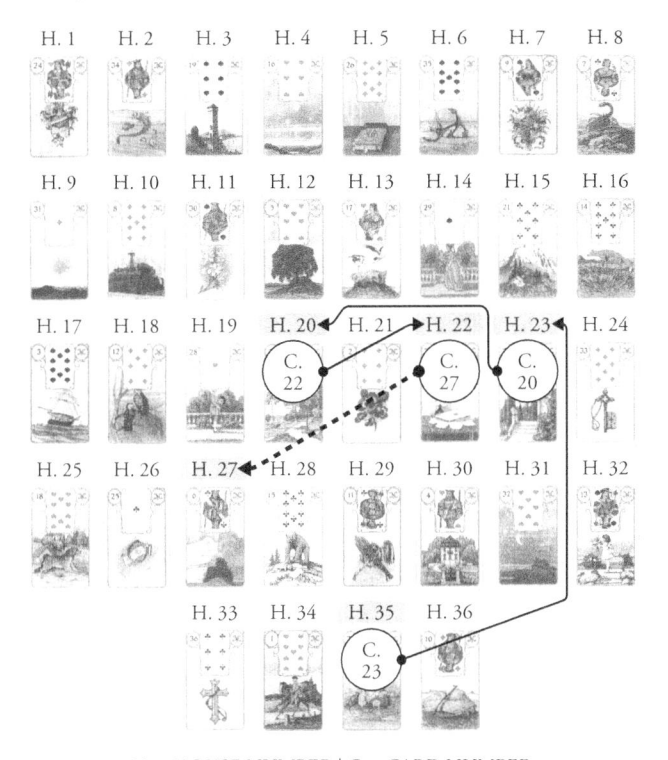

H. = HOUSE NUMBER | C. = CARD NUMBER

The house no. 27 means a written communication, including emails, chats, or messages. And the card that falls in the house no. 27 is The Clouds. When this card shows up in a reading, it means:

- Anxiety;
- Instability;
- A warning about something unclear;
- Disappointments.

My interpretation:
My querent may experience a sense of despair due to unclear news.

Step 6

Continue the process by locating the natural house of the card in the house no. 27, The Clouds.

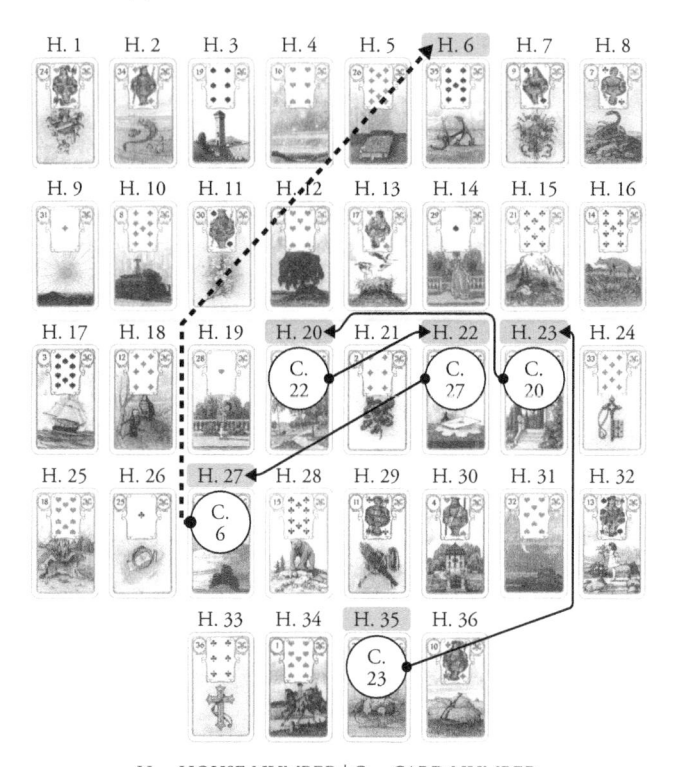

H. = HOUSE NUMBER | C. = CARD NUMBER

The Anchor card falls in the house no. 6. Even though The Anchor is the theme card in the reading, it must be interpreted with all its divinatory attributes.

The house no. 6 represents uncertainty and annoyance, and the card lying in this house will reveal what the querent fears, causing him to feel aimless and insecure

In a reading, The Anchor brings a guarantee of hope, stability, and security, but it can also produce resistance or reflect the state or attribute of the house in which it falls. In this example, Anchor falls in the house no. 6, indicating that my querent's professional situation may remain uncertain for a long time.

Once the theme card is found, the chaining technique is completed. At this point, it's essential to summarize all the information gathered from the various links, houses, and cards that make up the chaining. The traditional chaining technique may involve one or more cards, making it difficult to memorize all the houses with their respective cards and consequences, which can lead to a confusing and inaccurate reading. For this reason, I recommend writing down all the houses and cards in the order you read them in a notebook or sheet of paper. I have a notebook where I write down all my readings from the Grand Tableau and prepare a list for the chaining technique as follows:

The houses and cards obtained in the chaining technique.

Houses	Cards	Interpretation
35	The Mice	Worries about reduction of work.
23	The Garden	Decrease in customers or staff.
20	The Crossroads	Employees selection process.
22	The Letter	News related to some decisions.
27	The Clouds	Uncertain and worrying news.
6	The Anchor	Prolonged distress.

Here's my interpretation:

My client is feeling discouraged and concerned about his current professional situation, which is quite fragile. His workload has significantly decreased, and there is a possibility for the company where he works to downsize his staff. This situation is causing him considerable distress, especially as rumors are circulating among his colleagues about who may be laid off. Nevertheless, a final decision has not yet been made and will take some time. Therefore, my querent needs to stay calm and understand that all aspects of this issue are being carefully evaluated.

The Simplified Chaining of Houses Techniques

I often use this technique in my readings because it allows me to follow my intuition at the moment. Let me share a specific consultation I did on January 6, 2014. During this reading, my client asked me about the probability of receiving a payment from Spain for goods sold online. He had been waiting for the money to be transferred to his bank account for over a week, and he was starting to worry that he had been scammed.

Step 1

When analyzing the querent's question, I immediately focused on the house no. 34, the theme house for financial matters. To make it easier to understand, I'll only show a part of the Grand Tableau that is relevant to this question.

H. = HOUSE NUMBER | C. = CARD NUMBER

In the house no. 34 lies The Mountain card, whose primary meanings are blockages, delays, and major obstacles to achieving something. The Mountain in this position confirms my querent's concern about the delay in transferring the money from Spain.

Step 2

The next step, as in the traditional chain technique, is to move to the natural house of the card that falls in the house no. 34, which is The Mountain. The house no. 21 means serious problems, difficulties, obstacles, and prolonged delays.

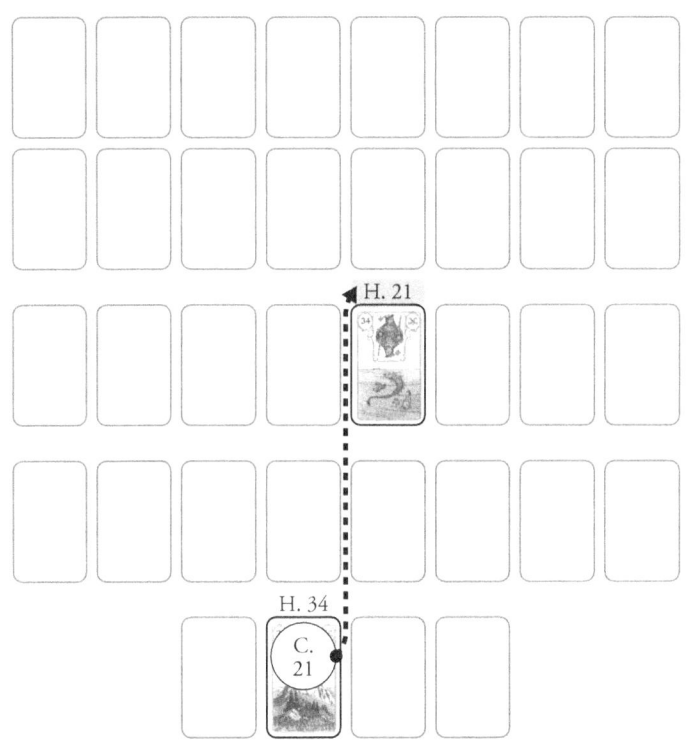

H. = HOUSE NUMBER | C. = CARD NUMBER

The Fish card is positioned in the house no. 21. In this case, the chain ends here since we found the theme card. However, in the simplified technique, the chain is never complete unless it happens exactly as in this example.

In the simplified technique, the houses that are "open" are the following:
- The natural house of the card that falls in the theme house;
- The house where the theme card is located.

While reading these houses, some doubts may arise, and you may need to clarify some gaps, as shown below.

Step 3

Before proceeding with the reading for my querent, I decided to investigate why the buyer hadn't paid yet. I checked out the house no. 29, representing the other person involved in the transaction, even though both parties were men. The house no. 28 already represented my querent, so I chose the house no. 29 to represent the other.

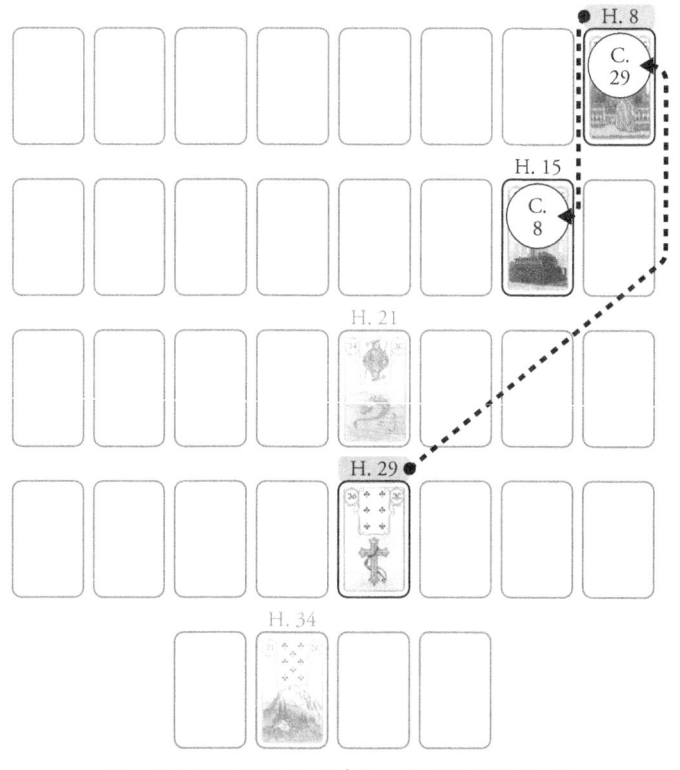

H. = HOUSE NUMBER | C. = CARD NUMBER

The Cross card fell in the house no. 29, indicating suffering, pain, and sadness. And we have the buyer's card in the house no. 8, associated with sickness, deep losses, and wrapping up things.

After examining both houses, I concluded that the buyer was going through a time of intense suffering that had destabilized him. To better understand the situation, I looked for The Coffin card, the natural card of the house no. 8 where the buyer was positioned. It was found in the house no. 15, which means power, strength, and authority figures like parents, bosses, and superiors.

At this point, I already had the scenario of the situation to guide my querent. The reason why the buyer couldn't transfer the money was that he was experiencing a period of great distress, probably due to the loss of an older person, maybe one of his parents. But, of course, I had other cards next to The Coffin that backed up my theory.

I advised my querent to get in touch with the buyer to check my information. He followed my suggestion immediately and contacted the buyer, who confirmed that he was in Funchal, Madeira Island, for his father's funeral. Unfortunately, he passed away after a severe and unexpected disease.

The buyer informed my querent he'd only return to Spain in two weeks. This confirmed what I had seen in the cards, showing that the simplified chaining technique can provide information far beyond the traditional approach. It allows for a more intuitive and personalized reading of the Grand Tableau.

The Knighting Technique

Now our Grand Tableau turns into a chessboard. Although this may seem intimidating due to its association with a complex game like chess, but with some patience and practice, you'll find that the knighting technique is not rocket science and is accessible to everyone.

The Knighting technique aims to uncover relevant facts and events that the querent may have overlooked. It provides additional information that, along with the information obtained from the surrounding cards and the cards in the present line, starting from the significator card, helps to create an overall picture of the current events.

> **Important Note:**
> The knighting should be used when the querent needs to explore a life area or topic in more depth.

How does it work? The Knighting is applied using a significator card as a starting point. Therefore, you must be familiar with it to use it correctly.

Before diving into the technique, I'd like to answer a commonly asked question: "Where should I start knighting in a reading? Up, down, or at the sides?". There is no correct answer here; it's up to you. I chose to knight in a clockwise direction, starting at 12 o'clock and continuing around the clock, as you can see in the illustration. As indicated by the arrows, you can knight in four possible directions (12, 3, 6, and 9 o'clock).

However, The number of knight's move options can vary based on the position of the significator card. The options can sometimes be reduced to 7, 6, 5, 4, 3, or 2 moves, as demonstrated in the following examples.

CHAPTER 7: THE GRAND TABLEAU

Step 1

In the Grand Tableau, the Knighting can begin from any significator card. In this example, I've chosen The Man card. Start moving clockwise from The Man Card (12 o'clock) and "jump" over two houses (the houses no. 13 and no. 5). Then turn right up to land in the 6th house.

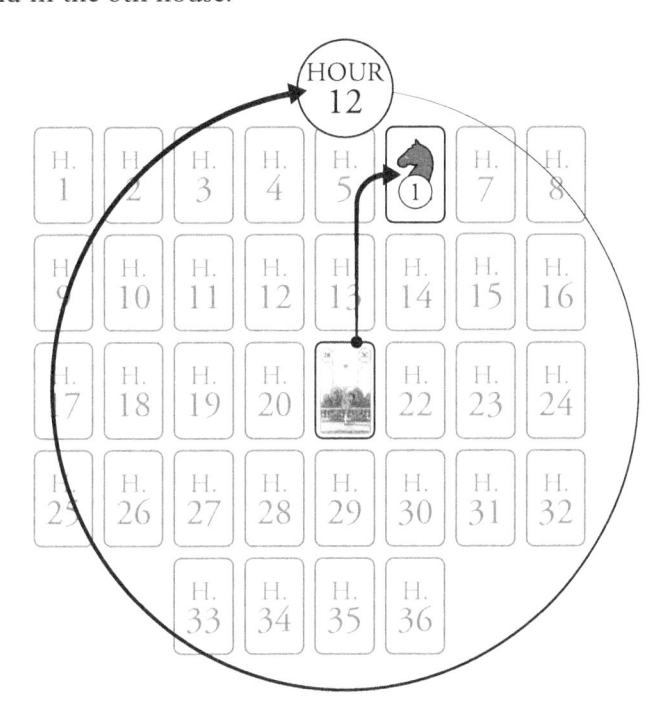

As you can see, the Knighting starts from the significator card, "jumps" over two houses, turns right, and lands in the house next to the house no. 2, forming an inverted L shape

Important Note:

In the reading, you must only consider the houses where the knight lands and ignore the houses that the knight "jumps" over.

Step 2

Start by moving clockwise the significator card (3 o'clock), then jump two houses (in the example, no. 22 and no. 23 houses). Next, move upward and land in the house no. 15. Repeat the process, always starting from the significator card at 3 o'clock, jumping two houses (houses no. 22 and no. 23), but this time move downward to the house no. 31.

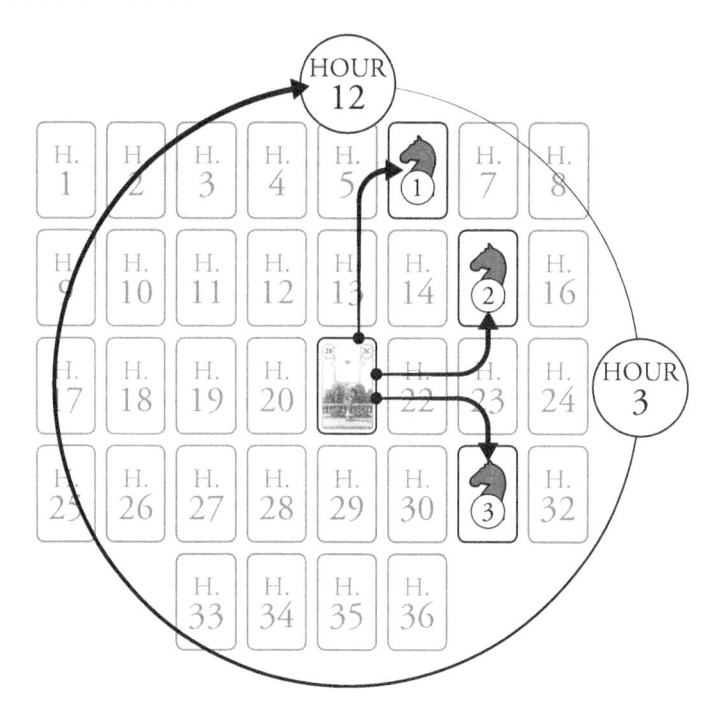

So, with the knighting, it's possible to obtain two final positions:
1. The left and right position;
2. The top and bottom position

Step 3

At 6 o'clock, follow the same procedure: jumping two houses (houses no. 29 and 35), turning right, and placing the Knight in the house no. 36. Then, repeat the previous process, but turn left this time and land the Knight in the house no. 34.

CHAPTER 7: THE GRAND TABLEAU

Step 4

In the position corresponding to 9 o'clock, repeat the same procedure by jumping two houses (houses no. 20 and no. 19) and turning downward, landing the Knight in the house no. 27. Then do the process again, but turn upward this time and place the Knight in the house no. 11.

Step 5

Repeat the process clockwise from 12 o'clock, turn left, jump two houses (houses no. 13 and no. 5), and then land the Knight in the house no. 4.

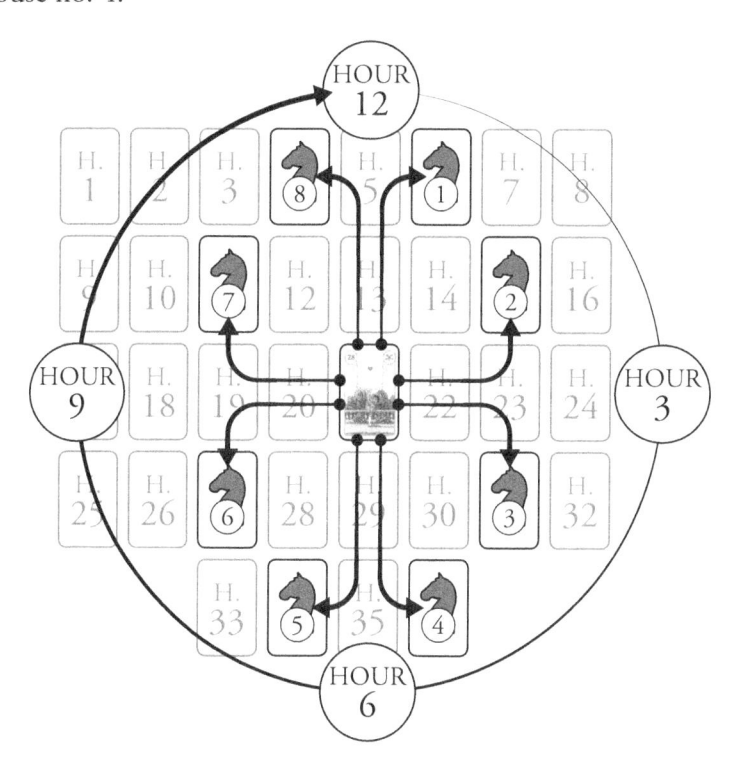

Note that the significator card in this position has eight positions, which means that eight cards will be read clockwise, starting from the first card drawn at the 12 o'clock position. These two cards will be combined to create a cohesive narrative.

| S.C. | H. 6 | H. 15 | H. 31 | H. 36 | H. 34 | H. 27 | H. 11 | H. 4 |

S.C. = SIGNIFICATOR CARD

During the reading, it's crucial to take into account the combination between the house and the card to obtain additional information and details.

As previously explained, the number of the cards obtained in the knighting will vary depending on the position of the SC in the Grand Tableau, ranging minimum of two cards to a maximum of eight cards, as in the examples below.

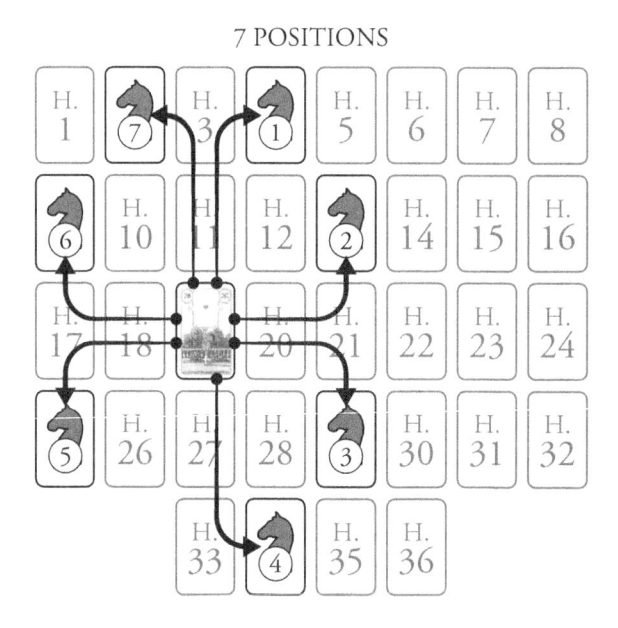

7 POSITIONS

CHAPTER 7: THE GRAND TABLEAU

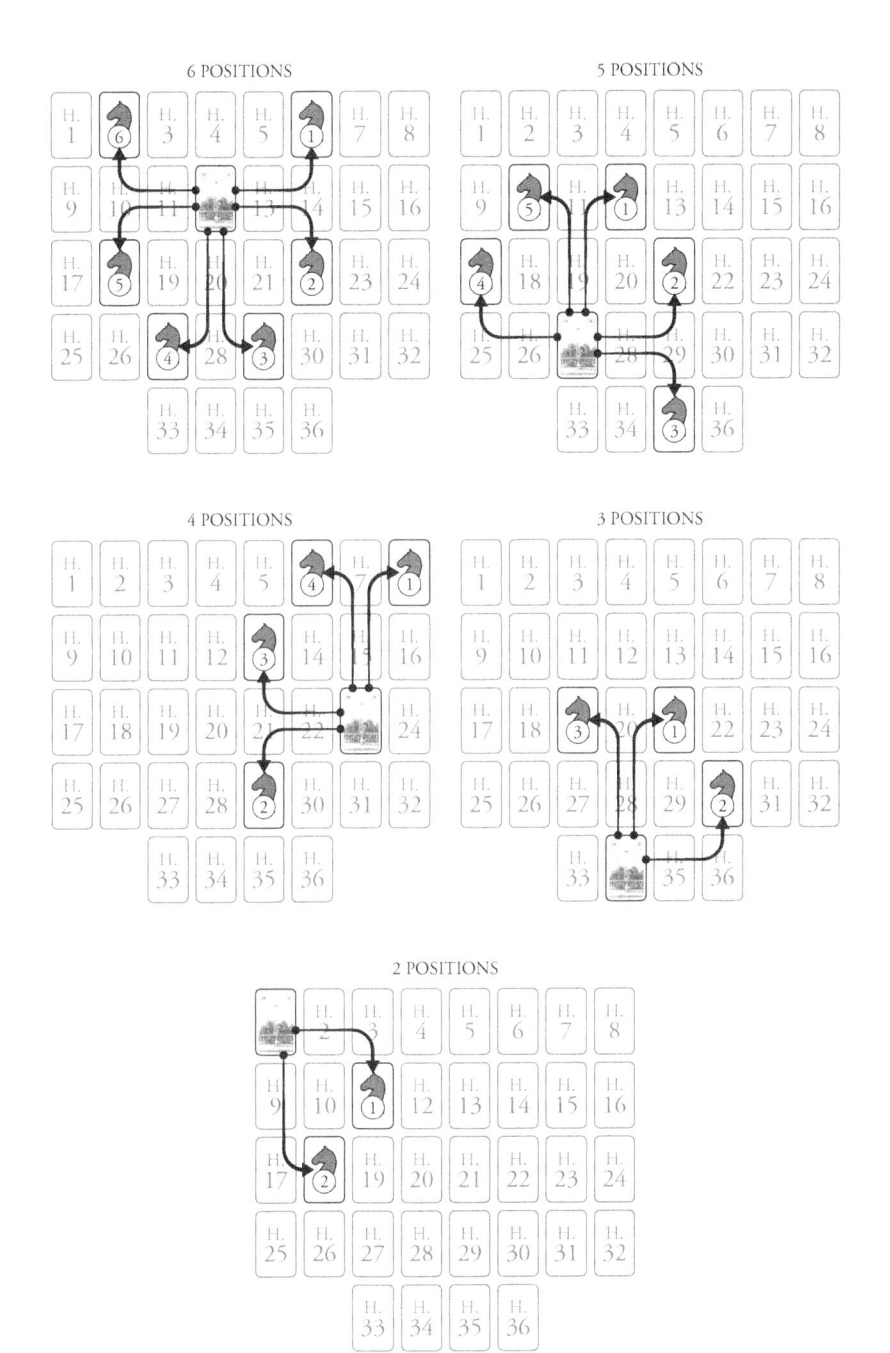

6 POSITIONS

5 POSITIONS

4 POSITIONS

3 POSITIONS

2 POSITIONS

559

Take a look at the table below, which illustrate clockwise movement and the knight's positions, starting from the 36 houses of the Grand Tableau:

House no.	Knighting Houses	House no.	Knighting Houses
1	11 and 18	19	4, 13, 29, 34, 25, 9 and 2
2	12, 19 and 17	20	5, 14, 30, 35, 33, 26, 10 and 3
3	13, 20, 18 and 9	21	6, 15, 31, 36, 34, 27, 11 and 4
4	14, 21, 19 and 10	22	7, 16, 32, 35, 28, 12 and 5
5	15, 22, 20 and 11	23	8, 29, 13 and 6
6	16, 23, 21 and 12	24	30, 14 and 7
7	24, 22 and 13	25	10, 19 and 33
8	23 and 14	26	11, 20, 34 and 9
9	3, 19 and 26	27	12, 21, 35, 17 and 10
10	4, 20, 27 and 25	28	13, 22, 36, 18 and 11
11	5, 21, 28, 26 and 17	29	14, 23, 33, 19 and 12
12	6, 22, 29, 27, 18 and 2	30	15, 24, 34, 20 and 13
13	7, 23, 30, 28, 19 and 3	31	16, 35, 21 and 14
14	8, 24, 31, 29, 20 and 4	32	36, 22 and 15
15	32, 30, 21 and 5	33	20, 29 and 18
16	31, 22 and 6	34	21, 30 and 19
17	2, 11 and 27	35	22, 28 and 20
18	3, 12, 28 and 1	36	23, 28 and 21

The Queen's Movement Technique

When giving guidance and advice in a reading, it's necessary to cover a wide range of topics and life areas. In my effort to accomplish this, I experimented with various techniques, but most of them didn't produce satisfactory outcomes. My passion for chess motivated me to explore some chess techniques, and the Queen's Movement perfectly matched what I was looking for. After trying the technique in my readings in 2011, I started teaching it to my students in the advanced Grand Tableau course.

Once again, the Grand Tableau transforms into a chessboard, and it's now the queen's turn to move.

But what's the purpose of using this technique in a reading?
It helps the querent to find balance or decide what action to take in a particular life area.

However, the Queen's movement technique should be distinct from The Heart of the Grand Tableau technique (houses no. 12, no. 13, no. 20, and no. 21). Although both serve the same purpose of guiding and advising the querent by pointing out the life area they should focus on during reading's time frame, each technique has its specific application:

- The Heart of Tableau provides overall guidance for the entire Grand Tableau.
- The Queen's Movement is used to guide specific topics in different life areas, such as relationships, family, work, finances, and health, without requiring a new Grand Tableau for each area.

How does this technique work?

Step 1

Find the significator card in the Grand Tableau that represents the specific area or subject on which the querent is seeking advice.

Step 2

Similar to the knighting technique, the reading is done clockwise, starting from the significator card at 12 o'clock. However, the queen's movement forms straight lines vertically, horizontally, and diagonally to the right and left of the significator card. All the last cards placed at the end of each line are then read.

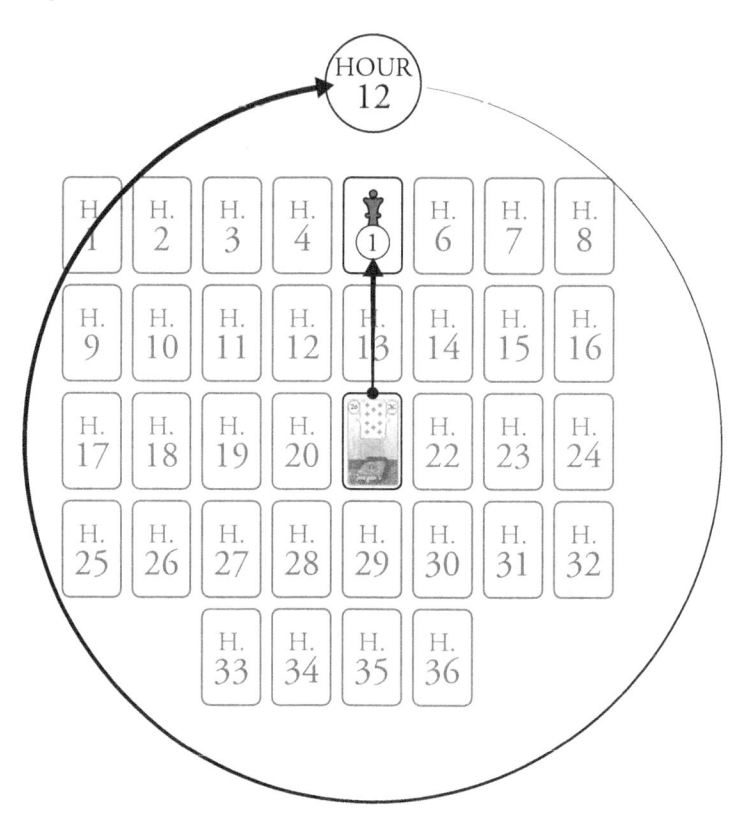

In this example, with The Book card, jump the no. 13 and set the queen in the no. 5 house. The card in this position is the first card to be read.

Step 3

Next, move the queen diagonally, jumping the house no. 14 and placing it in the house no. 7. The card in this position will be the second card chosen for the reading.

Step 4

Now the Queen's Movement continues horizontally, "jumping" the houses no. 22 and no. 23, and lands on house no. 24, which will be the third card chosen.

Step 5

Repeat the procedure, but this time move diagonally, finding the 4th card in the house no. 30. Keep moving clockwise until you complete the entire turn and reach the same point where the movement started (12 o'clock).

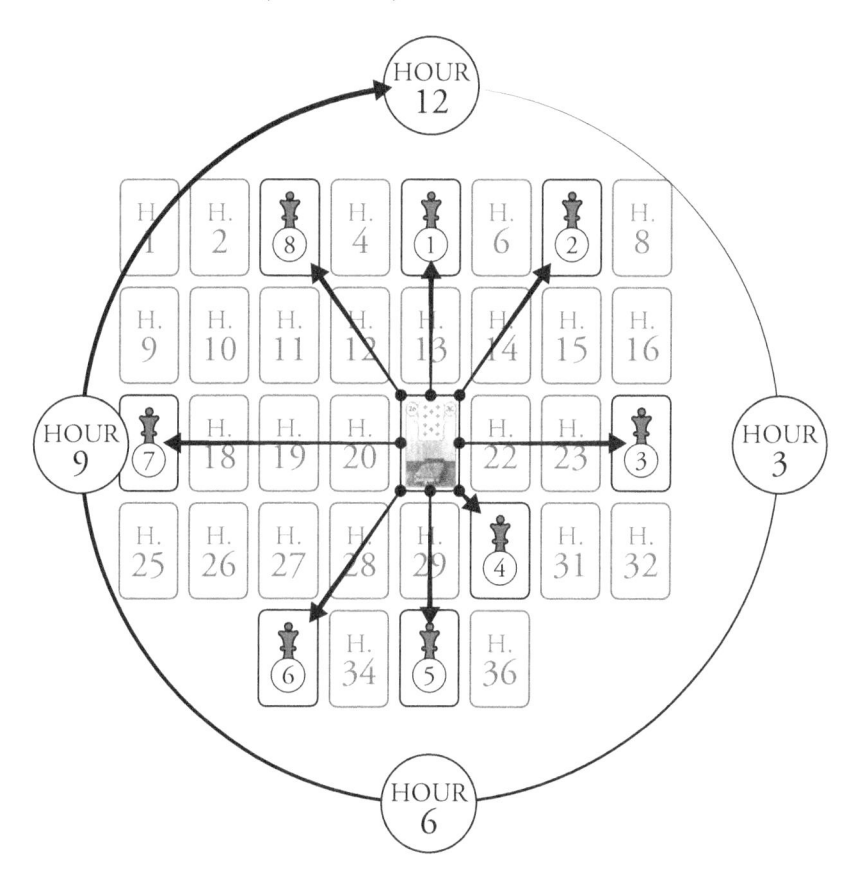

As you'll notice, the number of positions obtained in the Grand Tableau can range from 3 to 8, depending on the significator card's position.

THE COMPLETE BOOK OF THE PETIT LENORMAND

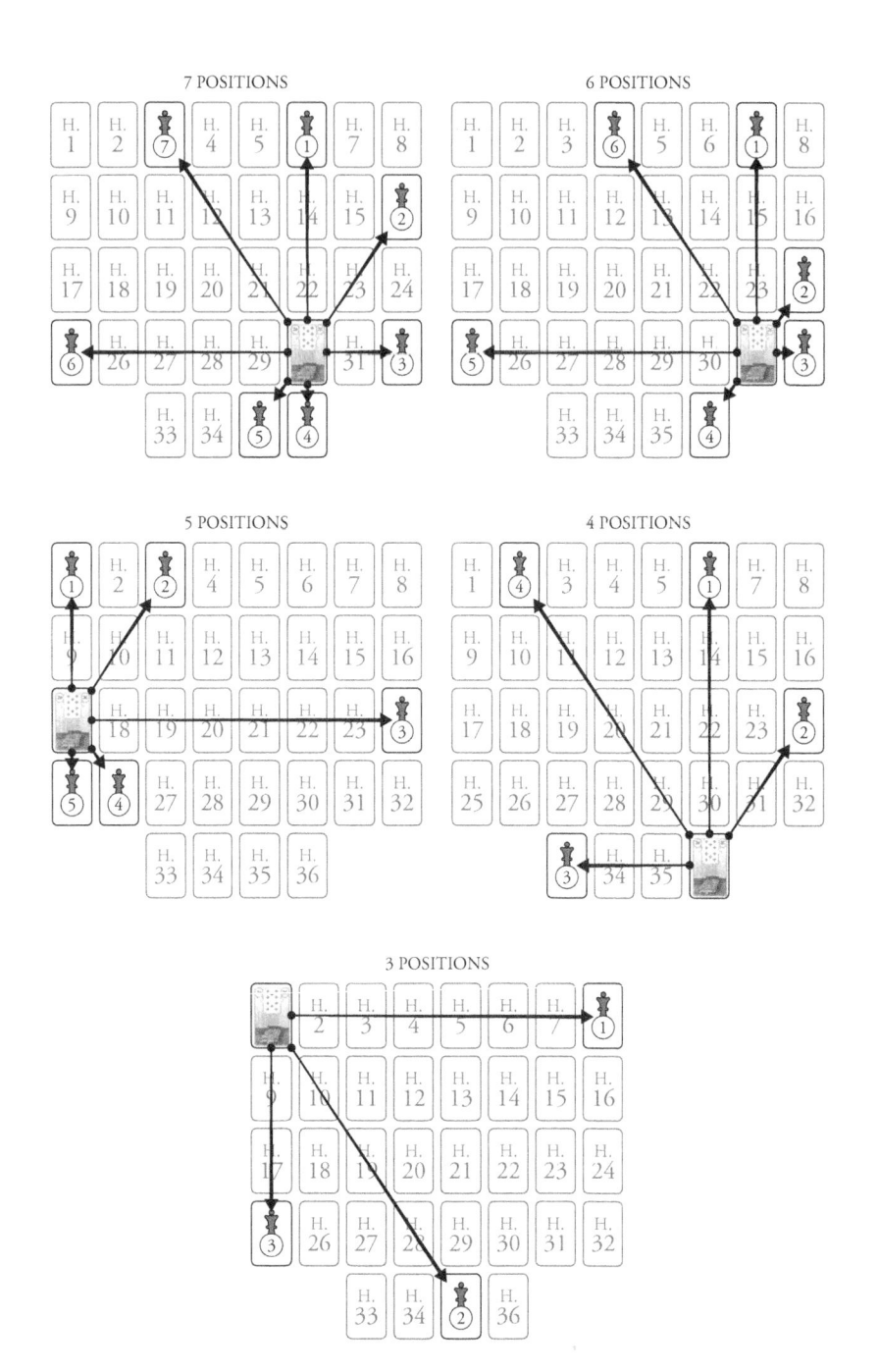

7 POSITIONS

6 POSITIONS

5 POSITIONS

4 POSITIONS

3 POSITIONS

The cards obtained must be read in the order they were pulled (the 1st card + the 2nd card; the 2nd card + the 3rd card, and so on), disregarding the positions of the houses in the Grand Tableau.

The table below illustrates clockwise the queen's movement, starting from the 36 houses of the Grand Tableau:

House no.	Queen's Movement houses	House no.	Queen's Movement houses
1	8, 35 and 25	13	5, 6, 16, 31, 35, 27, 9 and 4
2	8, 36, 26, 9 and 1	14	6, 7, 16, 32, 36, 33, 9 and 5
3	8, 30, 33, 17 and 1	15	7, 8, 16, 24, 31, 34, 9 and 6
4	8, 31, 34, 25 and 1	16	8, 32, 35, 9 and 7
5	8, 32, 35, 26 and 1	17	1, 3, 24, 33 and 25
6	8, 24, 36, 27 and 1	18	2, 4, 24, 34, 26, 25, 17 and 9
7	8, 16, 31, 33 and 1	19	3, 5, 24, 35, 33, 26, 17 and 1
8	8, 32, 34 and 1	20	4, 6, 24, 36, 34, 27, 17 and 2
9	1, 2, 16, 34 and 25	21	5, 7, 24, 30, 35, 33, 17 and 3
10	2, 3, 16, 35, 26, 17, 9 and 1	22	6, 8, 24, 31, 36, 34, 17 and 4
11	3, 4, 16, 36, 33, 25, 9 and 2	23	7, 16, 24, 32, 31, 35, 17 and 5
12	4, 5, 16, 30, 34, 26, 9 and 3	24	8, 32, 31, 17 and 6

House no.	Queen's Movement houses	House no.	Queen's Movement houses
25	1, 4 and 32	31	7, 24, 32, 36, 25 and 4
26	2, 5, 32, 33, 25 and 17	32	8, 25 and 5
27	3, 6, 32, 34, 33, 25 and 9	33	3, 7, 36 and 17
28	4, 7, 32, 35, 34, 33, 25 and 1	34	4, 8, 36, 33 and 9
29	5, 8, 32, 36, 35, 34, 25 and 2	35	5, 16, 36, 33 and 1
30	6, 16, 32, 36, 35, 25 and 3	36	6, 24, 33 and 2

The Mirroring Technique

Mirroring is an ancient technique used by fortune tellers in the last century. Etteilla (Jean-Baptiste Alliette), a French fortune teller and occultist, described in his book "Etteilla, ou la seule maniere de tirer les cartes"(p.50), published in 1773, how this technique works in a demonstrative reading using a line of 9 to 15 cards.

Jean-Baptiste Alliette (Etteilla)
1738 – 1791

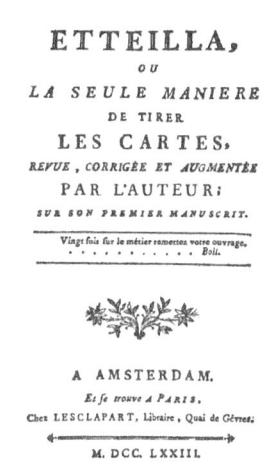

This technique has been successfully applied in the 3, 5, or 7 card-line methods, as well as in Grand Tableau; however, it should be noted that the procedure differs when applying this technique in the Grand Tableau.

What's the function of the mirroring in a reading?

I use this technique when I need additional information about a particular card or life area. The mirroring cards reveal concealed details, such as intentions and motives that are not always evident in the cards surrounding the card being read.

The technique step by step

To find the mirroring houses, first fold the tableau in half: vertically and horizontally. This technique can be best understood by breaking it into two phases to make it easier to follow the procedure.

STEP 1: THE VERTICAL MIRRORING

Imagine that the Grand Tableau is a sheet of A4 paper and fold it in half vertically, creating two parts of 18 cards each, as shown in the diagram.

- The left side includes the house numbers 1, 2, 3, 4, 9, 10, 11, 12, 17, 18, 19, 20, 25, 26, 27, 28, 33, and 34;
- And the right side includes the houses numbers: 5, 6, 7, 8, 13, 14, 15, 16, 21, 22, 23, 24, 29, 30, 31, 32, 35, and 36.

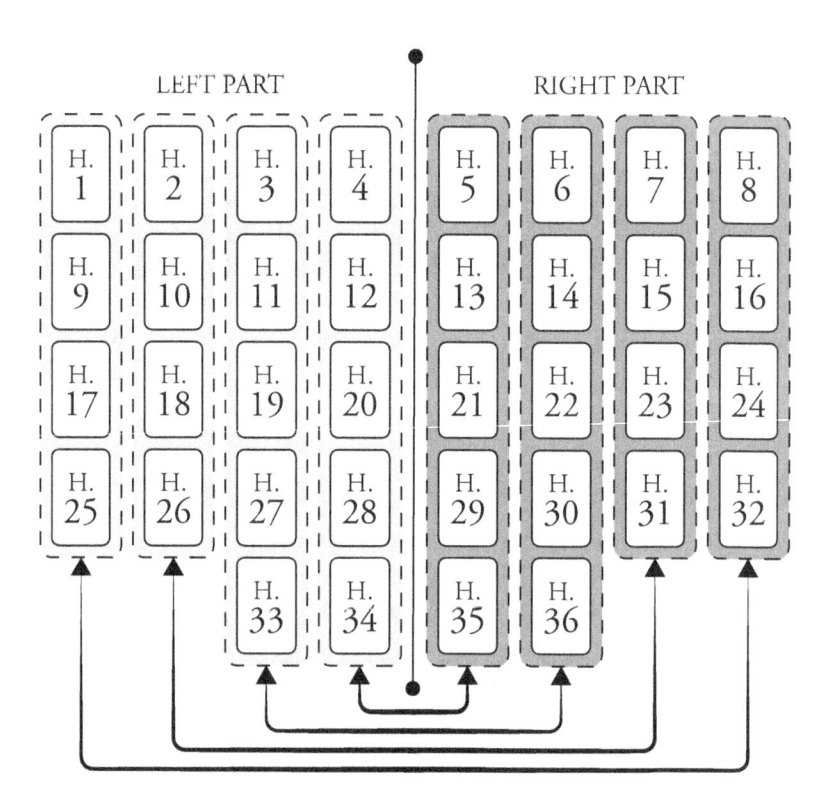

When you fold the Grand Tableau in half vertically, you'll notice that the house no. 1 meets the house no. 8, as shown in the illustration below. This is what we call mirroring in cartomancy, and we say that the house no. 1 mirrors the house no. 8:

House no.	Mirroring house no.	House no.	Mirroring house no.
1	8	18	23
2	7	19	22
3	6	20	21
4	5	25	32
9	16	26	31
10	15	27	30
11	14	28	29
12	13	33	36
17	24	34	35

In this first step, we find the vertical mirroring cards.

Step 2: The Horizontal Mirroring

In this second phase of the mirroring, it's essential to consider the four houses of the fifth row: the houses no. 33, no. 34, no. 35, and no. 36. Imagine the Grand Tableau being folded in half horizontally, creating two groups of 16 cards each:

- The group of cards above includes the house numbers: 1, 2, 3, 4, 5, 6, 7, 8, 9, 10, 11, 12, 13, 14, 15, and 16;
- The group of cards below includes the house numbers: 17, 18, 19, 20, 21, 22, 23, 24, 25, 26, 27, 28, 29, 30, 31 and 32.

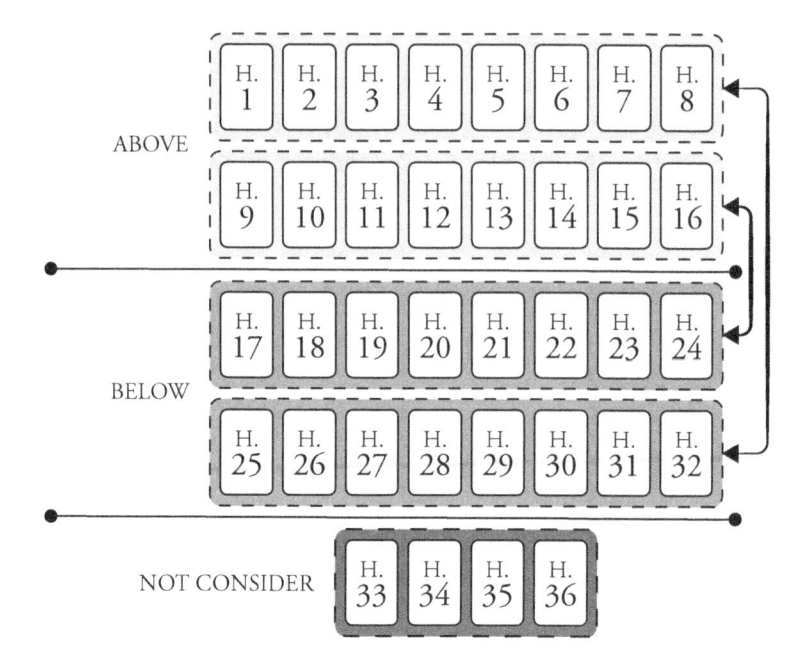

```
         ┌──────────────────────────────────┐
         │ H. │ H. │ H. │ H. │ H. │ H. │ H. │ H. │
         │ 1  │ 2  │ 3  │ 4  │ 5  │ 6  │ 7  │ 8  │
ABOVE    ├──────────────────────────────────┤
         │ H. │ H. │ H. │ H. │ H. │ H. │ H. │ H. │
         │ 9  │ 10 │ 11 │ 12 │ 13 │ 14 │ 15 │ 16 │
         └──────────────────────────────────┘

         ┌──────────────────────────────────┐
         │ H. │ H. │ H. │ H. │ H. │ H. │ H. │ H. │
         │ 17 │ 18 │ 19 │ 20 │ 21 │ 22 │ 23 │ 24 │
BELOW    ├──────────────────────────────────┤
         │ H. │ H. │ H. │ H. │ H. │ H. │ H. │ H. │
         │ 25 │ 26 │ 27 │ 28 │ 29 │ 30 │ 31 │ 32 │
         └──────────────────────────────────┘

                    ┌─────────────────┐
NOT CONSIDER        │ H. │ H. │ H. │ H. │
                    │ 33 │ 34 │ 35 │ 36 │
                    └─────────────────┘
```

When you fold the Grand Tableau horizontally, you'll notice that the houses in the first row match the houses in the fourth row, and the houses in the second row match those in the third row. This means that the house no. 1 mirrors the house no. 25, and the house no. 9 mirrors the house no. 17. Therefore, the mirroring is:

House no.	Mirroring house no.	House no.	Mirroring house no.
1	25	9	17
2	26	10	18
3	27	11	19
4	28	12	20
5	29	13	21
6	30	14	22
7	31	15	23
8	32	16	24

Finally, fold the inner of the Grand Tableau horizontally to find the four vertical mirrors of the four houses in the fifth row (no. 33, no. 34, no. 35, and no. 36 houses.

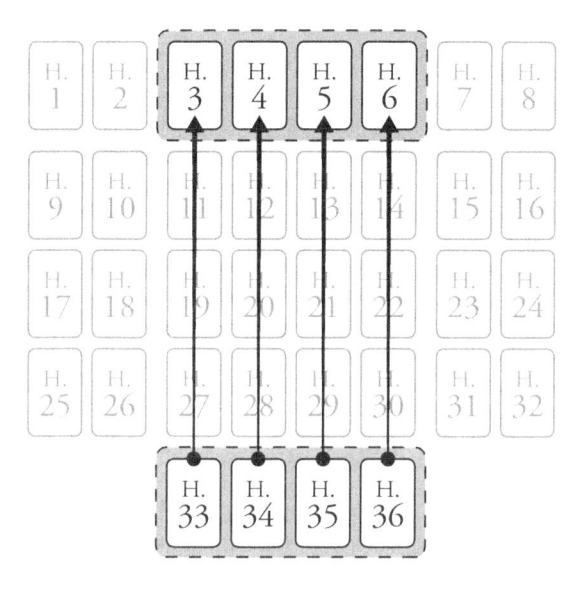

Consequently:
- The house no. 33 mirrors the house no. 3
- The house no. 34 mirrors the house no. 4
- The house no. 35 mirrors the house no. 5
- The house no. 36 mirrors the house no. 6

Have you noticed that each house has two mirroring houses.

STEP 3: MIRRORING

At this point, every card in the Grand Tableau will have two mirroring cards: one horizontally and one vertically. So, for example, if the card being read is in the house no. 3, it'll mirror horizontally with the house no. 6 and vertically with the house no. 27.

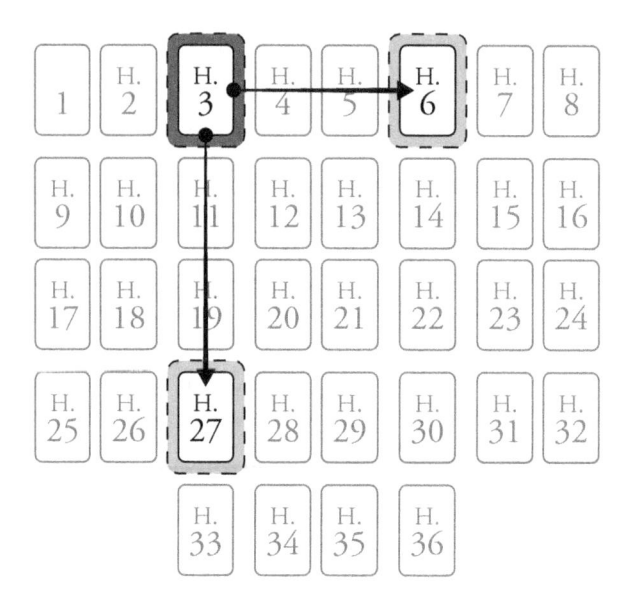

H. 1	H. 2	H. 3	H. 4	H. 5	H. 6	H. 7	H. 8
H. 9	H. 10	H. 11	H. 12	H. 13	H. 14	H. 15	H. 16
H. 17	H. 18	H. 19	H. 20	H. 21	H. 22	H. 23	H. 24
H. 25	H. 26	H. 27	H. 28	H. 29	H. 30	H. 31	H. 32
		H. 33	H. 34	H. 35	H. 36		

Table of Houses and Mirroring

House no.	Mirroring house no.	House no.	Mirroring house no.
1	8 and 25	13	12 and 21
2	7 and 26	14	11 and 22
3	6 and 27	15	10 and 23
4	5 and 28	16	9 and 24
5	4 and 29	17	24 and 9
6	3 and 30	18	23 and 10
7	2 and 31	19	22 and 11
8	1 and 32	20	21 and 12
9	16 and 17	21	20 and 13
10	15 and 18	22	19 and 14
11	14 and 19	23	18 and 15
12	13 and 20	24	17 and 16

House no.	Mirroring house no.	House no.	Mirroring house no.
25	32 and 1	31	26 and 7
26	31 and 2	32	25 and 8
27	30 and 3	33	36 and 3
28	29 and 4	34	35 and 4
29	28 and 5	35	34 and 5
30	27 and 6	36	33 and 6

The Counting of 7

This is an old technique in cartomancy. I remember my grandmother used the counting in her readings. Many fortune tellers use the 3, 4, or 5 counting, and all of them are equally valid. The only difference is the number of cards obtained at the end. Choosing one or the other counting technique is a matter of personal preference. Once you've decided, I recommend that you stick with it in the future. Here, I present the counting technique I've learned, use personally, and teach to my students in my courses.

What is the function of counting rounds in a reading?

The Counting of 7 technique is used to gain insight into past or future events related to a specific life area. This technique is commonly used in readings involving multiple issues, such as conflicts, breakups, or life areas like work, finances, health, family, and so on. It can help you determine the outcomes of an action or the direction a question will take in the future. It can also help you understand the origins of the factors.

Important Note:

The counting is applied to the querent's card only when it's placed at one end of the Grand Tableau and has no past or future.

The Counting of 7 For The Future

Step 1

First, locate the significator card in the Grand Tableau representing the person or the subject you want to investigate. In this example, The Anchor card is the significator card symbolizing the querent's professional area. Start counting at the significator card (The Anchor), and move towards your right hand, from left to right. Once you reach the end of the row, continue counting in the row below, starting at the first card positioned at the beginning of the row. The counting stops at the seventh card.

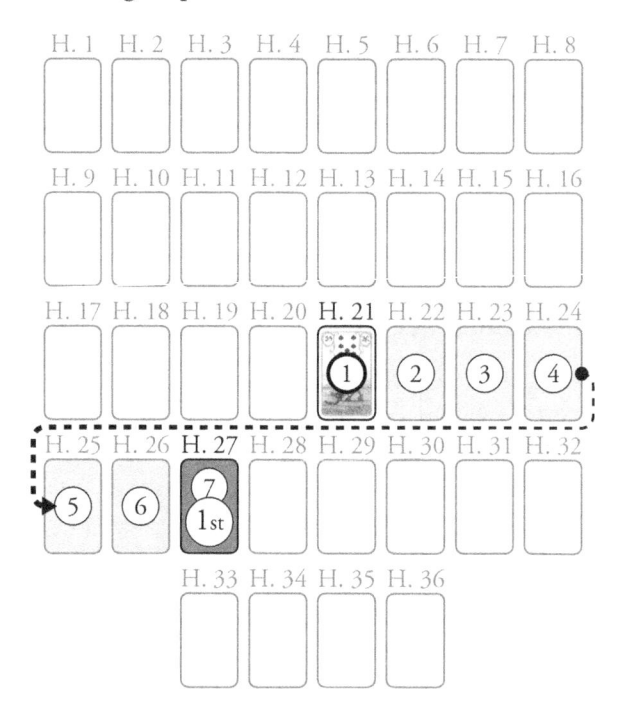

Step 2

Continue counting from the seventh card of the first counting (1st card) and proceed with a new counting of seven cards. The procedure of changing rows during the counting is the same as previously explained. If you still have trouble understanding the explanation, follow the arrows shown in the illustration.

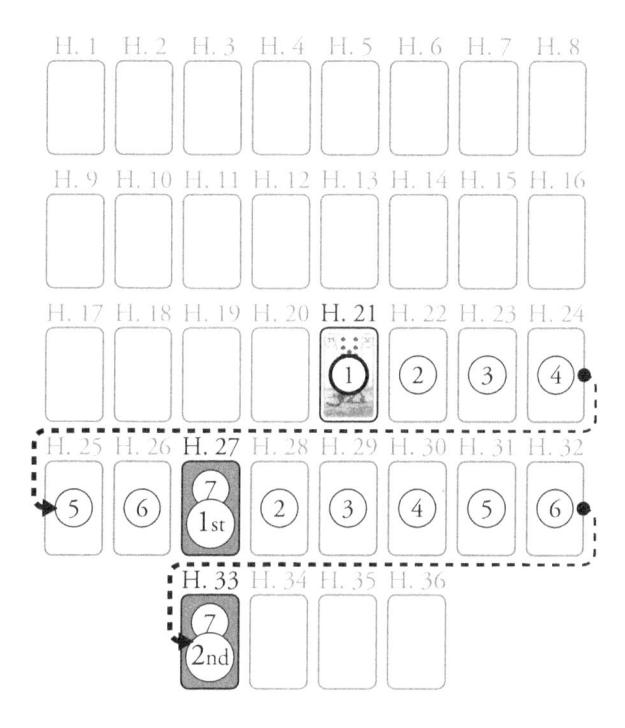

Step 3

Repeat the counting starting at the 7th card of the second counting (2nd card).

Step 4

Repeat the counting from the seventh card of the third counting (3rd card). As you can see, the counting in the fifth row follows your counting in the first row in the Grand Tableau. Again, note the direction of the arrow in the example.

Step 5

Repeat the counting from the seventh card of the fourth counting (4th card).

Step 6

Repeat the counting from with seventh card of the fourth counting (5th card).

Step 7

Continue the counting procedure, always starting from the seventh card (5th card) until you land back on the last seventh card that will coincide with the significator card. This is the end of the counting round of 7.

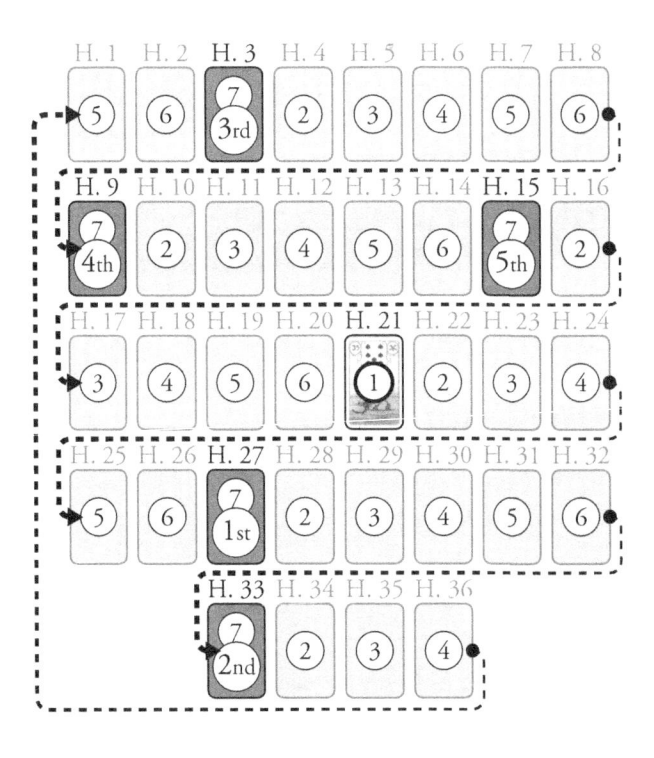

Important Note:

It may be difficult for you to remember the cards drawn in the counting. So I recommend writing down the cards in the counting order on paper.

How to "read" the counting round cards?

These six cards can be read as you identify the seventh card in each counting, starting from the significator card. To do this, combine the cards as follows:

- The significator card + the 1st card
- The 1st card + the 2nd card
- The 2nd card + the 3rd card
- The 3rd card + the 4th card
- The 4th card + the 5th card

When you are more familiar with the counting technique, you can move on to a more advanced level that involves considering the houses where the cards drawn in the counting are positioned. For example:

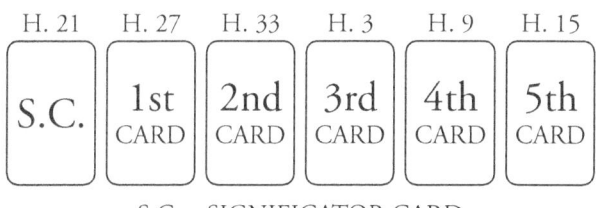

	H. 21	H. 27	H. 33	H. 3	H. 9	H. 15
	S.C.	1st CARD	2nd CARD	3rd CARD	4th CARD	5th CARD

S.C. = SIGNIFICATOR CARD

The reading is done combining the house with the card to get a more detailed picture of the question being investigated. It's crucial to pay close attention to the last card in the line (the 5th card), as it may indicate an estimated timeframe for the outcome of the question.

Table of the position of the seven cards in the houses of the Grand Tableau for the FUTURE

House no.	Counting of 7 houses	House no.	Counting of 7 houses
1	7, 13, 19, 25 and 31	19	25, 31, 1, 7 and 13
2	8, 14, 20, 26 and 32	20	26, 32, 2, 8 and 14
3	9, 15, 21, 27 and 33	21	27, 33, 3, 9 and 15
4	10, 16, 22, 28 and 34	22	28, 34, 4, 10 and 16
5	11, 17, 23, 29 and 35	23	29, 35, 5, 11 and 17
6	12, 18, 24, 30 and 36	24	30, 36, 6, 12 and 18
7	13, 19, 25, 31 and 1	25	31, 1, 7, 13 and 19
8	14, 20, 26, 32 and 2	26	32, 2, 8, 14 and 20
9	15, 21, 27, 33 and 3	27	33, 3, 9, 15 and 21
10	16, 22, 28, 34 and 4	28	34, 4, 10, 16 and 22
11	17, 23, 29, 35 and 5	29	35, 5, 11, 17 and 23
12	18, 24, 30, 36 and 6	30	36, 6, 12, 18 and 24
13	19, 25, 31, 1 and 7	31	1, 7, 13, 19 and 25
14	20, 26, 32, 2 and 8	32	2, 8, 14, 20 and 26
15	21, 27, 33, 3 and 9	33	3, 9, 15, 21 and 27
16	22, 28, 34, 4 and 10	34	4, 10, 16, 22 and 28
17	23, 29, 35, 5 and 11	35	5, 11, 17, 23 and 29
18	24, 30, 36, 6 and 12	36	6, 12, 18, 24 and 30

CHAPTER 7: THE GRAND TABLEAU

THE COUNTING OF 7 FOR THE PAST

STEP 1

To perform the counting for the past, follow the same procedure explained for counting for the future. But this time, in the opposite direction (from right to left). Start counting from the significator card (1st card) and keep counting the cards until you land on the seventh card, the first card in the counting. In this example, when you reach the fifth card, the counting continues on the second row, starting with the first card to its right, as indicated by the arrow in the.

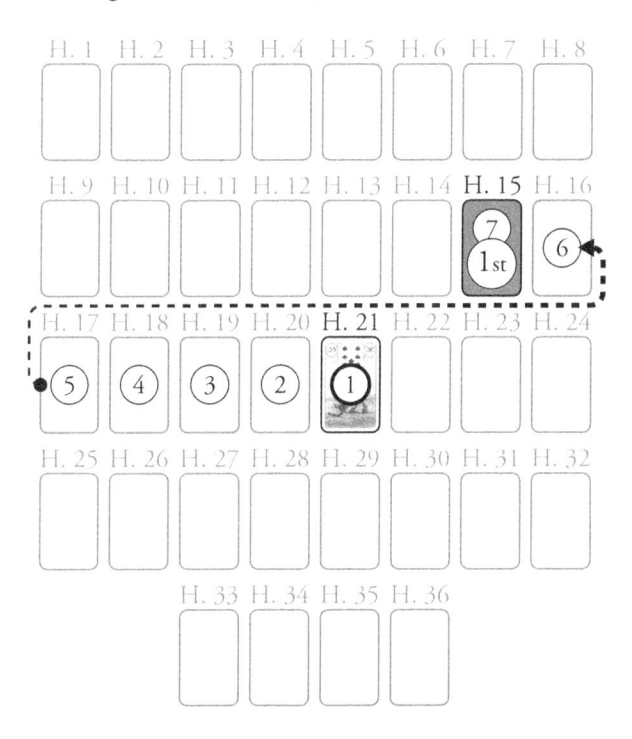

STEP 2

Start the second counting from the seventh card of the first counting (1st card) and get the 2nd card.

Step 3

Repeat the counting, starting at the seventh card of the second counting (2nd card), and you'll get the 3rd card.

Step 4

Start the counting again from the seventh card of the third counting (3rd card) and continue counting along until the 4th card. Notice how the counting from the first row continues in the fifth row, starting at the first card on the right and moving towards its left, as indicated by the arrow.

Step 5

Repeat the counting starting from the seventh card of the fourth counting (4th card) and get the 5th card. In this case, the counting continues on the fourth line, from right to left.

Step 6

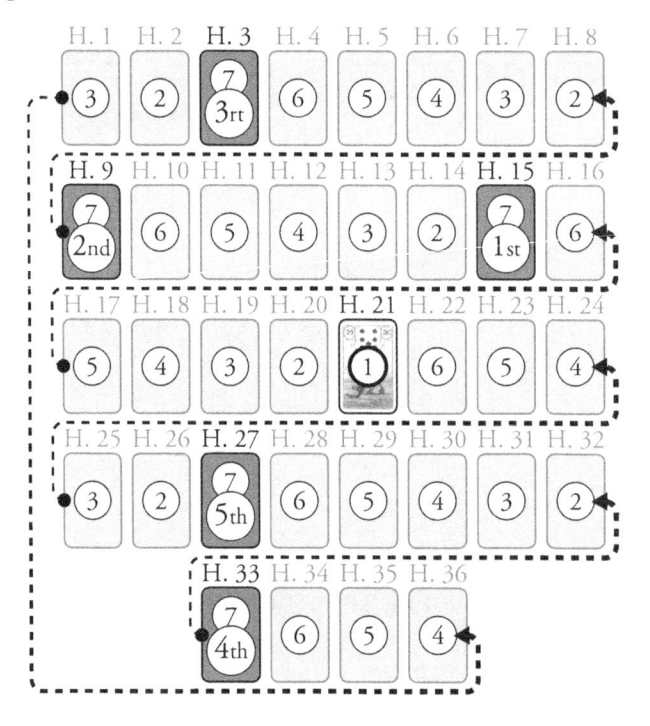

CHAPTER 7: THE GRAND TABLEAU

To continue with the counting, repeat the same process by starting from the seventh card of the fifth counting until you land back on the last seventh card that coincides with the significator card. This is the end of the counting of 7. The interpretation of the cards drawn in the counting follows the same guidelines as previously explained for the counting round for the future.

Table of the position of the seven cards in the houses of the Grand Tableau for the PAST

House no.	Counting of 7 houses	House no.	Counting of 7 houses
1	31, 25, 19, 13 and 7	19	13, 7, 1, 31 and 25
2	32, 26, 20, 14 and 8	20	14, 8, 2, 32 and 26
3	33, 27, 21, 15 and 9	21	15, 9, 3, 33 and 27
4	34, 28, 22, 16 and 10	22	16, 10, 4, 34 and 28
5	35, 29, 23, 17 and 11	23	17, 11, 5, 35 and 29
6	36, 30, 24, 18 and 12	24	18, 12, 6, 36 and 30
7	1, 31, 25, 19 and 13	25	19, 13, 7, 1 and 31
8	2, 32, 26, 20 and 14	26	20, 14, 8, 2 and 32
9	3, 33, 27, 21 and 15	27	21, 15, 9, 3 and 33
10	4, 34, 28, 22 and 16	28	22, 16, 10, 4 and 34
11	5, 35, 29, 23 and 17	29	23, 17, 11, 5 and 35
12	6, 36, 30, 24 and 18	30	24, 18, 12, 6 and 36
13	7, 1, 31, 25 and 19	31	25, 19, 13, 7 and 1
14	8, 2, 32, 26 and 20	32	26, 20, 14, 8 and 2
15	9, 3, 33, 27 and 21	33	27, 21, 15, 9 and 3
16	10, 4, 34, 28 and 22	34	28, 22, 16, 10 and 4
17	11, 5, 35, 29 and 23	35	29, 23, 17, 11 and 5
18	12, 6, 36, 30 and 24	36	30, 24, 18, 12 and 6

INTRODUCTION STEP-BY-STEP TO READ THE GRAND TABLEAU

Now that you've learned all the theories, it's time to perform your first reading of the Grand Tableau Lenormand. As previously mentioned, this complex reading method requires time and patience both in study and interpretation.

There are no strict rules for interpreting the Grand Tableau. However, based on my experience and how I learned fortune-telling, it would be helpful to create a guide to provide a clear structure and set of guidelines that may be useful to my students and, now, to you.

Preparing the Reading

What needs to be defined at the very beginning of the reading:

1. **The context:** At the beginning of the reading, it's crucial to understand the context by asking about the querent the reasons for seeking a consultation, the topics they'd like to explore, and any sensitive area they'd rather avoid. This will enable me to concentrate on the important points during the reading and focus to the querent's specific needs.

2. **The type of Grand Tableau to use:** Once the context has been established, it's necessary to clearly define which type of Grand Tableau reading is most appropriate:

    2.1. <u>General reading</u>: It's the ideal reading to get an overview of the querent's life and is traditionally performed at the beginning of a consultation, as it covers a wide range of life areas, including:

    ♣ Health (house no. 5)

    ♣ Family (house no. 30)

- ♣ Financial issues (house no. 34)
- ♣ and so on.

and other important additional issues:
- ♣ New events (house no. 1)
- ♣ Changes (house no. 17)
- ♣ Uncertainties and indecisions (house no. 22)
- ♣ Honor and acknowledgement (house no. 32)
- ♣ and so on.

2.2. <u>Specific reading</u>: This reading is recommended when you need to focus on a particular topic or life area, such as relationships, family, work, finances, etc. It's also used when a specific subject requires more attention and detail in a general reading.

2.3. <u>Annual horoscope</u>: This type of reading is done at the beginning of each year to predict the major influences the querent is likely to experience throughout the year.

2.4. <u>Monthly horoscope</u>: This reading is done at the beginning of each month to predict the significant events the querent may experience during the month.

3. **Timeframe:** it's necessary to set a timeframe for the information you want to gather. This timeframe could be a month or even several months, depending on the issue the querent wants to address.

Once I've clarified these three points, I can determine the best type of reading and the timeframe for the analysis. After that, I can begin the reading.

Step-by-Step Guide for a General Reading

Step 1 – Shuffling

To start reading, shuffle the cards and then focus on the querent's question, even if it's a general reading. It's crucial to have a clear question and set a timeframe (such as 1, 3, 6, 9, or 12 months) to link events with that specific time.

For general reading, you may ask, "What should (querent's name) be aware of in their life during the next (timeframe)?"

Step 2 – Cutting the Cards

(This step isn't mandatory.)

After shuffling the cards, cut them into two piles and turn over the last card in each pile. These cards will give you the initial insight about the querent's life but don't reveal this information immediately, as the meaning of these two cards will make more sense during the reading.

Step 3 – Laying the Cards on the Table

H. 1	H. 2	H. 3	H. 4	H. 5	H. 6	H. 7	H. 8
H. 9	H. 10	H. 11	H. 12	H. 13	H. 14	H. 15	H. 16
H. 17	H. 18	H. 19	H. 20	H. 21	H. 22	H. 23	H. 24
H. 25	H. 26	H. 27	H. 28	H. 29	H. 30	H. 31	H. 32
		H. 33	H. 34	H. 35	H. 36		

After cutting the deck, join the two piles together, keeping the same order. Then arrange the 36 cards in sequence from left to right to form the Grand Tableau. I suggest laying the cards out face-up during this process to activate your memory (techniques and knowledge you've acquired about the deck) and intuition immediately. These two components are essential for a successful reading.

Step 4 – Evaluating the querent's status

The first phase of the reading is very significant as it provides valuable information about how the querent is currently managing their life. This information, along with initial conversations with the querent, can help determine the appropriate language and approach to take during the reading. Therefore, before you start reading, I suggest you take a moment to reflect on the following points silently:

1. **The first and last cards:** These two cards help you to "feel" the "tone" of the reading. They serve as a guide and are like a GPS, pointing the way for the entire reading. (Chapter 7 - The Meaning of the First and Last Cards of the Grand Tableau)

2. **Natural house:** Check if any card is placed in its natural house. This could be a sign that something is very intense in the querent's life. For instance, if The Mountain card falls in the house no. 21, which is its natural house, it could mean that the querent is facing difficulties, problems, and adversities that require a lot of effort and concentration to overcome them. (Chapter 7 – Natural House).

3. **Personal indicators:** Verification houses: These cards are essential for understanding the querent's personal situation. To access this information, it's necessary to analyze the following houses:

    o <u>House no. 4</u>: This house is related to the querent's personal life and their inner resilience;

- House no. 24: This house is associated with the heart and emotions, revealing what is truly important to the querent, how they feel and deal with emotions;
- House no. 26: This house refers to the mind, showing the querent's mental state.

Once you have checked these three houses individually, now it's time to analyze them together.

Important Note:
The information gained by analyzing the three houses is not definitive, as a person's attitudes, behaviors, and emotional and mental states can change over time. Therefore, the three cards positioned in these houses will indicate the emotional and psychological state during the timeframe of the reading.

4. **The position of the querent's card in the Grand Tableau**

   4.1. In which columns (A, B, C, D, E, F, G, and H) and liness (1, 2, 3, 4, and 5) is the querent's card located? (Chapter 7 – The Querent's card position in the Grand Tableau).

   4.2. In which house is the querent's card? (Chapter 7 – The Querent's Card in The Houses). For example, if the querent's card is in the 17th house, representing changes, it indicates that the querent is going through significant changes. To understand the life area where these changes occur and the reasons behind them, I suggest analyzing:

   - ♣ Pay close attention to the house where The Storks card falls, especially if it's in a theme house, as it will indicate the life area where change is likely to happen.
   - ♣ The cards surrounding The Storks card provide insights into the motives and reasons behind the change.

   4.3. Which card falls in the querent's house? (Chapter 7 – The Querent's Card in The Houses). For instance, if The Broom and The Whip card falls in the querent's house, which stands for attacks and aggression, and the querent's card is in the house no. 8, representing the end of something, we can conclude that the querent is putting an end to the aggressions they've been suffering. For further information about the nature of the conflict, it's necessary to examine the cards surrounding The Broom and The Whip card and the house no. 11, which is the house of conflicts and disagreements.

5. **The Four Corner Cards:** The cards positioned in the four corners of the Grand Tableau represent the querent's current concerns. Generally, the four corner cards and the two court cards can indicate the life areas that require more attention. Let's take as examples the following cards: The Clouds, The Anchor, The Mice, and The Lilies.

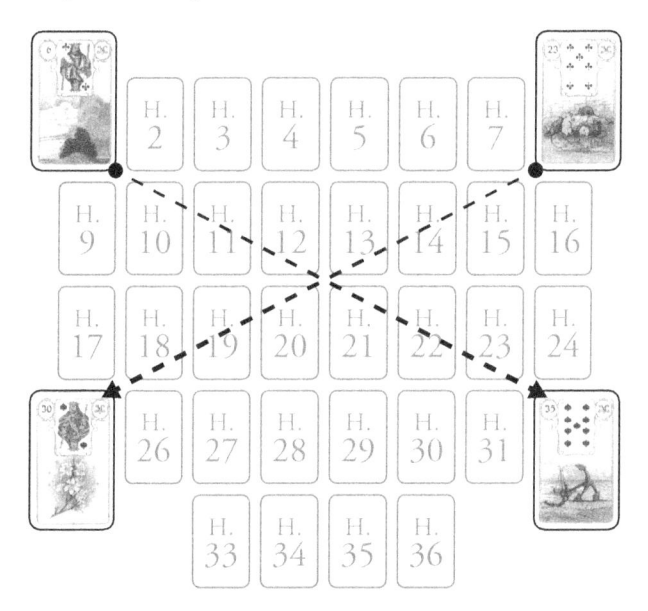

The querent is troubled (The Clouds) by work-related issues (The Anchor) that are taking away (The Mice) their peace (The Lilies). So, it suggests that the querent is currently worried about their work. More information about the four corner cards can be found in the surrounding cards. (Chapter 7 – The Timeline, The Four Corner Cards)

Now we have enough elements to start the reading. It's important to keep in mind the information you've gathered in this step throughout the entire reading!

Step 5: The Present – The current moment

The cards in this position reveal the querent's current events and conditions, showing the challenges they're experiencing and the actions they're taking to shape their future.

At this stage, consider the following three points:

1. **The cards surrounding the querent's card** (Chapter 4 - Philippe Lenormand's law), that is, all the cards that are very near and near to it:

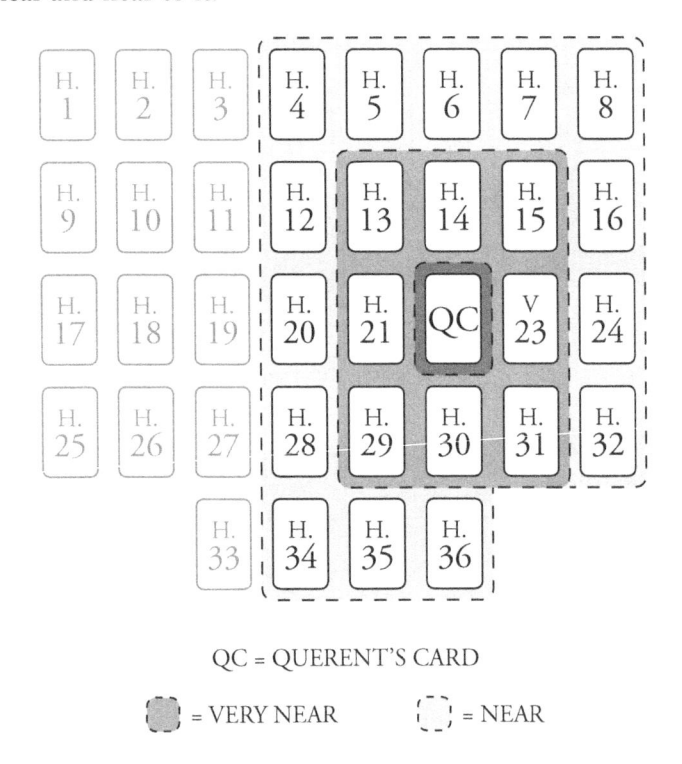

H. 1	H. 2	H. 3	H. 4	H. 5	H. 6	H. 7	H. 8
H. 9	H. 10	H. 11	H. 12	H. 13	H. 14	H. 15	H. 16
H. 17	H. 18	H. 19	H. 20	H. 21	QC	V 23	H. 24
H. 25	H. 26	H. 27	H. 28	H. 29	H. 30	H. 31	H. 32
	H. 33	H. 34	H. 35	H. 36			

QC = QUERENT'S CARD

▓ = VERY NEAR   ▒ = NEAR

As you examine these cards, pay attention to the following:

1.1. The dominant energies: they show the current energies:

- ♣ Which group of movement cards is dominant? Are they movement, slow or stop cards? For example, if the movement cards prevail, it denotes that some issues are still being worked out (for more details on the topic, see Chapter 4 – The Law of Movement);
- ♣ Which polarity prevails: positive, neutral, or negative? (Chapter 3 – the Polarity of the 36 cards);
- ♣ Which suite is dominant? (Chapter 4 – The Law of Predominance)
- ♣ Are there any court cards? If so, which suit do they belong to? Court cards represent people who play a significant role in the events; therefore, they have some influence or responsibility for them. For example, Heart court cards can indicate people close to the querent, possibly from their family, who believe in and support their points of view, harmonizing and minimizing any tension they may be experiencing. (Chapter 3 – The Court Cards);

1.2. Is there any significator card present? The significator cards indicate the active themes in the querent's life. For instance, if The Anchor card, the significator card for work, is next to the querent's card, it suggests that professional issues are presently a prior.

Important Note:

After locating a significator card, it's important to analyze not only the cards surrounding it but also the house in which it's placed as well as the theme house it represents - in this case, the house no.35. In this reading, it can be applied auxiliary techniques, such as chaining, knighting, or mirroring, depending on the information you want to obtain. These techniques are described in Chapter 7.

2. The Vertical Line – The Timeline

It's the line that goes vertically across the querent's card.

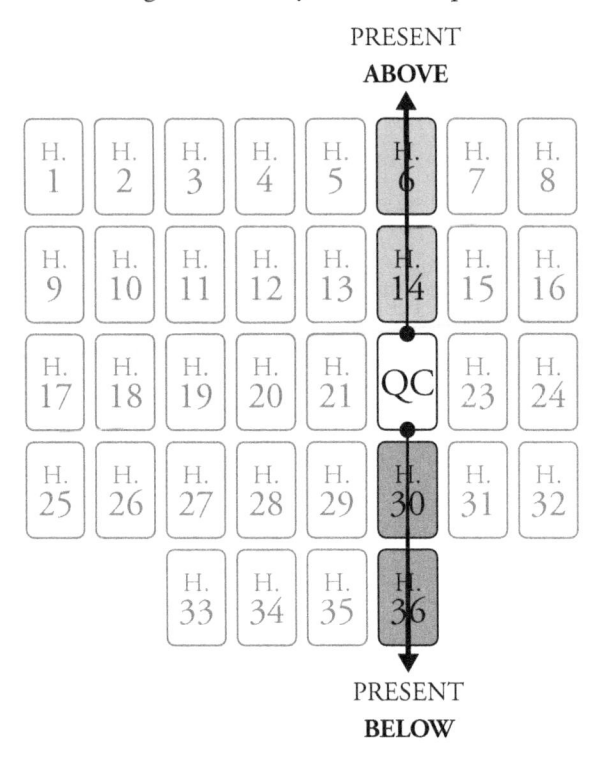

```
                    PRESENT
                     ABOVE
                       ↑
H.1  H.2  H.3  H.4  H.5  H.6  H.7  H.8
H.9  H.10 H.11 H.12 H.13 H.14 H.15 H.16
H.17 H.18 H.19 H.20 H.21 QC   H.23 H.24
H.25 H.26 H.27 H.28 H.29 H.30 H.31 H.32
               H.33 H.34 H.35 H.36
                       ↓
                    PRESENT
                     BELOW
```

When interpreting these cards, remember to take into account the cards that are next to them, as explained earlier in the study of the timeline. To interpret these cards, follow the guidelines (Chapter 7 – The timeline, The technique of reading the cards in the lines):

2.1. <u>The Present Line Above</u>: Mind: This line shows the thoughts, plans, and perception of the querent's current situation. It's essential to check the cards that are below the querent's card, as they will reveal how the thoughts may be influencing the querent's behavior at the moment.

Important Note:
This point must be analyzed together with the house no.26, which is the theme house for the mind.

2.2. <u>The Present Line Below</u>: Action. This line provides information about the challenges the querent is dealing with, their actions, and what they have under control. It may also show how the querent is using their potential at the moment.

Important Note:

When analyzing the present line, it's also crucial to check the Past and the Future lines. These lines provide insights into the origin of the current situation and the direction it may take as the result of the effort being made in the present. As this book is didactic, each argument is presented separately, but during a real reading, it's necessary to consider all the points together to get all the points together.

3. **The Theme Houses** – The life areas to be analyzed

   In a general reading, the querent often wants to know about the most significant areas of their life. Therefore, the main theme houses to be explored in a general reading are:
   - House no. 4 for HOME and PRIVATE LIFE
   - House no. 5 for HEALTH
   - House no. 16 for SPIRITUALITY
   - House no. 18 for FRIENDSHIP
   - House no. 20 for SOCIAL LIFE
   - House no. 24 for FEELINGS
   - House no. 25 for RELATIONSHIPS and CONTRACTS
   - House no. 26 for EDUCATION and STUDIES
   - House no. 30 for FAMILY and SEXUALITY
   - House no. 34 for FINANCES
   - House no. 35 for WORK
   - House no. 36 for RELIGION

Certainly, you don't need to read to all these houses for a 10-year-old querent. The relevant houses, in this case, would be:

o House no. 5 for HEALTH
o House no. 18 for FRIENDSHIP
o House no. 20 for SOCIAL LIFE
o House no. 26 for EDUCATION and STUDIES
o House no. 30 for the FAMILY

As you've learned, in a Grand Tableau, there are 36 houses representing different aspects of life. However, it's not advisable to focus on all of them, unless the querent has expressed specific areas of interest. This is due to the fact that trying to cover all of the houses can make the reading confusing and contradictory. Additionally, some houses may cover more than one subject or life area. For instance, the house no. 4 includes topics related to home, properties, and the querent's personal life, stability, and security. Another example is the house no. 30, which stands for both the family and the client's sexual life. So, It's important to clearly define these houses before reading to avoid confusion during the interpretation.

3.1. How to determine the past, present and future of a significator card in a general reading?

- For the past, use the counting of 7 technique.
- For the present, check the cards surrounding the significator card (very near and near); also consider the Chaining, the Knighting, and Mirroring Techniques.
- For the future, apply the counting of 7 technique.
- To provide guidance to the querent, consider the Queen's Movement Technique.

STEP 6: THE PAST – THE ORIGINS

The cards positioned in the past line reveal details about the origins of the events being experienced in the present. In this reading phase, the following points are considered:

1. **The Directional Facing Law:** As explained in Chapter 4, The Directional Facing Law determines the timeline of a reading (past, present, and future). It's applied to the querent's card and determines that the cards positioned in the direction where the figure is facing represent the present, while the cards on the "back" of the figure represent the past;

2. **The Timeline: Past**

   The past line points to past events that have led the querent to the present situation.

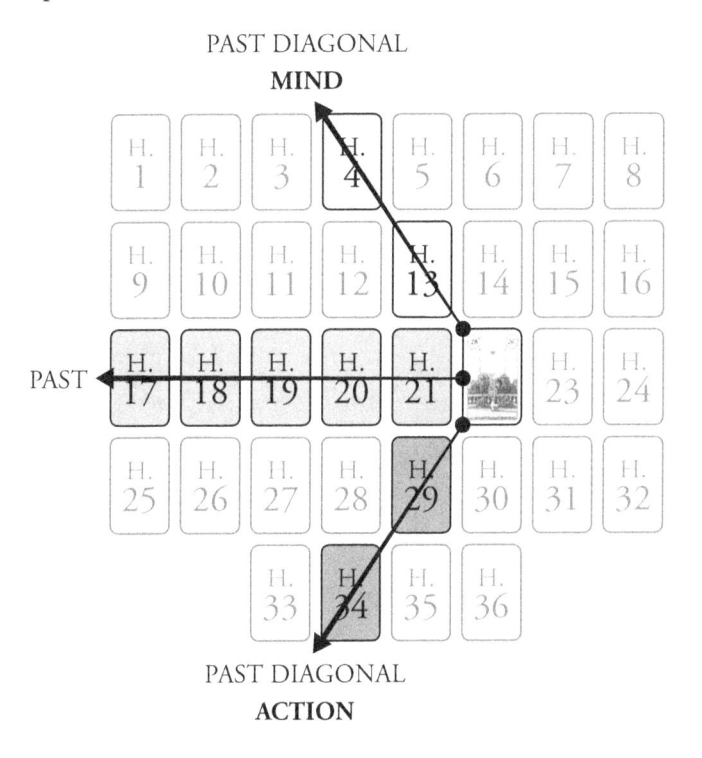

   PAST DIAGONAL
   MIND

   PAST →

   PAST DIAGONAL
   ACTION

   2.1. What has the querent lived? To identify the querent's past experiences, you need to analyze the cards behind their card. Keep in mind that the cards very near and near to the querent's card reveal recent past events and issues that may still be influencing the present, while the far and very far cards can indicate events and situations from a more distant past;

2.2. What has affected the querent? - The answer can be found in the past diagonal line in the mental zone.

2.3. What has the querent refused? - The answer can be found in the past diagonal line in the action zone.

STEP 7: THE FUTURE – GENERAL TRENDS FOR THE FUTURE

In this reading phase, consider the following points:

1. Future diagonal (mind): What are the querent's future plans, hopes, or fears?

2. What next steps will the querent take in the coming days? The answer can be found in the future diagonal line below the querent's card;

3. What can be expected? The answer can be found in the cards in front of the querent's card.

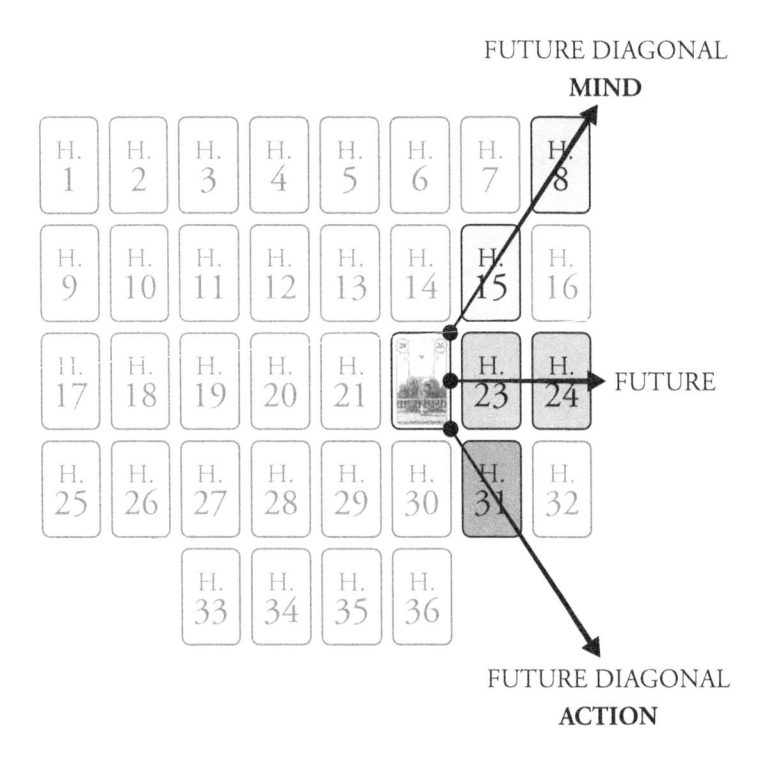

FUTURE DIAGONAL
MIND

H.1	H.2	H.3	H.4	H.5	H.6	H.7	H.8
H.9	H.10	H.11	H.12	H.13	H.14	H.15	H.16
H.17	H.18	H.19	H.20	H.21		H.23	H.24	→ FUTURE
H.25	H.26	H.27	H.28	H.29	H.30	H.31	H.32
	H.33	H.34	H.35	H.36			

FUTURE DIAGONAL
ACTION

To determine the timeframe of the future events, you need to divide the timeframe set for the reading by the number of cards in the future line. For instance, if the reading is for three months (90 days) and there are two cards in the future line, divide 90 by 2 to get 45 days for each card, right? So, the first card in the line will represent events that will occur in the first 45 days, and the second card will stand for the events that will happen in the last 45.

But if the reading is for November, which has 30 days, and there are five cards in the future line, divide 30 by 5 to get 6 days for each card.

STEP 8: THE FATE LINE

What events doesn't the querent have any control over? The answer lies in the Fate line (houses no. 33. no. 34, no. 35, and no. 36. I recommend paying attention to this line when reading the future line.

STEP 9: THE HEART OF THE GRAND TABLEAU – GUIDANCE OR ADVICE

It'll provide a general recommendation related to a specific life area or subject (if a significator card is present), which the querent should focus on during the period established for the reading.

Step-by-Step Guide for a Specific Reading

Preparing for the Reading

Before reading the Grand Tableau, it's essential to consider the following:

1. A Specific Reading in the Frand Tableau needs a specific context, that is, the specific topic or life area that the reading will focus on;
2. Choose the significator card and theme house that will represent the topic being addressed. (Chapter 3 – Choosing the Significator Card) and (Chapter 7 – The Theme Cards);
3. If the reading involves another person, such as in a relationship reading, it's crucial to "baptize" the card that will represent him or her in the reading. (Chapter 3 - The Two Consulting Cards in a Relationship Reading);
4. All the cards should be interpreted according to the context of the reading. For example, if the context is focused on finances, the cards should be analyzed according to the financial aspect of the cards. If it's a work-related context, the cards should be analyzed according to their professional aspect.

Step 1: Shuffling

Shuffle the cards and then focus on the specific question, which should include a timeframe varying from days to 1, 3, 6, 9, or 12 months to connect events with that particular timeframe. For instance, if the querent wants to know about their financial situation in the next six months, the appropriate question would be: "How will (querent's name) financial situation develop over the next six months?". Remember: the clearer the question, the more accurate the answer!

Step 2: Cutting The Cards
(This step isn't mandatory.)

After shuffling the cards, cut the deck into two piles and turn over the last card in each pile. These cards will give you the initial insight about the querent's life but don't reveal this information immediately. The meaning of these two cards will make more sense during the reading.

Step 3: Laying the cards on the table

Join the two piles together, keeping the same order. Then lay out the 36 cards in sequence from left to right to form the Grand Tableau (as shown in the graph in step 3 for general reading). I suggest laying the cards out face-up during this process to activate your memory and intuition immediately. Both are essential components to a successful reading, as well as the techniques and everything you've learned about the deck.

Step 4: Evaluating the querent's status

The first phase of the reading is very significant as it provides valuable information about how the querent is currently managing and facing their life in the reading period. Knowing this information in advance, along with the initial conversation with the querent, can help determine the appropriate language and approach to take during the reading. Therefore, before proceeding with the reading, I suggest that you take a moment to review the following points siently:

1. The first and last cards: These two cards help to "feel" the "tone" of the reading. However, I don't recommend focusing on them, but take them like a GPS, pointing the way for the entire reading. (Chapter 7 - The Importance of the First and Last Cards of the Grand Tableau).

2. Natural house: Check if any card is placed in its natural house. This could be a sign that something is very intense in the querent's life. (Chapter 7 – Natural House).

3. Personal indicators: Verification houses: These cards are essential for understanding the querent's personal situation. To access this information, it's necessary to analyze the following houses:
   - House no. 4: This house is related to the querent's personal life and his inner resilience;
   - House no. 24: This house is associated with the heart and emotions, revealing what is truly important to the querent, how they feel and deal with emotions;
   - House no. 26: This house refers to the mind, showing the querent's mental state.

Once you have analyzed these three houses individually, now it's necessary to analyze them together.

Important Note:
Keep in mind that the information gained by analyzing the three houses is not definitive, as a person's attitudes, behaviors, and emotional and mental states can change over time. Therefore, the three cards positioned in these houses will only indicate the emotional and psychological state during the timeframe of the reading.

4. **The position of the querent's card in the Grand Tableau**
   4.1. In which rows (1, 2, 3, 4, and 5) and columns (A, B, C, D, E, F, G, and H) is the querent's card located? (Chapter 7 – The querent's card position in the Grand Tableau).
   4.2. Which house does the querent's card land in? (Chapter 7 – The Querent's Card in The Houses). If it's in a theme house related to the question, the querent is putting all their energy into this life area.
   However, if the querent's card is in a different house, it reveals how the querent is responding to the present situation. For example, if the reading is about marriage,

and the querent's card lands in the house no.10, which is associated with dangers, risks, cuts, and separation, it's possible to conclude that the querent is going through a challenging situation that is putting them under pressure, and may result in a decision that will probably be irrevocable. Therefore, it's important to check the card in the house no.25, which stands for marriage, and the cards surrounding The Ring card to better understand the situation. However, if The Tower or The Scythe cards are in this position, it may suggest a potential divorce.

Now, if the querent's card is in the house no. 24, the theme house for love, it's possible that the querent is in a marriage where love is the main motivator and the actions are driven by feelings and respect for the partner.

4.3. Which card is in the querent's house? The card in this position will provide information about what motivates the querent to behave in a certain way. Taking the example above, (see point 4.2), if the querent's card is in the house no.10 and The Snake falls in the querent's house, representing betrayal, it's possible to infer that there are reasons for a potential breakup due to infidelity.

But be careful! To confirm betrayal, it's necessary to check if in the house no. 25, which stands for marriage, in the house no.7, for betrayal, and in the house no. 26, for hidden matters are positioned The Clouds, The Fox, The Book, The Ring (houses no. 7 and no. 25). Observe the distance between the querent's and The Snake cards to determine which side the betrayal is coming from. If the querent's card is very near or near The Snake card, it may indicate an unfaithful person.

5. **The position of the significator card in the Grand Tableau.**
    5.1. Which row (1, 2, 3, 4, and 5) and column (A, B, C, D, E, F, G, and H) does the significator card land in?
    5.2. Which house does the significator card fall in?

5.3. Which house is in the theme house?

For a specific reading to evaluate the progress of a relationship, such as marriage, family, romantic, professional, or any other type, it's common to use more than one significator card. For instance, if a male querent wants to know the state of his marriage, the following significator cards may be used in the reading:

♣ Card no. 28, The Man, representing the querent (the person who's asking for the consultation)

♣ Card no. 29, The Woman, representing the querent's partner (the other querent);

♣ Card no. 24, The Heart, the significator card for feelings;

♣ Card no.25, The Ring, the significator card for marriage.

Therefore, the following points should be observed:
» Which row (1, 2, 3, 4, e 5) and column (A, B, C, D, E, F, G, and H) are the two querent's cards in?
» Which house are located the two querent's cards?
» Which card is in the querent's houses (28th and 29th houses)?
» Which row (1, 2, 3, 4, e 5) and column (A, B, C, D, E, F, G, and H) are the significator cards in?
» Which house is the significator cards in?
» Which card is in the theme houses?

6. Analyzing the position between the querent's card and the significator card – The Law of Influence

Is the querent's card above or below the significator card? As explained in Chapter 4 – The Law of Influence, the card above controls the card below. Therefore, this technique shows if the querent is influencing or controlling the situation (the querent's card above the significator card) or being controlled by the situation (the querent's card below the significator card).

However, when the reading involves more than one significator card and another querent (see point 5), it's necessary to consider the following:

6.1. Is the querent's card (the person who's seeking the consultation) above or below the other querent's card

6.2. Is the querent's card above or below the significator card?

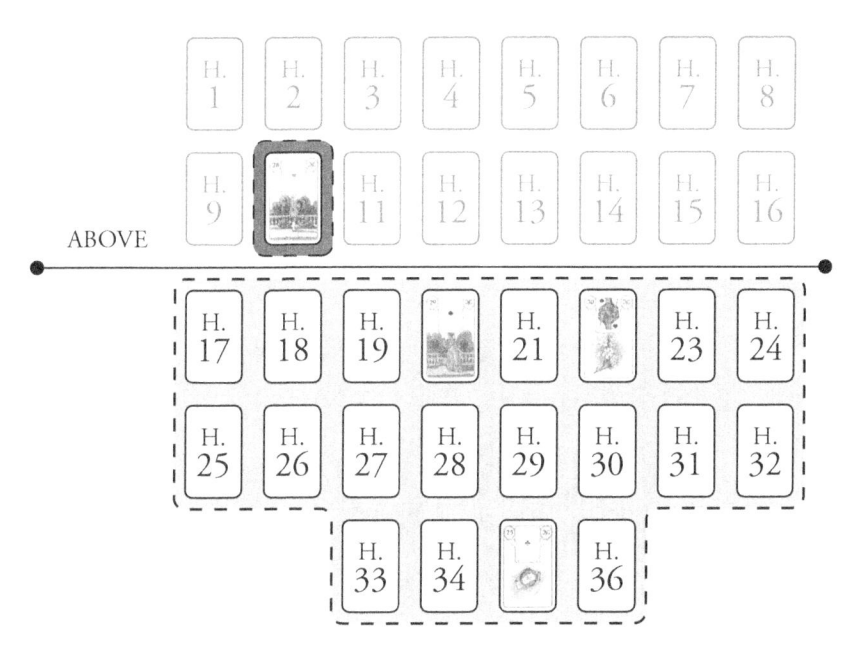

ABOVE

| H.1 | H.2 | H.3 | H.4 | H.5 | H.6 | H.7 | H.8 |
| H.9 | [H.10] | H.11 | H.12 | H.13 | H.14 | H.15 | H.16 |

H.17	H.18	H.19	[H.20]	H.21	[H.22]	H.23	H.24
H.25	H.26	H.27	H.28	H.29	H.30	H.31	H.32
	H.33	H.34	[H.35]	H.36	

In the example illustrated in the graph, the querent's card (The Man card) is positioned above the other cards (The Woman, The Heart, and The Ring card), indicating that he has complete control of the situation. This means that he'll be able to defend his rights and face any challenge with confidence and determination.

7. **If the reading is for two people** – The directional facing law: Are the two figures in the querent's cards facing each other, or do they have their backs turned? This will determine the "mood" between the two people. (Chapter 4 – How to interpret the querent's card).

THE COMPLETE BOOK OF THE PETIT LENORMAND

8. The distance between the querent's card and the Significator card – Philippe Lenormand's law

What's the distance between the querent's card and the significator card? Are they very near, near, far or very far from each other? This will define the level of the querent's "commitment" to the issue.

However, when the reading involves another person and other significant cards, it's important to determine the distance between them. In the example below, a male querent wants to inquire about his marriage, consider the following:

8.1. What's the distance between the querent's card and the other significator cards? Are they very near, near, far, or very far from each other?

H. 1	H. 2	H. 3	H. 4	H. 5	H. 6	H. 7	H. 8
H. 9	H. 10	H. 11	H. 12	H. 13	H. 14	H. 15	H. 16
H. 17	H. 18	H. 19	H. 20	H. 21	H. 22	H. 23	H. 24
H. 25	H. 26	H. 27	H. 28	H. 29	H. 30	H. 31	H. 32
		H. 33	H. 34	H. 35	H. 36		

■ = NEAR   □ = FAR   ⋮ = VERY FAR

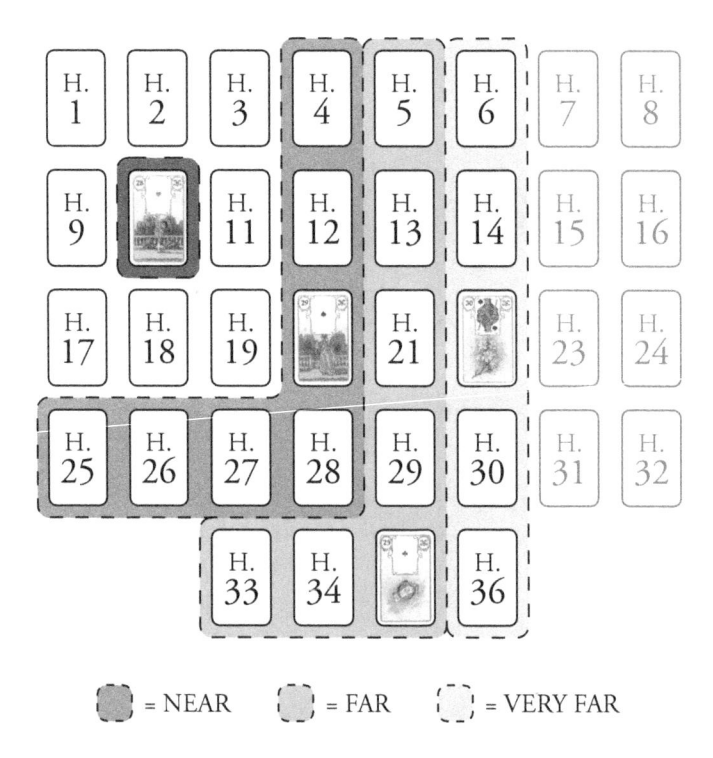

CHAPTER 7: THE GRAND TABLEAU

8.2. What's the distance between the other Querent's card and the Significator cards?

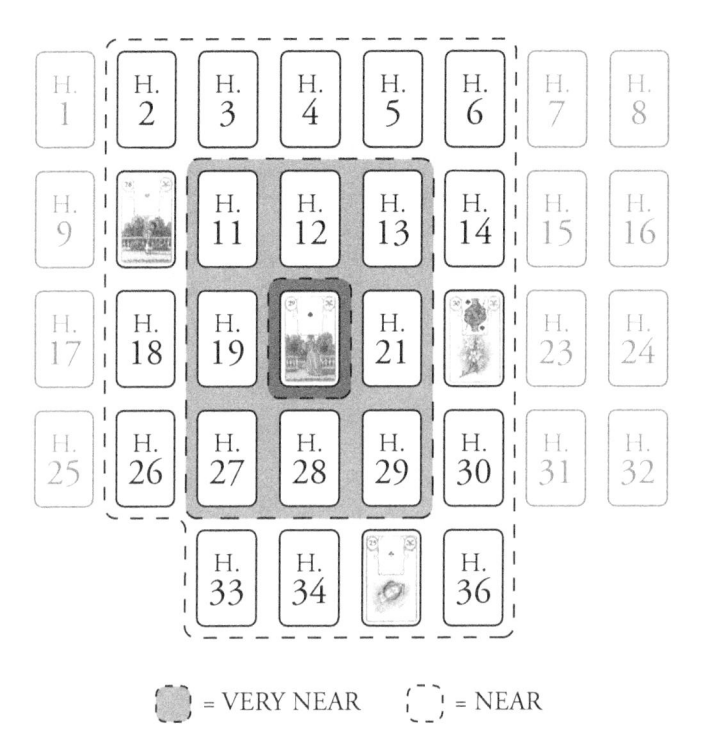

H. 1	H. 2	H. 3	H. 4	H. 5	H. 6	H. 7	H. 8
H. 9	H. 10	H. 11	H. 12	H. 13	H. 14	H. 15	H. 16
H. 17	H. 18	H. 19	H. 20	H. 21	H. 22	H. 23	H. 24
H. 25	H. 26	H. 27	H. 28	H. 29	H. 30	H. 31	H. 32
		H. 33	H. 34	H. 35	H. 36		

■ = VERY NEAR   □ = NEAR

What's the conclusion from the analysis of the two graphs above? Based on the analysis, we can conclude that the wife is more emotionally interested in the marriage than the querent, who seems to maintain a certain distance from the relationship, preferring only to keep in touch with his wife (as evidenced by the other card in a nearby zone). The reasons for this behavior can be found in the example in step 5.3.

9. **The four corner cards:** The cards positioned in the four corners of the Grand Tableau represent the querent's current concerns. The four corner cards and the two court cards can indicate the life areas that require more attention.

Now that we have enough information to start the reading. It's important to keep in mind the information you've gathered in this step throughout the entire reading!

STEP 5: THE PRESENT – THE CURRENT MOMENT

These cards reveal the querent's current events and conditions, showing the challenges they're experiencing and the actions they're taking to shape their future.

In this phase, consider the following points:

1. **The cards surrounding the querent's card** (Chapter 4 - Philippe Lenormand's Law): These cards reveal the influences or events that the querent is experiencing at that moment. The same procedure should be followed if the reading involves another person.

2. **The cards surrounding the significator card:** They represent the actual situation of the question under investigation.

When analyzing points 1 and 2, pay close attention to the energies present at that moment.

- o Which group of movement cards is dominant? Are most of them movement, slow or stop cards? (for more details on the topic, see Chapter 4 – The Law of Movement);
- o Which polarity prevails: positive, neutral, or negative? (Chapter 3 – The Polarity of the 36 Cards);
- o Which suit is predominant? (Chapter 4 – The Law of Predominance);
- o Are there any court cards? If so, which suit do they belong to? Court cards represent people who play a significant role in the events; therefore, they have some influence or responsibility for them (Chapter 3 – The Court Cards);

3. If the reading involves another person and one or more significator cards, it's also important to **analyze the connecting cards between them** (Chapter 7 – The Bridge Technique).

CHAPTER 7: THE GRAND TABLEAU

Still analyzing the example of the male querent who is seeking information about his marriage, we can note that the cards The Child + The House form a bridge between him and his wife. This suggests that the issue connecting the couple refers to a young man who lives in their home, possibly their own son.

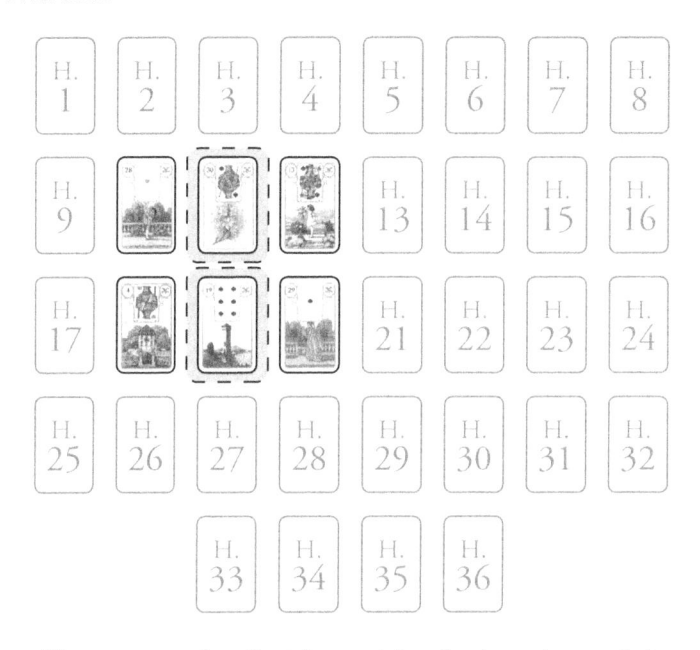

To get more details, it's crucial to look at the cards between the connecting cards, which, in this case, are The Lilies and The Tower. These cards indicate the involvement of an authority figure, which could imply a legal process to determine custody of their child, that is, deciding whether the child should stay with the father or the mother.

4. Repeat the same procedure in point 3 between the querent and significator cards separately. Again, I'll only use the male querent's card as an example and find the bridge between the querent's card and The Heart card:

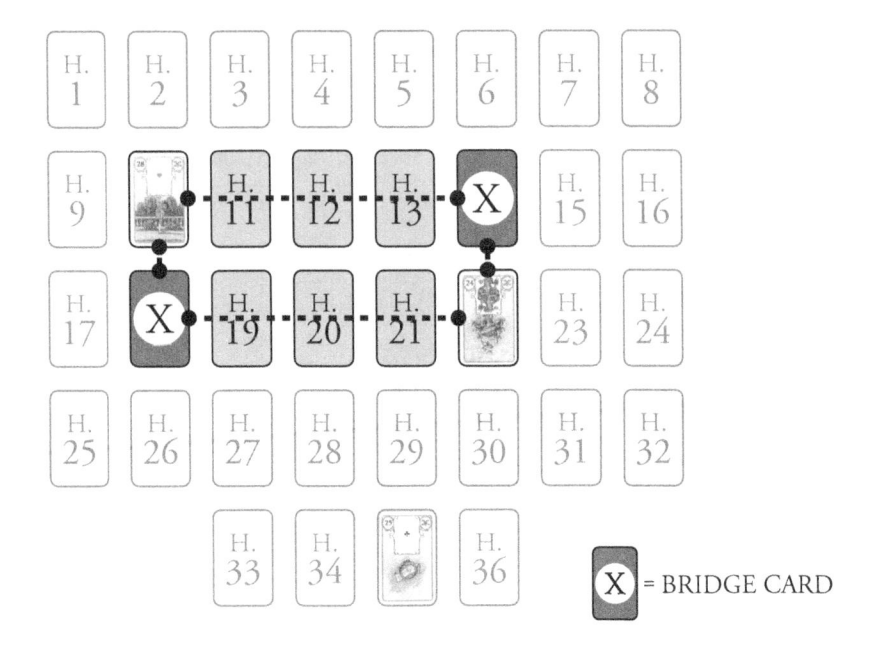

First read the two bridge cards and then the cards between them (in the example above, the gray cards). Proceed in the same way with the querent's card and The Ring card:

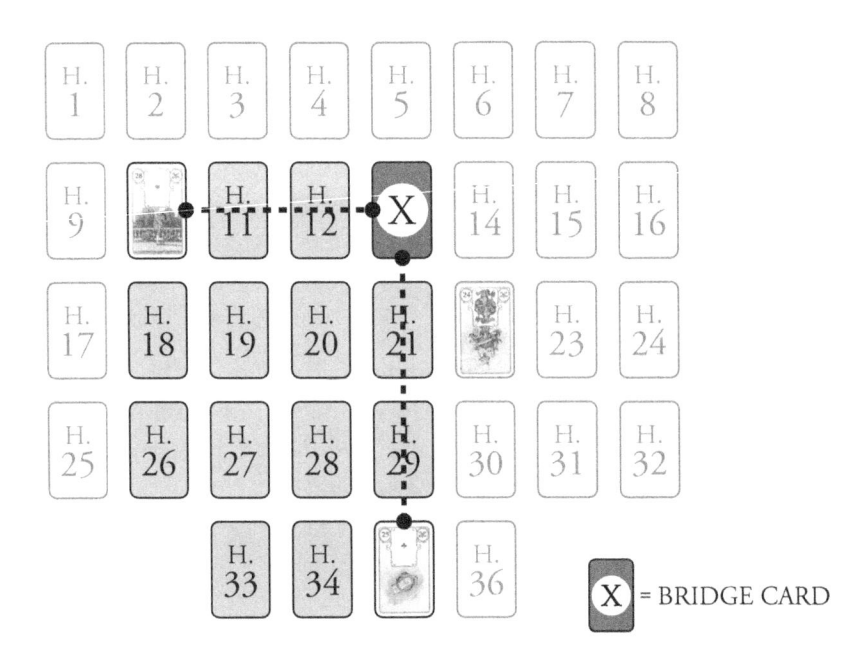

Then follow the same procedure with the other querent's card and the significator cards.

5. **The vertical line that goes across the querent's card** (Chapter 7 – The Timeline):

   Observe the vertical line to understand the querent's current thoughts. If the reading involves another person, repeat the same process with the other querent's card.

6. **Additional houses** – when reading a theme house, it's essential to make connections with other houses related to the theme or topic under analysis. For instance, when analyzing a question about marriage, the primary theme houses would be the house no.25, which is associated with marriage, the house no.28, representing the querent, and the house no.29 for the querent's partner.

7. Next, I recommend you adopt the habit of using the verification house technique in your reading whenever you feel it's necessary. This will enable you to answer any doubt or question the querent may have. (Chapter 7 – The Special Houses).

   For example:
   - House no. 01 – What's coming; what's likely to happen soon;
   - House no. 06 – What's not clear; what needs further clarification;
   - House no. 08 – What's over; it shows what the querent must let go to move forward;
   - House no. 13 – What's in the initial phase;
   - House no. 17 – What's changing or what needs to be changed;
   - House no. 26 – What's hidden or unknown to the querent;
   - House no. 33 – What's in the querent's hands or what they can do to achieve their objectives.

You can examine other houses if you need to delve deeper into a particular issue, such as:

- House no. 14 – What the querent shouldn't trust;
- House no. 18 – What the querent can trust;
- House no. 19 – What needs to be done;
- House no. 21 – What's causing a blockage;
- House no. 23 – What's losing its strength or what's querent's is losing.

Important Note:
When reading a theme card, consider the cards surrounding it and use the auxiliary techniques that can serve as excellent tools to provide further details for the interpretation.

STEP 6: THE PAST – THE ORIGINS

The cards positioned in the past line reveal details about the origins of the events being experienced in the present. In this reading phase, the following points are considered:

1. **The Directional Facing Law:** As previously explained (Chapter 4, The Directional Facing Law), to determine the timeline of a reading (past, present, and future), it's applied to the querent's card the directional facing law that determines that the cards positioned in the direction where the figure is facing represent the present, while the cards on the "back" of the figure represent the past.

   In a reading that involves two querent's cards, the past, and the future will always be determined using the directional facing law technique, as represented in the figure below:

CHAPTER 7: THE GRAND TABLEAU

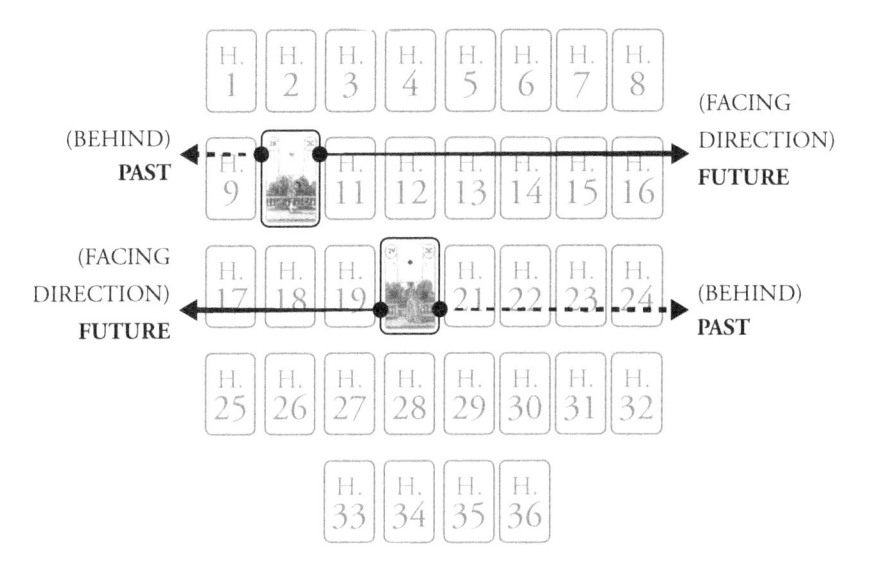

```
                H.  H.  H.  H.  H.  H.  H.  H.
                1   2   3   4   5   6   7   8
(BEHIND)                                         (FACING
 PAST   ◄────  H.  [H.] H.  H.  H.  H.  H.  H.  ─► DIRECTION)
               9   10  11  12  13  14  15  16    FUTURE

(FACING
 DIRECTION)    H.  H.  H.  [H.] H.  H.  H.  H.   (BEHIND)
 FUTURE ◄──── 17  18  19  20  21  22  23  24 ──► PAST

               H.  H.  H.  H.  H.  H.  H.  H.
               25  26  27  28  29  30  31  32

                    H.  H.  H.  H.
                    33  34  35  36
```

2. The timeline: Past

It indicates past events that have led the querent to the present situation.

When reading the past line, you need to consider:

2.1. What has the querent lived? This information is in the cards behind the querent's card. Keep in mind that the cards very near and near to the querent's card reveal recent past events, while the far and very far cards can indicate events and situations from a more distant past;

2.2. What has affected the querent? - The answer can be found in the past diagonal line in the mental zone.

2.3. What has the querent refused? - The answer can be found in the past diagonal line in the action zone.

Obviously, it's important to interpret all of these points according to the reading's context. For example, if the reading is about a marriage issue, all the points should refer to that particular topic.

Step 7: The Future – Trends for the Future

In this reading phase, consider the following points:
- The Timeline – Future
    - Future diagonal (mind): What are the querent's future plans, hopes, or desires?
    - What next steps will the querent take in the coming days? The answer can be found in the future diagonal line below the querent's card.
    - What can be expected? The answer can be found in the cards in front of the querent's card.

    To determine the timeframe of future events, you need to divide the timeframe set for the reading by the number of cards in the future line. For instance, if the reading is for three months (90 days) and there are two cards in the future line, divide 90 by 2 to get 45 days for each card, right? So, the first card in the line will represent events that will occur in the first 45 days of the month, and the second card will stand for the events that will happen in the last 45. But if the reading is for November, which has 30 days, and there are five cards in the future line, divide 30 by 5 to get 6 days for each card.

Step 8: The Fate Line

What events doesn't the querent have any control over? The answer lies in the Fate line (houses no.33, no.34, no.35, and no.36. I recommend paying attention to this line when reading the future line.

Step 9: The Heart of the Grand Tableau – for guidance or advice:

The cards in this position provide recommendation on a life area or a specific topic that the querent should focus on during the timeframe set for the reading.

REFERENCES

Droesbeke, Erna. (1978). La Divination par Les Cartes du Petit Lenormand. 1st edition, Editions Parsifal, Anvers.

Droesbeke, Erna. (1989). L' oracle de Mlle Lenormand: manuel d' interprétation du jeu de Mlle Lenormand. 1st edition, Editions Urania, Argovia.

Rinascimento Italian Art : rinascimentoitalianart.wordpress.com

Mary K. Greer : www.marykgreer.com

Robert M. Place : www.robertmplacetarot.com

Lenormand dictionary : www.lenormanddictionary.blogspot.com

British Museum : www.britishmuseum.org

THE AUTHOR

Odete Lopes Mazza

I was born in Mozambique and my family is originally from Goa, India, and I'm presently living in Ticino, Italian Switzerland. My family comes from a long line of fortune tellers, spanning four generations.

I started my journey in cartomancy when I was five years old, using a regular deck of playing cards. The following year, in 1971, my grandmother introduced me to the "little French cards", the name she called the Petit Lenormand deck, which had been first introduced to my family by my great-grandmother in Goa, who worked as a maid for an English family.

In those days, it was typical for the English ladies to gather for tea and chat in their living rooms in the afternoons. On these occasions, they used to consult the "little French cards" to get information about their children, husbands, lovers, and suitors. At these gatherings, my great-grandmother was introduced to the Petit Lenormand deck as she served the ladies.

According to my grandmother Sheyla, my great-grandmother immediately fell in love with card playing and asked her employer to teach her how to read cards, and in return, offered to teach her the art of card reading and palmistry.

Interestingly, the lady made an unexpected and unconventional request: in exchange for teaching the "little French cards", she wanted to learn Kamasutra! That's how my family came into contact with the Petit Lenormand deck. I drew my first Lenormand cards with a black pen on small cardboard sheets, and I continued to draw my own decks throughout the 80's. At that time, there were no esoteric stores, and finding any divinatory deck on the market was impossible. It was not until 1989 that I bought my first Lenormand deck, the Mlle. Lenormand Blue Owl, at an esoteric bookstore in Lugano, Switzerland, called The Prophet.

Three people played a significant role in my development with the Petit Lenormand: my grandmother Sheyla in 1971, Erna Droesbeke in 1989, who taught me the traditional Philippe Lenormand method (traditional method), and Angelique in 1990, who taught me the basics of the traditional German "method" and helped me define my path with Petit Lenormand. When I started, the Philippe-Lenormand method was quite limited, and finding a more content-rich view was extremely valuable for my growth.

I've noticed a significant improvement in the level of detail in my consultations, especially when analyzing specific events. For The Grand Tableau, I use techniques from two different schools. When I first started reading, I followed Philippe Lenormand's method based on my grandmother's teachings and Erna Droesbeke's studies. This approach allows me to quickly gain a thorough overview of the querent's life and begin the reading with greater confidence

As a fortune teller, I provide both in-person and phone consultations. I also teach professional training courses, both in-person and online, covering several areas, including the Petit Lenormand, La Vera Sibilla Italiana, traditional playing cards, Kipper, Belline, and Geomancy in Italian and Portuguese. In Italy, I'm a bestselling author of two books: "L'Oracolo della Vera Sibilla Italiana" (1999) and "L'Oracolo di Mademoiselle Lenormand" (2001), both released by Hermes Edizione in Rome. In 2015, I published the book "Petit Lenormand deck, Introduction to Combinations" (Capital Books) by Perse. bom.br (in Brazil). Furthermore, I co-authored the deck "A Sibila do Coração" with the Italian historian and writer Giordano Berti in 2015. In addition, in 2017, I founded and still manage the Lusitano Mistic Forum.

Contacts:

- Email: mazza.lopes.odete@gmail.com
- Instagram: Odete Lopes Mazza
- Facebook: Odete Lopes Mazza
- Website: www.odetelopesmazza.com

ACKNOWLEDGMENT

I am grateful to my family, friends, colleagues, and students for their encouragement to write and publish a book on this topic in English.

I want to express my sincere gratitude to Diogo Borges for the meticulous and skilled formatting of this book, to Alexsander Lepletier for the thorough revision, and to Tânia Regina Carvalho Leite for the outstanding English translation. I would also like to extend my heartfelt thanks to the esteemed Erna Droesbeke for her invaluable contribution to my understanding and mastery of Petit Lenormand, and to Andy Boroveshengra for his dedication in reviving the traditional Petit Lenormand.

2

Printed in France by Amazon
Brétigny-sur-Orge, FR